THE KASHF AL-MAHJUB

The oldest Persian Treatise on Sufism

كشف المحجوب

THE KASHF AL-MAHJUB

The oldest Persian Treatise on Sufism

'ALI B. 'UTHMAN AL-JULLABBI ALHUJWIRI

TRANSLATED FROM THE TEXT OF THE LAHORE EDITION. COMPARED WITH MSS. IN THE INDIA OFFICE AND BRITISH MUSEUM.

TRANSLATED BY

Reynold A. Nicholson.

SANG-E-MEEL PUBLICATIONS
25-LOWER MALL LAHORE-CHOWK URDU BAZAR LAHORE

297.4 Abu'l-Hassan Ali Hujwiri
The Kashf Al-Mahjub / tr. by
Reynold A. Nicholson. Lahore : Sang-e-
Meel Publications, 1996.
xii, 441p.
1. Sufism I. Reynold A. Nicholson -
tr. II. Title.

1996

Published by :
NIAZ AHMAD
Sang-e-Meel Publications
Lahore

Printed at:
Combine Printers
Lahore (Pakistan)

ISBN - 969 - 35 - 0720 - 7

PREFACE TO THE FIRST EDITION.

THIS translation of the most ancient and celebrated Persian treatise on Ṣúfiism will, I hope, be found useful not only by the small number of students familiar with the subject at first hand, but also by many readers who, without being Orientalists themselves, are interested in the general history of mysticism and may wish to compare or contrast the diverse yet similar manifestations of the mystical spirit in Christianity, Buddhism, and Islam. The origin of Ṣúfiism and its relation to these great religions cannot properly be considered here, and I dismiss such questions the more readily because I intend to deal with them on another occasion. It is now my duty to give some account of the author of the *Kashf al-Maḥjúb*, and to indicate the character of his work.

Abu 'l-Ḥasan 'Alí b. 'Uthmán b. 'Alí al-Ghaznawí al-Jullábí al-Hujwírí[1] was a native of Ghazna in Afghanistan.[2] Of his life very little is known beyond what he relates incidentally in the *Kashf al-Maḥjúb*. He studied Ṣúfiism under Abu 'l-Faḍl Muḥammad b. al-Ḥasan al-Khuttalí[3] (p. 166), who was a pupil of Abu 'l-Ḥasan al-Ḥuṣrí (ob. 371 A.H.), and under Abu 'l-'Abbás Aḥmad b. Muḥammad al-Ashqání or al-Shaqání[4] (p. 168). He

[1] Julláb and Hujwír were two suburbs of Ghazna. Evidently he resided for some time in each of them.

[2] Notices occur in the *Nafaḥát al-Uns*, No. 377; the *Safínat al-Awliyá*, No. 298 (Ethé's *Cat. of the Persian MSS. in the Library of the India Office*, i, col. 304); the *Riyáḍ al-Awliyá*, Or. 1745, f. 140a (Rieu's *Cat. of the Persian MSS. in the British Museum*, iii, 975). In the *khátimat al-ṭab'* on the last page of the Lahore edition of the *Kashf al-Maḥjúb* he is called Ḥaḍrat-i Dátá Ganj-bakhsh 'Alí al-Hujwírí.

[3] *Nafaḥát*, No. 376. Through al-Khuttalí, al-Ḥuṣrí, and Abú Bakr al-Shiblí the author of the *Kashf al-Maḥjúb* is spiritually connected with Junayd of Baghdád (ob. 297 A.H.).

[4] Ibid., No. 375. The *nisba* Shaqqání or Shaqání is derived from Shaqqán, a village near Níshápúr.

also received instruction from Abu 'l-Qásim Gurgání[1] (p. 169) and Khwája Muzaffar[2] (p. 170), and he mentions a great number of Shaykhs whom he had met and conversed with in the course of his wanderings. He travelled far and wide through the Muhammadan empire from Syria to Turkistán and from the Indus to the Caspian Sea. Among the countries and places which he visited were Ádharbáyaján (pp. 57 and 410), the tomb of Báyazíd at Bisṭám (p. 68), Damascus, Ramla, and Bayt al-Jinn in Syria (pp. 94, 167, 343), Ṭús and Uzkand (p. 234), the tomb of Abú Sa'íd b. Abi 'l-Khayr at Mihna (p. 235), Merv (p. 401), and the Jabal al-Buttam to the east of Samarcand (p. 407). He seems to have settled for a time in 'Iráq, where he ran deeply into debt (p. 345). It may be inferred from a passage on p. 364 that he had a short and unpleasant experience of married life. Finally, according to the *Riyáḍ al-Awliyá*, he went to reside at Lahore and ended his days in that city. His own statement, however, shows that he was taken there as a prisoner against his will (p. 91), and that in composing the *Kashf al-Maḥjúb* he was inconvenienced by the loss of the books which he had left at Ghazna. The date of his death is given as 456 A.H. (1063–4 A.D.) or 464 A.H. (1071–2 A.D.), but it is likely that he survived Abu 'l-Qásim al-Qushayrí, who died in 465 A.H. (1072 A.D.). Rieu's observation (*Cat. of the Persian MSS. in the British Museum*, i, 343) that the author classes Qushayrí with the Ṣúfís who had passed away before the time at which he was writing, is not quite accurate. The author says (p. 161): "Some of those whom I shall mention in this chapter are already deceased, and some are still living." But of the ten Ṣúfís in question only one, namely, Abu 'l-Qásim Gurgání, is referred to in terms which leave no doubt that he was alive when the author wrote. In the *Safínat al-Awliyá*, No. 71, it is stated that Abu 'l-Qásim Gurgání died in 450 A.H. If this date were correct, the *Kashf al-Maḥjúb* must have been written at least fifteen years before Qushayrí's death. On the other hand, my MS. of the *Shadharát al-Dhahab* records the

[1] *Nafaḥát*, No. 367. [2] Ibid., No. 368.

death of Abu 'l-Qásim Gurgání under the year 469 A.H., a date which appears to me more probable, and in that case the statement that the author survived Qushayrí may be accepted, although the evidence on which it rests is mainly negative, for we cannot lay much stress on the fact that Qushayrí's name is sometimes followed by the Moslem equivalent for "of blessed memory". I conjecture, then, that the author died between 465 and 469 A.H.[1] His birth may be placed in the last decade of the tenth or the first decade of the eleventh century of our era, and he must have been in the prime of youth when Sultan Maḥmúd died in 421 A.H. (1030 A.D.). The *Risála-i Abdáliyya*,[2] a fifteenth century treatise on the Muḥammadan saints by Ya'qúb b. 'Uthmán al-Ghaznawí, contains an anecdote, for which it would be hazardous to claim any historical value, to the effect that al-Hujwírí once argued in Maḥmúd's presence with an Indian philosopher and utterly discomfited him by an exhibition of miraculous powers. Be that as it may, he was venerated as a saint long after his death, and his tomb at Lahore was being visited by pilgrims when Bakhtáwar Khán wrote the *Riyáḍ al-Awliyá* in the latter half of the seventeenth century.

In the introduction to the *Kashf al-Maḥjúb* al-Hujwírí complains that two of his former works had been given to the public by persons who erased his name from the title-page, and pretended that they themselves were the authors. In order to guard against the repetition of this fraud, he has inserted his own name in many passages of the present work. His writings, to which he has occasion to refer in the *Kashf al-Maḥjúb*, are—

1. A *díwán* (p. 2).
2. *Minháj al-dín*, on the method of Ṣúfiism (p. 2). It comprised a detailed account of the Ahl-i Ṣuffa (p. 80) and a full biography of Ḥusayn b. Manṣúr al-Ḥalláj (p. 153).

[1] The date 465 A.H. is given by Ázád in his biographical work on the famous men of Balgrám, entitled *Ma'áthir al-Kirám*.

[2] See Ethé's *Cat. of the Persian MSS. in the India Office Library*, No. 1774 (2). The author of this treatise does not call al-Hujwírí the *brother* of Abú Sa'íd b. Abi 'l-Khayr, as Ethé says, but his *spiritual* brother (*birádar-i ḥaqíqat*).

3. *Asrár al-khiraq wa 'l-ma'únát*, on the patched frocks of the Ṣúfís (p. 56).

4. *Kitáb-i faná ú baqá*, composed "in the vanity and rashness of youth" (p. 60).

5. A work, of which the title is not mentioned, in explanation of the sayings of Ḥusayn b. Manṣúr al-Ḥalláj (p. 153).

6. *Kitáb al-bayán li-ahl al-'iyán*, on union with God (p. 259).

7. *Baḥr al-qulúb* (p. 259).

8. *Al-Ri'áyat li-ḥuqúq Allah*, on the Divine unity (p. 280).

9. A work, of which the title is not mentioned, on faith (p. 286).

None of these books has been preserved.

The *Kashf al-Maḥjúb*,[1] which belongs to the later years of the author's life, and, partly at any rate, to the period of his residence in Lahore, was written in reply to certain questions addressed to him by a fellow-townsman, Abú Sa'íd al-Hujwírí. Its object is to set forth a complete system of Ṣúfiism, not to put together a great number of sayings by different Shaykhs, but to discuss and expound the doctrines and practices of the Ṣúfís. The author's attitude throughout is that of a teacher instructing a pupil. Even the biographical section of the work (pp. 70–175) is largely expository. Before stating his own view the author generally examines the current opinions on the same topic and refutes them if necessary. The discussion of mystical problems and controversies is enlivened by many illustrations drawn from his personal experience. In this respect the *Kashf al-Maḥjúb* is more interesting than the *Risála* of Qushayrí, which is so valuable as a collection of sayings, anecdotes, and definitions, but which follows a somewhat formal and academic method on the orthodox lines. No one can read the present work without detecting, behind the scholastic terminology, a truly Persian flavour of philosophical speculation.

Although he was a Sunní and a Ḥanafite, al-Hujwírí, like many Ṣúfís before and after him, managed to reconcile his

[1] Its full title is *Kashf al-maḥjúb li-arbáb al-qulúb* (Ḥájjí Khalífa, v, 215).

theology with an advanced type of mysticism, in which the theory of "annihilation" (*faná*) holds a dominant place, but he scarcely goes to such extreme lengths as would justify us in calling him a pantheist. He strenuously resists and pronounces heretical the doctrine that human personality can be merged and extinguished in the being of God. He compares annihilation to burning by fire, which transmutes the quality of all things to its own quality, but leaves their essence unchanged. He agrees with his spiritual director, al-Khuttalí, in adopting the theory of Junayd that "sobriety" in the mystical acceptation of the term is preferable to "intoxication". He warns his readers often and emphatically that no Súfís, not even those who have attained the highest degree of holiness, are exempt from the obligation of obeying the religious law. In other points, such as the excitation of ecstasy by music and singing, and the use of erotic symbolism in poetry, his judgment is more or less cautious. He defends al-Ḥalláj from the charge of being a magician, and asserts that his sayings are pantheistic only in appearance, but condemns his doctrines as unsound. It is clear that he is anxious to represent Ṣúfiism as the true interpretation of Islam, and it is equally certain that the interpretation is incompatible with the text.[1] Notwithstanding the homage which he pays to the Prophet we cannot separate al-Hujwírí, as regards the essential principles of his teaching, from his older and younger contemporaries, Abú Sa'íd b. Abi 'l-Khayr and 'Abdalláh Anṣárí.[2] These three mystics developed the distinctively Persian theosophy which is revealed in full-blown splendour by Faríd al-dín 'Aṭṭár and Jalál al-dín Rúmí.

The most remarkable chapter in the *Kashf al-Maḥjúb* is the fourteenth, "Concerning the Doctrines held by the different sects of Ṣúfís," in which the author enumerates twelve mystical

[1] The author's view as to the worthlessness of outward forms of religion is expressed with striking boldness in his chapter on the Pilgrimage (pp. 326–9).

[2] Many passages from the *Kashf al-Maḥjúb* are quoted, word for word, in Jámí's *Nafaḥát al-Uns*, which is a modernized and enlarged recension of 'Abdalláh Anṣárí's *Ṭabaqát al-Ṣúfiyya*.

schools and explains the special doctrine of each.[1] So far as I know, he is the first writer to do this. Only one of the schools mentioned by him, namely, that of the Malámatís, seems to be noticed in earlier books on Ṣúfiism; such brief references to the other schools as occur in later books, for example in the *Tadhkirat al-Awliyá*, are probably made on his authority. The question may be asked, "Did these schools really exist, or were they invented by al-Hujwírí in his desire to systematize the theory of Ṣúfiism?" I see no adequate ground at present for the latter hypothesis, which involves the assumption that al-Hujwírí made precise statements that he must have known to be false. It is very likely, however, that in his account of the special doctrines which he attributes to the founder of each school he has often expressed his own views upon the subject at issue and has confused them with the original doctrine. The existence of these schools and doctrines, though lacking further corroboration,[2] does not seem to me incredible; on the contrary, it accords with what happened in the case of the Mu'tazilites and other Muḥammadan schismatics. Certain doctrines were produced and elaborated by well-known Shaykhs, who published them in the form of tracts or were content to lecture on them until, by a familiar process, the new doctrine became the pre-eminent feature of a particular school. Other schools might then accept or reject it. In some instances sharp controversy arose, and the novel teaching gained so little approval that it was confined to the school of its author or was embraced only by a small minority of the Ṣúfí brotherhood. More frequently it would, in the course of time, be drawn into the common stock and reduced to its proper level. Dr. Goldziher has observed that Ṣúfiism cannot be regarded as a regularly organized sect within Islam, and that its dogmas

[1] A summary of these doctrines will be found in the abstract of a paper on "The Oldest Persian Manual of Ṣúfiism" which I read at Oxford in 1908 (*Trans. of the Third International Congress for the History of Religions*, i, 293-7).

[2] Some of al-Hujwírí's twelve sects reappear at a later epoch as orders of dervishes, but the pedigree of those orders which trace their descent from ancient Ṣúfís is usually fictitious.

cannot be compiled into a regular system.[1] That is perfectly true, but after allowing for all divergences there remains a fairly definite body of doctrine which is held in common by Ṣúfís of many different shades and is the result of gradual agglomeration from many different minds.

It is probable that oral tradition was the main source from which al-Hujwírí derived the materials for his work. Of extant treatises on Ṣúfiism he mentions by name only the *Kitáb al-Luma'* by Abú Naṣr al-Sarráj, who died in 377 or 378 A.H. This book is written in Arabic and is the oldest specimen of its class. Through the kindness of Mr. A. G. Ellis, who has recently acquired the sole copy that is at present known to Orientalists, I have been able to verify the reading of a passage quoted by al-Hujwírí (p. 341), and to assure myself that he was well acquainted with his predecessor's work. The arrangement of the *Kashf al-Maḥjúb* is partially based on that of the *Kitáb al-Luma'*, the two books resemble each other in their general plan, and some details of the former are evidently borrowed from the latter. Al-Hujwírí refers in his notice of Ma'rúf al-Karkhí (p. 114) to the biographies of Ṣúfís compiled by Abú 'Abd al-Raḥmán al-Sulamí and Abu 'l-Qásim al-Qushayrí. Although he does not give the titles, he is presumably referring to Sulamí's *Ṭabaqát al-Ṣúfiyya* and Qushayrí's *Risála*.[2] The *Kashf al-Maḥjúb* contains a Persian rendering of some passages in the *Risála* of Qushayrí, with whom al-Hujwírí seems to have been personally acquainted. A citation from 'Abdalláh Anṣárí occurs on p. 26.

Manuscripts of the *Kashf al-Maḥjúb* are preserved in several European libraries.[3] It has been lithographed at Lahore, and Professor Schukovski of St. Petersburg is now, as I understand, engaged in preparing a critical text. The Lahore edition is inaccurate, especially in the spelling of names, but most of

[1] *JRAS.*, 1904, p. 130.

[2] Cf., however, p. 114, note.

[3] See Ethé's *Cat. of the Persian MSS. in the India Office Library*, i, col. 970, where other MSS. are mentioned, and Blochet, *Cat. des manuscrits persans de la Bibliothèque Nationale*, i, 261 (No. 401).

its mistakes are easy to emend, and the text agrees closely with two MSS. in the Library of the India Office (Nos. 1773 and 1774 in Ethé's *Catalogue*), with which I have compared it. I have also consulted a good MS. in the British Museum (Rieu's *Catalogue*, i, 342). The following abbreviations are used: L. to denote the Lahore edition, I. to denote the India Office MS. 1773 (early seventeenth century), J. to denote the India Office MS. 1774 (late seventeenth century), and B. to denote the British Museum MS. Or. 219 (early seventeenth century). In my translation I have, of course, corrected the Lahore text where necessary. While the doubtful passages are few in number, there are, I confess, many places in which a considerable effort is required in order to grasp the author's meaning and follow his argument. The logic of a Persian Ṣúfí must sometimes appear to European readers curiously illogical. Other obstacles might have been removed by means of annotation, but this expedient, if adopted consistently, would have swollen the volume to a formidable size.

The English version is nearly complete, and nothing of importance has been omitted, though I have not hesitated to abridge when opportunity offered. Arabists will remark an occasional discrepancy between the Arabic sayings printed in italics and the translations accompanying them: this is due to my having translated, not the original Arabic, but the Persian paraphrase given by al-Hujwírí.

REYNOLD A. NICHOLSON.

CONTENTS.

PREFACE TO THE SECOND EDITION.

THE abridged English version of the *Kashf al-Mahjúb*, first published in the Gibb Memorial Series in 1911, is now re-issued without alteration, but I have taken the opportunity to add a fresh list of corrections, together with a few explanatory notes. Any attempt to revise it throughout and explain obscure passages would entail an amount of labour I am not prepared to face, especially as the much fuller text edited by Schukovski (Leningrad, 1926), which provides ample material in the shape of variant readings, in some respects, unfortunately, is less useful than might have been hoped. Though Hujwírí was neither a profound mystic nor a precise thinker, his work on the whole forms an admirable introduction to the study of Súfiism: it covers a great deal of ground and has the merit—very rare in such books—of bringing us into immediate touch with the author himself, his views, experiences, and adventures, while incidentally it throws light on the manners of dervishes in various parts of the Moslem world. His exposition of Sufí doctrine and practice is distinguished not only by wide learning and first-hand knowledge but also by the strongly personal character impressed on everything he writes. We cannot help liking a Shaykh who tells us that after God had preserved him for eleven years from the dangers of matrimony, it was his destiny to fall in love with the description of a woman whom he had never seen, and that his faith was near being ruined in consequence. My thanks are due to Messrs. Luzac for making the English translation, which has long been out of print, available once more to students and others interested in the subject.

REYNOLD A. NICHOLSON.

Cambridge,
January, 1936.

KASHF AL-MAHJUB.

INTRODUCTION.

IN THE NAME OF GOD, THE MERCIFUL, THE COMPASSIONATE.

O Lord, bestow on us mercy from Thyself, and provide for us a right course of action!

Praise be to God, who hath revealed the secrets of His kingdom to His Saints, and hath disclosed the mysteries of His power to His intimates, and hath shed the blood of Lovers with the sword of His glory, and hath let the hearts of Gnostics taste the joy of His communion! He it is that bringeth dead hearts to life by the radiance of the perception of His eternity and His majesty, and reanimates them with the comforting spirit of knowledge by divulging His Names.

And peace be upon His Apostle, Muḥammad, and his family and his companions and his wives!

'Alí b. 'Uthmán b. 'Alí al-Jullábí al-Ghaznawí al-Hujwírí (may God be well pleased with him!) says as follows:—

I have asked God's blessing, and have cleared my heart of motives related to self, and have set to work in accordance with your invitation—may God make you happy!— and have firmly resolved to fulfil all your wishes by means of this book. I have entitled it "The Revelation of the Mystery". Knowing what you desire, I have arranged the book in divisions suitable to your purpose. Now I pray God to aid and prosper me in its completion, and I divest myself of my own strength and ability in word and deed. It is God that gives success.

Sẹction.

Two considerations have impelled me to put my name at the beginning of the book : one particular, the other general.[1] As regards the latter, when persons ignorant of this science see a new book, in which the author's name is not set down in several places, they attribute his work to themselves, and thus the author's aim is defeated, since books are compiled, composed, and written only to the end that the author's name may be kept alive and that readers and students may pronounce a blessing on him. This misfortune has already befallen me twice. A certain individual borrowed my poetical works, of which there was no other copy, and retained the manuscript in his possession, and circulated it, and struck out my name which stood at its head, and caused all my labour to be lost. May God forgive him! I also composed another book, entitled "The Highway of Religion" (*Minháj al-Dín*), on the method of Ṣúfiism—may God make it flourish! A shallow pretender, whose words carry no weight, erased my name from the title page and gave out to the public that he was the author, notwithstanding that connoisseurs laughed at his assertion. God, however, brought home to him the unblessedness of this act and erased *his* name from the register of those who seek to enter the Divine portal.

As regards the particular consideration, when people see a book, and know that its author is skilled in the branch of science of which it treats, and is thoroughly versed therein, they judge its merits more fairly and apply themselves more seriously to read and remember it, so that both author and reader are better satisfied. The truth is best known to God

Section.

In using the words "I have asked God's blessing" (p. 3), I wished to observe the respect due to God, who said to His

[1] The author's meaning appears to be that one consideration has a special reference to connoisseurs and competent persons, while the other has a general reference to the public at large.

Apostle: "*When you read the Koran, take refuge with God from the stoned Devil*" (Kor. xvi, 100). "To ask blessing" means "to commit all one's affairs to God and to be saved from the various sorts of contamination". The Prophet used to teach his followers to ask a blessing (*istikhárat*) just as he taught them the Koran. When a man recognizes that his welfare does not depend on his own effort and foresight, but that every good and evil that happens to him is decreed by God, who knows best what is salutary for him, he cannot do otherwise than surrender himself to Destiny and implore God to deliver him from the wickedness of his own soul.

SECTION.

As to the words "I have cleared my heart of all motives related to self" (p. 3), no blessing arises from anything in which selfish interest has a part. If the selfish man succeeds in his purpose, it brings him to perdition, for "the accomplishment of a selfish purpose is the key of Hell"; and if he fails, he will nevertheless have removed from his heart the means of gaining salvation, for "resistance to selfish promptings is the key of Paradise", as God hath said: "*Whoso refrains his soul from lust, verily Paradise shall be his abode*" (Kor. lxxix, 40-1). People act from selfish motives when they desire aught except to please God and to escape from Divine punishment. In fine, the follies of the soul have no limit and its manœuvres are hidden from sight. If God will, a chapter on this subject will be found at its proper place in the present book.

SECTION.

Now as to the words "I have set to work in accordance with your invitation, and have firmly resolved to fulfil all your wishes by means of this book" (p. 3), since you thought me worthy of being asked to write this book for your instruction, it was incumbent on me to comply with your request. Accordingly it behoved me to make an unconditional resolution that I would carry out my undertaking completely. When anyone begins an enterprise with the intention of finishing it, he may be excused if imperfections appear in his work; and for this reason the Prophet said: "The believer's intention is better than his performance." Great is the power of intention, through which a man advances from one category to another without any external change. For example, if anyone endures hunger for a while without having intended to fast, he gets no recompense (*thawáb*) for it in the next world; but if he forms in his heart the intention of fasting, he becomes one of the favourites of God (*muqarrabán*). Again, a traveller who stays for a time in a city does not become a resident until he has formed the intention to reside there. A good intention, therefore, is preliminary to the due performance of every act.

SECTION.

When I said that I had called this book "The Revelation of the Mystery" (p. 3), my object was that the title of the book should proclaim its contents to persons of insight. You must know that all mankind are veiled from the subtlety of spiritual truth except God's saints and His chosen friends; and inasmuch as this book is an elucidation of the Way of Truth, and an explanation of mystical sayings, and an uplifting of the veil of mortality, no other title is appropriate to it. Essentially, unveiling (*kashf*) is destruction of the veiled object, just as the veil destroys revelation (*mukáshafát*), and just as, for instance, one who is near cannot bear to be far, and one who is far cannot bear to be near; or as an animal which is generated from vinegar dies when it falls into any other substance, while those animals which are generated from other substances perish if they are put in vinegar. The spiritual path is hard to travel except for those who were created for that purpose. The Prophet said: "Everyone finds easy that for which he was created." There are two veils: one is the "veil of covering" (*ḥijáb-i rayní*), which can never be removed, and the other is the "veil of clouding" (*ḥijáb-i ghayní*), which is quickly removed. The explanation is as follows: one man is veiled from the Truth by his essence (*dhát*), so that in his view truth and falsehood are the same. Another man is veiled from the Truth by his attributes (*ṣifat*), so that his nature and heart continually seek the Truth and flee from falsehood. Therefore the veil of essence, which is that of "covering" (*rayní*), is never removed. *Rayn* is synonymous with *khatm* (sealing) and *ṭab*' (imprinting). Thus God hath said: "*By no means: but their deeds have spread a covering* (rána) *over their hearts*" (Kor. lxxxiii, 14); then He made the sense of this manifest and said: "*Verily it is all one to the unbelievers whether thou warnest them or no; they will not believe*" (Kor. ii, 5); then he explained the cause thereof, saying: "*God hath sealed up their hearts*" (Kor. ii, 6). But the veil of attributes, which is that of "clouding" (*ghayní*), may be removed at times, for essence does not admit of alteration, but the alteration of attributes is possible. The Ṣúfí Shaykhs have given many subtle hints on the subject of *rayn* and *ghayn*. Junayd said: *Al-rayn min jumlat al-waṭanát wa 'l-ghayn min jumlat al-khaṭarát*, "*Rayn* belongs to the class of abiding things and *ghayn* to the class of transient things." *Waṭan* is permanent and *khaṭar* is adventitious. For example, it is impossible to make a mirror out of a stone, though many polishers assemble to try their skill on it, but a rusty mirror can be made bright by polishing; darkness is innate in the stone, and brightness is innate in the mirror; since the essence is permanent, the temporary attribute does not endure.

Accordingly, I have composed this book for polishers of hearts which are infected by the veil of "clouding" but in which the substance of the light of the Truth is existent, in order that the veil may be lifted from them by the blessing of reading it, and that they may find their way to spiritual reality. Those whose being is compounded of denial of the truth and perpetration of falsehood will never find their way thither, and this book will be of no use to them.

Section.

Now with reference to my words "knowing what you desire, I have arranged the book in divisions suitable to your purpose" (p. 3), a questioner cannot be satisfied until he makes his want known to the person whom he interrogates. A question presupposes a difficulty, and a difficulty is insoluble until its nature is ascertained. Furthermore, to answer a question in general terms is only possible when he who asks it has full knowledge of its various departments and corollaries, but with a beginner one needs to go into detail, and offer diverse explanations and definitions; and in this case especially, seeing that you—God grant you happiness!—desired me to answer your questions in detail and write a book on the matter.

Section.

I said, "I pray God to aid and prosper me" (p. 3), because God alone can help a man to do good deeds. When God assists anyone to perform acts deserving recompense, this is truly "success given by God" (*tawfíq*). The Koran and the Sunna attest the genuineness of *tawfíq*, and the whole Moslem community are unanimous therein, except some Mu'tazilites and Qadarites, who assert that the expression *tawfíq* is void of meaning. Certain Ṣúfí Shaykhs have said, *Al-tawfíq huwa 'l-qudrat 'ala 'l-ṭá'at 'inda 'l-isti'mál*, "When a man is obedient to God he receives from God increased strength." In short, all human action and inaction is the act and creation of God: therefore the strength whereby a man renders obedience to God is called *tawfíq*. The discussion of this topic, however, would be out of place here. Please God, I will now return to the task which you have proposed, but before entering on it I will set down your question in its exact form.

The Question Proposed.

The questioner, Abú Sa'íd al-Hujwírí, said: "Explain to me the true meaning of the Path of Ṣúfiism and the nature of the 'stations' (*maqámát*) of the Ṣúfís, and explain their doctrines and sayings, and make clear to me their mystical allegories, and the nature of Divine Love and how it is manifested in human hearts, and why the intellect is unable to reach the essence thereof, and why the soul recoils from the reality thereof, and why the spirit is lulled in the purity thereof; and explain the practical aspects of Ṣúfiism which are connected with these theories."

Answer.

The person questioned, 'Alí b. 'Uthmán al-Jullábí-al-Hujwírí—may God have mercy on him!—says:—

Know that in this our time the science of Ṣúfiism is obsolete, especially in this country. The whole people is occupied with following its lusts and has turned its back on the path of quietism (*riḍá*), while the *'ulamá* and those who pretend to learning have formed a conception of Ṣúfiism which is quite contrary to its fundamental principles.

High and low alike are content with empty professions: blind conformity has taken the place of spiritual enthusiasm. The vulgar say, "We know God," and the elect, satisfied if they feel in their hearts a longing for the next world, say, "This desire is vision and ardent love." Everyone makes pretensions, none attains to reality. The disciples, neglecting their ascetic practices, indulge in idle thoughts, which they call "contemplation".

I myself (the author proceeds) have already written several books on Ṣúfiism, but all to no purpose. Some false pretenders picked out passages here and there in order to deceive the public, while they erased and destroyed the rest; others did not mutilate the books, but left them unread; others read them, but did not comprehend their meaning, so they copied the text and committed it to memory and said: "We can discourse on mystical science." Nowadays true spiritualism is as rare as the Philosopher's Stone (*kibrít-i aḥmar*); for it is natural to seek the medicine that fits the disease, and nobody wants to mix pearls and coral with common remedies like *shalíthá*[1] and *dawá al-misk.*[2] In time past the works of eminent Ṣúfís, falling into the hands of those who could not appreciate them, have been used to make lining for caps or binding for the poems of Abú Nuwás and the pleasantries of Jáḥiẓ. The royal falcon is sure to get its wings clipped when it perches on the wall of an old woman's cottage. Our contemporaries give the name of "law" to their lusts, pride and ambition they call "honour and learning", hypocrisy towards men "fear of God", concealment of anger "clemency", disputation "discussion", wrangling and foolishness "dignity", insincerity "renunciation", cupidity "devotion to God", their own senseless fancies "divine knowledge", the motions of the heart and affections of the animal soul "divine love", heresy "poverty", scepticism "purity", disbelief in positive religion (*zandaqa*) "self-annihilation", neglect of the Law of the Prophet "the mystic Path", evil communication with time-servers "exercise of piety". As Abú Bakr al-Wásiṭí said: "We are afflicted with a time in which there are neither the religious duties of Islam nor the morals of Paganism nor the virtues of Chivalry" (*aḥlám-i dhawi 'l-muruwwa*). And Mutanabbí says to the same effect:—[3]

"*God curse this world! What a vile place for any camel-rider to alight in!*
For here the man of lofty spirit is always tormented."

SECTION.

Know that I have found this universe an abode of Divine mysteries, which are deposited in created things. Substances accidents, elements, bodies, forms, and properties—all these are veils of Divine mysteries. From the standpoint of

[1] An electuary used as a remedy for paralysis of the tongue or mouth.
[2] See Dozy, *Supplément*, under *dawá*.
[3] Mutanabbí, ed. by Dieterici, p. 662, l. 4 from foot.

Unification (*tawḥíd*) it is polytheism to assert that any such veils exist, but in this world everything is veiled, by its being, from Unification, and the spirit is held captive by admixture and association with phenomenal being. Hence the intellect can hardly comprehend those Divine mysteries, and the spirit can but dimly perceive the marvels of nearness to God. Man, enamoured of his gross environment, remains sunk in ignorance and apathy, making no attempt to cast off the veil that has fallen upon him. Blind to the beauty of Oneness, he turns away from God to seek the vanities of this world and allows his appetites to domineer over his reason, notwithstanding that the animal soul, which the Koran (xii, 53) describes as "commanding to evil" (*ammárat^un bi 'l-sú'*), is the greatest of all veils between God and Man.

Now I will begin and explain to you, fully and lucidly, what you wish to know concerning the "stations" and the "veils", and I will interpret the expressions of the technicologists (*ahl-i ṣaná'i'*), and add thereto some sayings of the Shaykhs and anecdotes about them, in order that your object may be accomplished and that any learned doctors of law or others who look into this work may recognize that the Path of Ṣúfiism has a firm root and a fruitful branch, since all the Ṣúfí Shaykhs have been possessed of knowledge and have encouraged their disciples to acquire knowledge and to persevere in doing so. They have never been addicted to frivolity and levity. Many of them have composed treatises on the method of Ṣúfiism which clearly prove that their minds were filled with divine thoughts.

CHAPTER I.

ON THE AFFIRMATION OF KNOWLEDGE.

God hath said, describing the savants (*'ulamá*): "*Of those who serve God only the savants fear Him*" (Kor. xxxv, 25). The Prophet said: "To seek knowledge is obligatory on every Moslem man and woman;" and he said also: "Seek knowledge even in China." Knowledge is immense and life is short: therefore it is not obligatory to learn all the sciences, such as Astronomy and Medicine, and Arithmetic, etc., but only so much of each as bears upon the religious law: enough astronomy to know the times (of prayer) in the night, enough medicine to abstain from what is injurious, enough arithmetic to understand the division of inheritances and to calculate the duration of the *'iḍda*,[1] etc. Knowledge is obligatory only in so far as is requisite for acting rightly. God condemns those who learn useless knowledge (Kor. ii, 96), and the Prophet said: "I take refuge with Thee from knowledge that profiteth naught." Much may be done by means of a little knowledge, and knowledge should not be separated from action. The Prophet said: "The devotee without divinity is like a donkey turning a mill," because the donkey goes round and round over its own tracks and never makes any advance.

Some regard knowledge as superior to action, while others put action first, but both parties are wrong. Unless action is combined with knowledge, it is not deserving of recompense. Prayer, for instance, is not really prayer, unless performed with knowledge of the principles of purification and those

[1] The period within which a woman, who has been divorced or whose husband has died, may not marry again.

which concern the *qibla*,[1] and with knowledge of the nature of intention. Similarly, knowledge without action is not knowledge. Learning and committing to memory are acts for which a man is rewarded in the next world; if he gained knowledge without action and acquisition on his part, he would get no reward. Hence two classes of men fall into error: firstly, those who claim knowledge for the sake of public reputation but are unable to practise it, and in reality have not attained it; and secondly, those who pretend that practice suffices and that knowledge is unnecessary. It is told of Ibráhím b. Adham that he saw a stone on which was written, "Turn me over and read!" He obeyed, and found this inscription: "Thou dost not practise what thou knowest; why, then, dost thou seek what thou knowest not?" Anas b. Málik says: "The wise aspire to know, the foolish to relate." He who uses his knowledge as a means of winning power and honour and wealth is no savant. The highest pinnacle of knowledge is expressed in the fact that without it none can know God.

SECTION.

Knowledge is of two kinds: Divine and Human. The latter is worthless in comparison with the former, because God's knowledge is an attribute of Himself, subsisting in Him, whose attributes are infinite; whereas our knowledge is an attribute of ourselves, subsisting in us, whose attributes are finite. Knowledge has been defined as "comprehension and investigation of the object known", but the best definition of it is this: "A quality whereby the ignorant are made wise." God's knowledge is that by which He knows all things existent and non-existent: He does not share it with Man: it is not capable of division nor separable from Himself. The proof of it lies in the disposition of His actions (*tartíb-i fi'lash*), since action demands knowledge in the agent as an indispensable condition. The Divine knowledge penetrates what is hidden

[1] The point to which a Moslem turns his face when worshipping, viz. the Ka'ba.

and comprehends what is manifest. It behoves the seeker to contemplate God in every act, knowing that God sees him and all that he does.

Story. They relate that a leading man in Baṣra went to his garden. By chance his eye fell upon the beautiful wife of his gardener. He sent the fellow away on some business and said to the woman: "Shut the gates." She replied: "I have shut them all except one, which I cannot shut." He asked: "Which one is that?" "The gate," said she, "that is between us and God." On receiving this answer the man repented and begged to be forgiven.

Ḥátim al-Aṣamm said: "I have chosen four things to know, and have discarded all the knowledge in the world besides." He was asked: "What are they?" "One," he answered, "is this: I know that my daily bread is apportioned to me, and will neither be increased nor diminished; consequently I have ceased to seek to augment it. Secondly, I know that I owe to God a debt which no other person can pay instead of me; therefore I am occupied with paying it. Thirdly, I know that there is one pursuing me (i.e. Death) from whom I cannot escape; accordingly I have prepared myself to meet him. Fourthly, I know that God is observing me; therefore I am ashamed to do what I ought not."

SECTION.

The object of human knowledge should be to know God and His Commandments. Knowledge of "time" (*'ilm-i waqt*),[1] and of all outward and inward circumstances of which the due effect depends on "time", is incumbent upon everyone. This is of two sorts: primary and secondary. The external

[1] "Time" (*waqt*) is used by Muḥammadan mystics to denote the spiritual state in which anyone finds himself, and by which he is dominated at the moment. The expression *'ilm-i waqt* occurs again in the notice of Abú Sulaymán al-Dárání (chapter x, No. 17), where *waqt* is explained as meaning "the preservation of one's spiritual state". According to a definition given by Sahl b. 'Abdallah al-Tustarí, *waqt* is "search for knowledge of the state, i.e. the decision (*ḥukm*) of a man's state, which exists between him and God in this world and hereafter".

division of the primary class consists in making the Moslem's profession of faith, the internal division consists in the attainment of true cognition. The external division of the secondary class consists in the practice of devotion, the internal division consists in rendering one's intention sincere. The outward and inward aspects cannot be divorced. The exoteric aspect of Truth without the esoteric is hypocrisy, and the esoteric without the exoteric is heresy. So, with regard to the Law, mere formality is defective, while mere spirituality is vain.

The Knowledge of the Truth (*Ḥaqíqat*) has three pillars—

(1) Knowledge of the Essence and Unity of God.
(2) Knowledge of the Attributes of God.
(3) Knowledge of the Actions and Wisdom of God.

The Knowledge of the Law (*Sharí'at*) also has three pillars—

(1) The Koran.
(2) The Sunna.
(3) The Consensus (*ijmá'*) of the Moslem community.

Knowledge of the Divine Essence involves recognition, on the part of one who is reasonable and has reached puberty, that God exists externally by His essence, that He is infinite and not bounded by space, that His essence is not the cause of evil, that none of His creatures is like unto Him, that He has neither wife nor child, and that He is the Creator and Sustainer of all that your imagination and intellect can conceive.

Knowledge of the Divine Attributes requires you to know that God has attributes existing in Himself, which are not He nor a part of Him, but exist in Him and subsist by Him, e.g. Knowledge, Power, Life, Will, Hearing, Sight, Speech, etc.

Knowledge of the Divine Actions is your knowledge that God is the Creator of mankind and of all their actions, that He brought the non-existent universe into being, that He predestines good and evil and creates all that is beneficial and injurious.

Knowledge of the Law involves your knowing that God has sent us Apostles with miracles of an extraordinary nature; that our Apostle, Muḥammad (on whom be peace!), is a true Messenger, who performed many miracles, and that whatever he has told us concerning the Unseen and the Visible is entirely true.

SECTION.

There is a sect of heretics called Sophists (*Súfisṭá'iyán*), who believe that nothing can be known and that knowledge itself does not exist. I say to them: "You think that nothing can be known; is your opinion correct or not?" If they answer "It is correct", they thereby affirm the reality of knowledge; and if they reply "It is not correct", then to argue against an avowedly incorrect assertion is absurd. The same doctrine is held by a sect of heretics who are connected with Ṣúfiism. They say that, inasmuch as nothing is knowable, their negation of knowledge is more perfect than the affirmation of it. This statement proceeds from their folly and stupidity. The negation of knowledge must be the result either of knowledge or of ignorance. Now it is impossible for knowledge to deny knowledge; therefore knowledge cannot be denied except by ignorance, which is nearly akin to infidelity and falsehood; for there is no connexion between ignorance and truth. The doctrine in question is opposed to that of all the Ṣúfí Shaykhs, but is commonly attributed to the Ṣúfís in general by people who have heard it and embraced it. I commit them to God, with Whom it rests whether they shall continue in their error. If religion takes hold of them, they will behave more discreetly and will not misjudge the Friends of God in this way and will look more anxiously to what concerns themselves. Although some heretics claim to be Ṣúfís in order to conceal their own foulness under the beauty of others, why should it be supposed that all Ṣúfís are like these pretenders, and that it is right to treat them all with disdain and contumely? An individual who wished to pass for learned and orthodox, but really was devoid of knowledge and religion, once said to me in the course of debate: "There are twelve heretical sects, and one of them flourishes amongst those who profess Ṣúfiism" (*mutaṣawwifa*). I replied: "If one sect belongs to us, eleven belong to you; and the Ṣúfís can protect themselves from one better than you can from eleven." All this heresy springs from the corruption and degeneracy of the times, but God has always kept His Saints hidden from the multitude and apart from the ungodly. Well said that eminent spiritual guide, 'Alí b. Bundár al-Ṣayrafí[1]: "The depravity of men's hearts is in proportion to the depravity of the age."

Now in the following section I will cite some sayings of the Ṣúfís as an admonition to those sceptics towards whom God is favourably inclined.

SECTION.

Muḥammad b. Faḍl al-Balkhí says: "Knowledge is of three kinds—*from* God, *with* God, and *of* God." Knowledge *of* God is the science of Gnosis (*'ilm-i ma'rifat*), whereby He is known to all His prophets and saints. It cannot be acquired by ordinary means, but is the result of Divine guidance and information. Knowledge *from* God is the science of the Sacred Law (*'ilm-i sharí'at*), which He has commanded and made obligatory upon us. Knowledge *with* God is the science of the "stations" and the "Path" and the degrees of the saints. Gnosis is unsound without acceptance of the Law, and the Law is not practised rightly unless the "stations" are manifested. Abú 'Alí Thaqafí[2] says: *Al-'ilm ḥayát al-qalb min al-jahl wa-núr al-'ayn min al-ẓulmat*, "Knowledge is the life of the

[1] A famous Ṣúfí of Níshápúr, who died in 359 A.H. (*Nafaḥát*, No. 118).

[2] Also a native of Níshápúr. He died in 328 A.H. (*Nafaḥát*, No. 248).

heart, which delivers it from the death of ignorance: it is the light of the eye of faith, which saves it from the darkness of infidelity." The hearts of infidels are dead, because they are ignorant of God, and the hearts of the heedless are sick, because they are ignorant of His Commandments. Abú Bakr Warraq of Tirmidh says: "Those who are satisfied with disputation (*kalám*) about knowledge and do not practise asceticism (*zuhd*) become *zindíqs* (heretics); and those who are satisfied with jurisprudence (*fiqh*) and do not practise abstinence (*wara'*) become wicked." This means that Unification (*tawḥíd*), without works, is predestination (*jabr*), whereas the assertor of Unification ought to hold the doctrine of predestination but to act as though he believed in free will, taking a middle course between free will and predestination. Such is the true sense of another saying uttered by the same spiritual guide, viz.: "Unification is below predestination and above free will."

Lack of positive religion and of morality arises from heedlessness (*ghaflat*). Well said that great master, Yaḥyá b. Mu'ádh al-Rází: "Avoid the society of three classes of men—heedless savants, hypocritical Koran-readers, and ignorant pretenders to Ṣúfiism." The heedless savants are they who have set their hearts on worldly gain and paid court to governors and tyrants, and have been seduced by their own cleverness to spend their time in subtle disputations, and have attacked the leading authorities on religion. The hypocritical Koran-readers are they who praise whatever is done in accordance with their desire, even if it is bad, and blame whatever they dislike, even if it is good: they seek to ingratiate themselves with the people by acting hypocritically. The ignorant pretenders to Ṣúfiism are they who have never associated with a spiritual director (*pír*), nor learned discipline from a shaykh, but without any experience have thrown themselves among the people, and have donned a blue mantle (*kabúdí*), and have trodden the path of unrestraint.

Abú Yazíd Bisṭámí says: "I strove in the spiritual combat for thirty years, and I found nothing harder to me than knowledge and its pursuit." It is more easy for human nature to walk on fire than to follow the road of knowledge, and an ignorant heart will more readily cross the Bridge (*Ṣiráṭ*) a thousand times than learn a single piece of knowledge; and the wicked man would rather pitch his tent in Hell than put one item of knowledge into practice. Accordingly you must learn knowledge and seek perfection therein. The perfection of human knowledge is ignorance of Divine knowledge. You must know enough to know that you do not know. That is to say, human knowledge is alone possible to Man, and humanity is the greatest barrier that separates him from Divinity. As the poet says:—

Al-'ajzu 'an daraki 'l-idráki idráku
Wa 'l-waqfu fí ṭuruqi 'l-akhyári ishráku.

"True perception is to despair of attaining perception,
But not to advance on the paths of the virtuous is polytheism."

He who will not learn and perseveres in his ignorance is a polytheist, but to the learner, when his knowledge becomes perfect, the reality is revealed, and he perceives that his knowledge is no more than inability to know what his end shall be, since realities are not affected by the names bestowed upon them.

CHAPTER II.

ON POVERTY.

Know that Poverty has a high rank in the Way of Truth, and that the poor are greatly esteemed, as God said: "(Give alms) *unto the poor, who are kept fighting in God's cause and cannot go to and fro on the earth; whom the ignorant deem rich forasmuch as they refrain* (from begging)."[1] And again: "*Their sides are lifted from their beds while they call on their Lord in fear and hope*" (Kor. xxxii, 16). Moreover, the Prophet chose poverty and said: "O God, make me live lowly and die lowly and rise from the dead amongst the lowly!" And he also said: "On the day of Resurrection God will say, 'Bring ye My loved ones nigh unto Me;' then the angels will say, 'Who are Thy loved ones?' and God will answer them, saying, 'The poor and destitute.'" There are many verses of the Koran and Traditions to the same effect, which on account of their celebrity need not be mentioned here. Among the Refugees (*Muhájirín*) in the Prophet's time were poor men (*fuqará*) who sat in his mosque and devoted themselves to the worship of God, and firmly believed that God would give them their daily bread, and put their trust (*tawakkul*) in Him. The Prophet was enjoined to consort with them and take due care of them; for God said: "*Do not repulse those who call on their Lord in the morning and in the evening, desiring His favour*" (Kor. vi, 52). Hence, whenever the Prophet saw one of them, he used to say: "May my father and mother be your sacrifice! since it was for your sakes that God reproached me."

God, therefore, has exalted Poverty and has made it a special distinction of the poor, who have renounced all things external

[1] Kor. ii, 274.

and internal, and have turned entirely to the Causer; whose poverty has become their pride, so that they lamented its going and rejoiced at its coming, and embraced it and deemed all else contemptible.

Now, Poverty has a form (*rasm*) and an essence (*ḥaqíqat*). Its form is destitution and indigence, but its essence is fortune and free choice. He who regards the form rests in the form and, failing to attain his object, flees from the essence; but he who has found the essence averts his gaze from all created things, and, in complete annihilation, seeing only the All-One he hastens towards the fullness of eternal life (*ba-faná-yi kull andar ru'yat-i kull ba-baqá-yi kull shitáft*). The poor man (*faqír*) has nothing and can suffer no loss. He does not become rich by having anything, nor indigent by having nothing: both these conditions are alike to him in respect of his poverty. It is permitted that he should be more joyful when he has nothing, for the Shaykhs have said: "The more straitened one is in circumstances, the more expansive (cheerful and happy) is one's (spiritual) state," because it is unlucky for a dervish to have property: if he "imprisons" anything (*dar band kunad*) for his own use, he himself is "imprisoned" in the same proportion. The friends of God live by means of His secret bounties. Worldly wealth holds them back from the path of quietism (*riḍá*).

Story. A dervish met a king. The king said: "Ask a boon of me." The dervish replied: "I will not ask a boon from one of my slaves." "How is that?" said the king. The dervish said: "I have two slaves who are thy masters: covetousness and expectation."

The Prophet said: "Poverty is glorious to those who are worthy of it." Its glory consists in this, that the poor man's body is divinely preserved from base and sinful acts, and his heart from evil and contaminating thoughts, because his outward parts are absorbed in (contemplation of) the manifest blessings of God, while his inward parts are protected by invisible grace, so that his body is spiritual (*rúḥání*) and his heart divine (*rabbání*). Then no relation subsists between him and mankind: this world and the next weigh less than a gnat's wing in the scales of his poverty: he is not contained in the two worlds for a single moment.

SECTION.

The Ṣúfí Shaykhs differ in opinion as to whether poverty or wealth is superior, both being regarded as human attributes; for true wealth (*ghiná*) belongs to God, who is perfect in all His attributes. Yaḥyá b. Mu'ádh al-Rází, Aḥmad b. Abi 'l-Ḥawárí, Ḥárith al-Muḥásibí, Abu 'l-'Abbás b. 'Aṭá, Ruwaym, Abu 'l-Ḥasan b. Sim'ún,[1] and among the moderns the Grand Shaykh Abú Sa'íd Faḍlallah b. Muḥammad al-Mayhaní, all hold the view that wealth is superior to poverty. They argue that wealth is an attribute of God, whereas poverty cannot be ascribed to Him: therefore an attribute common to God and Man is superior to one that is not applicable to God. I answer: "This community of designation is merely nominal, and has no existence in reality: real community involves mutual resemblance, but the Divine attributes are eternal and the human attributes are created; hence your proof is false." I, who am 'Alí b. 'Uthmán al-Jullábí, declare that wealth is a term that may fitly be applied to God, but one to which Man has no right; while poverty is a term that may properly be applied to Man, but not to God. Metaphorically a man is called "rich", but he is not really so. Again, to give a clearer proof, human wealth is an effect due to various causes, whereas the wealth of God, who Himself is the Author of all causes, is not due to any cause. Therefore there is no community in regard to this attribute. It is not allowable to associate anything with God either in essence, attribute, or name. The wealth of God consists in His independence of anyone and in His power to do whatsoever He wills: such He has always been and such He shall be for ever. Man's

[1] See *Nafaḥát*, No. 291, where his "name of honour" is given as Abu 'l-Ḥusayn.

wealth, on the other hand, is, for example, a means of livelihood, or the presence of joy, or the being saved from sin, or the solace of contemplation; which things are all of phenomenal nature and subject to change.

Furthermore, some of the vulgar prefer the rich man to the poor, on the ground that God has made the former blest in both worlds and has bestowed the benefit of riches on him. Here they mean by "wealth" abundance of worldly goods and enjoyment of pleasures and pursuit of lusts. They argue that God has commanded us to be thankful for wealth and patient in poverty, i.e. patient in adversity and thankful in prosperity; and that prosperity is essentially better than adversity. To this I reply that, when God commanded us to be thankful for prosperity He made thankfulness the means of increasing our prosperity; but when He commanded us to be patient in adversity He made patience the means of drawing nigh unto Himself. He said: "*Verily, if ye return thanks, I will give you an increase*" (Kor. xiv, 7), and also, "*God is with the patient*" (Kor. ii, 148).

The Shaykhs who prefer wealth to poverty do not use the term "wealth" in its popular sense. What they intend is not "acquisition of a benefit" but "acquisition of the Benefactor"; to gain union (with God) is a different thing from gaining forgetfulness (of God). Shaykh Abú Sa'íd[1]—God have mercy on him!—says: "Poverty is wealth in God" (*al-faqr huwa 'l-ghiná billáh*), i.e. everlasting revelation of the Truth. I answer to this, that revelation (*mukáshafat*) implies the possibility of a veil (*ḥijáb*); therefore, if the person who enjoys revelation is veiled from revelation by the attribute of wealth, he either becomes in need of revelation or he does not; if he does not, the conclusion is absurd, and if he does, need is incompatible with wealth; therefore that term cannot stand. Besides, no one has "wealth in God" unless his attributes are permanent and his object is invariable; wealth cannot coincide with the subsistence of an object or

[1] See Chapter XII, No. 5.

with the affirmation of the attributes of human nature, inasmuch as the essential characteristics of mortality and phenomenal being are need and indigence. One whose attributes still survive is not rich, and one whose attributes are annihilated is not entitled to any name whatever. Therefore "the rich man is he who is enriched by God" (*al-ghaní man aghnáhu 'lláh*), because the term "rich in God" refers to the agent (*fá'il*), whereas the term "enriched by God" denotes the person acted upon (*maf'úl*); the former is self-subsistent, but the latter subsists through the agent; accordingly self-subsistence is an attribute of human nature, while subsistence through God involves the annihilation of attributes. I, then, who am 'Alí b. 'Uthmán al-Jullábí, assert that true wealth is incompatible with the survival (*baqá*) of any attribute, since human attributes have already been shown to be defective and subject to decay; nor, again, does wealth consist in the annihilation of these attributes, because a name cannot be given to an attribute that no longer exists, and he whose attributes are annihilated cannot be called either "poor" or "rich"; therefore the attribute of wealth is not transferable from God to Man, and the attribute of poverty is not transferable from Man to God.

All the Ṣúfí Shaykhs and most of the vulgar prefer poverty to wealth for the reason that the Koran and the Sunna expressly declare it to be superior, and herein the majority of Moslems are agreed. I find, among the anecdotes which I have read, that on one occasion this question was discussed by Junayd and Ibn 'Aṭá. The latter maintained the superiority of the rich. He argued that at the Resurrection they would be called to account for their wealth, and that such an account (*ḥisáb*) entails the hearing of the Divine Word, without any mediation, in the form of reproach (*'itáb*): and reproach is addressed by the Beloved to the lover. Junayd answered: "If He will call the rich to account, He will ask the poor for their excuse; and asking an excuse is better than calling to account." This is a very subtle point. In true love excuse is "otherness" (*bégánagí*) and reproach is contrary to unity (*yagánagí*). Lovers regard both these things as a blemish, because excuse is made for some disobedience to the command of the Beloved and reproach is made on the same score; but both are impossible in true love, for then neither does the Beloved require an expiation from the lover nor does the lover neglect to perform the will of the Beloved.

Every man is "poor", even though he be a prince. Essentially the wealth of Solomon and the poverty of Solomon are one. God said to Job in the extremity of his patience, and likewise to Solomon in the plenitude of his dominion: "*Good servant that thou art!*"[1] When God's pleasure was accomplished, it made no difference between the poverty and the wealth of Solomon.

The author says: "I have heard that Abu 'l-Qásim Qushayrí —God have mercy on him!—said: 'People have spoken much concerning poverty and wealth, and have chosen one or the other for themselves, but I choose whichever state God chooses for me and keeps me in; if He keeps me rich I will not be forgetful, and if He wishes me to be poor I will not be covetous and rebellious.'" Therefore, both wealth and poverty are Divine gifts: wealth is corrupted by forgetfulness, poverty by covetousness. Both conceptions are excellent, but they differ in practice. Poverty is the separation of the heart from all but God, and wealth is the preoccupation of the heart with that which does not admit of being qualified. When the heart is cleared (of all except God), poverty is not better than wealth nor is wealth better than poverty. Wealth is abundance of worldly goods and poverty is lack of them: all goods belong to God: when the seeker bids farewell to property, the antithesis disappears and both terms are transcended.

SECTION.

All the Ṣúfí Shaykhs have spoken on the subject of poverty. I will now cite as many of their sayings as it is possible to include in this book.

[1] Kor. xxxviii, 29, 44.

One of the moderns says: *Laysa 'l-faqír man khalá min al-zád: innama 'l-faqír man khalá min al-murád*, "The poor man is not he whose hand is empty of provisions, but he whose nature is empty of desires." For example, if God gives him money and he desires to keep it, then he is rich; and if he desires to renounce it, he is rich no less, because poverty consists in ceasing to act on one's own initiative. Yaḥyá b. Mu'ádh al-Rázi says: *Al-faqr khawf al-faqr*, "It is a sign of true poverty that, although one has reached the perfection of saintship and contemplation and self-annihilation, one should always be dreading its decline and departure." And Ruwaym says: *Min na't al-faqír ḥifẓu sirrihi wa-ṣiyánatu nafsihi wa-adá'u farídatihi*, "It is characteristic of the poor man that his heart is protected from selfish cares, and that his soul is guarded from contaminations, and that he performs the obligatory duties of religion:" that is to say, his inward meditations do not interfere with his outward acts, nor *vice versâ*; which is a sign that he has cast off the attributes of mortality. Bishr Ḥáfí says: *Afḍal al-maqámát i'tiqád al-ṣabr 'ala 'l-faqr ila 'l-qabr*, "The best of 'stations' is a firm resolution to endure poverty continually." Now poverty is the annihilation of all "stations": therefore the resolution to endure poverty is a sign of regarding works and actions as imperfect, and of aspiring to annihilate human attributes. But in its obvious sense this saying pronounces poverty to be superior to wealth, and expresses a determination never to abandon it. Shiblí says: *Al-faqír man lá yastaghní bi-shay'in dúna 'lláh*, "The poor man does not rest content with anything except God," because he has no other object of desire. The literal meaning is that you will not become rich except by Him, and that when you have gained Him you have become rich. Your being, then, is other than God; and since you cannot gain wealth except by renouncing "other", your "you-ness" is a veil between you and wealth: when that is removed, you are rich. This saying is very subtle and obscure. In the opinion of advanced spiritualists (*ahl-i ḥaqíqat*) it means: *Al-faqr an lá yustaghná 'anhu*, "Poverty consists in never being independent of poverty." This is what the Pír, i.e. Master 'Abdalláh Anṣárí[1]—may God be well-pleased with him!—meant when he said that our sorrow is everlasting, that our aspiration never reaches its goal, and that our sum (*kulliyyat*) never becomes non-existent in this world or the next, because for the fruition of anything homogeneity is necessary, but God has no congener, and for turning away from Him forgetfulness is necessary, but the dervish is not forgetful. What an endless task, what a difficult road! The dead (*fání*) never become living (*báqí*), so as to be united with Him; the living never become dead, so as to approach His presence. All that His lovers do and suffer is entirely a probation (*miḥnat*); but in order to console themselves they have invented a fine-sounding phraseology (*'ibárati muzakhraf*) and have produced "stations" and "stages" and a "path". Their symbolic expressions, however, begin and end in themselves, and their "stations" do not rise beyond their own *genus*, whereas God is exempt from every human attribute and relationship. Abu 'l-Ḥasan Núrí says: *Na't al-faqír al-sukún 'indą 'l-'adam wa 'l-badhl 'inda 'l-wujúd*; and he says also: *Al-iḍṭiráb 'inda 'l-wujúd*, "When he gets nothing he is silent, and when he gets something he regards another person as better entitled to it than himself, and therefore gives it away." The practice enunciated in this saying is of great importance. There are two meanings: (1) His quiescence when he gets nothing is satisfaction (*riḍá*), and his liberality when he gets something is love (*maḥabbat*), because "satisfied" means "accepting a robe of honour" (*qábil-i khil'at*), and the robe of honour is a token of proximity (*qurbat*), whereas the lover (*muḥibb*) rejects the robe of honour inasmuch as it is a token of severance (*furqat*); and (2) his quiescence when he gets nothing is expectation of getting something, and when he has got it, that "something" is other than God: he cannot be satisfied with anything other than God; therefore he rejects it. Both these meanings are implicit in the saying of the Grand

[1] The celebrated mystic of Herát, who died in 481 A.H. See Professor Browne's *Literary History of Persia*, vol. ii, p. 269.

Shaykh, Abu 'l-Qásim Junayd: *Al-faqr khuluww al-qalb 'an al-ashkál*, "When his heart is empty of phenomena he is poor." Since the existence of phenomena is "other" (than God), rejection is the only course possible. Shiblí says: *Al-faqr bahr al-balá wa-balá'uhu kulluhu 'izz*[un], "Poverty is a sea of trouble, and all troubles for His sake are glorious." Glory is a portion of "other". The afflicted are plunged in trouble and know nothing of glory, until they forget their trouble and regard the Author thereof. Then their trouble is changed into glory, and their glory into a spiritual state (*waqt*), and their spiritual state into love, and their love into contemplation, so that finally the brain of the aspirant becomes wholly a centre of vision through the predominance of his imagination: he sees without eye, and hears without ear. Again, it is glorious for a man to bear the burden of trouble laid upon him by his Beloved, for in truth misfortune is glory, and prosperity is humiliation. Glory is that which makes one present with God, and humiliation is that which makes one absent from God: the affliction of poverty is a sign of "presence", while the delight of riches is a sign of "absence". Therefore one should cling to trouble of any description that involves contemplation and intimacy. Junayd says: *Yá ma'shar al-fuqará innakum tu'rafúna billáh wa-tukramúna lilláh fa-'nzurú kayfa takúnúna ma'a 'lláh idhá khalawtum bihi*, "O ye that are poor, ye are known through God, and are honoured for the sake of God: take heed how ye behave when ye are alone with Him," i.e. if people call you "poor" and recognize your claim, see that you perform the obligations of the path of poverty; and if they give you another name, inconsistent with what you profess, do not accept it, but fulfil your professions. The basest of men is he who is thought to be devoted to God, but really is not; and the noblest is he who is not thought to be devoted to God, but really is. The former resembles an ignorant physician, who pretends to cure people, but only makes them worse, and when he falls ill himself needs another physician to prescribe for him; and the latter is like one who is not known to be a physician, and does not concern himself with other folk, but employs his skill in order to maintain his own health. One of the moderns has said: *Al-faqr 'adam^un bilá wujúd^in*, "Poverty is not-being without existence." To interpret this saying is impossible, because what is non-existent does not admit of being explained. On the surface it would seem that, according to this dictum, poverty is nothing, but such is not the case; the explanations and consensus of the Saints of God are not founded on a principle that is essentially non-existent. The meaning here is not "the not-being of the essence", but "the not-being of that which contaminates the essence"; and all human attributes are a source of contamination: when that is removed, the result is annihilation of the attributes (*faná-yi ṣifat*), which deprives the sufferer of the instrument whereby he attains, or fails to attain, his object; but his not-going to the essence (*'adam-i rawish ba-'ayn*) seems to him annihilation of the essence and casts him into perdition.

I have met with some scholastic philosophers who, failing to understand the drift of this saying, laughed at it and declared it to be nonsense; and also with certain pretenders (to Ṣúfiism) who made nonsense of it and were firmly convinced of its truth, although they had no grasp of the fundamental principle. Both parties are in the wrong: one ignorantly denies the truth, and the other makes ignorance a state (of perfection). Now the expressions "not-being" (*'adam*) and "annihilation" (*faná*), as they are used by Ṣúfís, denote the disappearance of a blameworthy instrument (*álat-i madhmúm*) and disapproved attribute in the course of seeking a praiseworthy attribute; they do not signify the search for non-reality (*'adam-i ma'ní*) by means of an instrument which exists.

Dervishhood in all its meanings is a metaphorical poverty, and amidst all its subordinate aspects there is a transcendent principle. The Divine mysteries come and go over the dervish, so that his affairs are acquired by himself, his actions attributed to himself, and his ideas attached to himself. But when his affairs are freed from the bonds of acquisition (*kasb*), his actions are no more attributed to himself. Then he is the Way, not the wayfarer, i.e. the dervish is a place over which something is passing, not a wayfarer following his own will. Accordingly, he neither draws anything to himself nor puts anything away from himself: all that leaves any trace upon him belongs to the essence.

I have seen false Ṣúfís, mere tonguesters (*arbáb al-lisán*), whose imperfect apprehension of this matter seemed to deny the existence of the essence of poverty, while their lack of desire for the reality of poverty seemed to deny the attributes of its essence. They called by the name of "poverty" and "purity" their failure to seek Truth and Reality, and it looked as though they affirmed their own fancies but denied all else. Every one of them was in some degree veiled from poverty, because the conceit of Ṣúfiism (*pindár-i ín ḥadíth*) betokens perfection of saintship, and the claim to be suspected of Ṣúfiism (*tawallá-yi tuhmat-i ín ḥadíth*) is the ultimate goal, i.e. this claim belongs only to the state of perfection. Therefore the seeker has no choice but to journey in their path and to traverse their "stations" and to know their symbolic expressions, in order that he may not be a plebeian (*'ámmí*) among the elect. Those who are ignorant of general principles (*'awámm-i uṣúl*) have no ground to stand on, whereas those who are ignorant only as regards the derivative branches are supported by the principles. I have said all this to encourage you to undertake this spiritual journey and occupy yourself with the due fulfilment of its obligations.

Now in the chapter on Ṣúfiism I will explain some of the principles and allegories and mystic sayings of this sect. Then I will mention the names of their holy men, and afterwards elucidate the different doctrines held by the Ṣúfí Shaykhs. In the next place, I will treat of the Verities, Sciences, and Laws of Ṣúfiism. Lastly, I will set forth their rules of discipline and the significance of their "stations", in order that the truth of this matter may become clear to you and to all my readers.

CHAPTER III.

ON ṢÚFIISM.

God, Almighty and Glorious, has said: "*And those who walk meekly on the earth, and when the ignorant speak to them answer 'Peace'*," (shall be rewarded with the highest place in Paradise).[1] And the Apostle has said: "He that hears the voice of Ṣúfís (*ahl al-taṣawwuf*) and does not say Amen to their prayer is inscribed before God among the heedless." The true meaning of this name has been much discussed and many books have been composed on the subject. Some assert that the Ṣúfí is so called because he wears a woollen garment (*jáma'-i ṣúf*); others that he is so called because he is in the first rank (*ṣaff-i awwal*); others say it is because the Ṣúfís claim to belong to the *Aṣḥáb-i Ṣuffa*,[2] with whom may God be well-pleased! Others, again, declare that the name is derived from *ṣafá* (purity). These explanations of the true meaning of Ṣúfiism are far from satisfying the requirements of etymology, although each of them is supported by many subtle arguments. *Ṣafá* (purity) is universally praised, and its opposite is *kadar*. The Apostle—on whom be peace!—said: "The *ṣafw* (pure part, i.e. the best) of this world is gone, and only its *kadar* (impurity) remains." Therefore, since the people of this persuasion have purged their morals and conduct, and have sought to free themselves from natural taints, on that account they are called Ṣúfís; and this designation of the sect is a proper name (*az asámi-yi a'lám*), inasmuch as the dignity of the Ṣúfís is too great for their transactions (*mu'ámalát*) to be hidden, so that their name should need a derivation. In this age, however, God has veiled most people from Ṣúfiism

[1] Kor. xxv, 64.

[2] See Chapter IX.

and from its votaries, and has concealed its mysteries from their hearts. Accordingly some imagine that it consists merely in the practice of outward piety without inward contemplation, and others suppose that it is a form and a system without essence and root, to such an extent that they have adopted the view of scoffers (*ahl-i hazl*) and theologians (*'ulamá*), who regard only the external, and have condemned Ṣúfiism altogether, making no attempt to discover what it really is. The people in general, blindly conforming to this opinion, have erased from their hearts the quest for inward purity and have discarded the tenets of the Ancients and the Companions of the Prophet. *Verily, purity is characteristic of the Ṣiddíq,*[1] *if thou desirest a true Ṣúfí*—because purity (*ṣafá*) has a root and a branch: its root being severance of the heart from "others" (*aghyár*), and its branch that the heart should be empty of this deceitful world. Both these are characteristic of the Greatest *Ṣiddíq*, (the Caliph) Abú Bakr 'Abdalláh b. Abí Quḥáfa, with whom may God be well-pleased! He is the leader (*imám*) of all the folk of this Path.

[The author then relates how, on Muḥammad's decease, when 'Umar threatened to decapitate anyone who asserted that the Prophet was dead, Abú Bakr stepped forth and cried with a loud voice: "Whoever worships Muḥammad, let him know that Muḥammad is dead; but whoever worships Muḥammad's Lord, let him know that HE is living and dieth not." Those who regarded Muḥammad with the eye of mortality ceased to venerate him as soon as he departed from this world, but to those who regarded him with the eye of reality his presence and absence were alike, because they attributed both to God; and looked, not at the particular change which had come to pass, but at the Author of all change; and venerated Muḥammad only

[1] The name *zaddíq* (an Aramaic word meaning "righteous") was given to the ascetics and spiritual adepts among the Manichæans. Its Arabic equivalent, *ṣiddíq*, which means "veracious", is a term that is frequently applied to Ṣúfís.

in proportion as God honoured him; and did not attach their hearts to anyone (except God); and did not open their eyes to gaze upon mankind, inasmuch as "he that beholdeth mankind waneth, but he that returneth unto God reigneth" (*man nazara ila 'l-khalq halak wa-man raja'a ila 'l-ḥaqq malak*). And Abú Bakr showed that his heart was empty of this deceitful world, for he gave away all his wealth and his clients (*mawálí*), and clad himself in a woollen garment (*gilím*), and came to the Apostle, who asked him what he had left for his family. Abú Bakr replied: "Only God and His Apostle." All this is characteristic of the sincere Ṣúfí.]

I said that *ṣafá* (purity) is the opposite of *kadar* (impurity), and *kadar* is one of the qualities of Man. The true Ṣúfí is he that leaves impurity behind. Thus, human nature (*bashariyyat*) prevailed in the women of Egypt as they gazed, enraptured, on the wondrous beauty of Yúsuf (Joseph), on whom be peace! But afterwards the preponderance was reversed, until at last they beheld him with their human nature annihilated (*ba-faná-yi bashariyyat*) and cried: "*This is no human being*" (Kor. xii, 31). They made him their object and gave expression to their own state. Hence the Shaykhs of this Path—God have mercy on them!—have said: *Laysa 'l-ṣafá min ṣifat al-bashar li'anna 'l-bashar madar wa'l-madar lá yakhlú min al-kadar*, "Purity is not one of the qualities of Man, for Man is clay, and clay involves impurity, and Man cannot escape from impurity." Therefore purity bears no likeness to acts (*af'ál*), nor can the human nature be destroyed by means of effort. The quality of purity is unrelated to acts and states, and its name is unconnected with names and nicknames—*purity is characteristic of the lovers* (of God), *who are suns without cloud*—because purity is the attribute of those who love, and the lover is he that is dead (*fání*) in his own attributes and living (*báqí*) in the attributes of his Beloved, and their "states" resemble the clear sun in the opinion of mystics (*arbáb-i ḥál*). The beloved of God, Muḥammad the Chosen One, was asked concerning the state of Ḥáritha. He answered: *'Abd nawwara 'lláh qalbahu bi 'l-ímán*, "He is a man whose heart is illumined by the light of faith, so that his face shines like the moon from the effect thereof, and he is formed by the Divine light." An eminent Ṣúfí says: *Ḍiyá al-shams wa'l-qamar idha 'shtaraká namúdhajun min ṣafá al-ḥubb wa 'l-tawḥíd idha 'shtabaká*, "The combination of the light of the sun and moon, when they are in conjunction, is like the purity of Love and Unification, when these are mingled together." Assuredly, the light of the sun and moon is worthless beside the light of the Love and Unification of God Almighty, and they should not be compared; but in this world there is no light more conspicuous than those two luminaries. The eye cannot see the light of the sun and moon with complete demonstration. During the sway of the sun and moon it sees the sky, whereas the heart (*dil*) sees the empyrean (*'arsh*) by the light of knowledge and unification and love, and while still in this world explores the world to come. All the Shaykhs of this Path are agreed that when a man has escaped from the captivity of "stations" (*maqámát*), and gets rid of the impurity of "states" (*aḥwál*), and is liberated from the abode of change and decay, and becomes endowed with all praiseworthy qualities, he is disjoined from all qualities. That is to say, he is not held in bondage by any praiseworthy quality of his own, nor does he regard it, nor is he made self-conceited thereby. His state is hidden from the perception of intelligences, and his time is exempt from the influence of thoughts. His presence (*ḥuḍúr*) with God has no end and his existence has no cause. And when he arrives at this degree, he becomes annihilated (*fání*) in this world and in the next, and is made divine (*rabbání*) in the disappearance of humanity; and gold and earth are the same in his eyes, and the ordinances which others find hard to keep become easy to him.

[Here follows the story of Ḥáritha, who declared that he had true faith in God. The Prophet asked: "What is the reality of thy faith?" Ḥáritha replied: "I have cut off and turned myself away from this world, so that its stones and its gold and its silver and its clay are equal in my sight. And I have passed my nights in wakefulness and my days in thirst until methinks I see the Throne of my Lord manifest, and the people of Paradise visiting one another, and the people of Hell wrestling with one another"[1] (or, according to an alternative reading: "making sudden attacks on one another").[2] The Prophet said, repeating the words thrice: "Thou knowest, therefore persevere."]

"Ṣúfí" is a name which is given, and has formerly been given, to the perfect saints and spiritual adepts. One of the Shaykhs says: *Man ṣaffáhu 'l-ḥubb fa-huwa ṣáf*^{in} *wa-man ṣaffáhu 'l-ḥabíb fa-huwa Ṣúfiyy*^{un}, "He that is purified by love is pure, and he that is absorbed in the Beloved and has abandoned all else is a 'Ṣúfí'." The name has no derivation answering to etymological requirements, inasmuch as Ṣúfiism is too exalted to have any genus from which it might be derived; for the derivation of one thing from another demands homogeneity (*mujánasat*). All that exists is the opposite of purity (*ṣafá*), and things are not derived from their opposites. To Ṣúfís the meaning of Ṣúfiism is clearer than the sun and does not need any explanation or indication. Since "Ṣúfí" admits of no explanation, all the world are interpreters thereof, whether they recognize the dignity of the name or no at the time when they learn its meaning. The perfect, then, among them are called *Ṣúfí*, and the inferior aspirants (*ṭálibán*) among them are called *Mutaṣawwif*; for *taṣawwuf* belongs to the form *tafa''ul*, which implies "taking trouble" (*takalluf*),[3] and is a branch of the original root. The difference both in meaning and in etymology

[1] *Yataṣára'ún.* B. has *yata'ádawn*, and in marg. *yatasára'ún.* The true reading is *yata'áwawn*, "barking (or 'growling') at one another." Cf. *Lisán*, xix, 343, 3.

[2] *Yataghháwárún.* This is the reading of J., I. has *yata'áwarún*, L. *yata'áwadún*, B. *yataghámazún*, and in marg. *yatasáwazún.*

[3] Examples of this signification of the form *ta'a''ul* are given in Wright's Arabic Grammar, vol. i, p. 37, Rem. *b.*

is evident. *Purity* (*ṣafá*) *is a saintship with a sign and a relation* (*riwáyat*), and *Ṣúfiism* (*taṣawwuf*) *is an uncomplaining imitation of purity* (*ḥikáyat*[un] *li'l-ṣafá bilá shikáyat*). Purity, then, is a resplendent and manifest idea, and Ṣúfiism is an imitation of that idea. Its followers in this degree are of three kinds: the *Ṣúfí*, the *Mutaṣawwif*, and the *Mustaṣwif*. The *Ṣúfí* is he that is dead to self and living by the Truth; he has escaped from the grip of human faculties and has really attained (to God). The *Mutaṣawwif* is he that seeks to reach this rank by means of self-mortification (*mujáhadat*) and in his search rectifies his conduct in accordance with their (the Ṣúfís') example. The *Mustaṣwif* is he that makes himself like them (the Ṣúfís) for the sake of money and wealth and power and worldly advantage, but has no knowledge of these two things.[1] Hence it has been said: *Al-mustaṣwif 'inda 'l-Ṣúfiyyat ka-'l-dhubáb wa-'inda ghayrihim ka-'l-dhi'áb*, "The *Mustaṣwif* in the opinion of the Ṣúfís is as despicable as flies, and his actions are mere cupidity; others regard him as being like a wolf, and his speech unbridled (*bé afsár*), for he only desires a morsel of carrion." Therefore the *Ṣúfí* is a man of union (*ṣáḥib wuṣúl*), the *Mutaṣawwif* a man of principles (*ṣáḥib uṣúl*), and the *Mustaṣwif* a man of superfluities (*ṣáḥib fuḍúl*). He that has the portion of union loses all end and object by gaining his end and reaching his object; he that has the portion of principle becomes firm in the "states" of the mystic path, and steadfastly devoted to the mysteries thereof; but he that has the portion of superfluity, is left devoid of all (worth having), and sits down at the gate of formality (*rasm*), and thereby he is veiled from reality (*ma'ní*), and this veil renders both union and principle invisible to him. The Shaykhs of this persuasion have given many subtle definitions of Ṣúfiism which cannot all be enumerated, but we shall mention some of them in this book, if God will, who is the Author of success.

[1] Viz., purity (*ṣafá*) and Ṣúfiism (*taṣawwuf*).

SECTION.

Dhu 'l-Nún, the Egyptian, says: *Al-Ṣúfí idhá naṭaqa bána nuṭquhu 'an al-ḥaqá'iq wa-in sakata naṭaqat 'anhu 'l-jawáriḥ bi-qaṭ' al-'alá'iq*, "The Ṣúfí is he whose language, when he speaks, is the reality of his state, i.e. he says nothing which he is not, and when he is silent his conduct explains his state, and his state proclaims that he has cut all worldly ties;" i.e. all that he says is based on a sound principle and all that he does is pure detachment from the world (*tajríd*); when he speaks his speech is entirely the Truth, and when he is silent his actions are wholly "poverty" (*faqr*). Junayd says: *Al-taṣawwuf na'tun uqíma 'l-'abd fíhi qíla na'tun li-'l-'abd am li-'l-ḥaqq faqála na't al-ḥaqq ḥaqíqatan wa-na't al-'abd rasman*, "Ṣúfiism is an attribute wherein is Man's subsistence." They said: "Is it an attribute of God or of mankind?" He replied: "Its essence is an attribute of God and its formal system is an attribute of mankind;" i.e. its essence involves the annihilation of human qualities, which is brought about by the everlastingness of the Divine qualities, and this is an attribute of God; whereas its formal system involves on the part of Man the continuance of self-mortification (*mujáhadat*), and this continuance of self-mortification is an attribute of Man. Or the words may be taken in another sense, namely, that in real Unification (*tawḥíd*) there are, correctly speaking, no human attributes at all, because human attributes are not constant but are only formal (*rasm*), having no permanence, for God is the agent. Therefore they are really the attributes of God. Thus (to explain what is meant), God commands His servants to fast, and when they keep the fast He gives them the name of "faster" (*ṣá'im*), and *nominally* this "fasting" (*ṣawm*) belongs to Man, but *really* it belongs to God. Accordingly God told His Apostle and said: *Al-ṣawm lí wa-ana ajzí bihi*, "Fasting is mine," because all His acts are His possessions, and when men ascribe things to themselves, the attribution is formal and metaphorical, not real. And Abu 'l-Ḥasan Núrí says: *Al-taṣawwuf tarku kulli ḥaẓẓin li-'l-nafs*, "Ṣúfiism is the renunciation of all selfish pleasures." This renunciation is of two kinds: formal and essential. For example, if one renounces a pleasure, and finds pleasure in the renunciation, this is formal renunciation; but if the pleasure renounces him, then the pleasure is annihilated, and this case falls under the head of true contemplation (*mushdhadat*). Therefore renunciation of pleasure is the act of Man, but annihilation of pleasure is the act of God. The act of Man is formal and metaphorical, while the act of God is real. This saying (of Núrí) elucidates the saying of Junayd which has been quoted above. And Abu 'l-Ḥasan Núrí also says: *Al-Ṣúfiyyat humu 'lladhína ṣafat arwáḥuhum fa-ṣárú fí 'l-ṣaff al-awwal bayna yadayi 'l-ḥaqq*, "The Ṣúfís are they whose spirits have been freed from the pollution of humanity, purified from carnal taint, and released from concupiscence, so that they have found rest with God in the first rank and the highest degree, and have fled from all save Him." And he also says: *Al-Ṣúfí alladhí lá yamlik wa-lá yumlak*, "The Ṣúfí is he that has nothing in his possession nor is himself possessed by anything." This denotes the essence of annihilation (*faná*), since one whose qualities are annihilated neither possesses nor is possessed, inasmuch as the term "possession" can properly be applied only to existent things. The meaning is, that the Ṣúfí does not make his own any good of this world or any glory of the next world, for he is not even in the possession and control of himself: he refrains from desiring authority over others, in order that others may not desire submission from him. This saying refers to a mystery of the Ṣúfís which they call "complete annihilation" (*faná-yi kullí*). If God will, we shall mention in this work, for your information, the points wherein they have fallen into error.

Ibn al-Jallá[1] says: *Al-taṣawwuf ḥaqíqatun lá rasm lahu*, "Ṣúfiism is an essence without form," because the form belongs

[1] So J. The Lahore edition has Ibn al-Jalálí, I. Ibn al-Jullábí. See Chapter X, No. 34.

to mankind in respect to their conduct (*mu'ámalát*), while the essence thereof is peculiar to God. Since Ṣúfiism consists in turning away from mankind, it is necessarily without form. And Abú 'Amr Dimashqí says: *Al-taṣawwuf ru'yat al-kawn bi-'ayn al-naqṣ, bal ghaḍḍ al-ṭarf 'an al-kawn*, "Ṣúfiism is: to see the imperfection of the phenomenal world (and this shows that human attributes are still existent), nay, to shut the eye to the phenomenal world" (and this shows that human attributes are annihilated; because the objects of sight are phenomena, and when phenomena disappear, sight also disappears). Shutting the eye to the phenomenal world leaves the spiritual vision subsistent, i.e. whoever becomes blind to self sees by means of God, because the seeker of phenomena is also a self-seeker, and his action proceeds from and through himself, and he cannot find any way of escaping from himself. Accordingly one sees himself to be imperfect, and one shuts his eye to self and does not see; and although the seer sees his imperfection, nevertheless his eye is a veil, and he is veiled by his sight, but he who does not see is not veiled by his blindness. This is a well-established principle in the Path of aspirants to Ṣúfiism and mystics (*arbáb-i ma'ání*), but to explain it here would be unsuitable. And Abú Bakr Shiblí says: *Al-taṣawwuf shirk^un li'annahu ṣiyánat al-qalb 'an ru'yat al-ghayr wa-lá ghayr*, "Ṣúfiism is polytheism, because it is the guarding of the heart from the vision of 'other', and 'other' does not exist." That is to say, vision of other (than God) in affirming the Unity of God is polytheism, and when "other" has no value in the heart, it is absurd to guard the heart from remembrance of "other". And Ḥuṣrí says: *Al-taṣawwuf ṣafá al-sirr min kudúrat al-mukhálafat*, "Ṣúfiism is the heart's being pure from the pollution of discord." The meaning thereof is that he should protect the heart from discord with God, because love is concord, and concord is the opposite of discord, and the lover has but one duty in the world, namely, to keep the commandment of the beloved; and if the object of desire is one, how can discord arise? And Muḥammad b. 'Alí b. al-Ḥusayn

b. 'Alí b. Abí Ṭálib—may God be pleased with them all!—says: *Al-taṣawwuf khulq^un fa-man záda 'alayka fí 'l-khulq záda 'alayka fí 'l-taṣawwuf*, "Ṣúfiism is goodness of disposition: he that has the better disposition is the better Ṣúfí." Now goodness of disposition is of two kinds: towards God and towards men. The former is acquiescence in the Divine decrees, the latter is endurance of the burden of men's society for God's sake. These two aspects refer to the seeker (*ṭálib*). God is independent of the seeker's acquiescence or anger, and these two qualities depend on consideration of His Unity. And Abú Muḥammad Murta'ish says: *Al-Ṣúfí lá yasbiqu himmatuhu khaṭwatahu*, "The Ṣúfí is he whose thought keeps pace with his foot," i.e. he is entirely present: his soul is where his body is, and his body where his soul is, and his soul where his foot is, and his foot where his soul is. This is the sign of presence without absence. Others say, on the contrary: "He is absent from himself and present with God." It is not so: he is present with himself and present with God. The expression denotes perfect union (*jam' al-jam'*), because there can be no absence from self so long as one regards one's self; when self-regard has ceased, there is presence (with God) without absence. In this particular sense the saying closely resembles that of Shiblí: *Al-Ṣúfí lá yará fí 'l-dárayn ma'a 'lláh ghayra 'lláh*, "The Ṣúfí is he that sees nothing except God in the two worlds." In short, human existence is "other", and when a man does not see "other" he does not see himself; and becomes totally void of self, whether "self" is affirmed or denied. And Junayd says: *Al-taṣawwuf mabniyy^un 'alá thamán khiṣál al-sakhá wa 'l-riḍá wa 'l-ṣabr wa 'l-ishárat wa 'l-ghurbat wa-labs al-ṣúf wa 'l-siyáḥat wa 'l-faqr amma 'l-sakhá fa-li-Ibráhím wa-amma 'l-riḍá fa-li-Isma'íl wa-amma 'l-ṣabr fa-li-Ayyúb wa-amma 'l-ishárat fa-li-Zakariyyá wa-amma 'l-ghurbat fa-li-Yaḥyá wa-ammá labs al-ṣúf fa-li-Músá wa-amma 'l-siyáḥat fa-li-'Ísá wa-amma 'l-faqr fa-li-Muḥammad ṣalla 'lláhu 'alayhi wa-sallama wa-'alayhim ajma'ín*, "Ṣúfiism is founded on eight qualities exemplified in eight Apostles:

the generosity of Abraham, who sacrificed his son; the acquiescence of Ishmael, who submitted to the command of God and gave up his dear life; the patience of Job, who patiently endured the affliction of worms and the jealousy of the Merciful; the symbolism of Zacharias, to whom God said, '*Thou shalt not speak unto men for three days save by signs*' (Kor. iii, 36), and again to the same effect, '*When he called upon his Lord with a secret invocation*' (Kor. xix, 2); the strangerhood of John, who was a stranger in his own country and an alien to his own kin amongst whom he lived; the pilgrimhood of Jesus, who was so detached therein from worldly things that he kept only a cup and a comb—the cup he threw away when he saw a man drinking water in the palms of his hands, and the comb likewise when he saw another man using his fingers instead of a toothpick; the wearing of wool by Moses, whose garment was woollen; and the poverty of Muḥammad, to whom God Almighty sent the key of all the treasures that are upon the face of the earth, saying: 'Lay no trouble on thyself, but procure every luxury by means of these treasures;' and he answered: 'O Lord, I desire them not; keep me one day full-fed and one day hungry.'" These are very excellent principles of conduct.

And Ḥuṣrí says: *Al-Ṣúfí la yújadu ba'da 'adamihi wa-lá yu'damu ba'da wujúdihi*, "The Ṣúfí is he whose existence is without non-existence and his non-existence without existence," i.e. he never loses that which he finds, and he never finds that which he loses. Another meaning is this, that his finding (*yáft*) has no not-finding (*ná-yáft*), and his not-finding has no finding at any time, so that there is either an affirmation without negation or a negation without affirmation. The object of all these expressions is that the Ṣúfí's state of mortality should entirely lapse, and that his bodily feelings (*shawáhid*) should disappear and his connexion with everything be cut off, in order that the mystery of his mortality may be revealed and his various parts united in his essential self, and that he may subsist through and in himself. The effect of this can be shown in two Apostles: firstly, Moses, in whose existence there was no non-existence, so that he said: "*O Lord, enlarge my breast and make my affair easy unto me*" (Kor. xx, 26, 27); secondly, the Apostle (Muḥammad), in whose non-existence there was no existence, so that God said: "*Did not We enlarge thy breast?*" (Kor. xciv, 1). The one asked for adornment and sought honour, but the other was adorned, since he had no request to make for himself.

And 'Alí b. Bundár al-Ṣayrafí of Níshápúr says: *Al-taṣawwuf isqáṭ al-ru'yat li-'l-ḥaqq záhir^an wa-báṭin^an*, "Ṣúfiism is this, that the Ṣúfí should not regard his own exterior and interior, but should regard all as belonging to God." Thus, if you look at the exterior, you will find an outward sign of God's blessing, and, as you look, outward actions will not have the weight even of a gnat's wing beside the blessing of God, and you will cease from regarding the exterior; and again, if you look at the interior, you will find an inward sign of God's aid, and, as you look, inward actions will not turn the scale by a single grain in comparison with the aid of God, and you will cease from regarding the interior, and will see that all belongs to God; and when you see that all is God's, you will see that you yourself have nothing.

Muḥammad b. Aḥmad al-Muqrí[1] says: *Al-taṣawwuf istiqámat al-aḥwál ma'a 'l-ḥaqq*, "Ṣúfiism is the maintenance of right states with God," i.e. "states" do not seduce the Ṣúfí from his (right) state, nor cast him into wrong, since he whose heart is devoted to the Author of states (*muḥawwil-i aḥwál*) is not cast down from the rank of rectitude nor hindered from attaining to the Truth.

SECTION.

Maxims of Conduct (*mu'ámalát*).

Abú Ḥafṣ Ḥaddád of Níshápúr says: *Al-taṣawwuf kulluhu ádáb^un li-kulli waqt^in adab^un wa-li-kulli maqám^in adab^un wa-li-kulli ḥál^in adab^un fa-man lazima ádáb al-awqát balagha mablagh*

[1] Died in 366 A.H. See *Nafaḥát*, No. 332.

al-rijál fa-man ḍayya'a 'l-ádáb fa-huwa ba'íd^un min ḥaythu yaẓunnu 'l-qurb wa-mardúd^un min ḥaythu yaẓunnu 'l-qabúl, "Ṣúfiism consists entirely of behaviour; every time, place, and circumstance have their own propriety; he that observes the proprieties of each occasion attains to the rank of holy men; and he that neglects the proprieties is far removed from the thought of nearness (to God) and is excluded from imagining that he is acceptable to God." The meaning of this is akin to the dictum of Abu 'l-Ḥasan Núrí: *Laysa 'l-taṣawwuf rusúm^an wa-lá 'ulúm^an wa-lákinnahu akhláq^un*, "Ṣúfiism is not composed of practices and sciences, but it is morals," i.e. if it consisted of practices, it could be acquired by effort, and if it consisted of sciences, it could be gained by instruction: hence it is morals, and it is not acquired until you demand from yourself the principles of morals, and make your actions square with them, and fulfil their just claims. The distinction between practices (*rusúm*) and morals (*akhláq*) is this, that practices are ceremonial actions proceeding from certain motives, actions devoid of reality, so that their form is at variance with their spirit, whereas morals are praiseworthy actions without ceremony or motive, actions devoid of pretension, so that their form is in harmony with their spirit.

Murta'ish says: *Al-taṣawwuf ḥusn al-khulq*, "Ṣúfiism is good nature." This is of three sorts: firstly, towards God, by fulfilling His Commandments without hypocrisy; secondly, towards men, by paying respect to one's superiors and behaving with kindness to one's inferiors and with justice to one's equals, and by not seeking recompense and justice from men in general; and thirdly, towards one's self, by not following the flesh and the devil. Whoever makes himself right in these three matters is a good-natured man. This which I have mentioned agrees with a story told of 'Á'isha the veracious (*ṣiddiqa*)—may God be well-pleased with her! She was asked concerning the nature of the Apostle. "Read from the Koran," she replied, "for God has given information in the place where He says: '*Use indulgence and order what is good and turn away from the ignorant'* (Kor. vii, 198)." And Murta'ish also says: *Hádhá madhhab^un kulluhu jidd^un fa-lá takhliṭúhu bi-shay'^in min al-hazl,* "This religion of Ṣúfiism is wholly earnest, therefore do not mix jest with it, and do not take the conduct of formalists (*mutarassimán*) as a model, and shun those who blindly imitate them." When the people see these formalists among the aspirants to Ṣúfiism in our time, and become aware of their dancing and singing and visiting the court of sultans and quarrelling for the sake of a pittance or a mouthful of food, their belief in the whole body of Ṣúfís is corrupted, and they say: "These are the principles of Ṣúfiism, and the tenets of the ancient Ṣúfís were just the same." They do not recognize that this is an age of weakness and an epoch of affliction. Consequently, since greed incites the sultan to acts of tyranny, and lust incites the savant to commit adultery and fornication, and ostentation incites the ascetic to hypocrisy, and vanity incites the Ṣúfí also to dance and sing—you must know that the evil lies in the men who hold the doctrines, not in the principles on which the doctrines are based; and that if some scoffers disguise their folly in the earnestness of true mystics (*aḥrár*), the earnestness of the latter is not thereby turned to folly. And Abú 'Alí Qarmíni[1] says: *Al-taṣawwuf huwa 'l-akhláq al-raḍiyyat,* "Ṣúfiism is good morals." Approved actions are such that the creature in all circumstances approves of God, and is content and satisfied. Abu 'l Ḥasan Núrí says: *Al-taṣawwuf huwa 'l-ḥurriyyat wa-'l-futuwwat wa-tark al-taklíf wa-'l-sakhá wa-badhl al-dunyá,* "Ṣúfiism is liberty, so that a man is freed from the bonds of desire; and generosity," i.e. he is purged from the conceit of generosity; "and abandonment of useless trouble," i.e. he does not strive after appurtenances and rewards; "and munificence," i.e. he leaves this world to the people of this world.

[1] IJ. Qazwíní. B. Abú 'Alí Kirmánsháhí Qurayshí. The Shaykh in question is probably Muẓaffar Kirmánsháhí Qarmíni (*Nafaḥát*, No. 270).

And Abu 'l-Ḥasan Fúshanja[1] — may God have mercy on him!—says: *Al-taṣawwuf al-yawma 'sm^un wa-lá ḥaqíqat^un wa-qad kána ḥaqíqat^an wa-la 'sm^an*, "To-day Ṣúfiism is a name without a reality, but formerly it was a reality without a name," i.e. in the time of the Companions and the Ancients—may God have mercy on them!—this name did not exist, but the reality thereof was in everyone; now the name exists, but not the reality. That is to say, formerly the practice was known and the pretence unknown, but nowadays the pretence is known and the practice unknown.

I have brought together and examined in this chapter on Ṣúfiism a number of the sayings of the Shaykhs, in order that this Path may become clear to you — God grant you felicity! — and that you may say to the sceptics: "What do you mean by denying the truth of Ṣúfiism?" If they deny only the name it is no matter, since ideas are unrelated to things which bear names; and if they deny the essential ideas, this amounts to a denial of the whole Sacred Law of the Apostle and his praised qualities. And I enjoin you in this book—God grant you the felicity with which He has blessed His Saints!—to hold these ideas in due regard and satisfy their just claims, so that you may refrain from idle pretensions and have an excellent belief in the Ṣúfís themselves. It is God that gives success.

[1] Generally written "Fúshanjí". See *Nafaḥát*, No. 279.

CHAPTER IV.

ON THE WEARING OF PATCHED FROCKS (*Muraqqa'át*).

Know that the wearing of a *muraqqa'a* (patched frock) is the badge of aspirants to Ṣúfiism. The wearing of these garments is a *Sunna* (custom of the Prophet), for the Apostle said: *'Alaykum bi-labs al-ṣúf tajidúna ḥaláwat al-ímán fí qulúbikum.* And, further, one of the Companions says: *Kána 'l-nabí salla 'lláh 'alayhi wa-sallama yalbasu 'l-ṣúf wa-yarkabu 'l-ḥimár.* And, moreover, the Apostle said to 'Á'isha: *Lá tuḍayyi'i 'l-thawb ḥattá turaqqi'íhi.* He said: "See that ye wear woollen raiment, that ye may feel the sweetness of faith." And it is related that the Apostle wore a garment of wool and rode on an ass, and that he said to 'Á'isha: "O 'Á'isha, do not let the garment be destroyed, but patch it." 'Umar, the son of Khaṭṭáb, wore, it is said, a *muraqqa'a* with thirty patches inserted on it. Of 'Umar, too, we are told that he said: "The best garment is that which gives the least trouble" (*ki ma'únat-i án sabuktar buvad*). It is related of the Commander of the Faithful, 'Alí, that he had a shirt of which the sleeves were level with his fingers, and if at any time he wore a longer shirt he used to tear off the ends of its sleeves. The Apostle also was commanded by God to shorten his garments, for God said: "*And purify thy garments*" (Kor. lxxiv, 4), i.e. shorten them. And Ḥasan of Baṣra says: "I saw seventy comrades who fought at Badr: all of them had woollen garments; and the greatest *Ṣiddíq* (Abú Bakr) wore a garment of wool in his detachment from the world" (*tajríd*). Ḥasan of Baṣra says further: "I saw Salmán (al-Fárisí) wearing a woollen frock (*gilím*) with patches." The Commander of the Faithful, 'Umar b. al-Khaṭṭáb, and the Commander of the Faithful, 'Alí, and Harim b. Ḥayyán relate that they saw Uways Qaraní with a woollen garment on which patches were inserted. Ḥasan of Baṣra and Málik Dínár and Sufyán Thawrí were owners of woollen patched frocks. And it is related of the Imám Abú Ḥanífa of Kúfa—this is written in the History of the Shaykhs composed by Muḥammad b. 'Alí Ḥakím Tirmidhí—that he at first clothed himself in wool and was on the point of retiring from the world, when he saw in a dream the Apostle, who said: "It behoves thee to live amidst the people, because thou art the means whereby my *Sunna* will be revived." Then Abú Ḥanífa refrained from solitude, but he never put on a garment of any value. And Dáwud Ṭá'í, who was one of the veritable adepts among the aspirants to Ṣúfiism (*yakí az muḥaqqiqán-i mutaṣawwifa*), enjoined the wearing of wool. And Ibráhím the son of Adham came to visit the most venerable Imám Abú Ḥanífa, clad in a garment of wool. The latter's disciples looked at him with contempt and disparagement, until Abú Ḥanífa said: "Our lord Ibráhím b. Adham has come." The disciples said: "The Imám utters no jests: how has he gained this lordship?" Abú Ḥanífa replied: "By continual devotion. He has been occupied in serving God while we have been engaged in serving our own bodies. Thus he has become our lord."

It may well be the case that at the present day some persons wear patched frocks and religious habits (*muraqqa'át ú khiraq*) for the sake of public honour and reputation, and that their hearts belie their external garb; for there may be but one champion in a host, and in every sect the genuine adepts are few. People, however, reckon as Ṣúfís all who resemble the Ṣúfís even in a single rule. The Apostle said: *Man tashabbaha bi-qawm^in^ fa-huwa minhum*, "He that makes himself akin to a party either in conduct or in belief, is one of that party." But while some regard only the outward forms of their practice, others direct attention to their spirit of inward purity.

Those who wish to associate with aspirants to Ṣúfiism fall into four classes: (1) He whose purity, enlightenment, subtlety, even balance of temperament, and soundness of character give him insight into the hearts of the Ṣúfís, so that he perceives the nearness of their spiritual adepts to God and the loftiness of their eminent men. He joins himself to them in hope of attaining to the same degree, and the beginning of his novitiate is marked by revelation of "states" (*kashf-i aḥwál*), and purgation from desire, and renunciation of self. (2) He whose health of body and continence of heart and quiet peace of mind enable him to see their outward practice, so that he fixes his gaze on their observance of the holy law and of the different sorts of discipline, and on the excellence of their conduct: consequently he seeks to associate with them and give himself up to the practice of piety, and the beginning of his novitiate is marked by self-mortification (*mujáhadat*) and good conduct. (3) He whose humanity and custom of social intercourse and goodness of disposition cause him to consider their actions and to see the virtue of their outward life: how they treat their superiors with respect and their inferiors with generosity and their equals as comrades, and how untroubled they are by thoughts of worldly gain and contented with what they have; he seeks their society, and renders easy to himself the hard path of worldly ambition, and makes himself at leisure one of the good. (4) He whose stupidity and feebleness of soul—his love of power without merit and of distinction without knowledge—lead him to suppose that the outward actions of the Ṣúfís are everything. When he enters their company they treat him kindly and indulgently, although they are convinced that he is entirely ignorant of God and that he has never striven to advance upon the mystic path. Therefore he is honoured by the people as if he were a real adept and is venerated as if he were one of God's saints, but his object is only to assume their dress and hide his deformity under their piety. He is like an ass laden with books (Kor. lxxii, 5). In this age the majority are impostors such as have been described. Accordingly, it behoves you not to seem to be anything except what you really are. It is inward glow (*ḥurqat*) that makes the Ṣúfí, not the religious habit (*khirqat*). To the true mystic there is no difference between the mantle (*'abá*) worn by dervishes, and the coat (*qabá*) worn by ordinary people. An eminent Shaykh was asked why he did not wear a patched frock (*muraqqa'a*). He replied: "It is hypocrisy to wear the garb of the Ṣúfís and not to bear the burdens which Ṣúfiism entails." If, by wearing this garb, you wish to make known to God that you are one of the elect, God knows that already; and if you wish to show to the people that you belong to God, should your claim be true, you are guilty of ostentation; and should it be false, of hypocrisy. The Ṣúfís are too great to need a special garment for this purpose. Purity (*ṣafá*) is a gift from God, whereas wool (*ṣúf*) is the clothing of animals. The Ṣúfí Shaykhs enjoined their disciples to wear patched frocks, and did the same themselves, in order that they might be marked men, and that all the people might keep watch over them: thus if they committed a transgression, every tongue would rebuke them, and if they wished to sin while clad in this garment, they would be held back by shame. In short, the *muraqqa'a* is the garb of God's saints. The vulgar use it merely as a means of gaining worldly reputation and fortune, but the elect prefer contumely to honour, and affliction to prosperity. Hence it is said "the *muraqqa'a* is a garb of happiness for the vulgar, but a mail-coat (*jawshan*) of affliction for the elect." You must seek what is spiritual, and shun what is external. The Divine is veiled by the human, and that veil is annihilated only by passing through the "states" and "stages" of the mystic Way. Purity (*ṣafá*) is the name given to such annihilation. How can he who has gained it choose one garment rather than another, or take pains to adorn himself at all? How should he care whether people call him a Ṣúfí or by some other name?

SECTION.

Muraqqa'as should be made with a view to ease and lightness, and when the original cloth is torn a patch should be inserted.

There are two opinions of the Shaykhs as to this matter. Some hold that it is improper to sew the patch on neatly and accurately, and that the needle should be drawn through the cloth at random,[1] and that no trouble should be taken. Others again hold that the stitches should be straight and regular, and that it is part of the practice of the dervishes to keep the stitches straight and to take pains therein; for sound practice indicates sound principles.

Now I, who am 'Alí b. 'Uthmán al-Jullábí, asked the Grand Shaykh, Abu 'l-Qásim Gurgání at Ṭús, saying: "What is the least thing necessary for a dervish in order that he may become worthy of poverty?" He replied: "A dervish must not have less than three things: first, he must know how to sew on a patch rightly; second, he must know how to listen rightly; third, he must know how to set his foot on the ground rightly." A number of dervishes were present with me when he said this. As soon as we came to the door each one began to apply this saying to his own case, and some ignorant fellows fastened on it with avidity. "This," they cried, "is poverty indeed," and most of them were hastening to sew patches on nicely and to set their feet on the ground correctly; and everyone of them imagined that he knew how to listen to sayings on Ṣúfiism. Wherefore, since my heart was devoted to that Sayyid, and I was unwilling that his words should fall to the ground, I said: "Come, let each of us say something upon this subject." So everyone stated his views, and when my turn came I said: "A right patch is one that is stitched for poverty, not for show; if it is stitched for poverty, it is right, even though it be stitched wrong. And a right word is one that is heard esoterically (*ba-ḥál*), not wilfully (*ba-munyat*), and is applied earnestly, not frivolously, and is apprehended by life, not by reason. And a right foot is one that is put on the ground with true rapture, not playfully and formally." Some of my remarks were reported to the Sayyid (Abu 'l-Qásim Gurgání), who said: "'Alí has spoken well—God

[1] Literally, "in whatever place it raises its head."

reward him!" The aim of this sect in wearing patched frocks is to alleviate the burden of this world and to be sincere in poverty towards God. It is related in the genuine Traditions that Jesus, son of Mary—God bless him!—was wearing a *muraqqa'a* when he was taken up to heaven. A certain Shaykh said: "I dreamed that I saw him clad in a woollen patched frock, and light was shining from every patch. I said: 'O Messiah, what are these lights on thy garment?' He answered: 'The lights of necessary grace; for I sewed on each of those patches through necessity, and God Almighty hath turned into a light every tribulation which He inflicted on my heart.'"

I saw in Transoxania an old man who belonged to the sect of Malámatís. He neither ate nor wore anything in which human beings had a hand. His food consisted of things thrown away by men, such as putrid vegetables, sour gourds, rotten carrots, and the like. His clothes were made of rags which he had picked up from the road and washed: of these he had made a *muraqqa'a*. And I have heard that among the mystics of recent times there was an old man of flourishing condition (*qawí ḥál*) and of excellent character, living at Marv al-Rúd, who had sewn so many patches, without taking pains, on his prayer-rug and cap, that scorpions brought forth their young in them. And my Shaykh—may God be well pleased with him!—wore for fifty-one years a single cloak (*jubba*), on which he used to sew pieces of cloth without taking any pains. I have found the following tale among the anecdotes of the (holy) men of 'Iráq. There were two dervishes, one a votary of the contemplative life (*ṣáḥib musháhadat*), and the other a votary of the purgative life (*ṣáḥib mujáhadat*). The former never clothed himself except in the pieces of cloth which were torn off by dervishes in a state of ecstasy (*samá'*) from their own garments, while the other used for the same purpose only the pieces torn off by dervishes who were asking forgiveness: thus the outward garb of each was in harmony with his inward disposition. This is observance of the "state" (*pás dáshtan-i ḥál*). Shaykh Muhammad b. Khafíf wore a coarse woollen frock (*palás*) for twenty years, and every year he used to undergo four fasts of forty days' duration (*chilla*), and every forty days he would compose a work on the mysteries of the Sciences of the Divine Verities. In his time there was an old man,[1] one of the adepts learned in the Way (*Ṭaríqat*) and the Truth (*Ḥaqíqat*), who resided at Parg[2] in Fárs and was called Muḥammad b. Zakariyyá.[3] He had never worn a *muraqqa'a*. Now Shaykh Muḥammad b. Khafíf was asked: "What is involved in wearing a *muraqqa'a*, and who is permitted to do so?" He replied: "It involves those obligations which are fulfilled by Muḥammad b. Zakariyyá in his white shirt, and the wearing of such a frock is permitted to him."

Section.

It is not the way of the Ṣúfís to abandon their customs. If they seldom wear garments of wool at the present day, there are two reasons for this fact: (1) that wools have deteriorated (*pashmhá shúrída shuda ast*) and the animals (which produce wool) have been carried off from one place to another by raiders; and (2) that a sect of heretics has adopted the woollen garment as a badge (*shi'ár*). And it is praiseworthy to depart from the badge of heretics, even although one departs at the same time from a traditional practice (*sunna*).

To take pains (*takalluf*) in sewing *muraqqa'as* is considered allowable by the Ṣúfís because they have gained a high reputation among the people; and since many imitate them and wear *muraqqa'as*, and are guilty of improper acts, and since the Ṣúfís dislike the society of others than themselves—for these reasons they have invented a garb which none but

[1] This story is related in 'Aṭṭár's *Tadhkirat al-Awliyá* (pt. ii, p. 125, l. 17 sqq.), where it is expressly said that the old man was *not* "learned in the Way".

[2] I. in margin has Park. The *Nuzhat al-Qulúb* gives the name as برک (Bark), and refers it to a village in the district of Kirmán.

[3] B., I., and J. have Dhakariyyá (Zakariyyá), L. ذکری. The MSS. of the *Tadhkirat al-Awliyá* vary between Dhakírí and ذکری.

themselves can sew, and have made it a mark of mutual acquaintance and a badge. So much so that when a certain dervish came to one of the Shaykhs wearing a garment on which the patch had been sewn with too wide stitches (*khaṭṭ ba-pahná áwarda búd*) the Shaykh banished him from his presence. The argument is that purity (*ṣafá*) is founded on delicacy of nature and fineness of temperament, and undoubtedly crookedness in one's nature is not good. It is natural to disapprove of incorrect actions, just as it is natural to derive no pleasure from incorrect poetry.

Others, again, do not trouble themselves about clothes at all. They wear either a religious habit (*'abá*) or an ordinary coat (*qabá*), whichever God may have given them; and if He keeps them naked, they remain in that state. I, who am 'Alí b. 'Uthmán al-Jullábí, approve of this doctrine, and I have practised it in my journeys. It is related that Aḥmad b. Khaḍrúya wore a coat when he visited Abú Yazíd, and that Sháh b. Shujá' wore a coat when he visited Abú Ḥafṣ. This was not their usual dress, for sometimes they wore a *muraqqa'a* and sometimes a woollen garment or a white shirt, as it might happen. The human soul is habituated to things, and fond of custom, and when anything has become habitual to the soul it soon grows natural, and when it has grown natural it becomes a veil. Hence the Apostle said: *Khayr al-ṣiyám ṣawm akhí Dáwud 'alayhi 'l-salám*, "The best of fasts is that of my brother David." They said: "O Apostle of God, what kind of fast is that?" He replied: "David used to keep his fast one day and break it on the next day," in order that his soul should not become accustomed either to keeping the fast or to breaking it, for fear that he might be veiled thereby. And, as regards this matter, Abú Ḥámid Dústán[1] of Merv was the most sound. His disciples used to put a garment on him, but those who wanted it used to seek him out when he was at leisure and alone, and divest him of it; and he would never say to the person who put it on him: "Why do you put it on?" nor to the

[1] See *Nafaḥát*, No. 350.

person who took it off: "Why do you take it off?" Moreover, at the present day there is at Ghazna—may God protect it!—an old man with the sobriquet Mu'ayyad, who has no choice or discrimination with respect to his clothes; and he is sound in that degree.

Now, as to their garments being mostly blue (*kabúd*), one of the reasons is that they have made wandering (*siyáḥat*) and travelling the foundation of their Path; and on journeys a white garment does not retain its original appearance, and is not easily washed, and besides, everyone covets it. Another cause is this, that a blue dress is the badge of the bereaved and afflicted, and the apparel of mourners; and this world is the abode of trouble, the pavilion of affliction, the den of sorrow, the house of parting, the cradle of tribulation: the (Ṣúfí) disciples, seeing that their heart's desire is not to be gained in this world, have clad themselves in blue and have sat down to mourn union (with God). Others behold in the practice (of devotion) only imperfection, in the heart only evil, in life only loss of time: therefore they wear blue; for loss (*fawt*) is worse than death (*mawt*). One wears blue for the death of a dear friend, another for the loss of a cherished hope.

A dervish was asked why he wore blue. He replied: "The Apostle left three things: poverty, knowledge, and the sword. The sword was taken by potentates, who misused it; knowledge was chosen by savants, who were satisfied with merely teaching it; poverty was chosen by dervishes, who made it a means of enriching themselves. I wear blue as a sign of mourning for the calamity of these three classes of men." Once Murta'ish was walking in one of the quarters of Baghdád. Being thirsty, he went to a door and asked for a drink of water. The daughter of the householder brought him some water in a jug. Murta'ish was smitten with her beauty and would not leave the spot until the master of the house came to him. "O sir," cried Murta'ish, "she gave me a drink of water and robbed me of my heart." The householder replied: "She is my daughter, and I give her to you in marriage." So Murta'ish went into the house, and the wedding was immediately solemnized. The bride's father, who was a wealthy man, sent Murta'ish to the bath, where they took off his patched frock (*muraqqa'a*) and clothed him in a night-dress. At nightfall he rose to say his prayers and engage in solitary devotion. Suddenly he called out, "Bring my patched frock." They asked, "What ails you?" He answered, "I heard a voice within, whispering: 'On account of one disobedient look We have removed thy *muraqqa'a*, the garb of piety, from thy body; if thou lookest again We shall remove the raiment of intimacy from thy heart.'" Only two kinds of men are fitted to wear the *muraqqa'a*: (1) those who are cut off from the world, and (2) those who feel a longing for the Lord (*mushtáqán-i mawlá*).

The Súfí Shaykhs observe the following rule. When a novice joins them, with the purpose of renouncing the world, they subject him to spiritual discipline for the space of three years. If he fulfil the requirements of this discipline, well and good; otherwise, they declare that he cannot be admitted to the Path (*Taríqat*). The first year is devoted to service of the people, the second year to service of God, and the third year to watching over his own heart. He can serve the people only when he places himself in the rank of servants and all other people in the rank of masters, i.e. he must regard all, without any discrimination, as being better than himself, and must consider it his duty to serve all alike; not in such a way as to deem himself superior to those whom he serves, for this is manifest perdition and evident fraud, and is one of the infectious cankers of the age (*az áfát-i zamána andar zamána yakí ínast*). And he can serve God Almighty only when he cuts off all his selfish interests relating either to this world or to the next, and worships God absolutely for His sake alone, inasmuch as whoever worships God for any thing's sake worships himself and not God. And he can watch over his heart only when his thoughts are collected and cares are dismissed from his heart, so that in the presence of intimacy (with God) he preserves his heart from the assaults of heedlessness. When these three qualifications are possessed by the novice, he may wear the *muraqqa'a* as a true mystic, not merely as an imitator of others.

Now as to the person who invests the novice with the *muraqqa'a*, he must be a man of rectitude (*mustaqím al-ḥál*) who has traversed all the hills and dales of the Path, and tasted the rapture of "states" and perceived the nature of actions, and experienced the severity of the Divine majesty and the clemency of the Divine beauty. Furthermore, he must examine the state of his disciples and judge what point they will ultimately reach: whether they will retire (*ráji'án*), or stand still (*wáqifán*), or attain (*bálighán*). If he knows that some day they will abandon this Path, he must forbid them to enter upon it; if they will come to a stand, he must enjoin them to practise devotion; and if they will reach the goal, he must give them spiritual nourishment. The Súfí Shaykhs are physicians of men's souls. When the physician is ignorant of the patient's malady he kills him by his art, because he does not know how to treat him and does not recognize the symptoms of danger, and prescribes food and drink unsuitable to his disease. The Apostle said: "The shaykh in his tribe is like the prophet in his nation." Accordingly, as the prophets showed insight in their call to the people, and kept everyone in his due degree, so the Shaykh likewise should show insight in his call, and should give to everyone his proper spiritual food, in order that the object of his call may be secured.

The adept, then, who has attained the perfection of saintship takes the right course when he invests the novice with the *muraqqa'a* after a period of three years during which he has educated him in the necessary discipline. In respect of the qualifications which it demands, the *muraqqa'a* is comparable to a winding-sheet (*kafan*): the wearer must resign all his hopes of the pleasures of life, and purge his heart of all sensual delights, and devote his life entirely to the service of God and completely renounce selfish desires. Then the Director (*Pír*) ennobles him by clothing him in that robe of honour, while he on his part fulfils the obligations which it involves, and strives with all his might to perform them, and deems it unlawful to satisfy his own wishes.

Many allegories (*ishárát*) have been uttered concerning the *muraqqa'a*. Shaykh Abú Ma'mar of Iṣfahán has written a book on the subject, and the generality of aspirants to Ṣúfiism display much extravagance (*ghuluww*) in this matter. My aim, however, in the present work is not to relate sayings, but to elucidate the difficulties of Ṣúfiism. The best allegory concerning the *muraqqa'a* is this, that its collar (*qabba*) is patience, its two sleeves fear and hope, its two gussets (*tiríz*) contraction and dilation, its belt self-abnegation, its hem (*kursí*)[1] soundness in faith, its fringe (*faráwíz*) sincerity. Better still is the following: "Its collar is annihilation of intercourse (with men), its two sleeves are observance (*ḥifẓ*) and continence (*'iṣmat*), its two gussets are poverty and purity, its belt is persistence in contemplation, its hem (*kursí*) is tranquillity in (God's) presence, and its fringe is settlement in the abode of union." When you have made a *muraqqa'a* like this for your spiritual self it behoves you to make one for your exterior also. I have composed a separate book on this subject, entitled "The Mysteries of Patched Frocks and Means of Livelihood" (*Asrár al-khiraq wa-'l-ma'únát*), of which the novice should get a copy.

If the novice, having donned the *muraqqa'a*, should be forced to tear it under compulsion of the temporal authority, this is permissible and excusable; but should he tear it of free will and deliberately, then according to the law of the sect he is not allowed to wear a *muraqqa'a* in future, and if he do so, he stands on the same footing as those in our time who are content to wear *muraqqa'as* for outward show, with no spiritual meaning. As regards the rending of garments the true doctrine is this, that when Ṣúfís pass from one stage to another they immediately change their dress in thankfulness for having gained a higher

[1] This conjectural translation of *kursí* was suggested to me by Colonel Ranking. The dictionaries give no explanation of the word as it is used here.

stage; but whereas every other garment is the dress of a single stage, the *muraqqa'a* is a dress which comprises all the stages of the Path of poverty and purity, and therefore to discard it is equivalent to renouncing the whole Path. I have made a slight allusion to this question, although this is not the proper place for it, in order to settle the particular point at issue; but, please God, I will give a detailed explanation of the principle in the chapter on rending (*kharq*), and in the revelation of the mystery of "audition" (*samá'*). Furthermore, it has been said that one who invests a novice with the *muraqqa'a* should possess such sovereign mystical powers that any stranger on whom he looks kindly should become a friend, and any sinner whom he clothes in this garment should become a saint.

Once I was travelling with my Shaykh in Ádharbáyaján, and we saw two or three persons wearing *muraqqa'as*, who were standing beside a wheat-barn and holding up their skirts in the hope that the farmer would throw them some wheat. On seeing this the Shaykh exclaimed: "*Those are they who have purchased error at the price of true guidance, but their traffic has not been profitable*" (Kor. ii, 15). I asked him how they had fallen into this calamity and disgrace. He said: "Their spiritual directors were greedy to gather disciples, and they themselves are greedy to collect worldly goods." It is related of Junayd that he saw at the Báb al-Ṭáq[1] a beautiful Christian youth and said: "O Lord, pardon him for my sake, for Thou hast created him exceeding fair." After a while the youth came to Junayd and made profession of Islam and was enrolled among the saints. Abú 'Alí Siyáh was asked: "Who is permitted to invest novices with the *muraqqa'a*?" He replied: "That one who oversees the whole kingdom of God, so that nothing happens in the world without his knowledge."

[1] A gate in the eastern quarter of Baghdád.

CHAPTER V.

On the Different Opinions held concerning Poverty and Purity.

The Doctors of the Mystic Path are not agreed as to the respective merits of Poverty (*faqr*) and Purity (*ṣafwat*). Some hold that Poverty is more perfect than Purity. Poverty, they say, is complete annihilation in which every thought ceases to exist, and Purity is one of the "stations" (*maqámát*) of Poverty: when annihilation is gained, all "stations" vanish into nothing. This is ultimately the same question as that touching Poverty and Wealth, which has already been discussed. Those who set Purity above Poverty say that Poverty is an existent thing (*shay ast mawjúd*) and is capable of being named, whereas Purity is the being pure (*ṣafá*) from all existing things: *ṣafá* is the essence of annihilation (*faná*), and Poverty is the essence of subsistence (*baqá*): therefore Poverty is one of the names of "stations", but Purity is one of the names of perfection. This matter has been disputed at great length in the present age, and both parties have resorted to far-fetched and amazing verbal subtleties; but it will be allowed on all sides that Poverty and Purity are not mere words and nothing else. The disputants have made up a doctrine out of words and have neglected to apprehend meanings: they have abandoned discussion of the Truth. Negation of arbitrary will they call negation of essence, and affirmation of desire they regard as affirmation of essence. The Mystic Path is far removed from such idle fictions. In short, the Saints of God attain to a place where place no longer exists, where all degrees and "stations" disappear, and where outward expressions fall off from the underlying realities, so that neither "spiritual delight" (*shurb*) is left, nor "taste" (*dhawq*), nor "sobriety" (*ṣaḥw*), nor "effacement" (*maḥw*). These controversialists, however, seek a forced name with which to cloak ideas that do not admit of being named or of being used as attributes; and everyone applies to them whatever name he thinks most estimable. Now, in dealing with the ideas themselves, the question of superiority does not arise, but when names are given to them, one will necessarily be preferred to another. Accordingly, to some people the name of Poverty seemed to be superior and of greater worth because it is connected with renunciation and humility, while others preferred Purity, and held it the more honourable because it comes nearer to the notion of discarding all that contaminates and annihilating all that has a taint of the world. They adopted these two names as symbols of an inexpressible idea, in order that they might converse with each other on that subject and make their own state fully known; and there is no difference of opinion in this sect (the Ṣúfís), although some use the term "Poverty" and others the term "Purity" to express the same idea. With the verbalists (*ahl-i 'ibárat*), on the contrary, who are ignorant of the true meaning of these ideas, the whole question is an affair of words. To conclude, whoever has made that idea his own and fixed his heart upon it, heeds not whether they call him "Poor" (*faqír*) or "Pure" (*Ṣúfí*), since both these appellations are forced names for an idea that cannot be brought under any name.

This controversy dates from the time of Abu 'l-Ḥasan Sumnún. He, on occasions when he was in a state of revelation (*kashf*) akin to subsistence (*baqá*), used to set Poverty above Purity; and on being asked by spiritualists (*arbáb-i ma'ání*) why he did so, he replied: "Inasmuch as I naturally delight in annihilation and abasement, and no less in subsistence and exaltation, I prefer Purity to Poverty when I am in a state akin to annihilation, and Poverty to Purity when I am in a state akin to subsistence; for Poverty is the name of subsistence and Purity that of annihilation. In the latter state I annihilate from myself the sight (consciousness) of subsistence, and in the former state I annihilate from myself the sight of annihilation, so that my nature becomes dead both to annihilation and to subsistence." Now this, regarded as an explanation (*'ibárat*), is an excellent saying, but neither annihilation nor subsistence can be annihilated: every subsistent thing that suffers annihilation is annihilated from itself, and every annihilated thing that becomes subsistent is subsistent from itself. Annihilation is a term of which it is impossible to speak hyperbolically. If a person says that annihilation is annihilated, he can only be expressing hyperbolically the non-existence of any vestige of the idea of annihilation; but so long as any vestige of existence remains, annihilation has not yet come to pass; and when it has been attained, the "annihilation" thereof is nothing but self-conceit flattered by meaningless phrases. In the vanity and rashness of youth I composed a discourse of this kind, entitled the "Book of Annihilation and Subsistence" (*Kitáb-i Faná ú Baqá*), but in the present work I will set forth the whole matter with caution, please God the Almighty and Glorious.

This is the distinction between Purity and Poverty in the spiritual sense. It is otherwise when Purity and Poverty are considered in their practical aspect, namely, the denuding one's self of worldly things (*tajríd*) and the casting away of all one's possessions. Here the real point is the difference between Poverty (*faqr*) and Lowliness (*maskanat*). Some Shaykhs assert that the Poor (*faqír*) are superior to the Lowly (*miskín*), because God has said, "*the poor who are straitened in the way of Allah, unable to go to and fro on the earth*" (Kor. ii, 274): the Lowly possess means of livelihood, which the Poor renounce: therefore Poverty is honour and Lowliness abasement, for, according to the rule of the Mystic Path, he who possesses the means of livelihood is base, as the Apostle said: "Woe befall those who worship the dínár and the dirhem, woe befall those who worship garments with a nap!" He who renounces the means of livelihood is honoured, inasmuch as he depends on God, while he who has means depends on them. Others, again, declare the Lowly to be superior, because the Apostle said: "Let me live lowly, and let me die lowly, and raise me from the dead among the lowly!" whereas, speaking of Poverty, he said, "Poverty is near to being unbelief." On this account the Poor are dependent on a means, but the Lowly are independent. In the domain of Sacred Law, some divines hold that the Poor are those who have a sufficiency (*ṣáḥib bulgha*), and the Lowly those who are free from worldly cares (*mujarrad*); but other divines hold the converse of this view. Hence the name "Ṣúfí" is given to the Lowly by followers of the Path (*ahl-i maqámát*) who adopt the former opinion: they prefer Purity (*ṣafwat*) to Poverty. Those Ṣúfís who accept the latter view prefer Poverty to Purity, for a similar reason.

CHAPTER VI.

ON BLAME (*Malámat*).

The path of Blame has been trodden by some of the Ṣúfí Shaykhs. Blame has a great effect in making love sincere. The followers of the Truth (*ahl-i ḥaqq*) are distinguished by their being the objects of vulgar blame, especially the eminent ones of this community. The Apostle, who is the exemplar and leader of the adherents of the Truth, and who marches at the head of the lovers (of God), was honoured and held in good repute by all until the evidence of the Truth was revealed to him and inspiration came upon him. Then the people loosed their tongues to blame him. Some said, "He is a soothsayer;" others, "He is a poet;" others, "He is a madman;" others, "He is a liar;" and so forth. And God says, describing the true believers: "*They fear not the blame of anyone; that is the grace of God which He bestows on whomsoever He pleases; God is bounteous and wise*" (Kor. v, 59). Such is the ordinance of God, that He causes those who discourse of Him to be blamed by the whole world, but preserves their hearts from being preoccupied by the world's blame. This He does in His jealousy: He guards His lovers from glancing aside to "other" (*ghayr*), lest the eye of any stranger should behold the beauty of their state; and He guards them also from seeing themselves, lest they should regard their own beauty and fall into self-conceit and arrogance. Therefore He hath set the vulgar over them to loose the tongues of blame against them, and hath made the "blaming soul" (*nafs-i lawwáma*) part of their composition, in order that they may be blamed by others for whatever they do, and by themselves for doing evil or for doing good imperfectly.

Now this is a firm principle in the Way to God, for in this Path there is no taint or veil more difficult to remove than self-conceit. God in His kindness hath barred the way of error against His friends. Their actions, however good, are not approved by the vulgar, who do not see them as they really are; and they themselves do not regard their works of mortification, however numerous, as proceeding from their own strength and power: consequently they are not pleased with themselves and are protected from self-conceit. Whoever is approved by God is disapproved by the vulgar, and whoever is elected by himself is not among the elect of God. Thus Iblís was approved by mankind and accepted by the angels, and he was pleased with himself; but since God was not pleased with him, their approval only brought a curse upon him. Adam, on the other hand, was disapproved by the angels, who said: "*Wilt Thou place there* [on the earth] *one who will do evil therein?*" (Kor. ii, 28), and was not pleased with himself, for he said: "*O Lord, we have done ourselves a wrong*" (Kor. vii, 22); but since God was pleased with him, the disapproval of the angels and his own displeasure bore the fruit of mercy. Let all men, therefore, know that those accepted by us are rejected by the people, and that those accepted by the people are rejected by us. Hence the blame of mankind is the food of the friends of God, because it is a token of Divine approval; it is the delight of the saints of God, because it is a sign of nearness to Him: they rejoice in it even as other men rejoice in popularity. There is a Tradition, which the Apostle received from Gabriel, that God said: " My friends (saints) are under My cloak: save Me, none knoweth them except My friends."

SECTION.

Now blame (*malámat*) is of three kinds: it may result (1) from following the right way (*malámat-i rást raftan*), or (2) from an intentional act (*malámat-i qaṣd kardan*), or (3) from abandonment of the law (*malámat-i tark kardan*). In the first case, a man is blamed who minds his own business and performs his religious duties and does not omit any practice of devotion: he is entirely indifferent to the behaviour of the people towards him. In the second case a man is greatly honoured by the people and pointed out among them: his heart inclines to the honour in which he is held, and becomes attached to those by whom it is bestowed: he wishes to make himself independent of them and devote himself wholly to God; therefore he purposely incurs their blame by committing some act which is offensive to them but which is no violation of the law: in consequence of his behaviour they wash their hands of him. In the third case, a man is driven by his natural infidelity and erroneous beliefs to abandon the sacred law and abjure its observances, and say to himself, "I am treading the path of blame:" in this case his behaviour depends on himself alone.

He who follows the right way and refuses to act hypocritically, and refrains from ostentation, pays no heed to the blame of the vulgar, but invariably takes his own course: it is all one to him what name they call him by. I find among the anecdotes (of holy men) that one day Shaykh Abú Ṭáhir Ḥaramí was seen in the bazaar, riding a donkey and attended by one of his disciples. Some person cried out, "Here comes that old freethinker!" The indignant disciple rushed at the speaker, trying to strike him, and the whole bazaar was filled with tumult. The Shaykh said to his disciple: "If you will be quiet, I will show you something that will save you from trouble of this sort." When they returned home, he bade the disciple bring a certain box, which contained letters, and told him to look at them. "Observe," he said, "how the writers address me. One calls me 'the Shaykh of Islam', another 'the pure Shaykh', another 'the ascetic Shaykh', another 'the Shaykh of the two Sanctuaries', and so on. They are all titles, there is no mention of my name. I am none of these things, but every person gives me the title which accords with his belief concerning me. If that poor fellow did the same just now, why should you quarrel with him?"

He who incurs blame purposely and resigns honour and

withdraws from authority is like the Caliph 'Uthmán who, although he possessed four hundred slaves, one day came forth from his plantation of date-palms carrying a bundle of firewood on his head. On being asked why he did this, he answered: "I wish to make trial of myself." He would not let the dignity which he enjoyed hinder him from any work. A similar tale related of the Imám Abú Ḥanífa will be found in this treatise. And a story is told about Abú Yazíd, that, when he was entering Rayy on his way from the Ḥijáz, the people of that city ran to meet him in order that they might show him honour. Their attentions distracted him and turned his thoughts away from God. When he came to the bazaar, he took a loaf from his sleeve and began to eat. They all departed, for it was the month of Ramaḍán. He said to a disciple who was travelling with him: "You see! as soon as I perform a single article of the law,[1] they all reject me." In those days it was necessary, for incurring blame, to do something disapproved or extraordinary; but in our time, if anyone desires blame, he need only lengthen a little his voluntary prayers or fulfil the religious practices which are prescribed: at once everybody will call him a hypocrite and impostor.

He who abandons the law and commits an irreligious act, and says that he is following the rule of "blame", is guilty of manifest wrong and wickedness and self-indulgence. There are many in the present age who seek popularity by this means, forgetting that one must already have gained popularity before deliberately acting in such a way as to make the people reject him; otherwise, his making himself unpopular is a mere pretext for winning popularity. On a certain occasion I was in the company of one of these vain pretenders. He committed a wicked act and excused himself by saying that he did it for the sake of blame. One of the party said, "That is nonsense." He heaved a sigh. I said to him: "If you claim to be a Malámatí and are firm in your belief, this gentleman's

[1] Abú Yazíd, being at that time on a journey, was not legally bound to observe the fast.

disapproval of what you have done ought to encourage you to persevere; and since he is seconding you in your chosen course, why are you so unfriendly and angry with him? Your behaviour is more like pretence than pursuit of blame. Whoever claims to be guided by the Truth must give some proof of his assertion, and the proof consists in observing the *Sunna* (Ordinances of the Prophet). You make this claim, and yet I see that you have failed to perform an obligatory religious duty. Your conduct puts you outside the pale of Islam."

SECTION.

The doctrine of Blame was spread abroad in this sect by the Shaykh of his age, Ḥamdún Qaṣṣár. He has many fine sayings on the subject. It is recorded that he said: *Al-malámat tark al-salámat*, "Blame is the abandonment of welfare." If anyone purposely abandons his own welfare and girds himself to endure misfortune, and renounces his pleasures and familiar ties, in hope that the glory of God will be revealed to him, the more he is separated from mankind the more he is united to God. Accordingly, the votaries of Blame turn their backs on that thing, namely welfare (*salámat*), to which the people of this world turn their faces, for the aspirations of the former are Unitarian (*waḥdání*). Aḥmad b. Fátik relates that Ḥusayn b. Manṣúr, in reply to the question "Who is the Ṣúfí?" said: "He who is single in essence" (*waḥdání al-dhát*). Ḥamdún also said concerning Blame: "It is a hard way for the vulgar to follow, but I will tell one part thereof: the Malámatí is characterized by the hope of the Murjites and the fear of the Qadarites." This saying has a hidden meaning which demands explanation. It is the nature of man to be deterred by popularity more than any other thing from seeking access to God. Consequently he who fears this danger is always striving to avoid it, and there are two perils which confront him: firstly, the fear that he may be veiled from God by the favour of his fellow-creatures; and secondly, the fear of committing some act for which the people will blame him and thereby fall into sin. Accordingly, the Malámatí must, in the first instance, take care to have no quarrel with the people for what they say of him, either in this world or the next, and for the sake of his own salvation he must commit some act which, legally, is neither a great sin (*kabíra*) nor a trivial offence (*ṣaghíra*), in order that the people may reject him. Hence his fear in matters of conduct is like the fear of the Qadarites, and his hope in dealing with those who blame him is like the hope of the Murjites. In true love there is nothing sweeter than blame, because blame of the Beloved makes no impression on the lover's heart: he heeds not what strangers say, for his heart is ever faithful to the object of his love.

"*'Tis sweet to be reviled for passion's sake.*"

This sect (the Ṣúfís) are distinguished above all creatures in the universe by choosing to be blamed in the body on account of the welfare of their souls; and this high degree is not attained by the Cherubim or any spiritual beings, nor has it been reached by the ascetics, devotees, and seekers of God belonging to the nations of antiquity, but it is reserved for those of this nation who journey on the path of entire severance from the things of the world.

In my opinion, to seek Blame is mere ostentation, and ostentation is mere hypocrisy. The ostentatious man purposely acts in such a way as to win popularity, while the Malámatí purposely acts in such a way that the people reject him. Both have their thoughts fixed on mankind and do not pass beyond that sphere. The dervish, on the contrary, never even thinks of mankind, and when his heart has been broken away from them he is as indifferent to their reprobation as to their favour: he moves unfettered and free. I once said to a Malámatí of Transoxania, with whom I had associated long enough to feel at my ease: "O brother, what is your object in these perverse actions?" He replied: "To make the people non-existent in regard to myself." "The people," I said, "are many, and during a lifetime you will not be able to make them non-existent in regard to yourself; rather make yourself non-existent in regard to the people, so that you may be saved from all this trouble. Some who are occupied with the people imagine that the people are occupied with them. If you wish no one to see you, do not see yourself. Since all your evils arise from seeing yourself, what business have you with others? If a sick man whose remedy lies in abstinence seeks to indulge his appetite, he is a fool." Others, again, practise the method of Blame from an ascetic motive: they wish to be despised by the people in order that they may mortify themselves, and it is their greatest delight to find themselves wretched and abased. Ibráhím b. Adham was asked, "Have you ever attained your desire?" He answered: "Yes, twice; on one occasion I was in a ship where nobody knew me. I was clad in common clothes and my hair was long, and my guise was such that all the people in the ship mocked and laughed at me. Among them was a buffoon, who was always coming and pulling my hair and tearing it out, and treating me with contumely after the manner of his kind. At that time I felt entirely satisfied, and I rejoiced in my garb. My joy reached its highest pitch one day when the buffoon rose from his place and *super me minxit*. On the second occasion I arrived at a village in heavy rain, which had soaked the patched frock on my body, and I was overcome by the wintry cold. I went to a mosque, but was refused admittance. The same thing happened at three other mosques where I sought shelter. In despair, as the cold strengthened its grip on my heart, I entered a bath-house and drew my skirt close up to the stove. The smoke enveloped me and blackened my clothes and my face. Then also I felt entirely satisfied."

Once I, 'Alí b. 'Uthmán al-Jullábí, found myself in a difficulty. After many devotional exercises undertaken in the hope of clearing it away, I repaired—as I had done with success on a former occasion—to the tomb of Abú Yazíd, and stayed beside it for a space of three months, performing every day three ablutions and thirty purifications in the hope that my difficulty might be removed. It was not, however; so I departed and journeyed towards Khurásán. One night I arrived at a village in that country where there was a convent (*khánaqáh*) inhabited by a number of aspirants to Ṣúfiism. I was wearing a dark-blue frock (*muraqqa'-i khishan*), such as is prescribed by the *Sunna*;[1] but I had with me nothing of the Ṣúfí's regular equipment (*álat-i ahl-i rasm*) except a staff and a leathern water-bottle (*rakwa*). I appeared very contemptible in the eyes of these Ṣúfís, who did not know me. They regarded only my external habit and said to one another, "This fellow is not one of us." And so in truth it was: I was not one of them, but I had to pass the night in that place. They lodged me on a roof, while they themselves went up to a roof above mine, and set before me dry bread which had turned green, while I was drawing into my nostrils the savour of the viands with which they regaled themselves. All the time they were addressing derisive remarks to me from the roof. When they finished the food, they began to pelt me with the skins of the melons which they had eaten, by way of showing how pleased they were with themselves and how lightly they thought of me. I said in my heart: "O Lord God, were it not that they are wearing the dress of Thy friends, I would not have borne this from them." And the more they scoffed at me the more glad became my heart, so that the endurance of this burden was the means of delivering me from that difficulty which I have mentioned; and forthwith I perceived why the Shaykhs have always given fools leave to associate with them and for what reason they submit to their annoyance.

[1] I. adds in margin "for travellers".

CHAPTER VII.

Concerning their Imáms who belonged to the Companions.

1. The Caliph Abú Bakr, the Veracious (*al-Ṣiddíq*).

He is placed by the Ṣúfí Shaykhs at the head of those who have adopted the contemplative life (*musháhadat*), on account of the fewness of the stories and traditions which he related; while 'Umar is placed at the head of those who have adopted the purgative life (*mujáhadat*), because of his rigour and assiduity in devotion. It is written among the genuine Traditions, and is well known to scholars, that when Abú Bakr prayed at night he used to recite the Koran in a low voice, whereas 'Umar used to recite in a loud voice. The Apostle asked Abú Bakr why he did this. Abú Bakr replied: "He with whom I converse will hear." 'Umar, in his turn, replied: "I wake the drowsy and drive away the Devil." The one gave a token of contemplation, the other of purgation. Now purgation, compared with contemplation, is like a drop of water in a sea, and for this reason the Apostle said that 'Umar, the glory of Islam, was only (equivalent to) a single one of the good deeds of Abú Bakr (*hal anta illá ḥasanat^un min ḥasanáti Abí Bakr*). It is recorded that Abú Bakr said: "Our abode is transitory, our life therein is but a loan, our breaths are numbered, and our indolence is manifest." By this he signified that the world is too worthless to engage our thoughts; for whenever you occupy yourself with what is perishable, you are made blind to that which is eternal: the friends of God turn their backs on the world and the flesh which veil them from Him, and they decline to act as if they were owners of a thing that is really the property of another. And he said: "O God, give me plenty of the world and make me desirous of renouncing it!" This saying has a hidden sense, viz.: "First bestow on me worldly goods that I may give thanks for them, and then help me to abstain from them for Thy sake, so that I may have the treble merit of thanksgiving and liberality and abstinence, and that my poverty may be voluntary, not compulsory." These words refute the Director of mystical practice, who said: "He whose poverty is compulsory is more perfect than he whose poverty is voluntary; for if it be compulsory, he is the creature (*ṣan'at*) of poverty, and if it be voluntary, poverty is his creature; and it is better that his actions should be free from any attempt to gain poverty for himself than that he should seek to acquire it by his own effort." I say in answer to this: The creature of poverty is most evidently that person who, while enjoying independence, is possessed by the desire for poverty, and labours to recover it from the clutches of the world; not that person who, in the state of poverty, is possessed by the desire for independence and has to go to the houses of evildoers and the courts of governors for the sake of earning money. The creature of poverty is he who falls from independence to poverty, not he who, being poor, seeks to become powerful. Abú Bakr is the foremost of all mankind after the prophets, and it is not permissible that anyone should take precedence of him, for he set voluntary poverty above compulsory poverty. This doctrine is held by all the Ṣúfí Shaykhs except the spiritual Director whom we have mentioned.

Zuhrí relates that, when Abú Bakr received the oaths of allegiance as Caliph, he mounted the pulpit and pronounced an oration, in the course of which he said: "By God, I never coveted the command nor desired it even for a day or a night, nor ever asked God for it openly or in secret, nor do I take any pleasure in having it." Now, when God causes anyone to attain perfect sincerity and exalts him to the rank of fixity (*tamkín*) he waits for Divine inspiration, that it may guide him; and according as he is bidden, he will be either a beggar or a prince, without exercising his own choice and will. Thus

Abú Bakr, the Veracious, resigned himself to the will of God from first to last. Hence the whole sect of Ṣúfís have made him their pattern in stripping themselves of worldly things, in fixity (*tamkín*), in eager desire for poverty, and in longing to renounce authority. He is the Imám of the Moslems in general, and of the Ṣúfís in particular.

2. The Caliph 'Umar b. al-Khaṭṭáb.

He was specially distinguished by sagacity and resolution, and is the author of many fine sayings on Ṣúfiism. The Apostle said: "The Truth speaks by the tongue of 'Umar;" and again, "There have been inspired relaters (*muḥaddath*[un]) in the peoples of antiquity, and if there be any such in my people, it is 'Umar." 'Umar said: "Retirement (*'uzlat*) is a means of relieving one's self of bad company." Retirement is of two sorts: firstly, turning one's back on mankind (*i'ráḍ az khalq*), and secondly, entire severance from them (*inqiṭá' az íshán*). Turning one's back on mankind consists in choosing a solitary retreat, and in renouncing the society of one's fellow-creatures externally, and in quiet contemplation of the faults in one's own conduct, and in seeking release for one's self from intercourse with men, and in making all people secure from one's evil actions. But severance from mankind is a spiritual state, which is not connected with anything external. When a person is severed from mankind in spirit, he knows nothing of created beings and no thought thereof can take possession of his mind. Such a person, although he is living among the people, is isolated from them, and his spirit dwells apart from them. This is a very exalted station. 'Umar followed the right path herein, for externally he lived among the people as their Commander and Caliph. His words show clearly that although spiritualists may outwardly mix with mankind, their hearts always cling to God and return to Him in all circumstances. They regard any intercourse they may have with men as an affliction sent by God; and that intercourse does not divert them from God, since the world never becomes pure in the eyes of those whom God loves. 'Umar said: "An abode which is founded upon affliction cannot possibly be without affliction." The Ṣúfís make him their model in wearing a patched frock (*muraqqa'a*) and rigorously performing the duties of religion.

3. THE CALIPH 'UTHMÁN B. 'AFFÁN.

It is related by 'Abdalláh b. Rabáḥ and Abú Qatáda as follows: "We were with the Commander of the Faithful, 'Uthmán, on the day when his house was attacked. His slaves, seeing the crowd of rebels gathered at the door, took up arms. 'Uthmán said: 'Whoever of you does not take up arms is a free man.' We went forth from the house in fear of our lives. Ḥasan b. 'Alí met us on the way, and we returned with him to 'Uthmán, that we might know on what business he was going. After he had saluted 'Uthmán and condoled with him he said: 'O Prince of the Faithful, I dare not draw sword against Moslems without thy command. Thou art the true Imám. Give the order and I will defend thee.' 'Uthmán replied: 'O my cousin, go back to thy house and sit there until God shall bring His decree to pass. We do not wish to shed blood.'"

These words betoken resignation in the hour of calamity, and show that the speaker had attained the rank of friendship with God (*khullat*). Similarly, when Nimrod lit a fire and put Abraham in the sling (*pala*) [1] of a catapult, Gabriel came to Abraham and said, "Dost thou want anything?" He answered, "From thee, no." Gabriel said, "Then ask God." He answered, "Since He knows in what plight I am I need not ask Him." Here 'Uthmán was in the position of the Friend (Khalíl) [2] in the catapult, and the seditious mob was in the place of the fire, and Ḥasan was in the place of Gabriel; but Abraham was saved, while 'Uthmán perished. Salvation (*naját*) is connected with subsistence (*baqá*) and destruction (*halák*) with annihilation (*faná*): on this topic something has been said above. The

[1] Arabic *kiffat*. See Dozy, *Supplément*, ii, 476.
[2] Abraham is called by Moslems "the Friend of God" (*al-Khalíl*).

Ṣúfís take 'Uthmán as their exemplar in sacrificing life and property, in resigning their affairs to God, and in sincere devotion.

4. THE CALIPH 'ALÍ B. ABÍ ṬÁLIB.

His renown and rank in this Path (of Ṣúfiism) were very high. He explained the principles (*uṣúl*) of Divine truth with exceeding subtlety, so that Junayd said: "'Alí is our Shaykh as regards the principles and as regards the endurance of affliction," i.e. in the theory and practice of Ṣúfiism; for Ṣúfís call the theory of this Path "principles" (*uṣúl*), and its practice consists entirely in the endurance of affliction. It is related that some one begged 'Alí to give him a precept (*waṣiyyat*). 'Alí replied: "Do not let your wife and children be your chief cares; for if they be friends of God, God will look after His friends, and if they are enemies of God, why should you take care of God's enemies?" This question is connected with the severance of the heart from all things save God, who keeps His servants in whatever state He willeth. Thus Moses left the daughter of Shu'ayb[1] in a most miserable plight and committed her to God; and Abraham took Hagar and Ishmael and brought them to a barren valley and committed them to God. Both these prophets, instead of making wife and child their chief care, fixed their hearts on God. This saying resembles the answer which 'Alí gave to one who asked what is the purest thing that can be acquired. He said: "It is that which belongs to a heart made rich by God" (*ghaná al-qalb billáh*). The heart that is so enriched is not made poor by having no worldly goods nor glad by having them. This subject really turns on the theory regarding poverty and purity, which has been already discussed. 'Alí is a model for the Ṣúfís in respect to the truths of outward expressions and the subtleties of inward meanings, the stripping one's self of all property either of this world or of the next, and consideration of the Divine providence.

[1] Moses is said to have married one of the daughters of Shu'ayb. See Kor. xxviii, 22–8, where Shu'ayb, however, is not mentioned by name.

CHAPTER VIII.

Concerning their Imáms who belonged to the House of the Prophet.

1. Ḥasan b. 'Alí.

He was profoundly versed in Ṣúfiism. He said, by way of precept: "See that ye guard your hearts, for God knows your secret thoughts." "Guarding the heart" consists in not turning to others (than God) and in keeping one's secret thoughts from disobedience to the Almighty. When the Qadarites got the upper hand, and the doctrine of Rationalism became widely spread, Ḥasan of Baṣra wrote to Ḥasan b. 'Alí begging for guidance, and asking him to state his opinion on the perplexing subject of predestination and on the dispute whether men have any power to act (*istiṭá'at*). Ḥasan b. 'Alí replied that in his opinion those who did not believe in the determination (*qadar*) of men's good and evil actions by God were infidels, and that those who imputed their sins to God were miscreants, i.e. the Qadarites deny the Divine providence, and the Jabarites impute their sins to God; hence men are free to acquire their actions according to the power given them by God, and thus our religion takes the middle course between free-will and predestination. I have read in the Anecdotes that when Ḥasan b. 'Alí was seated at the door of his house in Kúfa, a Bedouin came up and reviled him and his father and his mother. Ḥasan rose and said: "O Bedouin, perhaps you are hungry or thirsty, or what ails you?" The Bedouin took no heed, but continued to abuse him. Ḥasan ordered his slave to bring a purse of silver, and gave it to the fellow, saying: "O Bedouin, excuse me, for there is nothing else in the house; had there been more, I should not have grudged it to you." On hearing this, the Bedouin exclaimed: "I bear witness that thou art the grandson of the Apostle of God. I came hither to make trial of thy mildness." Such are the true saints and Shaykhs who care not whether they are praised or blamed, and listen calmly to abuse.

2. Ḥusayn b. 'Alí.

He is the martyr of Karbalá, and all Ṣúfís are agreed that he was in the right. So long as the Truth was apparent, he followed it; but when it was lost he drew the sword and never rested until he sacrified his dear life for God's sake. The Apostle distinguished him by many tokens of favour. Thus 'Umar b. al-Khaṭṭáb relates that one day he saw the Apostle crawling on his knees, while Ḥusayn rode on his back holding a string, of which the other end was in the Apostle's mouth. 'Umar said: "What an excellent camel thou hast, O father of 'Abdalláh!" The Apostle replied: "What an excellent rider is he, O 'Umar!" It is recorded that Ḥusayn said: "Thy religion is the kindest of brethren towards thee," because a man's salvation consists in following religion, and his perdition in disobeying it.

3. 'Alí b. Ḥusayn b. 'Alí, called Zayn al-'Ábidín.

He said that the most blessed man in this world and in the next is he who, when he is pleased, is not led by his pleasure into wrong, and when he is angry, is not carried by his anger beyond the bounds of right. This is the character of those who have attained perfect rectitude (*kamál-i mustaqímán*). Ḥusayn used to call him 'Alí the Younger ('Alí Aṣghar). When Ḥusayn and his children were killed at Karbalá, there was none left except 'Alí to take care of the women; and he was ill. The women were brought unveiled on camels to Yazíd b. Mu'áwiya—may God curse him, but not his father!—at Damascus. Some one said to 'Alí: "How are ye this morning, O 'Alí and O members of the House of Mercy?" 'Alí replied: "We are in the same position among our people as the people of Moses among Pharaoh's folk, who slaughtered their sons and took their women alive; we do not know morning from evening on account of the reality of our affliction."

[The author then relates the well-known story of Hishám b. 'Abd al-Malik's encounter with 'Alí b. Ḥusayn at Mecca—how the Caliph, who desired to kiss the Black Stone but was unable to reach it, saw the crowd immediately make way for 'Alí and retire to a respectful distance; how a man of Syria asked the Caliph to tell him the name of this person who was held in so great veneration; how Hishám feigned ignorance, for fear that his partisans should be shaken in allegiance to himself; and how the poet Farazdaq stepped forward and recited the splendid encomium beginning—[1]

"*This is he whose footprint is known to the valley of Mecca,*
He whom the Temple knows, and the unhallowed territory and the holy ground.
This is the son of the best of all the servants of God,
This is the pious, the elect, the pure, the eminent."

Hishám was enraged and threw Farazdaq into prison. 'Alí sent to him a purse containing 12,000 dirhems; but the poet returned it, with the message that he had uttered many lies in the panegyrics on princes and governors which he was accustomed to compose for money, and that he had addressed these verses to 'Alí as a partial expiation for his sins in that respect, and as a proof of his affection towards the House of the Prophet. 'Alí, however, begged to be excused from taking back what he had already given away; and Farazdaq at last consented to receive the money.]

4. ABÚ JA'FAR MUḤAMMAD B. 'ALÍ B. ḤUSAYN AL-BÁQIR.

Some say that his "name of honour" was Abú 'Abdalláh. His nickname was Báqir. He was distinguished for his knowledge of the abstruse sciences and for his subtle indications as to the meaning of the Koran. It is related that on one occasion a king, who wished to destroy him, summoned him to his

[1] Twenty-five verses are quoted.

presence. When Báqir appeared, the king begged his pardon, bestowed gifts upon him, and dismissed him courteously. On being asked why he had acted in this manner, the king replied: "When he came in, I saw two lions, one on his right hand and one on his left, who threatened to destroy me if I should attempt to do him any harm." In his explanation of the verse, "*Whosoever believes in the* ṭághút *and believes in God*" (Kor. ii, 257), Báqir said: "Anything that diverts thee from contemplation of the Truth is thy *ṭághút*." One of his intimate friends relates that when a portion of the night had passed and Báqir had finished his litanies, he used to cry aloud to God: "O my God and my Lord, night has come, and the power of monarchs has ceased, and the stars are shining in the sky, and all mankind are asleep and silent, and the Banú Umayya have gone to rest and shut their doors and set guards to watch over them; and those who desired anything from them have forgotten their business. Thou, O God, art the Living, the Lasting, the Seeing, the Knowing. Sleep and slumber cannot overtake Thee. He who does not acknowledge that Thou art such as I have described is unworthy of Thy bounty. O Thou whom no thing withholds from any other thing, whose eternity is not impaired by Day and Night, whose doors of Mercy are open to all who call upon Thee, and whose entire treasures are lavished on those who praise Thee: Thou dost never turn away the beggar, and no creature in earth or heaven can prevent the true believer who implores Thee from gaining access to Thy court. O Lord, when I remember death and the grave and the reckoning, how can I take joy in this world? Therefore, since I acknowledge Thee to be One, I beseech Thee to give me peace in the hour of death, without torment, and pleasure in the hour of reckoning, without punishment."

5. Abú Muḥammad Ja'far b. Muḥammad Ṣádiq.

He is celebrated among the Ṣúfí Shaykhs for the subtlety of his discourse and his acquaintance with spiritual truths, and he has written famous books in explanation of Ṣúfiism. It is related that he said: "Whoever knows God turns his back on all else." The gnostic (*'árif*) turns his back on "other" (than God) and is cut off from worldly things, because his knowledge (*ma'rifat*) is pure nescience (*nakirat*), inasmuch as nescience forms part of his knowledge, and knowledge forms part of his nescience. Therefore the gnostic is separated from mankind and from thought of them, and he is joined to God. "Other" has no place in his heart, that he should pay any heed to them, and their existence has no worth for him, that he should fix the remembrance of them in his mind. And it is related that he said: "There is no right service without repentance, because God hath put repentance before service, and hath said, *Those who repent and serve*" (Kor. ix, 113). Repentance (*tawbat*) is the first of the "stations" in this Path, and service (*'ibádat*) is the last. When God mentioned the disobedient He called them to repentance and said, "*Repent unto God together*" (Kor. xxiv, 31); but when He mentioned the Apostle He referred to his "servantship" (*'ubúdiyyat*), and said, "*He revealed to His servant that which He revealed*" (Kor. liii, 10). I have read in the Anecdotes that Dáwud Ṭá'í came to Ja'far Ṣádiq and said: "O son of the Apostle of God, counsel me, for my mind is darkened." Ja'far replied: "O Abú Sulaymán, thou art the ascetic of thy time: what need hast thou of counsel from me?" He answered: "O son of the Apostle, thy family are superior to all mankind, and it is incumbent on thee to give counsel to all." "O Abú Sulaymán," cried Ja'far, "I am afraid that at the Resurrection my grandsire will lay hold on me, saying, 'Why didst not thou fulfil the obligation to follow in my steps?' This is not a matter that depends on authentic and sure affinity (to Muḥammad), but on good conduct in the presence of the Truth." Dáwud Ṭá'í began to weep and exclaimed: "O Lord God, if one whose clay is moulded with the water of Prophecy, whose grandsire is the Apostle, and whose mother is Fáṭima (*Batúl*)—if such a one is distracted by doubts, who am I that I should be pleased with my dealings (towards God)?" One day Ja'far said to his clients: "Come, let us take a pledge that whoever amongst us shall gain deliverance on the Day of Resurrection shall intercede for all the rest." They said: "O son of the Apostle, how canst thou have need of our intercession since thy grandsire intercedes for all mankind?" Ja'far replied: "My actions are such that I shall be ashamed to look my grandsire in the face on the Last Day." To see one's faults is a quality of perfection, and is characteristic of those who are established in the Divine presence, whether they be prophets, saints, or apostles. The Apostle said: "When God wishes a man well, He gives him insight into his faults." Whoever bows his head with humility, like a servant, God will exalt his state in both worlds.

Now I shall mention briefly the People of the Veranda (*Ahl-i Ṣuffa*). In a book entitled "The Highway of Religion" (*Minháj al-Dín*), which I composed before the present work, I have given a detailed account of each of them, but here it will suffice to mention their names and "names of honour".

CHAPTER IX.

CONCERNING THE PEOPLE OF THE VERANDA (*Ahl-i Ṣuffa*).

Know that all Moslems are agreed that the Apostle had a number of Companions, who abode in his Mosque and engaged in devotion, renouncing the world and refusing to seek a livelihood. God reproached the Apostle on their account and said: "*Do not drive away those who call unto their Lord at morn and eve, desiring His face*" (Kor. vi, 52). Their merits are proclaimed by the Book of God, and in many traditions of the Apostle which have come down to us. It is related by Ibn 'Abbás that the Apostle passed by the People of the Veranda, and saw their poverty and their self-mortification and said: "Rejoice! for whoever of my community perseveres in the state in which ye are, and is satisfied with his condition, he shall be one of my comrades in Paradise." Among the *Ahl-i Ṣuffa*[1] were Bilál b. Rabáḥ, Salmán al-Fárisí, Abú 'Ubayda b. al-Jarráḥ, Abu 'l-Yaqẓán 'Ammár b. Yásir, 'Abdalláh b. Mas'úd al-Hudhalí, his brother 'Utba b. Mas'úd, Miqdád b. al-Aswad, Khabbáb b. al-Aratt, Ṣuhayb b. Sinán, 'Utba b. Ghazwán, Zayd b. al-Khaṭṭáb, brother of the Caliph 'Umar; Abú Kabsha, the Apostle's client; Abu 'l-Marthad Kinána b. al-Ḥuṣayn al-'Adawí; Sálim, client of Hudhayfa al-Yamání; 'Ukkásha b. Miḥṣan; Mas'úd b. Rabí' al-Fárisí; Abú Dharr Jundab b. Junáda al-Ghifárí; 'Abdalláh b. 'Umar; Ṣafwán b. Bayḍá; Abú Dardá 'Uwaym b. 'Ámir; Abú Lubába b. 'Abd al-Mundhir; and 'Abdalláh b. Badr al-Juhaní.

Shaykh Abú 'Abd al-Raḥmán Muḥammad b. al-Ḥusayn al-Sulamí,[2] the traditionist (*naqqál*) of Ṣúfiism and transmitter

[1] I have corrected many of the following names, which are erroneously written in the Persian text, by reference to various Arabic works.

[2] See Brockelmann, i, 200.

of the sayings of the Ṣúfí Shaykhs, has written a separate history of the *Ahl-i Ṣuffa*, in which he has recorded their virtues and merits and names and "names of honour". He has included among them Misṭaḥ b. Uthátha b. 'Abbád, whom I dislike because he began the slanders about 'Á'isha, the Mother of the Believers. Abú Hurayra, and Thawbán, and Mu'ádh b. al-Ḥárith, and Sá'ib b. Khallád, and Thábit b. Wadí'at, and Abú 'Ísá 'Uwaym b. Sá'ida, and Sálim b. 'Umayr b. Thábit, and Abu 'l-Yasar Ka'b b. 'Amr, and Wahb b. Ma'qal, and 'Abdalláh b. Unays, and Ḥajjáj b. 'Umar al-Aslamí belonged to the *Ahl-i Ṣuffa*. Now and then they had recourse to some means of livelihood (*ta'alluq ba-sababí kardandí*), but all of them were in one and the same degree (of dignity). Verily, the generation of the Companions was the best of all generations; and they were the best and most excellent of mankind, since God bestowed on them companionship with the Apostle and preserved their hearts from blemish.

CHAPTER X.

Concerning their Imáms who belonged to the Followers (*al-Tábi'ún*).

1. Uways al-Qaraní.

He lived in the time of the Apostle, but was prevented from seeing him, firstly by the ecstasy which overmastered him, and secondly by duty to his mother. The Apostle said to the Companions: "There is a man at Qaran, called Uways, who at the Resurrection will intercede for a multitude of my people, as many as the sheep of Rabí'a and Muḍar." Then turning to 'Umar and 'Alí, he said: "You will see him. He is a lowly man, of middle height, and hairy; on his left side there is a white spot, as large as a dirhem, which is not from leprosy (*písti*), and he has a similar spot on the palm of his hand. When you see him, give him my greeting, and bid him pray for my people." After the Apostle's death 'Umar came to Mecca, and cried out in the course of a sermon: "O men of Najd, are there any natives of Qaran amongst you?" They answered, "Yes"; whereupon 'Umar sent for them and asked them about Uways. They said: "He is a madman who dwells in solitude and associates with no one. He does not eat what men eat, and he feels no joy or sorrow. When others smile he weeps, and when others weep he smiles." 'Umar said: "I wish to see him." They replied: "He lives in a desert, far from our camels." 'Umar and 'Alí set out in quest of him. They found him praying, and waited until he was finished. He saluted them and showed them the marks on his side and the palm of his hand. They asked his blessing and gave him the Apostle's greeting, and enjoined him to pray for the Moslem people. After they had stayed with him for a while, he said: "You have taken trouble (to see me); now return, for the Resurrection is near, when we shall see each other without having to say farewell. At present I am engaged in preparing for the Resurrection." When the men of Qaran came home, they exhibited great respect for Uways. He left his native place and came to Kúfa. One day he was seen by Harim b. Ḥayyán, but after that nobody saw him until the period of civil war. He fought for 'Alí, and fell a martyr at the battle of Ṣiffín.

It is related that he said: "Safety lies in solitude," because the heart of the solitary is free from thought of "other", and in no circumstances does he hope for anything from mankind. Let none imagine, however, that solitude (*waḥdat*) merely consists in living alone. So long as the Devil associates with a man's heart, and sensual passion holds sway in his breast, and any thought of this world or the next occurs to him in such a way as to make him conscious of mankind, he is not truly in solitude; since it is all one whether he takes pleasure in the thing itself or in the thought of it. Accordingly, the true solitary is not disturbed by society, but he who is preoccupied seeks in vain to acquire freedom from thought by secluding himself. In order to be cut off from mankind one must become intimate with God, and those who have become intimate with God are not hurt by intercourse with mankind.

2. HARIM B. ḤAYYÁN.

He went to visit Uways Qaraní, but on arriving at Qaran he found that Uways was no longer there. Deeply disappointed, he returned to Mecca, where he learned that Uways was living at Kúfa. He repaired thither, but could not discover him for a long time. At last he set out for Baṣra and on the way he saw Uways, clad in a patched frock, performing an ablution on the banks of the Euphrates. As soon as he came up from the shore of the river and combed his beard, Harim advanced to meet him and saluted him. Uways said: "Peace be with thee, O Harim b. Ḥayyán!" Harim cried: "How did you know that I am Harim?" Uways answered: "My spirit knew thy spirit." He said to Harim: "Keep watch over thy heart" (*'alayka bi-qalbika*), i.e. "Guard thy heart from thoughts of 'other'". This saying has two meanings: (1) "Make thy heart obedient to God by self-mortification", and (2) "Make thyself obedient to thy heart". These are two sound principles. It is the business of novices (*murídán*) to make their hearts obedient to God in order to purge them from familiarity with vain desires and passions, and sever them from unseemly thoughts, and fix them on the method of gaining spiritual health, on the keeping of the commandments, and on contemplation of the signs of God, so that their hearts may become the shrine of Love. To make one's self obedient to one's heart is the business of adepts (*kámilán*), whose hearts God has illumined with the light of Beauty, and delivered from all causes and means, and invested with the robe of proximity (*qurb*), and thereby has revealed to them His bounties and has chosen them to contemplate Him and to be near Him: hence He has made their bodies accordant with their hearts. The former class are masters of their hearts (*ṣáḥib al-qulúb*), the latter are under the dominion of their hearts (*maghlúb al-qulúb*); the former retain their attributes (*báqi 'l-ṣifat*), the latter have lost their attributes (*fáni 'l-ṣifat*). The truth of this matter goes back to the words of God: *Illá 'ibádaka minhumu 'l-mukhlaṣína*, "Except such of them as are Thy purified (chosen) servants" (Kor. xv, 40). Here some read *mukhliṣína* instead of *mukhlaṣína*. The *mukhliṣ* (purifying one's self) is active, and retains his attributes, but the *mukhlaṣ* (purified) is passive, and has lost his attributes. I will explain this question more fully elsewhere. The latter class, who make their bodies accordant with their hearts, and whose hearts abide in contemplation of God, are of higher rank than those who by their own effort make their hearts comply with the Divine commandments. This subject has its foundation in the principles of sobriety (*ṣahw*) and intoxication (*sukr*), and in those of contemplation (*mushāhadat*) and self-mortification (*mujáhadat*).

3. ḤASAN OF BAṢRA.

His "name of honour" was Abú 'Alí; according to others, Abú Muḥammad or Abú Sa'íd. He is held in high regard and esteem by the Ṣúfís. He gave subtle directions relating to the science of practical religion (*'ilm-i mu'ámalat*). I have read in the Anecdotes that a Bedouin came to him and asked him about patience (*ṣabr*). Ḥasan replied: "Patience is of two sorts: firstly, patience in misfortune and affliction; and secondly, patience to refrain from the things which God has commanded us to renounce and has forbidden us to pursue." The Bedouin said: "Thou art an ascetic; I never saw anyone more ascetic than thou art." "O Bedouin!" cried Ḥasan, "my asceticism is nothing but desire, and my patience is nothing but lack of fortitude." The Bedouin begged him to explain this saying, "for [said he] thou hast shaken my belief." Ḥasan replied: "My patience in misfortune and my submission proclaim my fear of Hell-fire, and this is lack of fortitude (*jaza'*); and my asceticism in this world is desire for the next world, and this is the quintessence of desire. How excellent is he who takes no thought of his own interest! so that his patience is for God's sake, not for the saving of himself from Hell; and his asceticism is for God's sake, not for the purpose of bringing himself into Paradise. This is the mark of true sincerity." And it is related that he said: "Association with the wicked produces suspicion of the good." This saying is very apt and suitable to the people of the present age, who all disbelieve in the honoured friends of God. The reason of their disbelief is that they associate with pretenders to Ṣúfiism, who have only its external forms; and perceiving their actions to be perfidious, their tongues false, their ears listening to idle quatrains, their eyes following pleasure and lust, and their hearts set on amassing unlawful or dubious lucre, they fancy that aspirants to Ṣúfiism behave in the same manner, or that this is the doctrine of the Ṣúfís themselves, whereas, on the contrary, the Ṣúfís act in obedience to God, and speak the word of God, and keep the love of God in their hearts and the voice (*samá'*) of God in their ears, and the beauty of Divine contemplation in their eyes, and all their thoughts are fixed on the gaining of holy mysteries in the place where Vision is vouchsafed to them. If evildoers have appeared among them and have adopted their practices, the evil must be referred to those who commit it. Anyone who associates with the wicked members of a community does so through his own wickedness, for he would associate with the good if there were any good in him.

4. SA'ÍD B. AL-MUSAYYIB.

It is said that he was a man of devout nature who made a show of hypocrisy, not a hypocrite who pretended to be devout. This way of acting is approved in Ṣúfiism and is held laudable by all the Shaykhs. He said: "Be content with a little of this world while thy religion is safe, even as some are content with much thereof while their religion is lost," i.e. poverty without injury to religion is better than riches with heedlessness. It is related that when he was at Mecca a man came to him and said: "Tell me a lawful thing in which there is nothing unlawful." He replied: "Praise (*dhikr*) of God is a lawful thing in which there is nothing unlawful, and praise of aught else is an unlawful thing in which there is nothing lawful," because your salvation lies in the former and your perdition in the latter.

CHAPTER XI.

Concerning their Imáms who lived subsequently to the Followers (*al-Tábi'ún*) down to our day.

1. Ḥabíb al-'Ajamí.

His conversion (*tawbat*) was begun by Ḥasan of Baṣra. At first he was a usurer and committed all sorts of wickedness, but God gave him a sincere repentance, and he learned from Ḥasan something of the theory and practice of religion. His native tongue was Persian (*'ajamí*), and he could not speak Arabic correctly. One evening Ḥasan of Baṣra passed by the door of his cell. Ḥabíb had uttered the call to prayer and was standing, engaged in devotion. Ḥasan came in, but would not pray under his leadership, because Ḥabíb was unable to speak Arabic fluently or recite the Koran correctly. The same night, Ḥasan dreamed that he saw God and said to Him: "O Lord, wherein does Thy good pleasure consist?" and that God answered: "O Ḥasan, you found My good pleasure, but did not know its value: if yesternight you had said your prayers after Ḥabíb, and if the rightness of his intention had restrained you from taking offence at his pronunciation, I should have been well pleased with you." It is common knowledge among Ṣúfís that when Ḥasan of Baṣra fled from Ḥajjáj he entered the cell of Ḥabíb. The soldiers came and said to Ḥabíb: "Have you seen Ḥasan anywhere?" Ḥabíb said: "Yes." "Where is he?" "He is in my cell." They went into the cell, but saw no one there. Thinking that Ḥabíb was making fun of them, they abused him and called him a liar. He swore that he had spoken the truth. They returned twice and thrice, but found no one, and at last departed. Ḥasan immediately came out and said to Ḥabíb:

"I know it was owing to thy benedictions that God did not discover me to these wicked men, but why didst thou tell them I was here?" Ḥabíb replied: "O Master, it was not on account of my benedictions that they failed to see thee, but through the blessedness of my speaking the truth. Had I told a lie, we both should have been shamed." Ḥabíb was asked: "With what thing is God pleased?" He answered: "With a heart which is not sullied by hypocrisy," because hypocrisy (*nifáq*) is the opposite of concord (*wifáq*), and the state of being well pleased (*riḍá*) is the essence of concord. There is no connexion between hypocrisy and love, and love subsists in the state of being well pleased (with whatever is decreed by God). Therefore acquiescence (*riḍá*) is a characteristic of God's friends, while hypocrisy is a characteristic of His enemies. This is a very important matter. I will explain it in another place.

2. MÁLIK B. DÍNÁR.

He was a companion of Ḥasan of Baṣra. Dínár was a slave, and Málik was born before his father's emancipation. His conversion began as follows. One evening he had been enjoying himself with a party of friends. When they were all asleep a voice came from a lute which they had been playing: "O Málik! why dost thou not repent?" Málik abandoned his evil ways and went to Ḥasan of Baṣra, and showed himself steadfast in repentance. He attained to such a high degree that once when he was in a ship, and was suspected of stealing a jewel, he no sooner lifted his eyes to heaven than all the fishes in the sea came to the surface, every one carrying a jewel in its mouth. Málik took one of the jewels, and gave it to the man whose jewel was missing; then he set foot on the sea and walked until he reached the shore. It is related that he said: "The deed that I love best is sincerity in doing," because an action only becomes an action in virtue of its sincerity. Sincerity bears the same relation to an action as the spirit to the body: as the body without the spirit is a lifeless thing, so an action without sincerity is utterly unsubstantial. Sincerity belongs to the class of internal actions, whereas acts of devotion belong to the class of external actions: the latter are completed by the former, while the former derive their value from the latter. Although a man should keep his heart sincere for a thousand years, it is not sincerity until his sincerity is combined with action; and although he should perform external actions for a thousand years, his actions do not become acts of devotion until they are combined with sincerity.

3. ABÚ ḤALÍM ḤABÍB B. SALÍM[1] AL-RÁ'Í.

He was a companion of Salmán Fárisí. He related that the Apostle said: "The believer's intentions are better than his acts." He had flocks of sheep, and his home was on the bank of the Euphrates. His religious Path (*ṭaríq*) was retirement from the world. A certain Shaykh relates as follows: "Once I passed by him and found him praying, while a wolf looked after his sheep. I resolved to pay him a visit, since he appeared to me to have the marks of greatness. When we had exchanged greetings, I said: 'O Shaykh! I see the wolf in accord with the sheep.' He replied: 'That is because the shepherd is in accord with God.' With those words he held a wooden bowl under a rock, and two fountains gushed from the rock, one of milk and one of honey. 'O Shaykh!' I cried, as he bade me drink, 'how hast thou attained to this degree?' He answered: 'By obedience to Muḥammad, the Apostle of God. O my son! the rock gave water to the people of Moses,[2] although they disobeyed him, and although Moses is not equal in rank to Muḥammad: why should not the rock give milk and honey to me, inasmuch as I am obedient to Muḥammad, who is superior to Moses?' I said: 'Give me a word of counsel.' He said: 'Do not make your heart a coffer of covetousness and your belly a vessel of unlawful things.'"

[1] L. Aslam. [2] Kor. vii, 160.

My Shaykh had further traditions concerning him, but I could not possibly set down more than this (*andar waqt-i man ḍíqí búd ú bísh az ín mumkin na-shud*), my books having been left at Ghazna—may God guard it!—while I myself had become a captive among uncongenial folk (*dar miyán-i nájinsán*) in the district of Laháwur, which is a dependency of Múltán. God be praised both in joy and sorrow!

4. Abú Ḥázim al-Madaní.

He was steadfast in poverty, and thoroughly versed in different kinds of self-mortification. 'Amr b. 'Uthmán al-Makkí, who shows great zeal on his behalf (*andar amr-i way ba-jidd báshad*), relates that on being asked what he possessed he answered: "Satisfaction (*riḍá*) with God and independence of mankind." A certain Shaykh went to see him and found him asleep. When he awoke he said: "I dreamed just now that the Apostle gave me a message to thee, and bade me inform thee that it is better to fulfil the duty which is owed to one's mother than to make the pilgrimage. Return, therefore, and try to please her." The person who tells the story turned back and did not go to Mecca. This is all that I have heard about Abú Ḥázim.

5. Muḥammad b. Wási'.

He associated with many of the Followers and with some of the ancient Shaykhs, and had a perfect knowledge of Ṣúfiism. It is related that he said: "I never saw anything without seeing God therein." This is an advanced stage (*maqám*) of Contemplation. When a man is overcome with love for the Agent, he attains to such a degree that in looking at His act he does not see the act but the Agent only and entirely, just as when one looks at a picture and sees only the painter. The true meaning of these words is the same as in the saying of Abraham, the Friend of God (*Khalíl*) and the Apostle, who said to the sun and moon and stars: "*This is my Lord*" (Kor. vi, 76–8), for he was then overcome with longing (*shawq*), so that the qualities of his beloved appeared to him in everything that he saw. The friends of God perceive that the universe is subject to His might and captive to His dominion, and that the existence of all created things is as nothing in comparison with the power of the Agent thereof. When they look thereon with longing, they do not see what is subject and passive and created, but only the Omnipotent, the Agent, the Creator. I shall treat of this in the chapter on Contemplation. Some persons have fallen into error, and have alleged that the words of Muḥammad b. Wási', "I saw God therein," involve a place of division and descent (*makán-i tajziya ú ḥulúl*), which is sheer infidelity, because place is homogeneous with that which is contained in it, and if anyone supposes that place is created the contained object must also be created; or if the latter be eternal the former also must be eternal: hence this assertion entails two evil consequences, both of which are infidelity, viz., either that created things are eternal (*qadím*) or that the Creator is non-eternal (*muḥdath*). Accordingly, when Muḥammad b. Wási' said that he saw God in things, he meant, as I have explained above, that he saw in those things the signs and evidences and proofs of God.

I shall discuss in the proper place some subtle points connected with this question.

6. Abú Ḥanífa Nu'mán b. Thábit al-Kharráz.

He is the Imám of Imáms and the exemplar of the Sunnites. He was firmly grounded in works of mortification and devotion, and was a great authority on the principles of Ṣúfiism. At first he wished to go into seclusion and abandon the society of mankind, for he had made his heart free from every thought of human power and pomp. One night, however, he dreamed that he was collecting the bones of the Apostle from the tomb, and choosing some and discarding others. He awoke in terror and asked one of the pupils of Muḥammad b. Sírín[1] (to interpret

[1] A well-known divine, who died in 110 A.H. See Ibn Khallikán, No. 576. An extant work on the interpretation of dreams is attributed to him (Brockelmann, i, 66).

the dream). This man said to him: "You will attain a high rank in knowledge of the Apostle and in preserving his ordinances (*sunnat*), so that you will sift what is genuine from what is spurious." Another time Abú Ḥanífa dreamed that the Apostle said to him: "You have been created for the purpose of reviving my ordinances." He was the master of many Shaykhs, e.g. Ibráhím b. Adham and Fuḍayl b. 'Iyáḍ and Dáwud Ṭá'í and Bishr Ḥáfí.

In the reign of the Caliph Manṣúr a plan was formed to appoint to the office of Cadi one of the following persons: Abú Ḥanífa, Sufyán Thawrí, Mis'ar b. Kidám, and Shurayḥ. While they were journeying together to visit Manṣúr, who had summoned them to his presence, Abú Ḥanífa said to his companions: "I will reject this office by means of a certain trick, Mis'ar will feign to be mad, Sufyán will run away, and Shurayḥ will be made Cadi." Sufyán fled and embarked in a ship, imploring the captain to conceal him and save him from execution. The others were ushered into the presence of the Caliph. Manṣúr said to Abú Ḥanífa: "You must act as Cadi." Abú Ḥanífa replied: "O Commander of the Faithful, I am not an Arab, but one of their clients; and the chiefs of the Arabs will not accept my decisions." Manṣúr said: "This matter has nothing to do with lineage: it demands learning, and you are the most eminent doctor of the day." Abú Ḥanífa persisted that he was unfit to hold the office. "What I have just said shows it," he exclaimed; "for if I have spoken the truth I am disqualified, and if I have told a falsehood it is not right that a liar should be judge over Moslems, and that you should entrust him with the lives, property, and honour of your subjects." He escaped in this way. Then Mis'ar came forward and seized the Caliph's hand and said: "How are you, and your children, and your beasts of burden?" "Away with him," cried Manṣúr, "he is mad!" Finally, Shurayḥ was told that he must fill the vacant office. "I am melancholic," said he, "and light-witted," whereupon Manṣúr advised him to drink ptisanes and potions (*'aṣídahá-yi muwáfiq ú nabídhhá-yi muthallath*) until his intellect was fully restored. So Shurayḥ was made Cadi, and Abú Ḥanífa never spoke a word to him again. This story illustrates not only the sagacity of Abú Ḥanífa, but also his adherence to the path of righteousness and salvation, and his determination not to let himself be deluded by seeking popularity and worldly renown. It shows, moreover, the soundness of blame (*malámat*), since all these three venerable men resorted to some trick in order to avoid popularity. Very different are the doctors of the present age, who make the palaces of princes their *qibla* and the houses of evildoers their temple.

Once a doctor of Ghazna, who claimed to be a learned divine and a religious leader, declared it heresy to wear a patched frock (*muraqqa'a*). I said to him: "You do not call it heretical to wear robes of brocade,[1] which are made entirely of silk and, besides being in themselves unlawful for men to wear, have been begged with importunity, which is unlawful, from evildoers whose property is absolutely unlawful. Why, then, is it heretical to wear a lawful garment, procured from a lawful place, and purchased with lawful money? If you were not ruled by inborn conceit and by the error of your soul, you would express a more judicious opinion. Women may wear a dress of silk lawfully, but it is unlawful for men, and only permissible (*mubáḥ*) for lunatics. If you acknowledge the truth of both these statements you are excused (for condemning the patched frock). God save us from lack of fairness!"

Yaḥyá b. Mu'ádh al-Rází relates as follows: "I dreamed that I said to the Apostle, 'O Apostle of God, where shall I seek thee?' He answered: 'In the science of Abú Ḥanífa.'"

Once, when I was in Syria, I fell asleep at the tomb of Bilál the Muezzin,[2] and dreamed that I was at Mecca, and that the Apostle came in through the gate of the Banú Shayba, tenderly

[1] The text has *jáma-i ḥashishí ú dibaqí*. Apparently the former word should be written "*khashishí*". It is described in Vullers's Persian Dictionary as "a kind of garment".

[2] Bilál b. Rabáḥ, the Prophet's Muezzin, was buried at Damascus.

clasping an old man to his bosom in the same fashion as people are wont to carry children; and that I ran to him and kissed the back of his foot, and stood marvelling who the old man might be; and that the Apostle was miraculously aware of my secret thought and said to me, "This is thy Imám and the Imám of thy countryman," meaning Abú Ḥanífa. In consequence of this dream I have great hopes for myself and also for the people of my country. It has convinced me, moreover, that Abú Ḥanífa was one of those who, having annihilated their natural qualities, continue to perform the ordinances of the sacred law, as appears from the fact that he was carried by the Apostle. If he had walked by himself, his attributes must have been subsistent, and such a one may either miss or hit the mark; but inasmuch as he was carried by the Apostle, his attributes must have been non-existent while he was sustained by the living attributes of the Apostle. The Apostle cannot err, and it is equally impossible that one who is sustained by the Apostle should fall into error.

When Dáwud Ṭá'í had acquired learning and become a famous authority, he went to Abú Ḥanífa and said to him: "What shall I do now?" Abú Ḥanífa replied: "Practise what you have learned, for theory without practice is like a body without a spirit." He who is content with learning alone is not learned, and the truly learned man is not content with learning alone.

Similarly, Divine guidance (*hidáyat*) involves self-mortification (*mujáhadat*), without which contemplation (*musháhadat*) is unattainable. There is no knowledge without action, since knowledge is the product of action, and is brought forth and developed and made profitable by the blessings of action. The two things cannot be divorced in any way, just as the light of the sun cannot be separated from the sun itself.

7. 'ABDALLÁH B. MUBÁRAK AL-MARWAZÍ.

He was the Imám of his time and consorted with many eminent Shaykhs. He is the author of celebrated works and famous miracles. The occasion of his conversion is related as follows:

He was in love with a girl, and one night in winter he stationed himself at the foot of the wall of her house, while she came on to the roof, and they both stayed gazing at each other until day-break. When 'Abdalláh heard the call to morning prayers he thought it was time for evening prayers; and only when the sun began to shine did he discover that he had spent the whole night in rapturous contemplation of his beloved. He took warning by this, and said to himself: "Shame on thee, O son of Mubárak! Dost thou stand on foot all night for thine own pleasure, and yet become furious when the Imám reads a long chapter of the Koran?" He repented and devoted himself to study, and entered upon a life of asceticism, in which he attained such a high degree that once his mother found him asleep in the garden, while a great snake was driving the gnats away from him with a spray of basil which it held in its mouth. Then he left Merv and lived for some time in Baghdád, associating with the Ṣúfí Shaykhs, and also resided for some time at Mecca. When he returned to Merv, the people of the town received him with friendship and founded for him a professorial chair and a lecture hall (*dars ú majlis nihádand*). At that epoch half the population of Merv were followers of Tradition and the other half adherents of Opinion, just as at the present day. They called him *Raḍí al-faríqayn* because of his agreement with both sides, and each party claimed him as one of themselves. He built two convents (*ribáṭ*) at Merv—one for the followers of Tradition and one for the followers of Opinion—which have retained their original constitution down to the present day. Afterwards he went back to the Ḥijáz and settled at Mecca. On being asked what wonders he had seen, he replied: "I saw a Christian monk (*ráhib*), who was emaciated by self-mortification and bent double by fear of God. I asked him to tell me the way to God. He answered, 'If you knew God, you would know the way to Him.' Then he said, 'I worship Him although I do not know him, whereas you disobey Him although you know Him,' i.e. 'knowledge entails fear, yet I see that you are confident; and infidelity entails ignorance, yet I feel fear within myself'. I laid this to heart, and it restrained me from many ill deeds." It is related that 'Abdalláh b. Mubárak said: "Tranquillity is unlawful to the hearts of the Saints of God," for they are agitated in this world by seeking God (*ṭalab*) and in the next world by rapture (*ṭarab*); they are not permitted to rest here, while they are absent from God, nor there, while they enjoy the presence, manifestation, and vision of God. Hence this world is even as the next world in their eyes, and the next world even as this world, because tranquillity of heart demands two things, either attainment of one's aim or indifference to the object of one's desire. Since He is not to be attained in this world or the next, the heart can never have rest from the palpitation of love; and since indifference is unlawful to those who love Him, the heart can never have rest from the agitations of seeking Him. This is a firm principle in the path of spiritual adepts.

8. ABÚ 'ALÍ AL-FUḌAYL B. 'IYÁḌ.

He is one of the paupers (*ṣa'álík*) of the Ṣúfís, and one of their most eminent and celebrated men. At first he used to practise brigandage between Merv and Báward, but he was always inclined to piety, and invariably showed a generous and magnanimous disposition, so that he would not attack a caravan in which there was any woman, or take the property of anyone whose stock was small; and he let the travellers keep a portion of their property, according to the means of each. One day a merchant set out from Merv. His friends advised him to take an escort, but he said to them: "I have heard that Fuḍayl is a God-fearing man;" and instead of doing as they wished he hired a Koran-reader and mounted him on a camel in order that he might read the Koran aloud day and night during the journey. When they reached the place where Fuḍayl was lying in ambush, the reader happened to be reciting: "*Is not the time yet come unto those who believe, that their hearts should humbly submit to the admonition of God?*" (Kor. lvii, 15). Fuḍayl's heart was softened. He repented of the business in which he was engaged, and having a written list of those whom he had robbed he satisfied all their claims upon him. Then he went to Mecca and resided there for some time and became acquainted with certain saints of God. Afterwards he returned to Kúfa, where he associated with Abú Ḥanífa. He has handed down relations which are held in high esteem by Traditionists, and he is the author of lofty sayings concerning the verities of Ṣúfiism and Divine Knowledge. It is recorded that he said: "Whoever knows God as He ought to be known worships Him with all his might," because everyone who knows God acknowledges His bounty and beneficence and mercy, and therefore loves Him; and since he loves Him he obeys Him so far as he has the power, for it is not difficult to obey those whom one loves. Accordingly, the more one loves, the more one is obedient, and love is increased by true knowledge.[1] It is related that he said: "The world is a madhouse, and the people therein are madmen, wearing shackles and chains." Lust is our shackle and sin is our chain.

Faḍl b. Rabí' relates as follows: "I accompanied Hárún al-Rashíd to Mecca. When we had performed the pilgrimage, he said to me, 'Is there any man of God here that I may visit him?' I replied, 'Yes, there is 'Abd al-Razzáq Ṣan'ání.'[2] We went to his house and talked with him for a while. When we were about to leave, Hárún bade me ask him whether he had any debts. He said, 'Yes,' and Hárún gave orders that they should be paid. On coming out, Hárún said to me, 'O Faḍl, my heart still desires to see a man greater than this one.' I conducted him to Sufyán b. 'Uyayna.[3] Our visit ended in the same way. Hárún gave orders to pay his debts and departed. Then he said to me, 'I recollect that Fuḍayl b. 'Iyáḍ is here; let us go and see him.' We found him in an upper chamber, reciting a verse of the Koran. When we knocked at the door, he cried, 'Who is there?' I replied, 'The Commander of the Faithful.' 'What have I to do with the Commander of the

[1] Here the author relates two anecdotes illustrating the devotion of Muḥammad.
[2] He died in 211 A.H. See Ibn Khallikán, No. 409.
[3] Died in 168 A.H. See Ibn Khallikán, No. 266.

Faithful?' said he. I said, 'Is there not an Apostolic Tradition to the effect that no one shall seek to abase himself in devotion to God?' He answered, 'Yes, but acquiescence in God's will (*riḍá*) is everlasting glory in the opinion of quietists: you see my abasement, but I see my exaltation.' Then he came down and opened the door, and extinguished the lamp and stood in a corner. Hárún went in and tried to find him. Their hands met. Fuḍayl exclaimed, 'Alas! never have I felt a softer hand: 't will be very wonderful if it escape from the Divine torment.' Hárún began to weep, and wept so violently that he swooned. When he came to himself, he said, 'O Fuḍayl, give me a word of counsel.' Fuḍayl said: 'O Commander of the Faithful, thy ancestor ('Abbás) was the uncle of Muṣṭafá. He asked the Prophet to give him dominion over men. The Prophet answered, "O my uncle, I will give thee dominion for one moment over thyself," i.e. one moment of thy obedience to God is better than a thousand years of men's obedience to thee, since dominion brings repentance on the Day of Resurrection' (*al-imárat yawm al-qiyámat nadámat*). Hárún said, 'Counsel me further.' Fuḍayl continued: 'When 'Umar b. 'Abd al-'Azíz was appointed Caliph, he summoned Sálim b. 'Abdalláh and Rajá b. Ḥayát, and Muḥammad b. Ka'b al-Quraẓí, and said to them, "What am I to do in this affliction? for I count it an affliction, although people in general consider it to be a blessing." One of them replied: "If thou wouldst be saved to-morrow from the Divine punishment, regard the elders of the Moslems as thy fathers, and their young men as thy brothers, and their children as thy children. The whole territory of Islam is thy house, and its people are thy family. Visit thy father, and honour thy brother, and deal kindly with thy children."' Then Fuḍayl said: 'O Commander of the Faithful, I fear lest that handsome face of thine fall into Hell-fire. Fear God, and perform thy obligations to Him better than this.' Hárún asked Fuḍayl whether he had any debts. He answered, 'Yes, the debt which I owe to God, namely, obedience to Him; woe is me, if He call me to account for it!'

Hárún said, 'O Fuḍayl, I am speaking of debts to men.' He replied, 'God be praised! His bounty towards me is great, and I have no reason to complain of Him to His servants.' Hárún offered him a purse of a thousand dínárs, saying, 'Use the money for some purpose of thine own.' Fuḍayl said, 'O Commander of the Faithful, my counsels have done thee no good. Here again thou art behaving wrongly and unjustly.' Hárún exclaimed, 'How is that?' Fuḍayl said, 'I wish thee to be saved, but thou wouldst cast me into perdition: is not this unjust?' We took leave of him with tears in our eyes, and Hárún said to me, 'O Faḍl, Fuḍayl is a king indeed.'"

All this shows his hatred of the world and its people, and his contempt for its gauds, and his refusal to abase himself before worldlings for the sake of worldly gain.

9. Abu 'l-Fayḍ Dhu 'l-Nún b. Ibráhím al-Miṣrí.

He was the son of a Nubian, and his name was Thawbán. He is one of the best of this sect, and one of the most eminent of their hidden spiritualists (*'ayyárán*), for he trod the path of affliction and travelled on the road of blame (*malámat*). All the people of Egypt were lost in doubt as to his true state, and did not believe in him until he was dead. On the night of his decease seventy persons dreamed that they saw the Apostle, who said: "I have come to meet Dhu 'l-Nún, the friend of God." And after his death the following words were found inscribed on his forehead: *This is the beloved of God, who died in love of God, slain by God.* At his funeral the birds of the air gathered above his bier, and wove their wings together so as to shadow it. On seeing this, all the Egyptians felt remorse and repented of the injustice which they had done to him. He has many fine and admirable sayings on the verities of mystical knowledge. He says, for example: "The gnostic (*'árif*) is more lowly every day, because he is approaching nearer to his Lord every moment," inasmuch as he thereby becomes aware of the awfulness of the Divine Omnipotence, and when the majesty of God has taken possession of his heart, he sees how far he is from God and that there is no way of reaching Him; hence his lowliness is increased. Thus Moses said, when he conversed with God: "O Lord, where shall I seek Thee?" God answered: "Among those whose hearts are broken." Moses said: "O Lord, no heart is more broken and despairing than mine." God answered: "Then I am where thou art." Accordingly, anyone who pretends to know God without lowliness and fear is an ignorant fool, not a gnostic. The sign of true knowledge is sincerity of will, and a sincere will cuts off all secondary causes and severs all ties of relationship, so that nothing remains except God. Dhu 'l-Nún says: "Sincerity (*ṣidq*) is the sword of God on the earth: it cuts everything that it touches." Now sincerity regards the Causer, and does not consist in affirmation of secondary causes. To affirm the latter is to destroy the principle of sincerity.

Among the stories told of Dhu 'l-Nún I have read that one day he was sailing with his disciples in a boat on the River Nile, as is the custom of the people of Egypt when they desire recreation. Another boat was coming up, filled with merry-makers, whose unseemly behaviour so disgusted the disciples that they begged Dhu 'l-Nún to implore God to sink the boat. Dhu 'l-Nún raised his hands and cried: "O Lord, as Thou hast given these people a pleasant life in this world, give them a pleasant life in the next world too!" The disciples were astonished by his prayer. When the boat came nearer and those in it saw Dhu 'l-Nún, they began to weep and ask pardon, and broke their lutes and repented unto God. Dhu 'l-Nún said to his disciples: "A pleasant life in the next world is repentance in this world. You and they are all satisfied without harm to anyone." He acted thus from his extreme affection towards the Moslems, following the example of the Apostle, who, notwithstanding the ill-treatment which he received from the infidels, never ceased to say: "O God! direct my people, for they know not." Dhu 'l-Nún relates that as he was journeying from Jerusalem to Egypt he saw in the distance some one advancing towards him, and felt impelled to ask a question. When the person came near he perceived that it was an old woman carrying a staff (*'ukkáza*[1]), and wearing a woollen tunic (*jubba*). He asked her whence she came. She answered: "From God." "And whither goest thou?" "To God." Dhu 'l-Nún drew forth a piece of gold which he had with him and offered it to her, but she shook her hand in his face and cried: "O Dhu 'l-Nún, the notion which thou hast formed of me arises from the feebleness of thy intelligence. I work for God's sake, and accept nothing unless from Him. I worship Him alone and take from Him alone." With these words she went on her way.

The old woman's saying that she worked for God's sake is a proof of her sincerity in love. Men in their dealings with God fall into two classes. Some imagine that they work for God's sake when they are really working for themselves; and though their work is not done with any worldly motive, they desire a recompense in the next world. Others take no thought of reward or punishment in the next world, any more than of ostentation and reputation in this world, but act solely from reverence for the commandments of God. Their love of God requires them to forget every selfish interest while they do His bidding. The former class fancy that what they do for the sake of the next world they do for God's sake, and fail to recognize that the devout have a greater self-interest in devotion than the wicked have in sin, because the sinner's pleasure lasts only for a moment, whereas devotion is a delight for ever. Besides, what gain accrues to God from the religious exercises of mankind, or what loss from their non-performance? If all the world acted with the veracity of Abú Bakr, the gain would be wholly theirs, and if with the falsehood of Pharaoh, the loss would be wholly theirs, as God hath said: "*If ye do good, it is to yourselves, and if ye do evil, it is to yourselves*" (Kor. xvii, 7); and also: "*Whoever exerts himself* [in religion] *does so for his*

[1] According to a marginal gloss in I, *'ukkáza* is a tripod on which a leathern water-bottle is suspended.

own advantage. Verily, God is independent of created beings" (Kor. xxix, 5). They seek for themselves an everlasting kingdom and say, "We are working for God's sake"; but to tread the path of love is a different thing. Lovers, in fulfilling the Divine commandment, regard only the accomplishment of the Beloved's will, and have no eyes for anything else.

A similar topic will be discussed in the chapter on Sincerity (*ikhláṣ*).

10. Abú Isḥáq Ibráhím b. Adham b. Manṣúr.

He was unique in his Path, and the chief of his contemporaries. He was a disciple of the Apostle Khiḍr. He met a large number of the ancient Ṣúfí Shaykhs, and associated with the Imám Abú Ḥanífa, from whom he learned divinity (*'ilm*). In the earlier part of his life he was Prince of Balkh. One day he went to the chase, and having become separated from his suite was pursuing an antelope. God caused the antelope to address him in elegant language and say: "Wast thou created for this, or wast thou commanded to do this?" He repented, abandoned everything, and entered on the path of asceticism and abstinence. He made the acquaintance of Fuḍayl b. 'Iyáḍ and Sufyán Thawrí, and consorted with them. After his conversion he never ate any food except what he had earned by his own labour. His sayings on the verities of Ṣúfiism are original and exquisite. Junayd said: "Ibráhím is the key of the (mystical) sciences." It is related that he said: "Take God as thy companion and leave mankind alone," i.e. when anyone is rightly and sincerely turned towards God, the rightness of his turning towards God requires that he should turn his back on mankind, inasmuch as the society of mankind has nothing to do with thoughts of God. Companionship with God is sincerity in fulfilling His commands, and sincerity in devotion springs from purity of love, and pure love of God proceeds from hatred of passion and lust. Whoever is familiar with sensual affections is separated from God, and whoever is separated from sensual affections is dwelling with God. Therefore thou art all mankind in regard to thyself: turn away from thyself, and thou hast turned away from all mankind. Thou dost wrong to turn away from mankind and towards thyself, and to be concerned with thyself, whereas the actions of all mankind are determined by the providence and predestination of God. The outward and inward rectitude (*istiqámat*) of the seeker is founded on two things, one of which is theoretical and the other practical. The former consists in regarding all good and evil as predestined by God, so that nothing in the universe passes into a state of rest or motion until God has created rest or motion in that thing; the latter consists in performing the command of God, in rightness of action towards Him, and in keeping the obligations which he Has imposed. Predestination can never become an argument for neglecting His commands. True renunciation of mankind is impossible until thou hast renounced thyself. As soon as thou hast renounced thyself, all mankind are necessary for the fulfilment of the will of God; and as soon as thou hast turned to God, thou art necessary for the accomplishment of the decree of God. Hence it is not permissible to be satisfied with mankind. If thou wilt be satisfied with anything except God, at least be satisfied with another (*ghayr*), for satisfaction with another is to regard unification (*tawḥíd*), whereas satisfaction with thyself is to affirm the nullity of the Creator (*ta'ṭíl*). For this reason Shaykh Abu 'l-Ḥasan Sáliba[1] used to say that it is better for novices to be under the authority of a cat than under their own authority, because companionship with another is for God's sake, while companionship with one's self is calculated to foster the sensual affections. This topic will be discussed in the proper place. Ibráhím b. Adham tells the following story: "When I reached the desert, an old man came up and said to me, 'O Ibráhím, do you know what place this is, and where you are journeying without provisions and on foot?' I knew that he was Satan. I produced from the bosom of my shirt four *dániqs*—the price of a basket which I had sold in Kúfa—and cast them away and made a vow that I would perform a prayer

[1] See *Nafaḥát*, No. 347, where he is called Abu 'l-Ḥusayn Sáliba.

of four hundred genuflexions for every mile that I travelled. I remained four years in the desert, and God was giving me my daily bread without any exertion on my part. During that time Khiḍr consorted with me and taught me the Great Name of God. Then my heart became wholly empty of 'other' (*ghayr*)."

11. Bishr b. al-Ḥárith al-Ḥáfí.

He associated with Fuḍayl and was the disciple of his own maternal uncle, 'Alí b. Khashram. He was versed in the principal, as well as the derivative, sciences. His conversion began as follows. One day, when he was drunk, he found on the road a piece of paper on which was written: "*In the name of God, the Compassionate, the Merciful.*" He picked it up with reverence, perfumed it, and laid in a clean place. The same night he dreamed that God said to him: "O Bishr, as thou hast made My name sweet, I swear by My glory that I will make thy name sweet both in this world and the next." Thereupon he repented and took to asceticism. So intensely was he absorbed in contemplation of God that he never put anything on his feet. When he was asked the reason of this, he said: "The Earth is His carpet, and I deem it wrong to tread on His carpet while there is anything between my foot and His carpet." This is one of his peculiar practices: in the concentration of his mind on God a shoe seemed to him a veil (between him and God). It is related that he said: "Whoever desires to be honoured in this world and exalted in the next world, let him shun three things: let him not ask a boon of anyone, nor speak ill of anyone, nor accept an invitation to eat with anyone." No man who knows the way to God will ask a boon of human beings, since to do so is a proof of his ignorance of God: if he knew the Giver of all boons, he would not ask a boon from a fellow-creature. Again, the man who speaks ill of anyone is criticizing the decree of God, inasmuch as both the individual himself and his actions are created by God; and on whom can the blame for an action be thrown except on the agent? This does not apply, however, to the blame which God has commanded us to bestow upon infidels. Thirdly, as to his saying, "Do not eat of men's food," the reason is that God is the Provider. If He makes a creature the means of giving you daily bread, do not regard that creature, but consider that the daily bread which God has caused to come to you does not belong to him but to God. If he thinks that it is his, and that he is thereby conferring a favour on you, do not accept it. In the matter of daily bread one person does not confer on another any favour at all, because, according to the opinion of the orthodox, daily bread is food (*ghidhá*), although the Mu'tazilites hold it to be property (*milk*); and God, not any created being, nourishes mankind with food. This saying may be explained otherwise, if it be taken in a profane sense (*majáz*).

12. Abú Yazíd Ṭayfúr b. 'Ísá al-Bisṭámí.

He is the greatest of the Shaykhs in state and dignity, so that Junayd said: "Abú Yazíd holds the same rank among us as Gabriel among the angels." His grandfather was a Magian, and his father was one of the notables of Bisṭám. He is the author of many trustworthy relations concerning the Traditions of the Apostle, and he is one of the ten celebrated Imáms of Ṣúfiism. No one before him penetrated so deeply into the arcana of this science. In all circumstances he was a lover of theology and a venerator of the sacred law, notwithstanding the spurious doctrine which has been foisted on him by some persons with the object of supporting their own heresies. From the first, his life was based on self-mortification and the practice of devotion. It is recorded that he said: "For thirty years I was active in self-mortification, and I found nothing harder than to learn divinity and follow its precepts. But for the disagreement of divines I should have utterly failed in my endeavour. The disagreement of divines is a mercy save on the point of Unification." This is true indeed, for human nature is more prone to ignorance than to knowledge, and while many things can be done easily with ignorance, not a single step can be made easily with knowledge. The bridge of the sacred law is much narrower and more dangerous than the Bridge (*Ṣiráṭ*) in the next world. Therefore it behoves thee so to act in all circumstances that, if thou shouldst not attain a high degree and an eminent station, thou mayst at any rate fall within the pale of the sacred law. Even if thou lose all else, thy practices of devotion will remain with thee. Neglect of those is the worst mischief that can happen to a novice.

It is related that Abú Yazíd said: "Paradise hath no value in the eyes of lovers, and lovers are veiled (from God) by their love," i.e. Paradise is created, whereas love is an uncreated attribute of God. Whoever is detained by a created thing from that which is uncreated, is without worth and value. Created things are worthless in the eyes of lovers. Lovers are veiled by love, because the existence of love involves duality, which is incompatible with unification (*tawḥíd*). The way of lovers is from oneness to oneness, but there is in love this defect, that it needs a desirer (*muríd*) and an object of desire (*murád*). Either God must be the desirer and Man the desired, or *vice versâ*. In the former case, Man's being is fixed in God's desire, but if Man is the desirer and God the object of desire, the creature's search and desire can find no way unto Him: in either case the canker of being remains in the lover. Accordingly, the annihilation of the lover in the everlastingness of love is more perfect than his subsistence through the everlastingness of love.

It is related that Abú Yazíd said: "I went to Mecca and saw a House standing apart. I said, 'My pilgrimage is not accepted, for I have seen many stones of this sort.' I went again, and saw the House and also the Lord of the House. I said, 'This is not yet real unification.' I went a third time, and saw only the Lord of the House. A voice in my heart whispered, 'O Báyazíd, if thou didst not see thyself, thou wouldst not be a polytheist (*mushrik*) though thou sawest the whole universe; and since thou seest thyself, thou art a polytheist though blind to the whole universe.' Thereupon I repented, and once more

I repented of my repentance; and yet once more I repented of seeing my own existence."

This is a subtle tale concerning the soundness of his state, and gives an excellent indication to spiritualists.

13. ABÚ 'ABDALLÁH AL-ḤÁRITH B. ASAD AL-MUḤÁSIBÍ.

He was learned in the principal and derivative sciences, and his authority was recognized by all the theologians of his day. He wrote a book, entitled *Ri'áyat*,[1] on the principles of Ṣúfiism, as well as many other works. In every branch of learning he was a man of lofty sentiment and noble mind. He was the chief Shaykh of Baghdád in his time. It is related that he said: *Al-'ilm bi-ḥarakát al-qulúb fí muṭála'at al-ghuyúb ashraf min al-'amal bi-ḥarakát al-jawáriḥ*, i.e. he who is acquainted with the secret motions of the heart is better than he who acts with the motions of the limbs. The meaning is that knowledge is the place of perfection, whereas ignorance is the place of search, and knowledge at the shrine is better than ignorance at the door: knowledge brings a man to perfection, but ignorance does not even allow him to enter (on the way to perfection). In reality knowledge is greater than action, because it is possible to know God by means of knowledge, but impossible to attain to Him by means of action. If He could be found by action without knowledge, the Christians and the monks in their austerities would behold Him face to face and sinful believers would have no vision of Him. Therefore knowledge is a Divine attribute and action a human attribute. Some relaters of this saying have fallen into error by reading *al-'amal bi-ḥarakát al-qulúb*,[2] which is absurd, since human actions have nothing to do with the motions of the heart. If the author uses this expression to denote reflection and contemplation of the inward feelings, it is not strange, for the Apostle said: "A moment's reflection is better than sixty years of devotion,"

[1] Its full title is *Ri'áyat li-ḥuqúq Alláh*, "The observance of what is due to God."

[2] This reading is given in the *Ṭabaqát al-Ṣúfiyya* of Abú 'Abd al-Raḥmán al-Sulamí (British Museum MS., Add. 18,520, f. 13*a*).

and spiritual actions are in truth more excellent than bodily actions, and the effect produced by inward feelings and actions is really more complete than the effect produced by outward actions. Hence it is said: "The sleep of the sage is an act of devotion and the wakefulness of the fool is a sin," because the sage's heart is controlled (by God) whether he sleeps or wakes, and when the heart is controlled the body also is controlled. Accordingly, the heart that is controlled by the sway of God is better than the sensual part of Man which controls his outward motions and acts of self-mortification. It is related that Ḥárith said one day to a dervish, *Kun lilláh wa-illá lá takun*, "Be God's or be nothing," i.e. either be subsistent through God or perish to thine own existence; either be united with Purity (*ṣafwat*) or separated by Poverty (*faqr*); either in the state described by the words "*Bow ye down to Adam*" (Kor. ii, 32) or in the state described by the words "*Did there not come over Man a time when he was not anything worthy of mention?*" (Kor. lxxvi, 1). If thou wilt give thyself to God of thy own free choice, thy resurrection will be through thyself, but if thou wilt not, then thy resurrection will be through God.

14. Abú Ṣulaymán Dáwud b. Nuṣayr al-Ṭá'í.

He was a pupil of Abú Ḥanífa and a contemporary of Fuḍayl and Ibráhím b. Adham. In Ṣúfiism he was a disciple of Ḥabíb Rá'í. He was deeply versed in all the sciences and unrivalled in jurisprudence (*fiqh*); but he went into seclusion and turned his back on authority, and took the path of asceticism and piety. It is related that he said to one of his disciples: "If thou desirest welfare, bid farewell to this world, and if thou desirest grace (*karámat*), pronounce the *takbír*[1] over the next world," i.e. both these are places of veiling (places which prevent thee from seeing God). Every kind of tranquillity (*farághat*) depends on these two counsels. Whoever would be

[1] The *takbír*, i.e. the words *Allah akbar*, "God is most great," is pronounced four times in Moslem funeral prayers.

tranquil in body, let him turn his back on this world; and whoever would be tranquil in heart, let him clear his heart of all desire for the next world. It is a well-known story that Dáwud used constantly to associate with Muḥammad b. al-Ḥasan,[1] but would never receive the Cadi Abú Yúsuf. On being asked why he honoured one of these eminent divines but refused to admit the other to his presence, he replied that Muḥammad b. al-Ḥasan had become a theologian after being rich and wealthy, and theology was the cause of his religious advancement and worldly abasement, whereas Abú Yúsuf had become a theologian after being poor and despised, and had made theology the means of gaining wealth and power. It is related that Ma'rúf Karkhí said: "I never saw anyone who held worldly goods in less account than Dáwud Ṭá'í; the world and its people had no value whatsoever in his eyes, and he used to regard dervishes (*fuqará*) as perfect although they were corrupt."

15. ABU 'L-ḤASAN SARÍ B. MUGHALLIS AL-SAQAṬÍ.

He was the maternal uncle of Junayd. He was well versed in all the sciences and eminent in Ṣúfiism, and he was the first of those who have devoted their attention to the arrangement of "stations" (*maqámát*) and to the explanation of spiritual "states" (*aḥwál*). Most of the Shaykhs of 'Iráq are his pupils. He had seen Ḥabíb Rá'í and associated with him. He was a disciple of Ma'rúf Karkhí. He used to carry on the business of a huckster (*saqaṭ-firúsh*) in the bazaar at Baghdád. When the bazaar caught fire, he was told that his shop was burnt. He replied: "Then I am freed from the care of it." Afterwards it was discovered that his shop had not been burnt, although all the shops surrounding it were destroyed. On seeing this, Sarí gave all that he possessed to the poor and took the path of Ṣúfiism. He was asked how the change in him began. He answered: "One day Ḥabíb Rá'í passed my shop, and I gave him a crust of bread, telling him to give it to the poor.

[1] Muḥammad b. al-Ḥasan and Abú Yúsuf were celebrated lawyers of the Hanafite school. See Brockelmann, i, 171.

He said to me, 'May God reward thee!' From the day when I heard this prayer my worldly affairs never prospered again." It is related that Sarí said: "O God, whatever punishment Thou mayst inflict upon me, do not punish me with the humiliation of being veiled from Thee," because, if I am not veiled from Thee, my torment and affliction will be lightened by the remembrance and contemplation of Thee; but if I am veiled from Thee, even Thy bounty will be deadly to me. There is no punishment in Hell more painful and hard to bear than that of being veiled. If God were revealed in Hell to the people of Hell, sinful believers would never think of Paradise, since the sight of God would so fill them with joy that they would not feel bodily pain. And in Paradise there is no pleasure more perfect than unveiledness (*kashf*). If the people there enjoyed all the pleasures of that place and other pleasures a hundredfold, but were veiled from God, their hearts would be utterly broken. Therefore it is the custom of God to let the hearts of those who love Him have vision of Him always, in order that the delight thereof may enable them to endure every tribulation; and they say in their orisons: "We deem all torments more desirable than to be veiled from Thee. When Thy beauty is revealed to our hearts, we take no thought of affliction."

16. ABÚ 'ALÍ SHAQÍQ B. IBRÁHÍM AL-AZDÍ.

He was versed in all the sciences—legal, practical, and theoretical—and composed many works on various branches of Ṣúfiism. He consorted with Ibráhím b. Adham and many other Shaykhs. It is related that he said: "God hath made the pious living in their death, and hath made the wicked dead during their lives," i.e., the pious, though they be dead, yet live, since the angels utter blessings on their piety until they are made immortal by the recompense which they receive at the Resurrection. Hence, in the annihilation wrought by death they subsist through the everlastingness of retribution. Once an old man came to Shaqíq and said to him: "O Shaykh,

I have sinned much and now wish to repent." Shaqíq said: "Thou hast come late." The old man answered: "No, I have come soon. Whoever comes before he is dead comes soon, though he may have been long in coming." It is said that the occasion of Shaqíq's conversion was this, that one year there was a famine at Balkh, and the people were eating one another's flesh. While all the Moslems were bitterly distressed, Shaqíq saw a youth laughing and making merry in the bazaar. The people said: "Why do you laugh? Are not you ashamed to rejoice when everyone else is mourning?" The youth said: "I have no sorrow. I am the servant of a man who owns a village as his private property, and he has relieved me of all care for my livelihood." Shaqíq exclaimed: "O Lord God, this youth rejoices so much in having a master who owns a single village, but Thou art the King of kings, and Thou hast promised to give us our daily bread; and nevertheless we have filled our hearts with all this sorrow because we are engrossed with worldly things." He turned to God and began to walk in the way of the Truth, and never troubled himself again about his daily bread. Afterwards he used to say: "I am the pupil of a youth; all that I have learned I learned from him." His humility led him to say this.

17. ABÚ SULAYMÁN 'ABD AL-RAḤMÁN B. 'ATIYYA AL-DÁRÁNÍ.

He was held in honour by the Ṣúfís and was (called) the sweet basil of hearts (*rayḥán-i dilhá*). He is distinguished by his severe austerities and acts of self-mortification. He was versed in the science of "time" (*'ilm-i waqt*)[1] and in knowledge of the cankers of the soul, and had a keen eye for its hidden snares. He spoke in subtle terms concerning the practice of devotion, and the watch that should be kept over the heart and the limbs. It is related that he said: "When hope predominates over fear, one's 'time' is spoilt," because "time" is the preservation of one's "state" (*ḥál*), which is preserved only so long as one is possessed by fear. If, on the other hand, fear predominates

[1] See note on p. 13.

over hope, belief in Unity (*tawḥíd*) is lost, inasmuch as excessive fear springs from despair, and despair of God is polytheism (*shirk*). Accordingly, the maintenance of belief in Unity consists in right hope, and the maintenance of "time" in right fear, and both are maintained when hope and fear are equal. Maintenance of belief in Unity makes one a believer (*mu'min*), while maintenance of "time" makes one pious (*muṭí'*). Hope is connected entirely with contemplation (*musháhadat*), in which is involved a firm conviction (*i'tiqád*); and fear is connected entirely with purgation (*mujáhadat*), in which is involved an anxious uncertainty (*iḍṭiráb*). Contemplation is the fruit of purgation, or, to express the same idea differently, every hope is produced by despair. Whenever a man, on account of his actions, despairs of his future welfare, that despair shows him the way to salvation and welfare and Divine mercy, and opens to him the door of gladness, and clears away sensual corruptions from his heart, and reveals to it the Divine mysteries.

Aḥmad b. Abi 'l-Ḥawárí relates that one night, when he was praying in private, he felt great pleasure. Next day he told Abú Sulaymán, who replied: "Thou art a weak man, for thou still hast mankind in view, so that thou art one thing in private and another in public." There is nothing in the two worlds that is sufficiently important to hold man back from God. When a bride is unveiled to the people, the reason is that everyone may see her and that she may be honoured the more through being seen, but it is not proper that she should see anyone except the bridegroom, since she is disgraced by seeing anyone else. If all mankind should see the glory of a pious man's piety, he would suffer no harm, but if he sees the excellence of his own piety he is lost.

18. Abú Maḥfúẓ Ma'rúf b. Fíruz al-Karkhí.

He is one of the ancient and principal Shaykhs, and was famed for his generosity and devoutness. This notice of him should have come earlier in the book, but I have placed it here in accordance with two venerable persons who wrote before me, one of them a relater of traditions and the other an independent authority (*ṣáḥib taṣarruf*)—I mean Shaykh Abú 'Abd al-Raḥmán al-Sulamí, who in his work adopts the arrangement which I have followed, and the Master and Imám Abu 'l-Qásimal-Qushayrí, who has put the notice of Ma'rúf in the same order in the introductory portion of his book.[1] I have chosen this arrangement because Ma'rúf was the master of Sarí Saqaṭí and the disciple of Dáwud Ṭá'í. At first Ma'rúf was a non-Moslem (*bégána*), but he made profession of Islam to 'Alí b. Músá al-Riḍá, who held him in the highest esteem. It is related that he said: "There are three signs of generosity—to keep faith without resistance, to praise without being incited thereto by liberality, and to give without being asked." In men all these qualities are merely borrowed, and in reality they belong to God, who acts thus towards His servants. God keeps unresisting faith with those who love Him, and although they show resistance in keeping faith with Him, He only increases His kindness towards them. The sign of God's keeping faith is this, that in eternity past He called His servant to His presence without any good action on the part of His servant, and that to-day He does not banish His servant on account of an evil action. He alone praises without the incitement of liberality, for He has no need of His servant's actions, and nevertheless extols him for a little thing that he has done. He alone gives without being asked, for He is generous and knows the state of everyone and fulfils his desire unasked. Accordingly, when God gives a man grace and makes him noble, and distinguishes him by His favour, and acts towards him in the three ways mentioned above, and when that man, as far as lies in his

1 This statement is not accurate. The notice of Ma'rúf Karkhí is the fourth in Qushayrí's list of biographies at the beginning of his treatise on Ṣúfiism, and stands between the notices of Fuḍayl b. 'Iyáḍ and Sarí Saqaṭí. In the *Ṭabaqát al-Ṣúfiyya*, by Abú 'Abd al-Raḥmán al-Sulamí, the notice of Ma'rúf comes tenth in order, but occupies the same position as it does here in so far as it is preceded by the article on Abú Sulaymán Dáráni and is followed by the article on Ḥátim al-Aṣamm. It appears from the next sentence that al-Hujwírí intended to place the life of Ma'rúf between those of Dáwud Ṭá'í and Sarí Saqaṭí (Nos. 14 and 15), but neither of the two above-mentioned authorities has adopted this arrangement.

power, acts in the same way towards his fellow-creatures, then he is called generous and gets a reputation for generosity. Abraham the Apostle possessed these three qualities in very truth, as I shall explain in the proper place.

19. ABÚ 'ABD AL-RAḤMÁN ḤÁTIM B. 'ULWÁN[1] AL-AṢAMM.

He was one of the great men of Balkh and one of the ancient Shaykhs of Khurásán, a disciple of Shaqíq and the teacher of Aḥmad Khaḍrúya. In all his circumstances, from beginning to end, he never once acted untruthfully, so that Junayd said: "Ḥátim al-Aṣamm is the veracious one (*ṣiddíq*) of our time." He has lofty sayings on the subtleties of discerning the cankers of the soul and the weaknesses of human nature, and is the author of famous works on ethics (*'ilm-i mu'ámalát*). It is related that he said: "Lust is of three kinds—lust in eating, lust in speaking, and lust in looking. Guard thy food by trust in God, thy tongue by telling the truth, and thine eye by taking example (*'ibrat*)." Real trust in God proceeds from right knowledge, for those who know Him aright have confidence that He will give them their daily bread, and they speak and look with right knowledge, so that their food and drink is only love, and their speech is only ecstasy, and their looking is only contemplation. Accordingly, when they know aright they eat what is lawful, and when they speak aright they utter praise (of God), and when they look aright they behold Him, because no food is lawful except what He has given and permits to be eaten, and no praise is rightly offered to anyone in the eighteen thousand worlds except to Him, and it is not allowable to look on anything in the universe except His beauty and majesty. It is not lust when thou receivest food from Him and eatest by His leave, or when thou speakest of Him by His leave, or when thou seest His actions by His leave. On the other hand, it *is* lust when of thy own will thou eatest even lawful food, or of thy own will thou speakest even praise of Him, or of thy own will thou lookest even for the purpose of seeking guidance.

[1] LIJ. have عنوان.

20. ABÚ 'ABDALLÁH MUḤAMMAD B. IDRÍS AL-SHÁFI'Í.

While he was at Medína he was a pupil of the Imám Málik, and when he came to 'Iráq he associated with Muḥammad b. al-Ḥasan. He always had a natural desire for seclusion, and used to seek an intimate comprehension of this way of life, until a party gathered round him and followed his authority. One of them was Aḥmad b. Ḥanbal. Then Sháfi'í became occupied with seeking position and exercising his authority as Imám, and was unable to retire from the world. At first he was not favourably disposed towards aspirants to Ṣúfiism, but after seeing Sulaymán Rá'í and obtaining admission to his society, he continued to seek the truth wherever he went. It is related that he said: "When you see a divine busying himself with indulgences (*rukhaṣ*), no good thing will come from him," i.e. divines are the leaders of all classes of men, and no one may take precedence of them in any matter, and the way of God cannot be traversed without precaution and the utmost self-mortification, and to seek indulgences in divinity is the act of one who flees from self-mortification and prefers an alleviation for himself. Ordinary people seek indulgences to keep themselves within the pale of the sacred law, but the elect practise self-mortification to feel the fruit thereof in their hearts. Divines are among the elect, and when one of them is satisfied with behaving like ordinary people, nothing good will come from him. Moreover, to seek indulgences is to think lightly of God's commandment, and divines love God: a lover does not think lightly of the command of his beloved.

A certain Shaykh relates that one night he dreamed of the Prophet and said to him: "O Apostle of God, a tradition has come down to me from thee that God hath upon the earth saints of diverse rank (*awtád ú awliyá ú abrár*)." The Apostle said that the relater of the tradition had transmitted it correctly, and in answer to the Shaykh's request that he might see one of these holy men, he said: "Muḥammad b. Idrís is one of them."

21. THE IMÁM AḤMAD B. ḤANBAL.

He was distinguished by devoutness and piety, and was the guardian of the Traditions of the Apostle. Ṣúfís of all sects regard him as blessed. He associated with great Shaykhs, such as Dhu 'l-Nún of Egypt, Bishr al-Ḥáfí, Sarí al-Saqaṭí, Ma'rúf al-Karkhí, and others. His miracles were manifest and his intelligence sound. The doctrines attributed to him to-day by certain Anthropomorphists are inventions and forgeries; he is to be acquitted of all notions of that sort. He had a firm belief in the principles of religion, and his creed was approved by all the divines. When the Mu'tazilites came into power at Baghdád, they wished to extort from him a confession that the Koran was created, and though he was a feeble old man they put him to the rack and gave him a thousand lashes. In spite of all this he would not say that the Koran was created. While he was undergoing punishment his *izár* became untied. His own hands were fettered, but another hand appeared and tied it. Seeing this evidence, they let him go. He died, however, of the wounds inflicted on that occasion. Shortly before his death some persons visited him and asked what he had to say about those who flogged him. He answered: "What should I have to say? They flogged me for God's sake, thinking that I was wrong and that they were right. I will not claim redress from them at the Resurrection for mere blows." He is the author of lofty sayings on ethics. When questioned on any point relating to practice he used to answer the question himself, but if it was a point of mystical theory (*ḥaqá'iq*) he would refer the questioner to Bishr Ḥáfí. One day a man asked him: "What is sincerity (*ikhláṣ*)?" He replied: "To escape from the cankers of one's actions," i.e. let thy actions be free from ostentation and hypocrisy and self-interest. The questioner then asked: "What is trust (*tawakkul*)?" Aḥmad replied: "Confidence in God, that He will provide thy daily bread." The man asked: "What is acquiescence (*riḍá*)?" He replied: "To commit thy affairs to God." "And what is love (*maḥabbat*)?" Aḥmad said: "Ask this question of Bishr

Ḥáfí, for I will not answer it while he is alive." Aḥmad b. Ḥanbal was constantly exposed to persecution: during his life by the attacks of the Mu'tazilites, and after his death by the suspicion of sharing the views of the Anthropomorphists. Consequently the orthodox Moslems are ignorant of his true state and hold him suspect. But he is clear of all that is alleged against him.

22. Abu 'l-Ḥasan Aḥmad b. Abi 'l-Ḥawárí.

He was one of the most eminent of the Syrian Shaykhs and is praised by all the leading Ṣúfís. Junayd said: "Aḥmad b. Abi 'l-Ḥawárí is the sweet basil of Syria (*rayḥánat al-Shám*)." He was the pupil of Abú Sulaymán Dáráni, and associated with Sufyán b. 'Uyayna and Marwán b. Mu'áwiya the Koran-reader (*al-Qárí*).[1] He had been a wandering devotee (*sayyáḥ*). It is related that he said: "This world is a dunghill and a place where dogs gather; and one who lingers there is less than a dog, for a dog takes what he wants from it and goes, but the lover of the world never departs from it or leaves it at any time." At first he was a student and attained the rank of the Imáms, but afterwards he threw all his books into the sea, and said: "Ye were excellent guides, but it is impossible to occupy one's self with a guide after one has reached the goal," because a guide is needed only so long as the disciple is on the road: when the shrine comes into sight the road and the gate are worthless. The Shaykhs have said that Aḥmad did this in the state of intoxication (*sukr*). In the mystic Path he who says "I have arrived" has gone astray. Since arriving is non-accomplishment, occupation is (superfluous) trouble, and freedom from occupation is idleness, and in either case the principle of union (*wuṣúl*) is non-existence, for both occupation and its opposite are human qualities. Union and separation alike depend on the eternal will and providence of God. Hence it is

[1] Marwán b. Mu'áwiya al-Fazárí of Kúfa died in 193 A.H. See Dhahabí's *Ṭabaqát al-Ḥuffáẓ*, ed. by Wüstenfeld, p. 63, No. 44. Al-Qárí is probably a mistranscription of al-Fazárí.

impossible to attain to union with Him. The terms "nearness" and "neighbourhood" are not applicable to God. A man is united to God when God holds him in honour, and separated from God when God holds him in contempt. I, 'Alí b. 'Uthmán al-Jullábí, say that possibly that eminent Shaykh in using the word "union" (*wuṣúl*) may have meant "discovery of the way to God", for the way to God is not found in books; and when the road lies plain before one no explanation is necessary. Those who have attained true knowledge have no use for speech, and even less for books. Other Shaykhs have done the same thing as Aḥmad b. Abi 'l-Ḥawárí, for example the Grand Shaykh Abú Sa'íd Faḍlalláh b. Muḥammad al-Mayhaní, and they have been imitated by a number of formalists whose only object is to gratify their indolence and ignorance. It would seem that those noble Shaykhs acted as they did from the desire of severing all worldly ties and making their hearts empty of all save God. This, however, is proper only in the intoxication of commencement (*ibtidá*) and in the fervour of youth. Those who have become fixed (*mutamakkin*) are not veiled (from God) by the whole universe: how, then, by a sheet of paper? It may be said that the destruction of a book signifies the impossibility of expressing the real meaning (of an idea). In that case the same impossibility should be predicated of the tongue, because spoken words are no better than written ones. I imagine that Aḥmad b. Abi 'l-Ḥawárí, finding no listener in his fit of ecstasy, wrote down an explanation of his feelings on pieces of paper, and having amassed a large quantity, did not regard them as suitable to be divulged and accordingly cast them into the water. It is also possible that he had collected many books, which diverted him from his devotional practices, and that he got rid of them for this reason.

23. Abú Ḥámid Aḥmad b. Khaḍrúya al-Balkhí.

He adopted the path of blame (*malámat*) and wore a soldier's dress. His wife, Fáṭima, daughter of the Amír of Balkh, was renowned as a Ṣúfí. When she desired to repent (of her former life), she sent a message to Aḥmad bidding him ask her in marriage of her father. Aḥmad refused, whereupon she sent another message in the following terms: "O Aḥmad, I thought you would have been too manly to attack those who travel on the way to God. Be a guide (*ráhbar*), not a brigand (*ráhbur*)." Aḥmad asked her in marriage of her father, who gave her to him in the hope of receiving his blessing. Fáṭima renounced all traffic with the world and lived in seclusion with her husband. When Aḥmad went to visit Báyazíd she accompanied him, and on seeing Báyazíd she removed her veil and talked to him without embarrassment. Aḥmad became jealous and said to her: "Why dost thou take this freedom with Báyazíd?" She replied: "Because you are my natural spouse, but he is my religious consort; through you I come to my desire, but through him to God. The proof is that he has no need of my society, whereas to you it is necessary." She continued to treat Báyazíd with the same boldness, until one day he observed that her hand was stained with henna and asked her why. She answered: "O Báyazíd, so long as you did not see my hand and the henna I was at my ease with you, but now that your eye has fallen on me our companionship is unlawful." Then Aḥmad and Fáṭima came to Níshápúr and abode there. The people and Shaykhs of Níshápúr were well pleased with Aḥmad. When Yaḥyá b. Mu'ádh al-Rází passed through Níshápúr on his way from Rayy to Balkh, Aḥmad wished to give him a banquet, and consulted with Fáṭima as to what things were required. She told him to procure so many oxen and sheep, such and such a quantity of sweet herbs, condiments, candles, and perfumes, and added, "We must also kill twenty donkeys." Aḥmad said: "What is the sense of killing donkeys?" "Oh!" said she, "when a noble comes as guest to the house of a noble the dogs of the quarter have something too." Báyazíd said of her: "Whoever wishes to see a man disguised in women's clothes, let him look at Fáṭima!" And Abú Ḥafṣ Ḥaddád says: "But for Aḥmad b. Khaḍrúya generosity would not have been displayed." He has lofty sayings to his credit, and faultless utterances (*anfás-i muhadhdhab*), and is the author of famous works in every branch of ethics and of brilliant discourses on mysticism. It is related that he said: "The way is manifest and the truth is clear, and the shepherd has uttered his call; after this if anyone loses himself, it is through his own blindness," i.e., it is wrong to seek the way, since the way to God is like the blazing sun; do thou seek thyself, for when thou hast found thyself thou art come to thy journey's end, inasmuch as God is too manifest to admit of His being sought. He is recorded to have said: "Hide the glory of thy poverty," i.e., do not say to people, "I am a dervish," lest thy secret be discovered, for it is a great grace bestowed on thee by God. It is related that he said: "A dervish invited a rich man to a repast in the month of Ramaḍán, and there was nothing in his house except a loaf of dry bread. On returning home the rich man sent to him a purse of gold. He sent it back, saying, 'This serves me right for revealing my secret to one like you.' The genuineness of his poverty led him to act thus."

24. Abú Turáb 'Askar b. al-Ḥusayn al-Nakhshabí al-Nasafí.

He was one of the chief Shaykhs of Khurásán, and was celebrated for his generosity, asceticism, and devoutness. He performed many miracles, and experienced marvellous adventures without number in the desert and elsewhere. He was one of the most noted travellers among the Ṣúfís, and used to cross the deserts in complete disengagement from worldly things (*ba-tajríd*). His death took place in the desert of Baṣra. After many years had elapsed he was found standing erect with his face towards the Ka'ba, shrivelled up, with a bucket in front of him and a staff in his hand; and the wild beasts had not touched him or come near him. It is related that he said: "The food of the dervish is what he finds, and his clothing is what covers him, and his dwelling-place is wherever he alights," i.e. he does not choose his own food or his own dress, or make a home for himself. The whole world is afflicted by these three items, and personal initiative therein keeps us in a state of distraction (*mashghúlí*) while we make efforts to procure them. This is the practical aspect of the matter, but in a mystical sense the food of the dervish is ecstasy, and his clothing is piety, and his dwelling-place is the Unseen, for God hath said, "*If they stood firm in the right path, We should water them with abundant rain*" (Kor. lxxii, 16); and again, "*and fair apparel; but the garment of piety, that is better*" (Kor. vii, 25); and the Apostle said, "Poverty is to dwell in the Unseen."

25. Abú Zakariyyá Yaḥyá b. Mu'ádh al-Rází.

He was perfectly grounded in the true theory of hope in God, so that Ḥuṣrí says: "God had two Yaḥyás, one a prophet and the other a saint. Yaḥyá b. Zakariyyá trod the path of fear so that all pretenders were filled with fear and despaired of their salvation, while Yaḥyá b. Mu'ádh trod the path of hope so that he tied the hands of all pretenders to hope." They said to Ḥuṣrí: "The state of Yaḥyá b. Zakariyyá is well known, but what was the state of Yaḥyá b. Mu'ádh?" He replied: "I have been told that he was never in the state of ignorance (*jáhiliyyat*) and never committed any of the greater sins (*kabíra*)." In the practice of devotion he showed an intense perseverance which was beyond the power of anyone else. One of his disciples said to him: "O Shaykh, thy station is the station of hope, but thy practice is the practice of those who fear." Yaḥyá answered: "Know, my son, that to abandon the service of God is to go astray." Fear and hope are the two pillars of faith. It is impossible that anyone should fall into error through practising either of them. Those who fear engage in devotion through fear of separation (from God), and those who hope engage in it through hope of union (with God). Without devotion neither fear nor hope can be truly felt, but when devotion is there this fear and hope are altogether metaphorical; and metaphors (*'ibárat*) are useless where devotion (*'ibádat*) is required.

Yaḥyá is the author of many books, fine sayings, and original precepts. He was the first of the Shaykhs of this sect, after the Orthodox Caliphs, to mount the pulpit. I am very fond of his sayings, which are delicately moulded and pleasant to the ear and subtle in substance and profitable in devotion. It is related that he said: "This world is an abode of troubles (*ashghál*) and the next world is an abode of terrors (*ahwál*), and Man never ceases to be amidst troubles or terrors until he finds rest either in Paradise or in Hell-fire." Happy the soul that has escaped from troubles and is secure from terrors, and has detached its thoughts from both worlds, and has attained to God! Yahyá held the doctrine that wealth is superior to poverty. Having contracted many debts at Rayy, he set out for Khurásán. When he arrived at Balkh the people of that city detained him for some time in order that he might discourse to them, and they gave him a hundred thousand dirhems. On his way back to Rayy he was attacked by brigands, who seized the whole sum. He came in a destitute condition to Níshápúr, where he died. He was always honoured and held in respect by the people.

26. ABÚ ḤAFṢ 'AMR B. SÁLIM[1] AL-NÍSHÁPÚRÍ AL-ḤADDÁDÍ.[2]

He was an eminent Ṣúfí, who is praised by all the Shaykhs. He associated with Abú 'Abdalláh al-Abíwardí and Aḥmad b. Khaḍrúya. Sháh Shujá' came from Kirmán to visit him. He did not know Arabic, and when he went to Baghdád to visit the Shaykhs there, his disciples said to one another: "It is a great shame that the Grand Shaykh of Khurásán should need an interpreter to make him understand what they say." However, when he met the Shaykhs of Baghdád, including Junayd, in the Shúníziyya Mosque, he conversed with them in elegant Arabic, so that they despaired of rivalling his eloquence. They asked him: "What is generosity?" He

[1] *Nafaḥát*, No. 44, has "Salama". Qushayrí calls him 'Umar b. Maslama.

[2] So LIJ. B. has "al-Ḥaddád", which is the form generally used by his biographers.

said: "Let one of you begin and declare what it is." Junayd said: "In my opinion generosity consists in not regarding your generosity and in not referring it to yourself." Abú Ḥafṣ replied: "How well the Shaykh has spoken! but in my opinion generosity consists in doing justice and in not demanding justice." Junayd said to his disciples: "Rise! for Abú Ḥafṣ has surpassed Adam and all his descendants (in generosity)." His conversion is related as follows. He was enamoured of a girl, and on the advice of his friends sought help from a certain Jew living in the city (*shár̀istán*) of Níshápúr. The Jew told him that he must perform no prayers for forty days, and not praise God or do any good deed or form any good intention; he would then devise a means whereby Abú Ḥafṣ should gain his desire. Abú Ḥafṣ complied with these instructions, and after forty days the Jew made a talisman as he had promised, but it proved ineffectual. He said: "You have undoubtedly done some good deed. Think!" Abú Ḥafṣ replied that the only good thing of any sort that he had done was to remove a stone which he found on the road lest some one might stumble on it. The Jew said to him: "Do not offend that God who has not let such a small act of yours be wasted though you have neglected His commands for forty days." Abú Ḥafṣ repented, and the Jew became a Moslem.

Abú Ḥafṣ continued to ply the trade of a blacksmith until he went to Báward and took the vows of discipleship to Abú 'Abdalláh Báwardí. One day, after his return to Níshápúr, he was sitting in his shop listening to a blind man who was reciting the Koran in the bazaar. He became so absorbed in listening that he put his hand into the fire and, without using the pincers, drew out a piece of molten iron from the furnace. On seeing this the apprentice fainted. When Abú Ḥafṣ came to himself he left his shop and no longer earned his livelihood. It is related that he said: "I left work and returned to it; then work left me and I never returned to it again," because when anyone leaves a thing by one's own act and effort, the leaving of it is no better than the taking of it, inasmuch as all acquired acts (*aksáb*) are contaminated, and derive their value from the spiritual influence which flows from the Unseen without effort on our part; which influence, wherever it descends, is united with the choice of Man and loses its pure spirituality. Therefore Man cannot properly take or leave anything; it is God who in His providence gives and takes away, and Man only takes what God has given or leaves what God has taken away. Though a disciple should strive a thousand years to win the favour of God, it would be worth less than if God received him into favour for a single moment, since everlasting future happiness is involved in the favour of past eternity, and Man has no means of escape except by the unalloyed bounty of God. Honoured, then, is he from whose state the Causer has removed all secondary causes.

27. ABÚ ṢÁLIḤ ḤAMDÚN B. AḤMAD B. 'UMÁRA AL-QAṢṢÁR.

He belonged to the ancient Shaykhs, and was one of those who were scrupulously devout. He attained the highest rank in jurisprudence and divinity, in which sciences he was a follower of Thawrí.[1] In Ṣúfiism he was a disciple of Abú Turáb Nakhshabí and 'Alí Naṣrábádí. When he became renowned as a theologian, the Imáms and notables of Níshápúr urged him to mount the pulpit and preach to the people, but he refused, saying: "My heart is still attached to the world, and therefore my words will make no impression on the hearts of others. To speak unprofitable words is to despise theology and deride the sacred law. Speech is permissible to him alone whose silence is injurious to religion, and whose speaking would remove the injury." On being asked why the sayings of the early Moslems were more beneficial than those of his contemporaries to men's hearts, he replied: "Because they

[1] The words *madhhab-i Thawrí dásht* may refer either to Abú Thawr Ibráhím b. Khálid, a pupil of al-Sháfi'í, who died in 246 A.H., or to Sufyán al-Thawrí. See Ibn Khallikán, No. 143.

discoursed for the glory of Islam and the salvation of souls and the satisfaction of the Merciful God, whereas we discourse for the glory of ourselves and the quest of worldly gain and the favour of mankind." Whoever speaks in accordance with God's will and by Divine impulsion, his words have a force and vigour that makes an impression on the wicked, but if anyone speaks in accordance with his own will, his words are weak and tame and do not benefit his hearers.

28. Abu 'l-Sarí Manṣúr b. 'Ammár.

He belonged to the school of 'Iráq, but was approved by the people of Khurásán. His sermons were unequalled for beauty of language and elegance of exposition. He was learned in all the branches of divinity, in traditions, sciences, principles, and practices. Some aspirants to Ṣúfiism exaggerate his merits beyond measure. It is related that he said: "Glory be to Him who hath made the hearts of gnostics vessels of praise (*dhikr*), and the hearts of ascetics vessels of trust (*tawakkul*), and the hearts of those who trust (*mutawakkilín*) vessels of acquiescence (*riḍá*), and the hearts of dervishes (*fuqará*) vessels of contentment, and the hearts of worldlings vessels of covetousness!" It is worth while to consider that whereas God has placed in every member of the body and in every sense a homogeneous quality, e.g., in the hands that of seizing, in the feet that of walking, in the eye seeing, in the ear hearing, He has placed in each individual heart a diverse quality and a different desire, so that one is the seat of knowledge, another of error, another of contentment, another of covetousness, and so on: hence the marvels of Divine action are in nothing manifested more clearly than in human hearts. And it is related that he said: "All mankind may be reduced to two types—the man who knows himself, and whose business is self-mortification and discipline, and the man who knows his Lord, and whose business is to serve and worship and please Him." Accordingly, the worship of the former is discipline (*riyáḍat*), while the worship of the latter is sovereignty (*riyásat*): the former practises devotion in order that he may attain a high degree, but the latter practises devotion having already attained all. What a vast difference between the two! One subsists in self-mortification (*mujáhadat*), the other in contemplation (*mushâhadat*). And it is related that he said: "There are two classes of men: those who have need of God—and they hold the highest rank from the standpoint of the sacred law—and those who pay no regard to their need of God, because they know that God has provided for their creation and livelihood and death and life and happiness and misery: they need God alone, and having him are independent of all else." The former, through seeing their own need, are veiled from seeing the Divine providence, whereas the latter, through not seeing their own need, are unveiled and independent. The former enjoy felicity, but the latter enjoy the Giver of felicity.

29. ABÚ 'ABDALLÁH AḤMAD B. 'ÁṢIM AL-INṬÁKÍ.

He lived to a great age and associated with the ancient Shaykhs, and was acquainted with those who belonged to the third generation after the Prophet (*atbá' al-tábi'ín*). He was a contemporary of Bishr and Sarí, and a pupil of Ḥárith Muhásibí. He had seen Fuḍayl and consorted with him. It is related that he said: "The most beneficial poverty is that which you regard as honourable, and with which you are well pleased," i.e., the honour of the vulgar consists in affirmation of secondary causes, but the honour of the dervish consists in denying secondary causes and in affirming the Causer, and in referring everything to Him, and in being well pleased with His decrees. Poverty is the non-existence of secondary causes, whereas wealth is the existence of secondary causes. Poverty detached from a secondary cause is with God, and wealth attached to a secondary cause is with itself. Therefore secondary causes involve the state of being veiled (from God), while their absence involves the state of unveiledness. This is a clear explanation of the superiority of poverty to wealth.

30. Abú Muhammad 'Abdalláh b. Khubayq.

He was an ascetic and scrupulously devout. He has related trustworthy traditions, and in jurisprudence, as well as in the practice and theory of divinity, he followed the doctrine of Thawrí, with whose pupils he had associated. It is recorded that he said: "Whoever desires to be living in his life, let him not admit covetousness to dwell in his heart," because the covetous man is dead in the toils of his covetousness, which is like a seal on his heart; and the sealed heart is dead. Blessed is the heart that dies to all save God and lives through God, inasmuch as God has made His praise (*dhikr*) the glory of men's hearts, and covetousness their disgrace; and to this effect is the saying of 'Abdalláh b. Khubayq: "God created men's hearts to be the homes of His praise, but they have become the homes of lust; and nothing can clear them of lust except an agitating fear or a restless desire." Fear and desire (*shawq*) are the two pillars of faith. When faith is settled in the heart, praise and contentment accompany it, not covetousness and heedlessness. Lust and covetousness are the result of shunning the society of God. The heart that shuns the society of God knows nothing of faith, since faith is intimate with God and averse to associate with aught else.

31. Abu 'l-Qásim al-Junayd b. Muhammad b. al-Junayd al-Baghdádí.

He was approved by externalists and spiritualists alike. He was perfect in every branch of science, and spoke with authority on theology, jurisprudence, and ethics. He was a follower of Thawrí. His sayings are lofty and his inward state perfect, so that all Ṣúfís unanimously acknowledge his leadership. His mother was the sister of Sarí Saqaṭí, and Junayd was the disciple of Sarí. One day Sarí was asked whether the rank of a disciple is ever higher than that of his spiritual director. He replied: "Yes; there is manifest proof of this: the rank of Junayd is above mine." It was the humility and insight of Sarí that caused him to say this. As is well known, Junayd refused to discourse to his disciples so long as Sarí was alive, until one night he dreamed that the Apostle said to him: "O Junayd, speak to the people, for God hath made thy words the means of saving a multitude of mankind." When he awoke the thought occurred to him that his rank was superior to that of Sarí, since the Apostle had commanded him to preach. At daybreak Sarí sent a disciple to Junayd with the following message: "You would not discourse to your disciples when they urged you to do so, and you rejected the intercession of the Shaykhs of Baghdád and my personal entreaty. Now that the Apostle has commanded you, obey his orders." Junayd said: "That fancy went out of my head. I perceived that Sarí was acquainted with my outward and inward thoughts in all circumstances, and that his rank was higher than mine, since he was acquainted with my secret thoughts, whereas I was ignorant of his state. I went to him and begged his pardon, and asked him how he knew that I had dreamed of the Apostle. He answered: 'I dreamed of God, who told me that He had sent the Apostle to bid you preach.'" This anecdote contains a clear indication that spiritual directors are in every case acquainted with the inward experiences of their disciples.

It is related that he said: "The speech of the prophets gives information concerning presence (*ḥuḍúr*), while the speech of the saints (*ṣiddíqín*) alludes to contemplation (*musháhadat*)." True information is derived from sight, and it is impossible to give true information of anything that one has not actually witnessed, whereas allusion (*ishárat*) involves reference to another thing. Hence the perfection and ultimate goal of the saints is the beginning of the state of the prophets. The distinction between prophet (*nabí*) and saint (*walí*), and the superiority of the former to the latter, is plain, notwithstanding that two heretical sects declare the saints to surpass the prophets in excellence. It is related that he said: "I was eagerly desirous of seeing Iblís. One day, when I was standing in the mosque, an old man came through the door and turned his face towards me. Horror seized my heart. When he came near I said to him, 'Who art thou? for I cannot bear to look on thee, or think of thee.' He answered, 'I am he whom you desired to see.' I exclaimed, 'O accursed one! what hindered thee from bowing down to Adam?' He answered, 'O Junayd, how can you imagine that I should bow down to anyone except God?' I was amazed at his saying this, but a secret voice whispered: 'Say to him, *Thou liest. Hadst thou been an obedient servant thou wouldst not have transgressed His command.*' Iblís heard the voice in my heart. He cried out and said, 'By God, you have burnt me!' and vanished." This story shows that God preserves His saints in all circumstances from the guile of Satan. One of Junayd's disciples bore him a grudge, and after leaving him returned one day with the intention of testing him. Junayd was aware of this and said, replying to his question: "Do you want a formal or a spiritual answer?" The disciple said: "Both." Junayd said: "The formal answer is that if you had tested yourself you would not have needed to test me. The spiritual answer is that I depose you from your saintship." The disciple's face immediately turned black. He cried, "The delight of certainty (*yaqín*) is gone from my heart," and earnestly begged to be forgiven, and abandoned his foolish self-conceit. Junayd said to him: "Did not you know that God's saints possess mysterious powers? You cannot endure their blows." He cast a breath at the disciple, who forthwith resumed his former purpose and repented of criticizing the Shaykhs.

32. Abu 'l-Ḥasan Aḥmad b. Muḥammad al-Núrí.

He has a peculiar doctrine in Ṣúfiism and is the model of a number of aspirants to Ṣúfiism, who follow him and are called Núrís. The whole body of aspirants to Ṣúfiism is composed of twelve sects, two of which are condemned (*mardúd*), while the remaining ten are approved (*maqbúl*). The latter are the Muḥásibís, the Qaṣṣárís, the Ṭayfúrís, the Junaydís, the Núrís, the Sahlís, the Ḥakímís, the Kharrázís, the Khafífís, and the Sayyárís. All these assert the truth and belong to the mass of orthodox Moslems. The two condemned sects are, firstly, the Ḥulúlís,[1] who derive their name from the doctrine of incarnation (*ḥulúl*) and incorporation (*imtizáj*), and with whom are connected the Sálimí sect of anthropomorphists;[2] and secondly, the Ḥallájís, who have abandoned the sacred law and have adopted heresy, and with whom are connected the Ibáḥatís[3] and the Fárisís.[4] I shall include in this book a chapter on the twelve sects and shall explain their different doctrines.

Núrí took a praiseworthy course in rejecting flattery and indulgence and in being assiduous in self-mortification. It is related that he said: "I came to Junayd and found him seated in the professorial chair (*muṣaddar*). I said to him: 'O Abu 'l-Qásim, thou hast concealed the truth from them and they have put thee in the place of honour; but I have told them the truth and they have pelted me with stones,'" because flattery is compliance with one's desire and sincerity is opposition to it, and men hate anyone who opposes their desires and love anyone who complies with their desires. Núrí was the companion of Junayd and the disciple of Sarí. He had associated with many Shaykhs, and had met Aḥmad b. Abi 'l-Ḥawárí. He is the author of subtle precepts and fine sayings on various branches of the mystical science. It is related that he said: "Union with God is separation from all else, and separation from all else is union with Him," i.e., anyone whose mind is united with God is separated from all besides, and *vice versâ*: therefore union of the mind with God is separation from the thought of created things, and to be rightly turned away from phenomena is to be rightly turned towards God. I have read in the Anecdotes that once Núrí stood in his chamber for three days and nights, never moving

[1] B. has "the Ḥulmánís", i.e. the followers of Abú Ḥulmán of Damascus. See Shahristání, Haarbrücker's translation, ii, 417.

[2] The Sálimís are described (ibid.) as "a number of scholastic theologians (*mutakallimún*) belonging to Baṣra".

[3] "Ibáḥatí" or "Ibáḥí" signifies "one who regards everything as permissible".

[4] See the eleventh section of the fourteenth chapter.

from his place or ceasing to wail. Junayd went to see him and said: "O Abu 'l-Ḥasan, if thou knowest that crying aloud to God is of any use, tell me, in order that I too may cry aloud; but if thou knowest that it avails naught, surrender thyself to acquiescence in God's will, in order that thy heart may rejoice." Núrí stopped wailing and said: "Thou teachest me well, O Abu 'l-Qásim!" It is related that he said: "The two rarest things in our time are a learned man who practises what he knows and a gnostic who speaks from the reality of his state," i.e., both learning and gnosis are rare, since learning is not learning unless it is practised, and gnosis is not gnosis unless it has reality. Núrí referred to his own age, but these things are rare at all times, and they are rare to-day. Anyone who should occupy himself in seeking for learned men and gnostics would waste his time and would not find them. Let him be occupied with himself in order that he may see learning everywhere, and let him turn from himself to God in order that he may see gnosis everywhere. Let him seek learning and gnosis in himself, and let him demand practice and reality from himself. It is related that Núrí said: "Those who regard things as determined by God turn to God in everything," because they find rest in regarding the Creator, not created objects, whereas they would always be in tribulation if they considered things to be the causes of actions. To do so is polytheism, for a cause is not self-subsistent, but depends on the Causer. When they turn to Him they escape from trouble.

33. ABÚ 'UTHMÁN SA'ÍD B. ISMÁ'ÍL AL-ḤÍRÍ.

He is one of the eminent Ṣúfís of past times. At first he associated with Yaḥyá b. Mu'ádh; then he consorted for a while with Sháh Shujá' of Kirmán, and accompanied him to Níshápúr on a visit to Abú Ḥafṣ, with whom he remained to the end of his life. It is related on trustworthy authority that he said: "In my childhood I was continually seeking the Truth, and the externalists inspired me with a feeling of abhorrence. I perceived that the sacred law concealed a mystery under the superficial forms which are followed by the vulgar. When I grew up I happened to hear a discourse by Yaḥyá b. Mu'ádh of Rayy, and I found there the mystery that was the object of my search. I continued to associate with Yaḥyá until, on hearing reports of Sháh Shujá' Kirmání from a number of persons who had been in his company, I felt a longing to visit him. Accordingly I quitted Rayy and set out for Kirmán. Sháh Shujá', however, would not admit me to his society. 'You have been nursed,' said he, 'in the doctrine of hope (*rajá*), on which Yaḥyá takes his stand. No one who has imbibed this doctrine can tread the path of purgation, because a mechanical belief in hope produces indolence.' I besought him earnestly, and lamented and stayed at his door for twenty days. At length he admitted me, and I remained in his society until he took me with him to visit Abú Ḥafṣ at Níshápúr. On this occasion Sháh Shujá' was wearing a coat (*qabá*). When Abú Ḥafṣ saw him he rose from his seat and advanced to meet him, saying, 'I have found in the coat what I sought in the cloak ('*abá*).' During our residence in Níshápúr I conceived a strong desire to associate with Abú Ḥafṣ, but was restrained from devoting myself to attendance on him by my respect for Sháh Shujá'. Meanwhile I was imploring God to make it possible for me to enjoy the society of Abú Ḥafṣ without hurting the feelings of Sháh Shujá', who was a jealous man; and Abú Ḥafṣ was aware of my wishes. On the day of our departure I dressed myself for the journey, although I was leaving my heart with Abú Ḥafṣ. Abú Ḥafṣ said familiarly to Sháh Shujá', 'I am pleased with this youth; let him stay here.' Sháh Shujá' turned to me and said, 'Do as the Shaykh bids thee.' So I remained with Abú Ḥafṣ and experienced many wonderful things in his company." God caused Abú 'Uthmán to pass through three "stations" by means of three spiritual directors, and these "stations", which he indicated as belonging to them, he also made his own: the "station" of hope through associating with Yaḥyá, the "station" of jealousy through associating with Sháh Shujá', and the "station" of affection (*shafaqat*) through associating with Abú Ḥafṣ. It is allowable for a disciple to associate with five or six or more directors and to have a different "station" revealed to him by each one of them, but it is better that he should not confuse his own "station" with theirs. He should point to their perfection in that "station" and say: "I gained this by associating with them, but they were superior to it." This is more in accordance with good manners, for spiritual adepts have nothing to do with "stations" and "states".

To Abú 'Uthmán was due the divulgation of Ṣúfiism in Níshápúr and Khurásán. He consorted with Junayd, Ruwaym, Yúsuf b. al-Ḥusayn, and Muḥammad b. Faḍl al-Balkhí, and no Shaykh ever derived as much spiritual advantage from his directors as he did. The people of Níshápúr set up a pulpit that he might discourse to them on Ṣúfiism. He is the author of sublime treatises on various branches of this science. It is related that he said: "It behoves one whom God hath honoured with gnosis not to dishonour himself by disobedience to God." This refers to actions acquired by Man and to his continual effort to keep the commandments of God, because, even though you recognize that it is worthy of God not to dishonour by disobedience anyone whom He has honoured with gnosis, yet gnosis is God's gift and disobedience is Man's act. It is impossible that one who is honoured with God's gift should be dishonoured by his own act. God honoured Adam with knowledge: He did not dishonour him on account of his sin.

34. Abú 'Abdalláh Aḥmad b. Yaḥyá al-Jallá.

He associated with Junayd and Abu 'l-Ḥasan Núrí and other great Shaykhs. It is recorded that he said: "The mind of the gnostic is fixed on his Lord; he does not pay attention to anything else," because the gnostic knows nothing except gnosis, and since gnosis is the whole capital of his heart, his thoughts are entirely bent on vision (of God), for distraction of thought produces cares, and cares keep one back from God. He tells the following story: "One day I saw a beautiful

Christian boy. I was amazed at his loveliness and stood still opposite him. Junayd passed by me. I said to him, 'O master, will God burn a face like this in Hell-fire?' He answered: 'O my son, this is a trick of the flesh, not a look by which one takes warning. If you look with due consideration, the same marvel is existent in every atom of the universe. You will soon be punished for this want of respect.' When Junayd turned away from me I immediately forgot the Koran, and it did not come back to my memory until I had for years implored God to help me and had repented of my sin. Now I dare not pay heed to any created object or waste my time by looking at things."

35. Abú Muḥammad Ruwaym b. Aḥmad.

He was an intimate friend of Junayd. In jurisprudence he followed Dáwud,[1] and he was deeply versed in the sciences relating to the interpretation and reading of the Koran. He was famed for the loftiness of his state and the exaltedness of his station, and for his journeys in detachment from the world (*tajríd*), and for his severe austerities. Towards the end of his life he hid himself among the rich and gained the Caliph's confidence, but such was the perfection of his spiritual rank that he was not thereby veiled from God. Hence Junayd said: "We are devotees occupied (with the world), and Ruwaym is a man occupied (with the world) who is devoted (to God)." He wrote several works on Ṣúfiism, one of which, entitled *Ghalaṭ al-Wájidín*,[2] deserves particular mention. I am exceedingly fond of it. One day he was asked, "How are you?" He replied: "How is he whose religion is his lust and whose thought is (fixed on) his worldly affairs, who is neither a pious God-fearing man nor a gnostic and one of God's elect?" This refers to the vices of the soul that is subject to passion and regards lust as its religion. Sensual men consider anyone to be devout who complies with their

[1] Dáwud of Iṣfahán, the founder of the Ẓáhirite school (Brockelmann, i, 183).
[2] i.e. "The Error of Ecstatic Persons".

inclinations, even though he be a heretic, and anyone to be irreligious who thwarts their desires, even though he be a pietist. This is a widely spread disease at the present time. God save us from associating with any such person! Ruwaym doubtless gave this answer in reference to the inward state of the questioner, which he truly diagnosed, or it may be that God had temporarily allowed him to fall into that condition, and that he described himself as he then was in reality.

36. Abú Ya'qúb Yúsuf b. al-Ḥusayn al-Rází.

He was one of the ancient Shaykhs and great Imáms of his age. He was a disciple of Dhu 'l-Nún the Egyptian, and consorted with a large number of Shaykhs and performed service to them all. It is related that he said: "The meanest of mankind is the covetous dervish and he who loves his beloved, and the noblest of them is the veracious (*al-ṣiddíq*)." Covetousness renders the dervish ignominious in both worlds, because he is already despicable in the eyes of worldlings, and only becomes more despicable if he builds any hopes on them. Wealth with honour is far more perfect than poverty with disgrace. Covetousness causes the dervish to incur the imputation of sheer mendacity. Again, he who loves his beloved is the meanest of mankind, since the lover acknowledges himself to be very despicable in comparison with his beloved and abases himself before her, and this also is the result of desire. So long as Zulaykhá desired Yúsuf, she became every day more mean: when she cast desire away, God gave her beauty and youth back to her. It is a law that when the lover advances, the beloved retires. If the lover is satisfied with love alone, then the beloved draws near. In truth, the lover has honour only while he has no desire for union. Unless his love diverts him from all thought of union or separation, his love is weak.

37. Abu 'l-Ḥasan Sumnún b. 'Abdalláh al-Khawwáṣ.

He was held in great esteem by all the Shaykhs. They called him Sumnún the Lover (*al-Muḥibb*), but he called himself Sumnún the Liar (*al-Kadhdháb*). He suffered much persecution at the hands of Ghulám al-Khalíl,[1] who had made himself known to the Caliph and courtiers by his pretended piety and Ṣúfiism. This hypocrite spoke evil of the Shaykhs and dervishes, hoping to bring about their banishment from Court and to establish his own power. Fortunate indeed were Sumnún and those Shaykhs to have only one adversary of this sort. In the present day there are a hundred Ghulám al-Khalíls for every true spiritualist, but what matter? Carrion is fit food for vultures. When Sumnún gained eminence and popularity in Baghdád, Ghulám al-Khalíl began to intrigue. A woman had fallen in love with Sumnún and made proposals to him, which he refused. She went to Junayd, begging him to advise Sumnún to marry her. On being sent away by Junayd, she came to Ghulám al-Khalíl and accused Sumnún of having attempted her virtue. He listened eagerly to her slanders, and induced the Caliph to command that Sumnún should be put to death. When the Caliph was about to give the word to the executioner his tongue stuck in his throat. The same night he dreamed that his empire would last no longer than Sumnún's life. Next day he asked his pardon and restored him to favour. Sumnún is the author of lofty sayings and subtle indications concerning the real nature of love. On his way from the Ḥijáz the people of Fayd requested him to discourse to them about this subject. He mounted the pulpit, but while he was speaking all his hearers departed. Sumnún turned to the lamps and said: "I am speaking to you." Immediately all the lamps collapsed and broke into small bits. It is related that he said: "A thing can be explained only by what is more subtle than itself: there is nothing subtler than love: by what, then, shall love

[1] Abú 'Abdalláh Aḥmad b. Muḥammad b. Ghálib b. Khálid al-Baṣrí al-Báhilí, generally known as Ghulám Khalíl, died in 275 A.H. He is described by Abu 'l-Maḥásin (*Nujúm*, ii, 79, 1 ff.) as a traditionist, ascetic, and saint. According to the *Tadhkirat al-Awliyá* (ii, 48, 4 ff.), he represented to the Caliph that Junayd, Núrí, Shiblí, and other eminent Ṣúfís were freethinkers and heretics, and urged him to put them to death.

be explained?" The meaning of this is that love cannot be explained because explanation is an attribute of the explainer. Love is an attribute of the Beloved, therefore no explanation of its real nature is possible.

38. Abu 'l-Fawáris Sháh Shujá' al-Kirmání.

He was of royal descent. He associated with Abú Turáb Nakhshabí and many other Shaykhs. Something has been said of him in the notice of Abú 'Uthmán al-Ḥírí. He composed a celebrated treatise on Ṣúfiism as well as a book entitled *Mir'át al-Ḥukamá*.[1] It is recorded that he said: "The eminent have eminence until they see it, and the saints have saintship until they see it," i.e., whoever regards his eminence loses its reality, and whoever regards his saintship loses its reality. His biographers relate that for forty years he never slept; then he fell asleep and dreamed of God. "O Lord," he cried, "I was seeking Thee in nightly vigils, but I have found Thee in sleep." God answered: "O Sháh, you have found Me by means of those nightly vigils: if you had not sought Me there, you would not have found Me here."

39. 'Amr b. 'Uthmán al-Makkí.

He was one of the principal Ṣúfís, and is the author of celebrated works on the mystical sciences. He became a disciple of Junayd after he had seen Abú Sa'íd Kharráz and had associated with Nibájí.[2] He was the Imám of his age in theology. It is related that he said: "Ecstasy does not admit of explanation, because it is a secret between God and the true believers." Let men seek to explain it as they will, their explanation is not that secret, inasmuch as all human power and effort is divorced from the Divine mysteries. It is said that when 'Amr came to Iṣfahán a young man associated with him against the wish of his father. The young man fell into a sickness. One day the Shaykh with

[1] i.e. "The Mirror of the Sages".

[2] Sa'íd (Abú 'Abdalláh) b. Yazíd al-Nibájí. See *Nafaḥát*, No. 86.

a number of friends came to visit him. He begged the Shaykh to bid the singer (*qawwál*) chant a few verses, whereupon 'Amr desired the singer to chant—

Má lí mariḍtu wa-lam ya'udní 'á'id
Minkum wa-yamraḍu 'abdukum fa-a'údu.

"How is it that when I fell ill none of you visited me,
Though I visit your slave when he falls ill?"

On hearing this the invalid left his bed and sat down, and the violence of his malady was diminished. He said: "Give me some more." So the singer chanted—

Wa-ashaddu min maraḍí 'alayya ṣudúdukum
Wa-ṣudúdu 'abdikumú 'alayya shadídu.

"Your neglect is more grievous to me than my sickness;
It would grieve me to neglect your slave."

The young man's sickness departed from him. His father permitted him to associate with 'Amr and repented of the suspicion which he had harboured in his heart, and the youth became an eminent Ṣúfí.

40. Abú Muḥammad Sahl b. 'Abdalláh al-Tustarí.

His austerities were great and his devotions excellent. He has fine sayings on sincerity and the defects of human actions. The formal divines say that he combined the Law and the Truth (*jama'a bayn al-sharí'at wa 'l-ḥaqíqat*). This statement is erroneous, for the two things have never been divided. The Law is the Truth, and the Truth is the Law. Their assertion is founded on the fact that the sayings of this Shaykh are more intelligible and easy to apprehend than is sometimes the case. Inasmuch as God has joined the Law to the Truth, it is impossible that His saints should separate them. If they be separated, one must inevitably be rejected and the other accepted. Rejection of the Law is heresy, and rejection of the Truth is infidelity and polytheism. Any (proper) separation between them is made, not to establish a difference of meaning, but to affirm the Truth, as when it is said: "The words *there is no god save Allah* are Truth, and the words *Muḥammad is the Apostle of Allah* are Law." No one can separate the one from the other without impairing his faith, and it is vain to wish to do so. In short, the Law is a branch of the Truth: knowledge of God is Truth, and obedience to His command is Law. These formalists deny whatever does not suit their fancy, and it is dangerous to deny one of the fundamental principles of the Way to God. Praise be to Allah for the faith which He has given us! And it is related that he said: "The sun does not rise or set upon anyone on the face of the earth who is not ignorant of God, unless he prefers God to his own soul and spirit and to his present and future life," i.e., if anyone cleaves to self-interest, that is a proof that he is ignorant of God, because knowledge of God requires abandonment of forethought (*tadbír*), and abandonment of forethought is resignation (*taslím*), whereas perseverance in forethought arises from ignorance of predestination.

41. Abú Muḥammad 'Abdalláh Muḥammad b. al-Faḍl al-Balkhí.

He was approved by the people of 'Iráq as well as by those of Khurásán. He was a pupil of Aḥmad b. Khaḍrúya, and Abú 'Uthmán of Ḥíra had a great affection for him. Having been expelled from Balkh by fanatics on account of his love of Ṣúfiism, he went to Samarcand, where he passed his life. It is related that he said: "He that has most knowledge of God is he that strives hardest to fulfil His commandments, and follows most closely the custom of His Prophet." The nearer one is to God the more eager one is to do His bidding, and the farther one is from God the more averse one is to follow His Apostle. It is related that he said: "I wonder at those who cross deserts and wildernesses to reach His House and Sanctuary, because the traces of His prophets are to be found there: why do not they cross their own passions and lusts to reach their hearts, where they will find the traces of their Lord?" That is to say, the heart is the seat of knowledge of God and is more venerable than the Ka'ba, to which men turn in devotion. Men are ever looking towards the Ka'ba, but God is ever looking towards the heart. Wherever the heart is, my Beloved is there; wherever His decree is, my desire is there; wherever the traces of my prophets[1] are, the eyes of those whom I love are directed there.

42. ABÚ 'ABDALLÁH MUḤAMMAD B. 'ALÍ AL-TIRMIDHÍ.

He is the author of many excellent books which, by their eloquence, declare the miracles vouchsafed to him, e.g., the *Khatm al-Wiláyat*,[2] the *Kitáb al-Nahj*,[3] the *Nawádir al-Uṣúl*,[4] and many more, such as the *Kitáb al-Tawḥíd*[5] and the *Kitáb 'Adháb al-Qabr*[6]: it would be tedious to mention them all. I hold him in great veneration and am entirely devoted to him. My Shaykh said: "Muḥammad is a union pearl that has no like in the whole world." He has also written works on the formal sciences, and is a trustworthy authority for the traditions of the Prophet which he related. He began a commentary on the Koran, but did not live long enough to finish it. The completed portion is widely circulated among theologians. He studied jurisprudence with an intimate friend of Abú Ḥanífa. The inhabitants of Tirmidh call him Muḥammad Ḥakím, and the Ḥakímís, a Ṣúfí sect in that region, are his followers. Many remarkable stories are told of him, as for instance that he associated with the Apostle Khiḍr. His disciple, Abú Bakr Warráq, relates that Khiḍr used to visit him every Sunday, and that they conversed with each other. It is recorded that he said: "Anyone who is ignorant of the nature of servantship (*'ubúdiyyat*) is yet more ignorant of the nature of lordship (*rubúbiyyat*)," i.e., whoever does not know the way to knowledge of himself does not know the way to

[1] So in all the texts.
[2] "The Seal of Saintship."
[3] "The Book of the Highway."
[4] "Choice Principles."
[5] "The Book Unification."
[6] "The Book of the Torment of the Tomb."

knowledge of God, and whoever does not recognize the contamination of human qualities does not recognize the purity of the Divine attributes, inasmuch as the outward is connected with the inward, and he who claims to possess the former without the latter makes an absurd assertion. Knowledge of the nature of lordship depends on having right principles of servantship, and is not perfect without them. This is a very profound and instructive saying. It will be fully explained in the proper place.

43. Abú Bakr Muḥammad b. 'Umar al-Warráq.

He was a great Shaykh and ascetic. He had seen Aḥmad b. Khaḍrúya and associated with Muḥammad b. 'Alí. He is the author of books on rules of discipline and ethics. The Ṣúfí Shaykhs have called him "The Instructor of the Saints" (*mu'addib al-awliyá*). He relates the following story: "Muḥammad b. 'Alí handed to me some of his writings with the request that I should throw them into the Oxus. I had not the heart to do so, but placed them in my house and came to him and told him that I had carried out his order. He asked me what I had seen. I replied, 'Nothing.' He said, 'You have not obeyed me; return and throw them into the river.' I returned, doubting the promised sign, and cast them into the river. The waters parted and a chest appeared, with its lid open. As soon as the papers fell into it, the lid closed and the waters joined again and the chest vanished. I went back to him and told him what had occurred. He answered, 'Now you have thrown them in.' I begged him to explain the mystery. He said: 'I composed a work on theology and mysticism which could hardly be comprehended by the intellect. My brother Khiḍr desired it of me, and God bade the waters bring it to him.'"

It is related that Abú Bakr Warráq said: "There are three classes of men—divines (*'ulamá*) and princes (*umará*) and dervishes (*fuqará*). When the divines are corrupt, piety and religion are vitiated; when the princes are corrupt, men's livelihood is spoiled; and when the dervishes are corrupt, men's morals are depraved." Accordingly, the corruption of the divines consists in covetousness, that of the princes in injustice, and that of the dervishes in hypocrisy. Princes do not become corrupt until they turn their backs on divines, and divines do not become corrupt until they associate with princes, and dervishes do not become corrupt until they seek ostentation, because the injustice of princes is due to want of knowledge, and the covetousness of divines is due to want of piety, and the hypocrisy of dervishes is due to want of trust in God.

44. ABÚ SA'ÍD AHMAD B. 'ÍSÁ AL-KHARRÁZ.

He was the first who explained the doctrine of annihilation (*faná*) and subsistence (*baqá*). He is the author of brilliant compositions and sublime sayings and allegories. He had met Dhu 'l-Nún of Egypt, and associated with Bishr and Sarí. It is related that concerning the words of the Apostle, "Hearts are naturally disposed to love him who acts kindly towards them," he said: "Oh! I wonder at him who sees none acting kindly towards him except God, how he does not incline to God with his whole being," inasmuch as true beneficence belongs to the Lord of phenomenal objects and is conferred only upon those who have need of it; how can he who needs beneficence from others bestow it upon anyone? God is the King and Lord of all and hath need of none. Recognizing this, the friends of God behold in every gift and benefit the Giver and Benefactor. Their hearts are wholly taken captive by love of Him and turned away from everything else.

45. ABU 'L-ḤASAN 'ALÍ B. MUḤAMMAD AL-IṢFAHÁNÍ.

According to others, his name is 'Alí b. Sahl. He was a great Shaykh. Junayd and he wrote exquisite letters to one another, and 'Amr b. 'Uthmán Makkí went to Iṣfahán to visit him. He consorted with Abú Turáb and Junayd. He followed a praiseworthy Path in Ṣúfiism and one that was peculiarly his own. He was adorned with acquiescence in God's will and self-discipline, and was preserved from mischiefs and contaminations. He spoke eloquently on the theory and practice of mysticism, and lucidly explained its difficulties and symbolical allusions. It is related that he said: "Presence (*ḥuḍúr*) is better than certainty (*yaqín*), because presence is an abiding state (*waṭanát*), whereas certainty is a transient one (*khaṭarát*)," i.e., presence makes its abode in the heart and does not admit forgetfulness, while certainty is a feeling that comes and goes: hence those who are "present" (*ḥáḍirán*) are in the sanctuary, and those who have certainty (*múqinán*) are only at the gate. The subject of "absence" and "presence" will be discussed in a separate chapter of this book.

And he said also: "From the time of Adam to the Resurrection people cry, 'The heart, the heart!' and I wish that I might find some one to describe what the heart is or how it is, but I find none. People in general give the name of 'heart' (*dil*) to that piece of flesh which belongs to madmen and ecstatics and children, who really are without heart (*bédil*). What, then, is this heart, of which I hear only the name?" That is to say, if I call intellect the heart, it is not the heart; and if I call spirit the heart, it is not the heart; and if I call knowledge the heart, it is not the heart. All the evidences of the Truth subsist in the heart, yet only the name of it is to be found.

46. Abu 'l-Ḥasan Muḥammad b. Ismá'íl Khayr al-Nassáj.

He was a great Shaykh, and in his time discoursed with eloquence on ethics and preached excellent sermons. He died at an advanced age. Both Shiblí and Ibráhím Khawwáṣ were converted in his place of meeting. He sent Shiblí to Junayd, wishing to observe the respect due to the latter. He was a pupil of Sarí, and was contemporary with Junayd and Abu 'l-Ḥasan Núrí. Junayd held him in high regard, and Abú Ḥamza of Baghdád treated him with the utmost consideration. It is related that he was called Khayr al-Nassáj from the following circumstance. He left Sámarrá, his native town, with the intention of performing the pilgrimage. At the gate of Kúfa, which lay on his route, he was seized by a weaver of silk, who cried out: "You are my slave, and your name is Khayr." Deeming this to come from God, he did not contradict the weaver, and remained many years in his employment. Whenever his master said "Khayr!" he answered, "At thy service" (*labbayk*), until the man repented of what he had done and said to Khayr: "I made a mistake; you are not my slave." So he departed and went to Mecca, where he attained to such a degree that Junayd said: "Khayr is the best of us" (*Khayr khayruná*). He used to prefer to be called Khayr, saying: "It is not right that I should alter a name which has been bestowed on me by a Moslem." They relate that when the hour of his death approached, it was time for the evening prayer. He opened his eyes and looked at the Angel of Death and said: "Stop! God save thee! Thou art only a servant who has received His orders, and I am the same. That which thou art commanded to do (viz. to take my life) will not escape thee, but that which I am commanded to do (viz. to perform the evening prayer) will escape me: therefore let me do as I am bidden, and then do as thou art bidden." He then called for water and cleansed himself, and performed the evening prayer and gave up his life. On the same night he was seen in a dream and was asked: "What has God done to thee?" He answered: "Do not ask me of this, but I have gained release from your world."

It is related that he said in his place of meeting: "God hath expanded the breasts of the pious with the light of certainty, and hath opened the eyes of the possessors of certainty with the light of the verities of faith." Certainty is indispensable to the pious, whose hearts are expanded with the light of certainty, and those who have certainty cannot do without the verities of faith, inasmuch as their intellectual vision consists in the light of faith. Accordingly, where faith is certainty is there, and where certainty is piety is there, for they go hand in hand with each other.

47. ABÚ ḤAMZA AL-KHURÁSÁNÍ.

He is one of the ancient Shaykhs of Khurásán. He associated with Abú Turáb, and had seen Kharráz.[1] He was firmly grounded in trust in God (*tawakkul*). It is a well-known story that one day he fell into a pit. After three days had passed a party of travellers approached. Abú Ḥamza said to himself: "I will call out to them." Then he said: "No; it is not good that I seek aid from anyone except God, and I shall be complaining of God if I tell them that my God has cast me into a pit and implore them to rescue me." When they came up and saw an open pit in the middle of the road, they said: "For the sake of obtaining Divine recompense (*thawáb*) we must cover this pit lest anyone should fall into it." Abú Ḥamza said: "I became deeply agitated and abandoned hope of life. After they blocked the mouth of the pit and departed, I prayed to God and resigned myself to die, and hoped no more of mankind. When night fell I heard a movement at the top of the pit. I looked attentively. The mouth of the pit was open, and I saw a huge animal like a dragon, which let down its tail. I knew that God had sent it and that I should be saved in this way. I took hold of its tail and it dragged me out. A heavenly voice cried to me, 'This is an excellent escape of thine, O Abú Ḥamza! We have saved thee from death by means of a death'" (i.e. a deadly monster).

He was asked, "Who is the stranger (*gharíb*)?" He replied, "He who shuns society," because the dervish has no home or society either in this world or the next, and when he is dissociated from phenomenal existence he shuns everything, and then he is a stranger; and this is a very lofty degree.

48. ABU 'L-'ABBÁS AḤMAD B. MASRÚQ.

He was one of the great men of Khurásán, and the Saints of God are unanimously agreed that he was one of the *Awtád*. He

[1] See No. 44.

associated with the *Quṭb*, who is the pivot of the universe. On being asked to say who the *Quṭb* was, he did not declare his name but hinted that Junayd was that personage. He had done service to the Forty who possess the rank of fixity (*ṣáḥib tamkín*) and received instruction from them. It is related that he said: "If anyone takes joy in aught except God, his joy produces sorrow, and if anyone is not intimate with the service of his Lord, his intimacy produces loneliness (*waḥshat*)," i.e., all save Him is perishable, and whoever rejoices in what is perishable, when that perishes becomes stricken with sorrow; and except His service all else is vain, and when the vileness of created objects is made manifest, his intimacy (with them) is wholly turned to loneliness: hence, the sorrow and loneliness of the entire universe consist in regarding that which is other (than God).

49. Abú 'Abdalláh Muḥammad[1] b. Ismá'íl al-Maghribí.

In his time he was an approved teacher and a careful guardian of his disciples. Both Ibráhím Khawwáṣ and Ibráhím Shaybání were pupils of his. He has lofty sayings and shining evidences, and he was perfectly grounded in detachment from this world. It is related that he said: "I never saw anyone more just than the world: if you serve her she will serve you, and if you leave her she will leave you," i.e. as long as you seek her she will seek you, but when you turn away from her and seek God she will flee from you, and worldly thoughts will no more cling to your heart.

50. Abú 'Alí al-Ḥasan b. 'Alí al-Júzajání.

He wrote brilliant works on the science of ethics and the detection of spiritual cankers. He was a pupil of Muḥammad b. 'Alí al-Tirmidhí, and a contemporary of Abú Bakr Warráq. Ibráhím Samarqandí was a pupil of his. It is related that he said: "All mankind are galloping on the race-courses of

[1] LB. have "Aḥmad".

heedlessness, relying upon idle fancies, while they suppose themselves to be versed in the Truth and to be speaking from Divine revelation." This saying alludes to natural self-conceit and to the pride of the soul. Men, though they are ignorant, have a firm belief in their ignorance, especially ignorant Ṣúfís, who are the vilest creatures of God, just as wise Ṣúfís are the noblest. The latter possess the Truth and are without conceit, whereas the former possess conceit and are without the Truth. They graze in the fields of heedlessness and imagine that it is the field of saintship. They rely on fancy and suppose it to be certainty. They go about with form and think it is reality. They speak from their own lust and think it is a Divine revelation. This they do because conceit is not expelled from a man's head save by vision of the majesty or the beauty of God: for in the manifestation of His beauty they see Him alone, and their conceit is annihilated, while in the revelation of His majesty they do not see themselves, and their conceit does not intrude.

51. Abú Muḥammad Aḥmad b. al-Ḥusayn al-Jurayrí.

He was an intimate friend of Junayd, and also associated with Sahl b. 'Abdalláh. He was learned in every branch of science and was the Imám of his day in jurisprudence, besides being well acquainted with theology. His rank in Ṣúfiism was such that Junayd said to him: "Teach my pupils discipline and train them!" He succeeded Junayd and sat in his chair. It is related that he said: "The permanence of faith and the subsistence of religions and the health of bodies depend on three qualities: satisfaction (*iktifá*) and piety (*ittiqá*) and abstinence (*iḥtimá*): if one is satisfied with God, his conscience becomes good; and if one guards himself from what God has forbidden, his character becomes upright; and if one abstains from what does not agree with him, his constitution is brought into good order. The fruit of satisfaction is pure knowledge of God, and the result of piety is excellence of moral character, and the end of abstinence is equilibrium of constitution." The Apostle said,

"He that prays much by night, his face is fair by day," and he also said that the pious shall come at the Resurrection "with resplendent faces on thrones of light".

52. ABU 'L-'ABBÁS AḤMAD B. MUḤAMMAD B. SAHL AL-ÁMULÍ.

He was always held in great respect by his contemporaries. He was versed in the sciences of Koranic exegesis and criticism, and expounded the subtleties of the Koran with an eloquence and insight peculiar to himself. He was an eminent pupil of Junayd, and had associated with Ibráhím Máristání. Abú Sa'íd Kharráz regarded him with the utmost veneration, and used to declare that no one deserved the name of Ṣúfí except him. It is related that he said: "Acquiescence in natural habits prevents a man from attaining to the exalted degrees of spirituality," because natural dispositions are the instruments and organs of the sensual part (*nafs*), which is the centre of "veiling" (*ḥijáb*), whereas the spiritual part (*ḥaqíqat*) is the centre of revelation. Natural dispositions become attached to two things: firstly, to this world and its accessories, and secondly, to the next world and its circumstances: to the former in virtue of homogeneousness, and to the latter through imagination and in virtue of heterogeneousness and non-cognition. Therefore they are attached to the notion of the next world, not to its true idea, for if they knew it in reality, they would break off connexion with this world, and nature would then have lost all her power and spiritual things would be revealed. There can be no harmony between the next world and human nature until the latter is annihilated, because "in the next world is that which the heart of man never conceived". The worth (*khaṭar*) of the next world lies in the fact that the way to it is full of danger (*khaṭar*). A thing that only comes into one's thoughts (*khawáṭir*) has little worth; and inasmuch as the imagination is incapable of knowing the reality of the next world, how can human nature become familiar with the true idea (*'ayn*) thereof? It is certain that our natural faculties can be acquainted only with the notion (*pindásht*) of the next world.

53. ABU 'L-MUGHÍTH AL-ḤUSAYN B. MANṢÚR AL-ḤALLÁJ.

He was an enamoured and intoxicated votary of Ṣúfiism. He had a strong ecstasy and a lofty spirit. The Ṣúfí Shaykhs are at variance concerning him. Some reject him, while others accept him. Among the latter class are 'Amr b. 'Uthmán al-Makkí, Abú Ya'qúb Nahrajúrí, Abú Ya'qúb Aqṭa', 'Alí b. Sahl Iṣfahání, and others. He is accepted, moreover, by Ibn 'Aṭá, Muḥammad b. Khafíf, Abu 'l-Qásim Naṣrábádí, and all the moderns. Others, again, suspend their judgment about him, e.g. Junayd and Shiblí and Jurayrí and Ḥuṣrí. Some accuse him of magic and matters coming under that head, but in our days the Grand Shaykh Abú Sa'íd b. Abi 'l-Khayr and Shaykh Abu 'l-Qásim Gurgání and Shaykh Abu 'l-'Abbás Shaqání looked upon him with favour, and in their eyes he was a great man. The Master Abu 'l-Qásim Qushayrí remarks that if al-Ḥalláj was a genuine spiritualist he is not to be banned on the ground of popular condemnation, and if he was banned by Ṣúfiism and rejected by the Truth he is not to be approved on the ground of popular approval. Therefore we leave him to the judgment of God, and honour him according to the tokens of the Truth which we have found him to possess. But of all these Shaykhs only a few deny the perfection of his merit and the purity of his spiritual state and the abundance of his ascetic practices. It would be an act of dishonesty to omit his biography from this book. Some persons pronounce his outward behaviour to be that of an infidel, and disbelieve in him and charge him with trickery and magic, and suppose that Ḥusayn b. Manṣúr Ḥalláj is that heretic of Baghdád who was the master of Muḥammad b. Zakariyyá[1] and the companion of Abú Sa'íd the Carmathian; but this Ḥusayn whose character is in dispute was a Persian and a native of Bayḍá, and his rejection by the

[1] The famous physician Abú Bakr Muḥammad b. Zakariyyá al-Rází, who died about 320 A.H. See Brockelmann, i, 233.

Shaykhs was due, not to any attack on religion and doctrine, but to his conduct and behaviour. At first he was a pupil of Sahl b. 'Abdalláh, whom he left, without asking permission, in order to attach himself to 'Amr b. 'Uthmán Makkí. Then he left 'Amr b. 'Uthmán, again without asking permission, and sought to associate with Junayd, but Junayd would not receive him. This is the reason why he is banned by all the Shaykhs. Now, one who is banned on account of his conduct is not banned on account of his principles. Do you not see that Shiblí said: "Al-Ḥalláj and I are of one belief, but my madness saved me, while his intelligence destroyed him"? Had his religion been suspected, Shiblí would not have said: "Al-Ḥalláj and I are of one belief." And Muḥammad b. Khafíf said: "He is a divinely learned man" (*'álim-i rabbání*). Al-Ḥalláj is the author of brilliant compositions and allegories and polished sayings in theology and jurisprudence. I have seen fifty works by him at Baghdád and in the neighbouring districts, and some in Khúzistán and Fárs and Khurásán. All his sayings are like the first visions of novices; some of them are stronger, some weaker, some easier, some more unseemly than others. When God bestows a vision on anyone, and he endeavours to describe what he has seen with the power of ecstasy and the help of Divine grace, his words are obscure, especially if he expresses himself with haste and self-admiration: then they are more repugnant to the imaginations, and incomprehensible to the minds, of those who hear them, and then people say, "This is a sublime utterance," either believing it or not, but equally ignorant of its meaning whether they believe or deny. On the other hand, when persons of true spirituality and insight have visions, they make no effort to describe them, and do not occupy themselves with self-admiration on that account, and are careless of praise and blame alike, and are undisturbed by denial and belief.

It is absurd to charge al-Ḥalláj with being a magician. According to the principles of Muḥammadan orthodoxy, magic is real, just as miracles are real; but the manifestation of magic in the state of perfection is infidelity, whereas the manifestation of miracles in the state of perfection is knowledge of God (*ma'rifat*), because the former is the result of God's anger, while the latter is the corollary of His being well pleased. I will explain this more fully in the chapter on the affirmation of miracles. By consent of all Sunnites who are endowed with perspicacity, no Moslem can be a magician and no infidel can be held in honour, for contraries never meet. Ḥusayn, as long as he lived, wore the garb of piety, consisting in prayer and praise of God and continual fasts and fine sayings on the subject of Unification. If his actions were magic, all this could not possibly have proceeded from him. Consequently, they must have been miracles, and miracles are vouchsafed only to a true saint. Some orthodox theologians reject him on the ground that his sayings are pantheistic (*ba-ma'ni-yi imtizáj ú ittiḥád*), but the offence lies solely in the expression, not in the meaning. A person overcome with rapture has not the power of expressing himself correctly; besides, the meaning of the expression may be difficult to apprehend, so that people mistake the writer's intention, and repudiate, not his real meaning, but a notion which they have formed for themselves. I have seen at Baghdád and in the adjoining districts a number of heretics who pretend to be the followers of al-Ḥalláj and make his sayings an argument for their heresy (*zandaqa*) and call themselves Ḥallájís. They spoke of him in the same terms of exaggeration (*ghuluww*) as the Ráfiḍís (Shí'ites) apply to 'Alí. I will refute their doctrines in the chapter concerning the different Ṣúfí sects. In conclusion, you must know that the sayings of al-Ḥalláj should not be taken as a model, inasmuch as he was an ecstatic (*maghlúb andar ḥál-i khud*), not firmly settled (*mutamakkin*), and a man needs to be firmly settled before his sayings can be considered authoritative. Therefore, although he is dear to my heart, yet his "path" is not soundly established on any principle, and his state is not fixed in any position, and his experiences are largely mingled with error. When my own visions began I derived much support from him, that is to say, in the way of evidences (*baráhín*). At an earlier time I composed a book in explanation of his sayings and demonstrated their sublimity by proofs and arguments. Furthermore, in another work, entitled *Minháj*, I have spoken of his life from beginning to end; and now I have given some account of him in this place. How can a doctrine whose principles require to be corroborated with so much caution be followed and imitated? Truth and idle fancy never agree. He is continually seeking to fasten upon some erroneous theory. It is related that he said: *Al-alsinat mustanṭiqát taḥta nuṭqihá mustahlikát*,[1] i.e. "speaking tongues are the destruction of silent hearts". Such expressions are entirely mischievous. Expression of the meaning of reality is futile. If the meaning exists it is not lost by expression, and if it is non-existent it is not created by expression. Expression only produces an unreal notion and leads the student mortally astray by causing him to imagine that the expression is the real meaning.

54. Abú Isḥáq Ibráhím b. Aḥmad al-Khawwáṣ.

He attained a high degree in the doctrine of trust in God (*tawakkul*). He met many Shaykhs, and many signs and miracles were vouchsafed to him. He is the author of excellent works on the ethics of Ṣúfiism. It is related that he said: "All knowledge is comprised in two sentences: 'do not trouble yourself with anything that is done for you, and do not neglect anything that you are bound to do for yourself,'" i.e., do not trouble yourself with destiny, for what is destined from eternity will not be changed by your efforts, and do not neglect His commandment, for you will be punished if you neglect it. He was asked what wonders he had seen. "Many wonders," he replied, "but the most wonderful was that the Apostle Khiḍr begged me to let him associate with me, and I refused. Not that I desired any better companion, but I feared that I should depend on him rather than on God, and that my trust in God

[1] Literally, "The tongues desire to speak, (but) under their speech they desire to perish."

would be impaired by consorting with him, and that in consequence of performing a work of supererogation I should fail to perform a duty incumbent on me." This is the degree of perfection.

55. Abú Ḥamza al-Baghdádí al-Bazzáz.

He was one of the principal Ṣúfí scholastic theologians (*mutakallimán*). He was a pupil of Ḥárith Muḥásibí, and associated with Sarí and was contemporary with Núrí and Khayr Nassáj. He used to preach in the Ruṣáfa mosque at Baghdád. He was versed in Koranic exegesis and criticism, and related Apostolic Traditions on trustworthy authority. It was he who was with Núrí when the latter was persecuted and when God delivered the Ṣúfís from death. I will tell this story in the place where Núrí's doctrine is explained. It is recorded that Abú Ḥamza said: "If thy 'self' (*nafs*) is safe from thee, thou hast done all that is due to it; and if mankind are safe from thee, thou hast paid all that is due to them," i.e., there are two obligations, one which thou owest to thy "self" and one which thou owest to others. If thou refrain thy "self" from sin and seek for it the path of future salvation, thou hast fulfilled thy obligation towards it; and if thou make others secure from thy wickedness and do not wish to injure them, thou hast fulfilled thy obligation towards them. Endeavour that no evil may befall thy "self" or others from thee: then occupy thyself with fulfilling thy obligation to God.

56. Abú Bakr Muḥammad b. Músá al-Wásiṭí.

He was a profound theosophist, praiseworthy in the eyes of all the Shaykhs. He was one of the early disciples of Junayd. His abstruse manner of expression caused his sayings to be regarded with suspicion by formalists (*ẓáhiriyán*). He found peace in no city until he came to Merv. The inhabitants of Merv welcomed him on account of his amiable disposition—for he was a virtuous man—and listened to his sayings; and he passed his life there. It is related that he said: "Those who remember their praise of God (*dhikr*) are more heedless than those who forget their praise," because if anyone forgets the praise, it is no matter; but it does matter if he remembers the praise and forgets God. Praise is not the same thing as the object of praise. Neglect of the object of praise combined with thought of the praise approximates to heedlessness more closely than neglect of the praise without thought. He who forgets, in his forgetfulness and absence, does not think that he is present (with God), but he who remembers, in his remembrance and absence from the object of praise, thinks that he is present (with God). Accordingly, to think that one is present when one is not present comes nearer to heedlessness than to be absent without thinking that one is present, for conceit (*pindásht*) is the ruin of those who seek the Truth. The more conceit, the less reality, and *vice versâ*. Conceit really springs from the suspiciousness (*tuhmat*) of the intellect, which is produced by the insatiable desire (*nahmat*) of the lower soul; and holy aspiration (*himmat*) has nothing in common with either of these qualities. The fundamental principle of remembrance of God (*dhikr*) is either in absence (*ghaybat*) or in presence (*ḥuḍúr*). When anyone is absent from himself and present with God, that state is not presence, but contemplation (*mushâhadat*); and when anyone is absent from God and present with himself, that state is not remembrance of God (*dhikr*), but absence; and absence is the result of heedlessness (*ghaflat*). The truth is best known to God.

57. Abú Bakr b. Dulaf b. Jaḥdar al-Shiblí.

He was a great and celebrated Shaykh. He had a blameless spiritual life and enjoyed perfect communion with God. He was subtle in the use of symbolism, wherefore one of the moderns says: "The wonders of the world are three: the symbolical utterances (*ishárát*) of Shiblí, and the mystical sayings (*nukat*) of Murta'ish, and the anecdotes (*ḥikáyát*) of Ja'far."[1] At first he was chief chamberlain to the Caliph, but he was converted in the assembly-room (*majlis*) of Khayr al-Nassáj and became

[1] See No. 58.

a disciple of Junayd. He made the acquaintance of a large number of Shaykhs. It is related that he explained the verse "*Tell the believers to refrain their eyes*" (Kor. xxiv, 30) as follows: "O Muḥammad, tell the believers to refrain their bodily eyes from what is unlawful, and to refrain their spiritual eyes from everything except God," i.e. not to look at lust and to have no thought except the vision of God. It is a mark of heedlessness to follow one's lusts and to regard unlawful things, and the greatest calamity that befalls the heedless is that they are ignorant of their own faults; for anyone who is ignorant here shall also be ignorant hereafter: "*Those who are blind in this world shall be blind in the next world*" (Kor. xvii, 74). In truth, until God clears the desire of lust out of a man's heart the bodily eye is not safe from its hidden dangers, and until God establishes the desire of Himself in a man's heart the spiritual eye is not safe from looking at other than Him.

It is related that one day when Shiblí came into the bazaar, the people said, "This is a madman." He replied: "You think I am mad, and I think you are sensible: may God increase my madness and your sense!" i.e., inasmuch as my madness is the result of intense love of God, while your sense is the result of great heedlessness, may God increase my madness in order that I may become nearer and nearer to Him, and may He increase your sense in order that you may become farther and farther from Him. This he said from jealousy (*ghayrat*) that anyone should be so beside one's self as not to separate love of God from madness and not to distinguish between them in this world or the next.

58. Abú Muḥammad Ja'far b. Nuṣayr al-Khuldí.

He is the well-known biographer of the Saints. One of the most eminent and oldest of Junayd's pupils, he was profoundly versed in the various branches of Ṣúfiism and paid the utmost respect to the Shaykhs. He has many sublime sayings. In order to avoid spiritual conceit, he attributed to different persons the anecdotes which he composed in illustration of each topic. It is related that he said: "Trust in God is equanimity whether you find anything or no," i.e., you are not made glad by having daily bread or sorrowful by not having it, because it is the property of the Lord, who has a better right than you either to preserve or to destroy: do not interfere, but let the Lord dispose of His own. Ja'far relates that he went to Junayd and found him suffering from a fever. "O Master," he cried, "tell God in order that He may restore thee to health." Junayd said: "Last night I was about to tell Him, but a voice whispered in my heart, 'Thy body belongs to Me: I keep it well or ill, as I please. Who art thou, that thou shouldst interfere with My property.'"

59. Abú 'Alí Muḥammad b. al-Qásim al-Rúdbárí.

He was a great Ṣúfí and of royal descent. Many signs and virtues were vouchsafed to him. He discoursed lucidly on the arcana of Ṣúfiism. It is related that he said: "He who desires (*muríd*) desires for himself only what God desires for him, and he who is desired (*murád*) does not desire anything in this world or the next except God." Accordingly, he who is satisfied with the will of God must abandon his own will in order that he may desire, whereas the lover has no will of his own that he should have any object of desire. He who desires God desires only what God desires, and he whom God desires desires only God. Hence satisfaction (*riḍá*) is one of the "stations" (*maqámát*) of the beginning, and love (*maḥabbat*) is one of the "states" (*aḥwál*) of the end. The "stations" are connected with the realization of servantship (*'ubúdiyyat*), while ecstasy (*mashrab*) leads to the corroboration of Lordship (*rubúbiyyat*). This being so, the desirer (*muríd*) subsists in himself, and the desired (*murád*) subsists in God.

60. Abu 'l-'Abbás Qásim b. al-Mahdí[1] al-Sayyárí.

He associated with Abú Bakr Wásiṭí and derived instruction from many Shaykhs. He was the most accomplished (*aẓraf*) of the Ṣúfís in companionship (*ṣuḥbat*) and the most sparing

[1] *Nafaḥát*, No. 167, has "Qásim b. al-Qásim al-Mahdí".

(*azhad*) of them in friendship (*ulfat*). He is the author of lofty sayings and praiseworthy compositions. It is related that he said: "Unification (*al-tawhíd*) is this: that nothing should occur to your mind except God." He belonged to a learned and influential family of Merv. Having inherited a large fortune from his father, he gave the whole of it in return for two of the Apostle's hairs. Through the blessing of those hairs God bestowed on him a sincere repentance. He fell into the company of Abú Bakr Wásití, and attained such a high degree that he became the leader of a Súfí sect. When he was on the point of death, he gave directions that those hairs should be placed in his mouth. His tomb is still to be seen at Merv, and people come thither to seek what they desire; and their prayers are granted.

61. Abú 'Abdalláh Muhammad b. Khafíf.

He was the Imám of his age in diverse sciences. He was renowned for his mortifications and for his convincing elucidation of mystical truths. His spiritual attainments are clearly shown by his compositions. He was acquainted with Ibn 'Atá and Shiblí and Husayn b. Mansúr and Jurayrí, and associated at Mecca with Abú Ya'qúb Nahrajúrí. He made excellent journeys in detachment from the world (*tajríd*). He was of royal descent, but God bestowed on him repentance, so that he turned his back on the glories of this world. He is held in high esteem by spiritualists. It is related that he said: "Unification consists in turning away from nature," because the natures of mankind are all veiled from the bounties and blind to the beneficence of God. Hence no one can turn to God until he has turned away from nature, and the "natural" man (*sáhib tab'*) is unable to apprehend the reality of Unification, which is revealed to you only when you see the corruption of your own nature.

62. Abú 'Uthmán Sa'íd b. Sallám al-Maghribí.

He was an eminent spiritualist of the class who have attained "fixity" (*ahl-i tamkín*), and was profoundly versed in various departments of knowledge. He practised austerities, and is the author of many notable sayings and excellent proofs concerning the observation of spiritual blemishes (*ru'yat-i áfát*). It is related that he said: "Whenever anyone prefers association with the rich to sitting with the poor God afflicts him with spiritual death." The terms "association" (*ṣuḥbat*) and "sitting with" (*mujálasat*) are employed, because a man turns away from the poor only when he has sat with them, not when he has associated with them; for there is no turning away in association. When he leaves off sitting with the poor in order to associate with the rich, his heart becomes dead to supplication (*niyáz*) and his body is caught in the toils of covetousness (*áz*). Since the result of turning away from *mujálasat* is spiritual death, how should there be any turning away from *ṣuḥbat*? The two terms are clearly distinguished from each other in this saying.

63. ABU 'L-QÁSIM IBRÁHÍM B. MUḤAMMAD B. MAḤMÚD AL-NAṢRÁBÁDÍ.

He was like a king in Níshápúr, save that the glory of kings is in this world, while his was in the next world. Original sayings and exalted signs were vouchsafed to him. Himself a pupil of Shiblí, he was the master of the later Shaykhs of Khurásán. He was the most learned and devout man of his age. It is recorded that he said: "Thou art between two relationships: one to Adam, the other to God. If thou claim relationship to Adam, thou wilt enter the arenas of lust and the places of corruption and error; for by this claim thou seekest to realize thy humanity (*bashariyyat*). God hath said: '*Verily, he was unjust and foolish*' (Kor. xxxiii, 72). If, however, thou claim relationship to God, thou wilt enter the stations of revelation and evidence and protection (from sin) and saintship; for by this c aim thou seekest to realize thy servantship (*'ubúdiyyat*). God hath said: '*The servants of the Merciful are those who walk on the earth meekly*' (Kor. xxv, 64)." Relationship to Adam ends at the Resurrection, whereas the relationship of being a servant of God subsists always and is unalterable. When a man refers himself to himself or to Adam, the utmost that he can reach is to say: "*Verily, I have injured myself*" (Kor. xxviii, 15); but when he refers himself to God, the son of Adam is in the same case as those of whom God hath said: "*O My servants, there is no fear for you this day*" (Kor. xliii, 68).

64. Abu 'l-Ḥasan 'Alí b. Ibráhím al-Ḥuṣrí.

He is one of the great Imáms of the Ṣúfís and was unrivalled in his time. He has lofty sayings and admirable explanations in all spiritual matters. It is related that he said: "Leave me alone in my affliction! Are not ye children of Adam, whom God formed with His own hand and breathed a spirit into him and caused the angels to bow down to him? Then He commanded him to do something, and he disobeyed. If the first of the wine-jar is dregs, what will its last be?" That is to say: "When a man is left to himself he is all disobedience, but when Divine favour comes to his help he is all love. Now regard the beauty of Divine favour and compare with it the ugliness of thy behaviour, and pass thy whole life in this."

I have mentioned some of the ancient Ṣúfís whose example is authoritative. If I had noticed them all and had set forth their lives in detail and had included the anecdotes respecting them, my purpose would not have been accomplished, and this book would have run to great length. Now I will add some account of the modern Ṣúfís.

CHAPTER XII.

CONCERNING THE PRINCIPAL ṢÚFÍS OF RECENT TIMES.

You must know that in our days there are some persons who cannot endure the burden of discipline (*riyáḍat*), and seek authority (*riyásat*) without discipline, and think that all Ṣúfís are like themselves; and when they hear the sayings of those who have passed away and see their eminence and read of their devotional practices they examine themselves, and finding that they are far inferior to the Shaykhs of old they no longer attempt to emulate them, but say: "We are not as they, and there is none like them in our time." Their assertion is absurd, for God never leaves the earth without a proof (*ḥujjat*) or the Moslem community without a saint, as the Apostle said: "One sect of my people shall continue in goodness and truth until the hour of the Resurrection." And he said also: "There shall always be in my people forty who have the nature of Abraham."

Some of those whom I shall mention in this chapter are already deceased, and some are still living.

1. ABU 'L-'ABBÁS AḤMAD B. MUḤAMMAD AL-QAṢṢÁB.

He associated with the leading Shaykhs of Transoxania. He was famed for his lofty spiritual endowments, his true sagacity, his abundant evidences, ascetic practices, and miracles. Abú 'Abdalláh Khayyáṭí, the Imám of Ṭabaristán, says of him: "It is one of God's bounties that He has made a person who was never taught able to answer our questions about any difficulty touching the principles of religion and the subtleties of Unification." Although Abu 'l-'Abbás Qaṣṣáb was illiterate (*ummí*), he discoursed in sublime fashion concerning the science of Ṣúfiism and theology. I have heard many stories of him, but my rule in this book is brevity. One day a camel, with a heavy burden, was going through the market-place at Ámul, which is always muddy. The camel fell and broke its leg. While the lad in charge of it was lamenting and lifting his hands to implore the help of God, and the people were about to take the load off its back, the Shaykh passed by, and asked what was the matter. On being informed, he seized the camel's bridle and turned his face to the sky and said: "O Lord! make the leg of this camel whole. If Thou wilt not do so, why hast Thou let my heart be melted by the tears of a lad?" The camel immediately got up and went on its way.

It is stated that he said: "All mankind, whether they will or no, must reconcile themselves to God, or else they will suffer pain," because, when you are reconciled to Him in affliction, you see only the Author of affliction, and the affliction itself does not come; and if you are not reconciled to Him, affliction comes and your heart is filled with anguish. God having predestined our satisfaction and dissatisfaction, does not alter His predestination: therefore our satisfaction with His decrees is a part of our pleasure. Whenever anyone reconciles himself to Him, that man's heart is rejoiced; and whenever anyone turns away from Him, that man is distressed by the coming of destiny.

2. Abú 'Alí Ḥasan b. Muḥammad al-Daqqáq.

He was the leading authority in his department (of science) and had no rival among his contemporaries. He was lucid in exposition and eloquent in speech as regards the revelation of the way to God. He had seen many Shaykhs and associated with them. He was a pupil of Naṣrábádí[1] and used to be a preacher (*tadhkír kardí*). It is related that he said: "Whoever becomes intimate with anyone except God is weak in his (spiritual) state, and whoever speaks of anyone except God is false in his speech," because intimacy with anyone except God springs from not knowing God sufficiently, and intimacy with Him is friendlessness in regard to others, and the friendless man does not speak of others.

[1] See Chapter XI, No. 63.

I heard an old man relate that one day he went to the place where al-Daqqáq held his meetings, with the intention of asking him about the state of those who trust in God (*mutawakkilán*). Al-Daqqáq was wearing a fine turban manufactured in Ṭabaristán, which the old man coveted. He said to al-Daqqáq: "What is trust in God?" The Shaykh replied: "To refrain from coveting people's turbans." With these words he flung his turban in front of the questioner.

3. ABU 'L-ḤASAN 'ALÍ B. AḤMAD AL-KHURQÁNÍ.

He was a great Shaykh and was praised by all the Saints in his time. Shaykh Abú Sa'íd visited him, and they conversed with each other on every topic. When he was about to take leave he said to al-Khurqání: "I choose you to be my successor." I have heard from Ḥasan Mu'addib, who was the servant of Abú Sa'íd, that when Abú Sa'íd came into the presence of al-Khurqání, he did not speak another word, but listened and only spoke by way of answering what was said by the latter. Ḥasan asked him why he had been so silent. He replied: "One interpreter is enough for one theme." And I heard the Master, Abu 'l-Qásim Qushayrí, say: "When I came to Khurqán, my eloquence departed and I no longer had any power to express myself, on account of the veneration with which that spiritual director inspired me; and I thought that I had been deposed from my own saintship."

It is related that he said: "There are two ways, one wrong and one right. The wrong way is Man's way to God, and the right way is God's way to Man. Whoever says he has attained to God has not attained; but when anyone says that he has been made to attain to God, know that he has really attained." It is not a question of attaining or not attaining, and of salvation or non-salvation, but one of being *caused* to attain or not to attain, and of being *given* salvation or being not given salvation.

4. Abú 'Abdalláh Muḥammad b. 'Alí, generally known as al-Dástání.

He resided at Bisṭám. He was learned in various branches of science, and is the author of polished discourses and fine symbolical indications. He found an excellent successor in Shaykh Sahlagí, who was the Imám of those parts. I have heard from Sahlagí some of his spiritual utterances (*anfás*), which are very sublime and admirable. He says, for example: "Unification, coming from thee, is existent (*mawjúd*), but thou in unification art non-existent (*mafqúd*)," i.e. unification, when it proceeds from thee, is faultless (*durust*), but thou art faulty in unification, because thou dost not fulfil its requirements. The lowest degree in unification is the negation of thy personal control over anything that thou hast, and the affirmation of thy absolute submission to God in all thy affairs. Shaykh Sahlagí relates as follows: "Once the locusts came to Bisṭám in such numbers that every tree and field was black with them. The people cried aloud for help. The Shaykh asked me: 'What is all this pother?' I told him that the locusts had come and that the people were distressed in consequence. He rose and went up to the roof and looked towards heaven. The locusts immediately began to fly away. By the hour of the afternoon prayer not one was left, and nobody lost even a blade of grass."

5. Abú Sa'íd Faḍlalláh b. Muḥammad al-Mayhaní.

He was the sultan of his age and the ornament of the Mystic Path. All his contemporaries were subject to him, some through their sound perception, and some through their excellent belief, and some through the strong influence of their spiritual feelings. He was versed in the different branches of science. He had a wonderful religious experience and an extraordinary power of reading men's secret thoughts. Besides this he had many remarkable powers and evidences, of which the effects are manifest at the present day. In early life he left Mihna (Mayhana) and came to Sarakhs in order to study. He attached himself to Abú 'Alí Záhir, from whom he learned in one day as much as is contained in three lectures, and he used to spend in devotion the three days that he had saved in this manner. The saint of Sarakhs at that time was Abu 'l-Faḍl Ḥasan. One day, when Abú Sa'íd was walking by the river of Sarakhs, Abu 'l-Faḍl met him and said: "Your way is not that which you are taking: take your own way." The Shaykh did not attach himself to him, but returned to his native town and engaged in asceticism and austerities until God opened to him the door of guidance and raised him to the highest rank. I heard the following story from Shaykh Abú Muslim Fárisí: "I had always," he said, "been on unfriendly terms with the Shaykh. Once I set out to pay him a visit. My patched frock was so dirty that it had become like leather. When I entered his presence, I found him sitting on a couch, dressed in a robe of Egyptian linen. I said to myself: 'This man claims to be a dervish (*faqír*) with all these worldly encumbrances (*'alá'iq*), while I claim to be a dervish with all this detachment from the world (*tajríd*). How can I agree with this man?' He read my thoughts, and raising his head cried: 'O Abú Muslim, in what *díwán* have you found that the name of dervish is applied to anyone whose heart subsists in the contemplation of God?' i.e. those who contemplate God are rich in God, whereas dervishes (*fuqará*) are occupied with self-mortification. I repented of my conceit and asked God to pardon me for such an unseemly thought."

And it is related that he said: "Ṣúfiism is the subsistence of the heart with God without any mediation." This alludes to contemplation (*musháhadat*), which is violence of love, and absorption of human attributes in realizing the vision of God, and their annihilation by the everlastingness of God. I will discuss the nature of contemplation in the chapter which treats of the Pilgrimage.

On one occasion Abú Sa'íd set out from Níshápúr towards Ṭús. While he was passing through a mountainous ravine his feet felt cold in his boots. A dervish who was then with him says: "I thought of tearing my waist-cloth (*fúṭa*) into two halves and wrapping them round his feet; but I could not bring myself to do it, as my *fúṭa* was a very fine one. When we arrived at Ṭús I attended his meeting and asked him to tell me the difference between suggestions of the Devil (*waswás*) and Divine inspiration (*ilhám*). He answered: 'It was a Divine inspiration that urged you to tear your *fúṭa* into two pieces for the sake of warming my feet; and it was a diabolic suggestion that hindered you from doing so.'" He performed a whole series of miracles of this kind which are wrought by spiritual adepts.

6. Abu 'l-Faḍl Muḥammad b. al-Ḥasan al-Khuttalí.

He is the teacher whom I follow in Ṣúfiism. He was versed in the science of Koranic exegesis and in traditions (*riwáyát*). In Ṣúfiism he held the doctrine of Junayd. He was a pupil of Ḥuṣrí[1] and a companion of Sírawání, and was contemporary with Abú 'Amr Qazwíní and Abu 'l-Ḥasan b. Sáliba. He spent sixty years in sincere retirement from the world, for the most part on Mount Lukám. He displayed many signs and proofs (of saintship), but he did not wear the garb or adopt the external fashions of the Ṣúfís, and he used to treat formalists with severity. I never saw any man who inspired me with greater awe than he did. It is related that he said: "The world is but a single day, in which we are fasting," i.e., we get nothing from it, and are not occupied with it, because we have perceived its corruption and its "veils" and have turned our backs upon it. Once I was pouring water on his hands in order that he might purify himself. The thought occurred to me: "Inasmuch as everything is predestined, why should free men make themselves the slaves of spiritual directors in the hope of having miracles vouchsafed to them?" The Shaykh said: "O my son, I know what you are thinking. Be assured that there is a cause for every decree of Providence. When God wishes to bestow a crown and a kingdom on a guardsman's son (*'awán-bacha*), He gives him repentance and employs him in the service of one

[1] See Chapter XI, No. 64.

of His friends, in order that this service may be the means of his obtaining the gift of miracles." Many such fine sayings he uttered to me every day. He died at Bayt al-Jinn, a village situated at the head of a mountain pass between Báníyás[1] and the river of Damascus. While he lay on his death-bed, his head resting on my bosom (and at that time I was feeling hurt, as men often do, by the behaviour of a friend of mine), he said to me: "O my son, I will tell thee one article of belief which, if thou holdest it firmly, will deliver thee from all troubles. Whatever good or evil God creates, do not in any place or circumstance quarrel with His action or be aggrieved in thy heart." He gave no further injunction, but yielded up his soul.

7. Abu 'l-Qásim 'Abd al-Karím b. Hawázin al-Qushayrí.

In his time he was a wonder. His rank is high and his position is great, and his spiritual life and manifold virtues are well known to the people of the present age. He is the author of many fine sayings and exquisite works, all of them profoundly theosophical, in every branch of science. God rendered his feelings and his tongue secure from anthropomorphism (*ḥashw*). I have heard that he said: "The Ṣúfí is like the disease called *birsám*, which begins with delirium and ends in silence; for when you have attained 'fixity' you are dumb." Ṣúfiism (*ṣafwat*) has two sides: ecstasy (*wajd*) and visions (*numúd*). Visions belong to novices, and the expression of such visions is delirium (*hadhayán*). Ecstasy belongs to adepts, and the expression of ecstasy, while the eestasy continues, is impossible. So long as they are only seekers they utter lofty aspirations, which seem delirium even to those who aspire (*ahl-i himmat*), but when they have attained they cease, and no more express anything either by word or sign. Similarly, since Moses was a beginner (*mubtadí*) all his desire was for vision of God; he expressed his desire and said, "*O Lord, show me that I may behold Thee*" (Kor. vii, 139). This expression of an unattained

[1] L. Báníyán, IJ. Máníyán.

desire seemed like delirium. Our Apostle, however, was an adept (*muntahí*) and firmly established (*mutamakkin*). When his person arrived at the station of desire his desire was annihilated, and he said, "I cannot praise Thee duly."

8. ABU 'L-'ABBÁS AḤMAD B. MUḤAMMAD AL-ASHQÁNÍ.

He was an Imám in every branch of the fundamental and derivative sciences, and consummate in all respects. He had met a great number of eminent Ṣúfís. His doctrine was based on "annihilation" (*faná*), and his recondite manner of expression was peculiarly his own; but I have seen some fools who imitated it and adopted his ecstatic phrases (*shaṭḥhá*). It is not laudable to imitate even a spiritual meaning: mark, then, how wrong it must be to imitate a mere expression! I was very intimate with him, and he had a sincere affection for me. He was my teacher in some sciences. During my whole life I have never seen anyone, of any sect, who held the religious law in greater veneration than he. He was detached from all created things, and only an Imám of profound insight could derive instruction from him, on account of the subtlety of his theological expositions. He always had a natural disgust of this world and the next, and was constantly exclaiming: *Ashtahí 'adam*[un] *lá wujúd lahu*, "I long for a non-existence that has no existence." And he used to say in Persian: "Every man has an impossible desire, and I too have an impossible desire, which I surely know will never be realized, namely, that God should bring me to a non-existence that will never return to existence." He wished this because "stations" and miracles are all centres of veiling (i.e. they veil man from God). Man has fallen in love with that which veils him. Non-existence in desire of vision is better than taking delight in veils. Inasmuch as Almighty God is a Being that is not subject to not-being, what loss would His kingdom suffer if I become a nonentity that shall never be endowed with existence? This is a sound principle in a real annihilation.

9. Abu 'l-Qásim b. 'Alí b. 'Abdalláh al-Gurgání (may God prolong his life for the benefit of us and of all Moslems !).

In his time he was unique and incomparable. His beginning (*ibtidá*) was very excellent and strong, and his journeys were performed with punctilious observance (of the sacred law). At that time the hearts of all initiates (*ahl-i dargáh*) were turned towards him, and all seekers (*ṭálibán*) had a firm belief in him. He possessed a marvellous power of revealing the inward experiences of novices (*kashf-i wáqi'a-i murídán*), and he was learned in various branches of knowledge. All his disciples are ornaments of the society in which they move. Please God, he will have an excellent successor, whose authority the whole body of Ṣúfís will recognize, namely, Abú 'Alí al-Faḍl b. Muḥammad al-Fármadhí (may God lengthen his days !),[1] who has not omitted to fulfil his duty towards his master, and has turned his back on all (worldly) things, and through the blessings of that (renunciation) has been made by God the spiritual mouthpiece (*zabán-i ḥál*) of that venerable Shaykh.

One day I was seated in the Shaykh's presence and was recounting to him my experiences and visions, in order that he might test them, for he had unrivalled skill in this. He was listening kindly to what I said. The vanity and enthusiasm of youth made me eager to relate those matters, and the thought occurred to me that perhaps the Shaykh, in his novitiate, did not enjoy such experiences, or he would not show so much humility towards me and be so anxious to inquire concerning my spiritual state. The Shaykh perceived what I was thinking. "My dear friend," he said, "you must know that my humility is not on account of you or your experiences, but is shown towards Him who brings experiences to pass. They are not peculiar to yourself, but common to all seekers of God." On hearing him say this I was utterly taken

[1] *Nafaḥát*, No. 428.

aback. He saw my confusion and said: "O my son, Man has no further relation to this Path except that, when he is attached to it, he imagines that he has found it, and when he is deposed from it he clothes his imagination in words. Hence both his negation and his affirmation, both his non-existence and existence, are imagination. Man never escapes from the prison of imagination. It behoves him to stand like a slave at the door and put away from himself every relation (*nisbat*) except that of manhood and obedience." Afterwards I had much spiritual conversation with him, but if I were to enter upon the task of setting forth his extraordinary powers my purpose would be defeated.

10. ABÚ AḤMAD AL-MUẒAFFAR B. AḤMAD B. ḤAMDÁN.

While he was seated on the cushion of authority (*riyásat*), God opened to him the door of this mystery (*Ṣúfiism*) and bestowed on him the crown of miracles. He spoke eloquently and discoursed with sublimity on annihilation and subsistence (*faná ú baqá*). The Grand Shaykh, Abú Sa'íd, said: "I was led to the court (of God) by the way of servantship (*bandagí*), but Khwája Muẓaffar was conducted thither by the way of lordship and dominion (*khwájagí*)," i.e. "I attained contemplation (*musháhadat*) by means of self-mortification (*mujáhadat*), whereas he came from contemplation to self-mortification". I have heard that he said: "That which great mystics have discovered by traversing deserts and wildernesses I have gained in the seat of power and pre-eminence (*bálish ú ṣadr*)." Some foolish and conceited persons have attributed this saying of his to arrogance, but it is never arrogant to declare one's true state, especially when the speaker is a spiritualist. At the present time Muẓaffar has an excellent and honoured successor in Khwája Aḥmad. One day, when I was in his company, a certain pretender of Níshápúr happened to use the expression: "He becomes annihilated and then becomes subsistent." Khwája Muẓaffar said: "How can subsistence (*baqá*) be predicated of annihilation (*faná*)? Annihilation means 'not-being', while subsistence refers to 'being': each term negates the other. We know what annihilation is, but when it is not, if it becomes 'being', its identity (*'ayn*) is lost. Essences are not capable of annihilation. Attributes, however, can be annihilated, and so can secondary causes. Therefore, when attributes and secondary causes are annihilated, the Object invested with attributes and the Author of secondary causes continues to subsist: His essence does not admit of annihilation." I do not recollect the precise words in which Muẓaffar expressed his meaning, but this was the purport of them. Now I will explain more clearly what he intended, in order that it may be more generally understood. A man's will (*ikhtiyár*) is an attribute of himself, and he is veiled by his will from the will of God. Therefore a man's attributes veil him from God. Necessarily, the Divine will is eternal and the human will phenomenal, and what is eternal cannot be annihilated. When the Divine will in regard to a man becomes subsistent (*baqá yábad*), his will is annihilated and his personal initiative disappears. But God knows best.

One day I came into his presence, when the weather was extremely hot, wearing a traveller's dress and with my hair in disorder. He said to me: "Tell me what you wish at this moment." I replied that I wished to hear some music (*samá'*). He immediately sent for a singer (*qawwál*) and a number of musicians. Being young and enthusiastic and filled with the ardour of a novice, I became deeply agitated as the strains of the music fell on my ear. After a while, when my transports subsided, he asked me how I liked it. I told him that I had enjoyed it very much. He answered: "A time will come when this music will be no more to you than the croaking of a raven. The influence of music only lasts so long as there is no contemplation, and as soon as contemplation is attained music has no power. Take care not to accustom yourself to this, lest it grow part of your nature and keep you back from higher things."

CHAPTER XIII.

A BRIEF ACCOUNT OF THE MODERN ṢÚFÍS IN DIFFERENT COUNTRIES.

I have not space enough to give biographies of them all, and if I omit some the object of this book will not be accomplished. Now, therefore, I will mention only the names of individual Ṣúfís and leading spiritualists who have lived in my time or are still alive, excluding the formalists (*ahl-i rusúm*).

1. SYRIA AND 'IRÁQ.

Shaykh Zakí b. al-'Alá was an eminent Shaykh. I found him to be like a flash of love. He was endowed with wonderful signs and evidences.

Shaykh Abú Ja'far Muḥammad b. al-Miṣbáḥ al-Ṣaydalání was one of the principal aspirants to Ṣúfiism. He discoursed eloquently on theosophy and had a great fondness for Ḥusayn b. Manṣúr (al-Ḥalláj), some of whose works I have read to him.

Shaykh Abu 'l-Qásim Suddí[1] was a director who mortified himself and led an excellent spiritual life. He cared tenderly for dervishes and had a goodly belief in them.

2. FÁRS.

The Grand Shaykh, Abu 'l-Ḥasan b. Sáliba,[2] spoke with the utmost elegance on Ṣúfiism and with extreme lucidity on Unification (*tawḥíd*). His sayings are well known.

The Shaykh and Director (*murshid*) Abú Isḥáq b. Shahriyár was one of the most venerable Ṣúfís and had complete authority.

Shaykh Abu 'l-Ḥasan 'Alí b. Bakrán was a great *mutaṣawwif*, and Shaykh Abú Muslim was highly esteemed in his time.

[1] IJ. Sudsí, B. Sundusí.

[2] See *Nafaḥát*, No. 347, where he is called Abu 'l-Ḥusayn Sáliba.

Shaykh Abu 'l-Fatḥ b. Sáliba is an excellent and hopeful successor to his father.

Shaykh Abú Ṭálib was a man enraptured by the words of the Truth.

I have seen all these except the Grand Shaykh, Abú Isḥáq.

3. Quhistán, Ádharbáyaján, Ṭabaristán, and Kish.[1]

Shaykh Faraj,[2] known as Akhí Zanjání, was a man of excellent disposition and admirable doctrine.

Shaykh Badr al-Dín is one of the great men of this sect, and his good deeds are many.

Pádsháh-i Tá'ib was profoundly versed in mysticism.

Shaykh Abú 'Abdalláh Junaydí was a revered director.

Shaykh Abú Ṭáhir Makshúf was one of the eminent of that time.

Khwája Ḥusayn Simnán is an enraptured and hopeful man.

Shaykh Sahlagí was one of the principal Ṣúfí paupers (*ṣa'álík*).

Aḥmad, son of Shaykh Khurqání, was an excellent successor to his father.

Adíb Kumandí was one of the chief men of the time.

4. Kirmán.

Khwája 'Alí b. al-Ḥusayn al-Sírgání was the wandering devotee (*sayyáḥ*) of his age and made excellent journeys. His son, Ḥakím, is held in honour.

Shaykh Muḥammad b. Salama was among the eminent of the time. Before him there have been hidden saints of God, and hopeful youths and striplings are still to be found.

5. Khurásán (where now is the shadow of God's favour).

The Shaykh and Mujtahid Abu 'l-'Abbás was the heart of spiritualism (*sirr-i ma'ání*) and had a goodly life.

Khwája Abú Ja'far Muḥammad b. 'Alí al-Ḥawárí is one of the eminent theosophists of this sect.

Khwája Abú Ja'far Turshízí was highly esteemed.

[1] B. Kumish.

[2] The texts have فرح or فرغ, but see *Nafaḥát*, No. 171.

Khwája Maḥmúd of Nísbápúr was regarded as an authority by his contemporaries. He was eloquent in discourse.

Shaykh Muḥammad Ma'shúq had an excellent spiritual state and was aglow with love.

Khwája Rashíd Muẓaffar, the son of Abú Sa'íd, will, it may be hoped, become an example to all Ṣúfís and a point to which their hearts will turn.

Khwája Shaykh Aḥmad Ḥammádí of Sarakhs was the champion of the time. He was in my company for a while, and I witnessed many wondrous experiences that he had.

Shaykh Aḥmad Najjár Samarqandí, who resided at Merv, was the sultan of his age.

Shaykh Abu 'l-Ḥasan 'Alí b. Abí 'Alí al-Aswad was an excellent successor to his father, and was unique in the sublimity of his aspiration and the sagacity of his intelligence.

It would be difficult to mention all the Shaykhs of Khurásán. I have met three hundred in that province alone who had such mystical endowments that a single man of them would have been enough for the whole world. This is due to the fact that the sun of love and the fortune of the Ṣúfí Path is in the ascendant in Khurásán.

6. TRANSOXANIA.

The Khwája and Imám, honoured by high and low, Abú Ja'far Muḥammad b. al-Ḥusayn[1] al-Ḥaramí, is an ecstatic (*mustami'*) and enraptured man, who has a great affection towards the seekers of God.

Khwája Abú Muḥammad Bángharí[2] had an excellent spiritual life, and there was no weakness in his devotional practices.

Aḥmad Íláqí was the Shaykh of his time. He renounced forms and habits.

Khwája 'Árif was unparalleled in his day.

'Alí b. Isḥáq was venerated and had an eloquent tongue.

I have seen all these Shaykhs and ascertained the "station" of each of them. They were all profound theosophists.

[1] IJ. Al-Ḥasan.

[2] This *nisba* is variously written "Bángharí" and "Báyghazí".

7. GHAZNA.

Abu 'l-Faḍl b. al-Asadí was a venerable director, with brilliant evidences and manifest miracles. He was like a flash of the fire of love. His spiritual life was based on concealment (*talbís*).

Ismá'íl al-Sháshí was a highly esteemed director. He followed the path of "blame" (*malámat*).

Shaykh Sálár-i Ṭabarí was one of the Ṣúfí divines and had an excellent state.

Shaykh Abú 'Abdalláh Muḥammad b. al-Ḥakím, known as Muríd, was a God-intoxicated man, and was not rivalled by any contemporary in his own line. His state was hidden from the vulgar, but his signs and evidences were conspicuous, and his state was better in companionship (*ṣuḥbat*) than in casual meeting (*dídár*).

Shaykh Sa'íd b. Abí Sa'íd al-'Ayyár was a recorder (*ḥáfiẓ*) of Apostolic Traditions. He had seen many Shaykhs and was a man of powerful spirituality and great knowledge, but he took the way of concealment and did not exhibit his true character.

Khwája Abu 'l-'Alá 'Abd al-Raḥím b. Aḥmad al-Sughdí is honoured by all Ṣúfís, and my heart is well-disposed towards him. His spiritual state is excellent, and he is acquainted with various branches of science.

Shaykh Awḥad Qaswarat b. Muḥammad al-Jardízí has a boundless affection for Ṣúfís and holds every one of them in reverence. He has seen many Shaykhs.

In consequence of the firm convictions of the people and divines of Ghazna, I have good hope that hereafter persons will appear in whom we shall believe, and that those wretches (*parágandagán*) who have found their way into this city and have made the externals of Ṣúfiism abominable will be cleared out, so that Ghazna will once more become the abode of saints and venerable men.

CHAPTER XIV.

Concerning the Doctrines held by the different sects of Ṣúfís.

I have already stated, in the notice of Abu 'l-Ḥasan Núrí, that the Ṣúfís are divided into twelve sects, of which two are reprobated and ten are approved. Every one of these ten sects has an excellent system and doctrine as regards both purgation (*mujáhadat*) and contemplation (*musháhadat*). Although they differ from each other in their devotional practices and ascetic disciplines, they agree in the fundamentals and derivatives of the religious law and Unification. Abú Yazíd said: "The disagreement of divines is a mercy except as regards the detachment (*tajríd*)[1] of Unification"; and there is a famous tradition to the same effect. The real essence of Ṣúfiism lies amidst the traditions (*akhbár*) of the Shaykhs, and is divided only metaphorically and formally. Therefore I will briefly divide their sayings in explanation of Ṣúfiism and unfold the main principle on which the doctrine of each one of them is based, in order that the student may readily understand this matter.

1. The Muḥásibís.

They are the followers of Abú 'Abdalláh Ḥárith b. Asad al-Muḥásibí, who by consent of all his contemporaries was a man of approved spiritual influence and mortified passions (*maqbúl al-nafas ú maqtúl al-nafs*), versed in theology, jurisprudence, and mysticism. He discoursed on detachment from the world and Unification, while his outward and inward dealings (with God) were beyond reproach. The peculiarity of his doctrine is this, that he does not reckon satisfaction

[1] i.e. the detachment of all phenomenal attributes from the Unity of God.

(*riḍá*) among the "stations" (*maqámát*), but includes it in the "states" (*aḥwál*). He was the first to hold this view, which was adopted by the people of Khurásán. The people of 'Iráq, on the contrary, asserted that satisfaction is one of the "stations", and that it is the extreme of trust in God (*tawakkul*). The controversy between them has gone on to the present day.[1]

Discourse on the true nature of Satisfaction and the explanation of this doctrine.

In the first place I will establish the true nature of satisfaction and set forth its various kinds; then, secondly, I will explain the real meaning of "station" (*maqám*) and "state" (*ḥál*) and the difference between them.

Satisfaction is of two kinds: (*a*) the satisfaction of God with Man, and (*b*) the satisfaction of Man with God. Divine satisfaction really consists in God's willing that Man should be recompensed (for his good works) and in His bestowing grace (*karámat*) upon him. Human satisfaction really consists in Man's performing the command of God and submitting to His decree. Accordingly, the satisfaction of God precedes that of Man, for until Man is divinely aided he does not submit to God's decree and does not perform His command, because Man's satisfaction is connected with God's satisfaction and subsists thereby. In short, human satisfaction is equanimity (*istiwá-yi dil*) towards Fate, whether it withholds or bestows, and spiritual steadfastness (*istiqámat*) in regarding events, whether they be the manifestation of Divine Beauty (*jamál*) or of Divine Majesty (*jalál*), so that it is all one to a man whether he is consumed in the fire of wrath or illuminated by the light of mercy, because both wrath and mercy are evidences of God, and whatever proceeds from God is good in His eyes. The Commander of the Faithful, Ḥusayn b. 'Alí, was asked about the saying of Abú Dharr Ghifárí: "I love poverty better than riches, and sickness better than health."

[1] According to Qushayrí (105, 21 ff.) the 'Iráqís held the doctrine which is here ascribed to the Khurásánís, and *vice versâ*.

Ḥusayn replied: "God have mercy on Abú Dharr! but I say that whoever surveys the excellent choice made by God for him does not desire anything except what God has chosen for him." When a man sees God's choice and abandons his own choice, he is delivered from all sorrow. This, however, does not hold good in absence from God (*ghaybat*); it requires presence with God (*ḥuḍúr*), because "satisfaction expels sorrows and cures heedlessness", and purges the heart of thoughts relating to other than God and frees it from the bonds of tribulation; for it is characteristic of satisfaction to deliver (*rahánídan*).

From the standpoint of ethics, satisfaction is the acquiescence of one who knows that giving and withholding are in God's knowledge, and firmly believes that God sees him in all circumstances. There are four classes of quietists: (1) those who are satisfied with God's gift (*'aṭá*), which is gnosis (*ma'rifat*); (2) those who are satisfied with happiness (*nu'má*), which is this world; (3) those who are satisfied with affliction (*balá*), which consists of diverse probations; and (4) those who are satisfied with being chosen (*iṣṭifá*), which is love (*maḥabbat*). He who looks away from the Giver to the gift accepts it with his soul, and when he has so accepted it trouble and grief vanish from his heart. He who looks away from the gift to the Giver loses the gift and treads the path of satisfaction by his own effort. Now effort is painful and grievous, and gnosis is only realized when its true nature is divinely revealed; and inasmuch as gnosis, when sought by effort, is a shackle and a veil, such gnosis is non-cognition (*nakirat*). Again, he who is satisfied with this world, without God, is involved in destruction and perdition, because the whole world is not worth so much that a friend of God should set his heart on it or that any care for it should enter his mind. Happiness is happiness only when it leads to the Giver of happiness; otherwise, it is an affliction. Again, he who is satisfied with the affliction that God sends is satisfied because in the affliction he sees the Author thereof and can endure its pain by contemplating Him who sent it; nay, he does not account it painful, such is his joy in contemplating his Beloved. Finally, those who are satisfied with being chosen by God are His lovers, whose existence is an illusion alike in His anger and His satisfaction; whose hearts dwell in the presence of Purity and in the garden of Intimacy; who have no thought of created things and have escaped from the bonds of "stations" and "states" and have devoted themselves to the love of God. Their satisfaction involves no loss, for satisfaction with God is a manifest kingdom.

SECTION.

It is related in the Traditions that Moses said: "O God, show me an action with which, if I did it, Thou wouldst be satisfied." God answered: "Thou canst not do that, O Moses!" Then Moses fell prostrate, worshipping God and supplicating Him, and God made a revelation to him, saying: "O son of 'Imrán, My satisfaction with thee consists in thy being satisfied with My decree," i.e. when a man is satisfied with God's decrees it is a sign that God is satisfied with him.

Bishr Ḥáfí asked Fuḍayl b. 'Iyáḍ whether renunciation (*zuhd*) or satisfaction was better. Fuḍayl replied: "Satisfaction, because he who is satisfied does not desire any higher stage," i.e. there is above renunciation a stage which the renouncer desires, but there is no stage above satisfaction that the satisfied man should wish for it. Hence the shrine is superior to the gate. This story shows the correctness of Muḥásibí's doctrine, that satisfaction belongs to the class of "states" and Divine gifts, not to the stages that are acquired (by effort). It is possible, however, that the satisfied man should have a desire. The Apostle used to say in his prayers: "O God, I ask of Thee satisfaction after the going forth of Thy ordinance (*al-riḍá ba'd al-qaḍá*)," i.e. "keep me in such a condition that when the ordinance comes to me from Thee, Destiny may find me satisfied with its coming". Here it is affirmed that satisfaction properly is posterior to the advent of Destiny, because, if it preceded, it would only be a resolution to be satisfied, which is not the same thing as actual satisfaction. Abu 'l-'Abbás b. 'Aṭá says: "Satisfaction is this, that the heart should consider the eternal choice of God on behalf of His creature," i.e. whatever befalls him, he should recognize it as the eternal will of God and His past decree, and should not be distressed, but should accept it cheerfully. Ḥárith Muḥásibí, the author of the doctrine, says: "Satisfaction is the quiescence (*sukún*) of the heart under the events which flow from the Divine decrees." This is sound doctrine, because the quiescence and tranquillity of the heart are not qualities acquired by Man, but are Divine gifts. And as an argument for the view that satisfaction is a "state", not a "station", they cite the story of 'Utba al-Ghulám, who one night did not sleep, but kept saying: "If Thou chastise me I love Thee, and if Thou have mercy on me I love Thee," i.e. "the pain of Thy chastisement and the pleasure of Thy bounty affect the body alone, whereas the agitation of love resides in the heart, which is not injured thereby". This corroborates the view of Muḥásibí. Satisfaction is the result of love, inasmuch as the lover is satisfied with what is done by the Beloved. Abú 'Uthmán Ḥírí says: "During the last forty years God has never put me in any state that I disliked, or transferred me to another state that I resented." This indicates continual satisfaction and perfect love. The story of the dervish who fell into the Tigris is well known. Seeing that he could not swim, a man on the bank cried out to him: "Shall I tell some one to bring you ashore?" The dervish said, "No." "Then do you wish to be drowned?" "No." "What, then, do you wish?" The dervish replied: "That which God wishes. What have I to do with wishing?"

The Ṣúfí Shaykhs have uttered many sayings on satisfaction, which differ in phraseology but agree in the two principles that have been mentioned.

The distinction between a "State" (ḥál) *and a "Station"* (maqám).

You must know that both these terms are in common use among Ṣúfís, and it is necessary that the student should be acquainted with them. I must discuss this matter here, although it does not belong to the present chapter.

"Station" (*maqám*) denotes anyone's "standing" in the Way of God, and his fulfilment of the obligations appertaining to that "station" and his keeping it until he comprehends its perfection so far as lies in a man's power. It is not permissible that he should quit his "station" without fulfilling the obligations thereof. Thus, the first "station" is repentance (*tawbat*), then comes conversion (*inábat*), then renunciation (*zuhd*), then trust in God (*tawakkul*), and so on: it is not permissible that anyone should pretend to conversion without repentance, or to renunciation without conversion, or to trust in God without renunciation.

"State" (*ḥál*), on the other hand, is something that descends from God into a man's heart, without his being able to repel it when it comes, or to attract it when it goes, by his own effort. Accordingly, while the term "station" denotes the way of the seeker, and his progress in the field of exertion, and his rank before God in proportion to his merit, the term "state" denotes the favour and grace which God bestows upon the heart of His servant, and which are not connected with any mortification on the latter's part. "Station" belongs to the category of acts, "state" to the category of gifts. Hence the man that has a "station" stands by his own self-mortification, whereas the man that has a "state" is dead to "self" and stands by a "state" which God creates in him.

Here the Shaykhs are at variance. Some hold that a "state" may be permanent, while others reject this view. Ḥárith Muḥásibí maintained that a "state" may be permanent. He argued that love and longing and "contraction" (*qabḍ*) and "expansion" (*basṭ*) are "states": if they cannot be permanent, then the lover would not be a lover, and until a man's "state" becomes his attribute (*ṣifat*) the name of that "state" is not properly applied to him. It is for this reason that he holds satisfaction to be one of the "states", and the same view is indicated by the saying of Abú 'Uthmán: "During the last forty years God has never put me in a 'state' that I disliked."

Other Shaykhs deny that a "state" can be permanent. Junayd says: "'States' are like flashes of lightning: their permanence is merely a suggestion of the lower soul (*nafs*)." Some have said, to the same effect: "'States' are like their name," i.e. they vanish almost as soon as they descend (*taḥillu*) on the heart. Whatever is permanent becomes an attribute, and attributes subsist in an object which must be more perfect than the attributes themselves; and this reduces the doctrine that "states" are permanent to an absurdity. I have set forth the distinction between "state" and "station" in order that you may know what is signified by these terms wherever they occur in the phraseology of the Ṣúfís or in the present work.

In conclusion, you must know that satisfaction is the end of the "stations" and the beginning of the "states": it is a place of which one side rests on acquisition and effort, and the other side on love and rapture: there is no "station" above it: at this point mortifications (*mujáhadát*) cease. Hence its beginning is in the class of things acquired by effort, its end in the class of things divinely bestowed. Therefore it may be called either a "station" or a "state".

This is the doctrine of Muḥásibí as regards the theory of Ṣúfiism. In practice, however, he made no difference, except that he used to warn his pupils against expressions and acts which, though sound in principle, might be thought evil. For example, he had a "king-bird" (*sháhmurghí*), which used to utter a loud note. One day Abú Ḥamza of Baghdád, who was Ḥárith's pupil and an ecstatic man, came to see him. The bird piped, and Abú Ḥamza gave a shriek. Ḥárith rose up and seized a knife, crying, "Thou art an infidel," and would have killed him if the disciples had not separated them. Then he said to Abú Ḥamza: "Become a Moslem, O miscreant!" The disciples exclaimed: "O Shaykh, we all know him to be one of the elect saints and Unitarians: why does the Shaykh regard him with suspicion?" Ḥárith replied: "I do not suspect him: his opinions are excellent, and I know that he is a profound Unitarian, but why should he do something which resembles the actions of those who believe in incarnation (*ḥulúliyán*) and has the appearance of being derived from their doctrine? If a senseless bird pipes after its fashion, capriciously, why should he behave as though its note were the voice of God? God is indivisible, and the Eternal does not become incarnate, or united with phenomena or commingled with them." When Abú Ḥamza perceived the Shaykh's insight, he said: "O Shaykh, although I am right in theory, nevertheless, since my action resembled the actions of heretics, I repent and withdraw."

May God keep my conduct above suspicion! But this is impossible when one associates with worldly formalists whose enmity is aroused by anyone who does not submit to their hypocrisy and sin.

2. The Qaṣṣárís.

They are the followers of Abú Ṣáliḥ Ḥamdún b. Aḥmad b. 'Umára al-Qaṣṣár, a celebrated divine and eminent Ṣúfí. His doctrine was the manifestation and divulgation of "blame" (*malámat*). He used to say: "God's knowledge of thee is better than men's knowledge," i.e. thy dealings with God in private should be better than thy dealings with men in public, for thy preoccupation with men is the greatest veil between thee and God. I have given some account of al-Qaṣṣár in the chapter on "Blame". He relates the following story: "One day, while I was walking in the river-bed in the Ḥíra quarter of Níshápúr, I met Núḥ, a brigand famous for his generosity, who was the captain of all the brigands of Níshápúr. I said to him, 'O Núḥ, what is generosity?' He replied, 'My generosity or yours?' I said, 'Describe both.' He replied: 'I put off the coat (*qabá*) and wear a patched frock and practise the conduct appropriate to that garment, in order that I may become a Ṣúfí and refrain from sin because of the shame that I feel before God; but you put off the patched frock in order that you may not be deceived by men, and that men may not be deceived by thee: accordingly, my generosity is formal observance of the religious law, while your generosity is spiritual observance of the Truth.'" This is a very sound principle.

3. The Ṭayfúrís.

They are the followers of Abú Yazíd Ṭayfúr b. Ísá b. Surúshán al-Bisṭámí, a great and eminent Ṣúfí. His doctrine is rapture (*ghalabat*) and intoxication (*sukr*). Rapturous longing for God and intoxication of love cannot be acquired by human beings, and it is idle to claim, and absurd to imitate, anything that lies beyond the range of acquisition. Intoxication is not an attribute of the sober, and Man has no power of drawing it to himself. The intoxicated man is enraptured and pays no heed to created things, that he should manifest any quality involving conscious effort (*taklíf*). The Ṣúfí Shaykhs are agreed that no one is a proper model for others unless he is steadfast (*mustaqím*) and has escaped from the circle of "states"; but there are some who allow that the way of rapture and intoxication may be trodden with effort, because the Apostle said: "Weep, or else make as though ye wept!" Now, to imitate others for the sake of ostentation is sheer polytheism, but it is different when the object of the imitator is that God may perchance raise him to the rank of those whom he has imitated, in accordance with the saying of the Apostle: "Whoever makes himself like unto a people is one of them." And one of the Shaykhs said: "Contemplations (*musháhadát*) are the result of mortifications (*mujáhadát*)." My own view is that, although mortifications are always excellent, intoxication and rapture cannot be acquired at all; hence they cannot be induced by mortifications, which in themselves never become a cause of intoxication. I will now set forth the different opinions of the Shaykhs concerning the true nature of intoxication (*sukr*) and sobriety (*ṣaḥw*), in order that difficulties may be removed.

Discourse on Intoxication and Sobriety.

You must know that "intoxication" and "rapture" are terms used by spiritualists to denote the rapture of love for God, while the term "sobriety" expresses the attainment of that which is desired. Some place the former above the latter, and some hold the latter to be superior. Abú Yazíd and his followers prefer intoxication to sobriety. They say that sobriety involves the fixity and equilibrium of human attributes, which are the greatest veil between God and Man, whereas intoxication involves the destruction of human attributes, like foresight and choice, and the annihilation of a man's self-control in God, so that only those faculties survive in him that do not belong to the human *genus*; and they are the most complete and perfect. Thus David was in the state of sobriety; an act proceeded from him which God attributed to him and said, "*David killed Goliath*" (Kor. ii, 252): but our Apostle was in the state of intoxication; an act proceeded from him which God attributed to Himself and said, "*Thou didst not throw, when thou threwest, but God threw*" (Kor. viii, 17). How great is the difference between these two men! The attribution of a man's act to God is better than the attribution of God's act to a man, for in the latter case the man stands by himself, while in the former case he stands through God.

Junayd and his followers prefer sobriety to intoxication. They say that intoxication is evil, because it involves the disturbance of one's normal state and loss of sanity and self-control; and inasmuch as the principle of all things is sought either by way of annihilation or subsistence, or of effacement or affirmation, the principle of verification cannot be attained unless the seeker is sane. Blindness will never release anyone from the bondage and corruption of phenomena. The fact that people remain in phenomena and forget God is due to their not seeing things as they really are; for if they saw, they would escape. Seeing is of two kinds: he who looks at anything sees it either with the eye of subsistence (*baqá*) or with the eye of annihilation (*faná*). If with the eye of subsistence, he perceives that the whole universe is imperfect in comparison with his own subsistence, for he does not regard phenomena as self-subsistent; and if he looks with the eye of annihilation, he perceives that all created things are non-existent beside the subsistence of God. In either case he turns away from created things. On this account the Apostle said in his prayer: "O God, show us things as they are," because whoever thus sees them finds rest. Now, such vision cannot be properly attained except in the state of sobriety, and the intoxicated have no knowledge thereof. For example, Moses was intoxicated; he could not endure the manifestation of one epiphany, but fell in a swoon (Kor. vii, 139): but our Apostle was sober; he beheld the same glory continuously, with ever-increasing consciousness, all the way from Mecca, until he stood at the space of two bow-lengths from the Divine presence (Kor. liii, 9).

My Shaykh, who followed the doctrine of Junayd, used to say that intoxication is the playground of children, but sobriety is the death-field of men. I say, in agreement with my Shaykh, that the perfection of the state of the intoxicated man is sobriety. The lowest stage in sobriety consists in regarding the powerlessness of humanity: therefore, a sobriety that appears to be evil is better than an intoxication that is really evil. It is related that Abú 'Uthmán Maghribí, in the earlier part of his life, passed twenty years in retirement, living in deserts where he never heard the sound of a human voice, until his frame was wasted and his eyes became as small as the eye of a sack-needle. After twenty years he was commanded to associate with mankind. He resolved to begin with the people of God who dwelt beside His Temple, since by doing so he would gain a greater blessing. The Shaykhs of Mecca were aware of his coming and went forth to meet him. Finding him so changed that he hardly seemed to be a human creature, they said to him: "O Abú 'Uthmán, tell us why you went and what you saw and what you gained and wherefore you have come back." He replied: "I went because of intoxication, and I saw the evil of intoxication, and I gained despair, and I have come back on account of weakness." All the Shaykhs said: "O Abú 'Uthmán, it is not lawful for anyone after you to explain the meaning of sobriety and intoxication, for you have done justice to the whole matter and have shown forth the evil of intoxication."

Intoxication, then, is to fancy one's self annihilated while the attributes really subsist; and this is a veil. Sobriety, on the other hand, is the vision of subsistence while the attributes are annihilated; and this is actual revelation. It is absurd for anyone to suppose that intoxication is nearer to annihilation than sobriety is, for intoxication is a quality that exceeds sobriety, and so long as a man's attributes tend to increase he is without knowledge; but when he begins to diminish them, seekers (of God) have some hope of him.

It is related that Yaḥyá b. Mu'ádh wrote to Abú Yazíd: "What do you say of one who drinks a single drop of the ocean of love and becomes intoxicated?" Báyazíd wrote in reply: "What do you say of one who, if all the oceans in the world were filled with the wine of love, would drink them all and still cry for more to slake his thirst?" People imagine that Yaḥyá was speaking of intoxication, and Báyazíd of sobriety, but the opposite is the case. The man of sobriety is he who is unable to drink even one drop, and the man of intoxication is he who drinks all and still desires more. Wine being the instrument of intoxication, but the enemy of sobriety, intoxication demands what is homogeneous with itself, whereas sobriety takes no pleasure in drinking.

There are two kinds of intoxication: (1) with the wine of affection (*mawaddat*) and (2) with the cup of love (*maḥabbat*). The former is "caused" (*ma'lúl*), since it arises from regarding the benefit (*ni'mat*); but the latter has no cause, since it arises from regarding the benefactor (*mun'im*). He who regards the benefit sees through himself and therefore sees himself, but he who regards the benefactor sees through Him and therefore does not see himself, so that, although he is intoxicated, his intoxication is sobriety.

Sobriety also is of two kinds: sobriety in heedlessness (*ghaflat*) and sobriety in love (*maḥabbat*). The former is the greatest of veils, but the latter is the clearest of revelations.

The sobriety that is connected with heedlessness is really intoxication, while that which is linked with love, although it be intoxication, is really sobriety. When the principle (*aṣl*) is firmly established, sobriety and intoxication resemble one another, but when the principle is wanting, both are baseless. In short, where true mystics tread, sobriety and intoxication are the effect of difference (*ikhtiláf*), and when the Sultan of Truth displays his beauty, both sobriety and intoxication appear to be intruders (*ṭufaylí*), because the boundaries of both are joined, and the end of the one is the beginning of the other, and beginning and end are terms that imply separation, which has only a relative existence. In union all separations are negated, as the poet says—

"*When the morning-star of wine rises,*
The drunken and the sober are as one."

At Sarakhs there were two spiritual directors, namely, Luqmán and Abu 'l-Faḍl Ḥasan. One day Luqmán came to Abu 'l-Faḍl and found him with a piece (of manuscript) in his hand. He said: "O Abu 'l-Faḍl, what are you seeking in this paper?" Abu 'l-Faḍl replied: "The same thing as you are seeking without a paper." Luqmán said: "Then why this difference?" Abu 'l-Faḍl answered: "You see a difference when you ask me what I am seeking. Become sober from intoxication and get rid of sobriety, in order that the difference may be removed from you and that you may know what you and I are in search of."

The Ṭayfúrís and Junaydís are at variance to the extent which has been indicated. As regards ethics, the doctrine of Báyazíd consists in shunning companionship and choosing retirement from the world, and he enjoined all his disciples to do the same. This is a praiseworthy and laudable Path.

4. The Junaydís.

They are the followers of Abu 'l-Qásim al-Junayd b. Muḥammad, who in his time was called the Peacock of the

Divines (*Ṭá'ús al-'Ulamá*). He is the chief of this sect and the Imám of their Imáms. His doctrine is based on sobriety and is opposed to that of the Ṭayfúrís, as has been explained. It is the best known and most celebrated of all doctrines, and all the Shaykhs have adopted it, notwithstanding that there is much difference in their sayings on the ethics of Ṣúfiism. Want of space forbids me to discuss it further in this book: those who wish to become better acquainted with it must seek information elsewhere.

I have read in the Anecdotes that when Ḥusayn b. Manṣúr (al-Ḥalláj) in his rapture broke off all relations with 'Amr b. 'Uthmán (al-Makkí) and came to Junayd, Junayd asked him for what purpose he had come to him. Ḥusayn said: "For the purpose of associating with the Shaykh." Junayd replied: "I do not associate with madmen. Association demands sanity; if that is wanting, the result is such behaviour as yours in regard to Sahl b. 'Abdalláh Tustarí and 'Amr." Ḥusayn said: "O Shaykh, sobriety and intoxication are two attributes of Man, and Man is veiled from his Lord until his attributes are annihilated." "O son of Manṣúr," said Junayd, "you are in error concerning sobriety and intoxication. The former denotes soundness of one's spiritual state in relation to God, while the latter denotes excess of longing and extremity of love, and neither of them can be acquired by human effort. O son of Manṣúr, in your words I see much foolishness and nonsense."

5. THE NÚRÍS.

They are the followers of Abu 'l-Ḥasan Aḥmad b. Muḥammad Núrí, one of the most eminent and illustrious Ṣúfí divines. The principle of his doctrine is to regard Ṣúfiism (*taṣawwuf*) as superior to poverty (*faqr*). In matters of conduct he agrees with Junayd. It is a peculiarity of his "path" that in companionship (*ṣuḥbat*) he prefers his companion's claim to his own, and holds companionship without preference (*íthár*) to be unlawful. He also holds that companionship is obligatory on dervishes, and that retirement (*'uzlat*) is not praiseworthy, and that everyone is bound to prefer his companion to himself. It is related that he said: "Beware of retirement! for it is in connexion with Satan; and cleave to companionship, for therein is the satisfaction of the Merciful God."

Now I will explain the true nature of preference, and when I come to the chapter on companionship and retirement I will set forth the mysteries of the subject in order to make it more generally instructive.

Discourse on Preference (íthár).

God said: "*And they prefer them to themselves, although they are indigent*" (Kor. lix, 9). This verse was revealed concerning the poor men among the Companions in particular. The true nature of preference consists in maintaining the rights of the person with whom one associates, and in subordinating one's own interest to the interest of one's friend, and in taking trouble upon one's self for the sake of promoting his happiness, because preference is the rendering of help to others, and the putting into practice of that which God commanded to His Apostle: "*Use indulgence and command what is just and turn away from the ignorant*" (Kor. vii, 198). This will be explained more fully in the chapter on the rules of companionship.

Now, preference is of two kinds: firstly, in companionship, as has been mentioned; and secondly, in love. In preferring the claim of one's companion there is a sort of trouble and effort, but in preferring the claim of one's beloved there is nothing but pleasure and delight. It is well known that when Ghulám al-Khalíl persecuted the Ṣúfís, Núrí and Raqqám and Abú Ḥamza were arrested and conveyed to the Caliph's palace. Ghulám al-Khalíl urged the Caliph to put them to death, saying that they were heretics (*zanádiqa*), and the Caliph immediately gave orders for their execution. When the executioner approached Raqqám, Núrí rose and offered himself in Raqqám's place with the utmost cheerfulness and submission. All the spectators were astounded. The executioner said:

"O young man, the sword is not a thing that people desire to meet so eagerly as you have welcomed it; and your turn has not yet arrived." Núrí answered: "Yes; my doctrine is founded on preference. Life is the most precious thing in the world: I wish to sacrifice for my brethren's sake the few moments that remain. In my opinion, one moment of this world is better than a thousand years of the next world, because this is the place of service (*khidmat*) and that is the place of proximity (*qurbat*), and proximity is gained by service." The tenderness of Núrí and the fineness of his saying astonished the Caliph (who was informed by a courier of what had passed) to such a degree, that he suspended the execution of the three Ṣúfís and charged the chief Cadi, Abu 'l-'Abbás b. 'Alí, to inquire into the matter. The Cadi, having taken them to his house and questioned them concerning the ordinances of the Law and the Truth, found them perfect, and felt remorse for his indifference to their fate. Then Núrí said: "O Cadi, though you have asked all these questions, you have not yet asked anything to the point, for God has servants who eat through Him, and drink through Him, and sit through Him, and live through Him, and abide in contemplation of Him: if they were cut off from contemplating Him they would cry out in anguish." The Cadi was amazed at the subtlety of his speech and the soundness of his state. He wrote to the Caliph: "If the Ṣúfís are heretics, who in the world is a Unitarian?" The Caliph called them to his presence and said: "Ask a boon." They replied: "The only boon we ask of thee is that thou shouldst forget us, and neither make us thy favourites nor banish us from thy court, for thy favour and displeasure are alike to us." The Caliph wept and dismissed them with honour.

It is related that Náfi'[1] said: "Ibn 'Umar[2] desired to eat a fish. I sought through the town, but did not find one until several days had passed. Having procured it, I gave orders

[1] A well-known traditionist, who died about 120 A.H.

[2] 'Abdalláh, son of the Caliph 'Umar.

that it should be placed on a cake of bread and presented it to him. I noticed an expression of joy on his face as he received it, but suddenly a beggar came to the door of his house and he ordered the fish to be given to him. The servant said: 'O master, you have been desiring a fish for several days; let us give the beggar something else.' Ibn 'Umar replied: 'This fish is unlawful to me, for I have put it out of my mind on account of a Tradition which I heard from the Apostle: *Whenever anyone feels a desire and repels it and prefers another to himself, he shall be forgiven.*'"

I have read in the Anecdotes that ten dervishes lost their way in the desert and were overtaken by thirst. They had only one cup of water, and everyone preferred the claim of the others, so that none of them would drink and they all died except one, who then drank it and found strength to escape. Some person said to him: "Had you not drunk, it would have been better." He replied: "The Law obliged me to drink; if I had not, I should have killed myself and been punished on that account." The other said: "Then did your friends kill themselves?" "No," said the dervish; "they refused to drink in order that their companions might drink, but when I alone survived I was legally obliged to drink."[1]

Among the Israelites there was a devotee who had served God for four hundred years. One day he said: "O Lord, if Thou hadst not created these mountains, wandering for religion's sake (*siyáḥat*) would have been easier for Thy servants." The Divine command came to the Apostle of that time to say to the devotee: "What business have you to interfere in My kingdom? Now, since you have interfered, I blot your name from the register of the blest and inscribe it in the register of the damned." On hearing this, the devotee trembled with joy and bowed to the ground in thanksgiving. The Apostle

[1] Here follow two stories illustrating the same topic: the first relates how 'Alí slept in the Prophet's bed on the night of the latter's emigration from Mecca, when the infidels were seeking to slay him; the second, how on the battle-field of Uḥud the wounded Moslems, though parched with thirst, preferred to die rather than drink the water which their comrades asked for.

said: "O fool, it is not necessary to bow down in thanksgiving for damnation." "My thanksgiving," the devotee replied: "is not for damnation, but because my name is at least inscribed in one of His registers. But, O Apostle, I have a boon to ask. Say unto God, 'Since Thou wilt send me to Hell, make me so large that I may take the place of all sinful Unitarians, and let them go to Paradise.'" God commanded the Apostle to tell the devotee that the probation which he had undergone was not for the purpose of humiliating him, but to reveal him to the people, and that on the Day of Resurrection both he and those for whom he had interceded would be in Paradise.

I asked Aḥmad Ḥammádí of Sarakhs what was the beginning of his conversion. He replied: "Once I set out from Sarakhs and took my camels into the desert and stayed there for a considerable time. I was always wishing to be hungry and was giving my portion of food to others, and the words of God—"*They prefer them to themselves, although they are indigent*" (Kor. lix, 9)—were ever fresh in my mind; and I had a firm belief in the Ṣúfís. One day a hungry lion came from the desert and killed one of my camels and retired to some rising ground and roared. All the wild beasts in the neighbourhood, hearing him roar, gathered round him. He tore the camel to pieces and went back to the higher ground without having eaten anything. The other beasts—foxes, jackals, wolves, etc.—began to eat, and the lion waited until they had gone away. Then he approached in order to eat a morsel, but seeing a lame fox in the distance he withdrew once more until the new-comer had eaten his fill. After that, he came and ate a morsel. As he departed he spoke to me, who had been watching from afar, and said: 'O Aḥmad, to prefer others to one's self in the matter of food is an act only worthy of dogs: a *man* sacrifices his life and his soul.' When I saw this evidence I renounced all worldly occupations, and that was the beginning of my conversion."

Ja'far Khuldí says: "One day, when Abu 'l-Ḥasan Núrí was praying to God in solitude I went to overhear him, for he was very eloquent. He was saying, 'O Lord, in Thy eternal knowledge and power and will Thou dost punish the people of Hell, whom Thou hast created; and if it be Thy inexorable will to make Hell full of mankind, Thou art able to fill that Hell and all its limbos with me alone and to send them to Paradise.' I was amazed by his speech, but I dreamed that some one came to me and said: 'God bids thee tell Abu 'l-Ḥasan that he has been forgiven on account of his compassion for God's creatures and his reverence for God.'"

He was called Núrí because when he spoke in a dark room the whole room was illuminated by the light (*núr*) of his spirituality. And by the light of the Truth he used to read the inmost thoughts of his disciples, so that Junayd said: "Abu 'l-Ḥasan is the spy on men's hearts (*jásús al-qulúb*)."

This is his peculiar doctrine. It is a sound principle, and one of great importance in the eyes of those who have insight. Nothing is harder to a man than spiritual sacrifice (*badhl-i rúḥ*) and to refrain from the object of his love, and God hath made this sacrifice the key of all good, as He said: "*Ye shall never attain to righteousness until ye give in alms of that which ye love*" (Kor. iii, 86). When a man's spirit is sacrificed, of what value are his wealth and his health and his frock and his food? This is the foundation of Ṣúfiism. Some one came to Ruwaym and asked him for direction. Ruwaym said: "O my son, the whole affair consists in spiritual sacrifice. If you are able for this, it is well; if not, do not occupy yourself with the futilities (*turrahát*) of the Ṣúfís," i.e. all except this is futile; and God said: "*Do not call dead those who are slain in the way of God. Nay, they are living*" (Kor. ii, 149). Eternal life is gained by spiritual sacrifice and by renunciation of self-interest in fulfilling God's commandment and by obedience to His friends. But from the standpoint of gnosis (*ma'rifat*) preference and free choice are separation (*tafriqat*), and real preference consists in union with God, for the true basis of self-interest is self-abandonment. So long as the seeker's progress is connected with acquisition (*kasb*) it is pernicious, but when the attracting influence (*jadhb*) of the Truth manifests its dominion all his actions are confounded, and he loses all power of expression; nor can any name be applied to him or any description be given of him or anything be imputed to him. On this subject Shiblí says in verse—

> "*I am lost to myself and unconscious,*
> *And my attributes are annihilated.*
> *To-day I am lost to all things:*
> *Naught remains but a forced expression.*"

6. THE SAHLÍS.

They are the followers of Sahl b. 'Abdalláh of Tustar, a great and venerable Ṣúfí, who has been already mentioned. His doctrine inculcates endeavour and self-mortification and ascetic training, and he used to bring his disciples to perfection in self-mortification (*mujáhadat*). It is related in a well-known anecdote that he said to one of his disciples: "Strive to say continuously for one day, 'O Allah! O Allah! O Allah!' and do the same next day and the day after that," until he became habituated to saying those words. Then he bade him repeat them at night also, until they became so familiar that he uttered them even during his sleep. Then he said: "Do not repeat them any more, but let all your faculties be engrossed in remembering God." The disciple did this, until he became absorbed in the thought of God. One day, when he was in his house, a piece of wood fell on his head and broke it. The drops of blood which trickled to the ground bore the legend "Allah! Allah! Allah!"

The "path" of the Sahlís is to educate disciples by acts of self-mortification and austerities; that of the Ḥamdúnís[1] is to serve and reverence dervishes; and that of the Junaydís is to keep watch over one's spiritual state (*muráqaba-i báṭin*).

[1] The followers of Ḥamdún al-Qaṣṣár, who are generally called Qaṣṣárís.

The object of all austerities and acts of self-mortification is resistance to the lower soul (*nafs*), and until a man knows his lower soul his austerities are of no use to him. Now, therefore, I will explain the knowledge and true nature of the lower soul, and in the next place I will lay down the doctrine concerning self-mortification and its principles.

Discourse touching the true nature of the Lower Soul (nafs) *and the meaning of Passion* (hawá).

You must know that *nafs*, etymologically, is the essence and reality of anything, but in popular language it is used to denote many contradictory meanings, e.g. "spirit", "virility" (*muruwwat*), "body", and "blood". The mystics of this sect, however, are agreed that it is the source and principle of evil, but while some assert that it is a substance (*'ayn*) located in the body, as the spirit (*rúḥ*) is, others hold it to be an attribute of the body, as life is. But they all agree that through it base qualities are manifested and that it is the immediate cause of blameworthy actions. Such actions are of two kinds, namely, sins (*ma'áṣí*) and base qualities (*akhláq-i daní*), like pride, envy, avarice, anger, hatred, etc., which are not commendable in law and reason. These qualities can be removed by discipline (*riyáḍat*): e.g., sins are removed by repentance. Sins belong to the class of external attributes, whereas the qualities above mentioned belong to the class of internal attributes. Similarly, discipline is an external act, and repentance is an internal attribute. A base quality that appears *within* is purged by excellent outward attributes, and one that appears *without* is purged by laudable inward attributes. Both the lower soul and the spirit are subtle things (*laṭá'if*) existing in the body, just as devils and angels and Paradise and Hell exist in the universe; but the one is the seat of good, while the other is the seat of evil. Hence, resistance to the lower soul is the chief of all acts of devotion and the crown of all acts of self-mortification, and only thereby can Man find the way to

God, because submission to the lower soul involves his destruction and resistance to it involves his salvation.[1]

Now, every attribute needs an object whereby it subsists, and knowledge of that attribute, namely, the soul, is not attained save by knowledge of the whole body, which knowledge in turn demands an explanation of the qualities of human nature (*insániyyat*) and the mystery thereof, and is incumbent upon all seekers of the Truth, because whoever is ignorant of himself is yet more ignorant of other things; and inasmuch as a man is bound to know God, he must first know himself, in order that by rightly perceiving his own temporality he may recognize the eternity of God, and may learn the everlastingness of God through his own perishableness. The Apostle said: "He who knows himself already knows his Lord," i.e., if he knows himself as perishable he knows God as everlasting, or if he knows himself as humble he knows God as Almighty, or if he knows himself as a servant he knows God as the Lord. Therefore one who does not know himself is debarred from knowledge of all things.

As regards the knowledge of human nature and the various opinions held on that topic, some Moslems assert that Man is nothing but spirit (*rúḥ*), of which this body is the cuirass and temple and residence, in order to preserve it from being injured by the natural humours (*ṭabáyi'*), and of which the attributes are sensation and intelligence. This view is false, because a body from which the soul (*ján*) has departed is still called "a human being" (*insán*); if the soul is joined with it it is "a live human being", and if the soul is gone it is "a dead human being". Moreover, a soul is located in the bodies of animals, yet they are not called "human beings". If the spirit (*rúḥ*) were the cause of human nature, it would follow that

[1] Here the author cites Kor. lxxix, 40, 41; ii, 81 (part of the verse); xii, 53; and the Traditions: "When God wishes well unto His servant He causes him to see the faults of his soul," and "God said to David, 'O David, hate thy soul, for My love depends on thy hatred of it.'"

the principle of human nature must exist in every creature possessed of a soul (*ján-dárí*); which is a proof of the falsity of their assertion. Others, again, have stated that the term "human nature" is applicable to the spirit and the body together, and that it no longer applies when one is separated from the other; e.g., when two colours, black and white, are combined on a horse, it is called "piebald" (*ablaq*), whereas the same colours, apart from each other, are called "black" and "white". This too is false, in accordance with God's word: "*Did there not come over Man a space of time during which he was not a thing worthy of mention?*" (Kor. lxxvi, 1): in this verse Man's clay, without soul—for the soul had not yet been joined to his body—is called "Man". Others aver that "Man" is an atom, centred in the heart, which is the principle of all human attributes. This also is absurd, for if anyone is killed and his heart is taken out of his body he does not lose the name of "human being"; moreover, it is agreed that the heart was not in the human body before the soul. Some pretenders to Ṣúfiism have fallen into error on this subject. They declare that "Man" is not that which eats and drinks and suffers decay, but a Divine mystery, of which this body is the vesture, situated in the interfusion of the natural humours (*imtizáj-i ṭab'*) and in the union (*ittiḥád*) of body and spirit. To this I reply, that by universal consent the name of "human being" belongs to sane men and mad, and to infidels and immoral and ignorant persons, in whom there is no such "mystery" and who suffer decay and eat and drink; and that there is not anything called "Man" in the body, either while it exists or after it has ceased to exist. God Almighty has given the name of "Man" to the sum of the substances which He compounded in us, excluding those things which are not to be found in some human beings, e.g. in the verses "*And We have created Man of the choicest clay,*" etc. (Kor. xxiii, 12–14). Therefore, according to the word of God, who is the most veracious of all who speak the Truth, this particular form, with all its ingredients and with all the changes which it undergoes, is "Man". In like manner, certain Sunnís have said that Man is a living creature whose form has these characteristics, and that death does not deprive him of this name, and that he is endowed with a definite physiognomy (*ṣúrat-i ma'húd*) and a distinct organ (*álat-i mawsúm*) both externally and internally. By "a definite physiognomy" they mean that he has either good or ill health, and by "a distinct organ" that he is either mad or sane. It is generally allowed that the more sound (*ṣaḥíḥ*) a thing is, the more perfect it is in constitution. You must know, then, that in the opinion of mystics the most perfect composition of Man includes three elements, viz. spirit, soul, and body; and that each of these has an attribute which subsists therein, the attribute of spirit being intelligence, of soul, passion, and of body, sensation. Man is a type of the whole universe. The universe is the name of the two worlds, and in Man there is a vestige of both, for he is composed of phlegm, blood, bile, and melancholy, which four humours correspond to the four elements of this world, viz. water, earth, air, and fire, while his soul (*ján*), his lower soul (*nafs*), and his body correspond to Paradise, Hell, and the place of Resurrection. Paradise is the effect of God's satisfaction, and Hell is the result of His anger. Similarly, the spirit of the true believer reflects the peace of knowledge, and his lower soul the error which veils him from God. As, at the Resurrection, the believer must be released from Hell before he can reach Paradise and attain to real vision and pure love, so in this world he must escape from his lower soul before he can attain to real discipleship (*irádat*), of which the spirit is the principle, and to real proximity (to God) and gnosis. Hence, whoever knows Him in this world and turns away from all besides and follows the highway of the sacred law, at the Resurrection he will not see Hell and the Bridge (*Ṣirát*). In short, the believer's spirit calls him to Paradise, of which it is a type in this world, and his lower soul calls him to Hell, of which it is a type in this world. Therefore it behoves those who seek God never to relax their resistance to the lower soul, in order that thereby they may reinforce the spirit and the intelligence, which are the home of the Divine mystery.

SECTION.

As regards what has been said by the Shaykhs concerning the lower soul, Dhu 'l-Nún the Egyptian says: "Vision of the lower soul and its promptings is the worst of veils," because obedience to it is disobedience to God, which is the origin of all veils. Abú Yazíd Bisṭámí says: "The lower soul is an attribute which never rests save in falsehood," i.e. it never seeks the Truth. Muḥammad b. 'Alí al-Tirmidhí says: "You wish to know God while your lower soul subsists in you; but your lower soul does not know itself, how should it know another?" Junayd says: "To fulfil the desires of your lower soul is the foundation of infidelity," because the lower soul is not connected with, and is always striving to turn away from, the pure truth of Islam; and he who turns away denies, and he who denies is an alien (*bégána*). Abú Sulaymán Dárání says: "The lower soul is treacherous and hindering (one who seeks to please God); and resistance to it is the best of actions."

Now I come to my main purpose, which is to set forth the doctrine of Sahl concerning the mortification and discipline of the lower soul, and to explain its true nature.

Discourse on the Mortification of the Lower Soul.

God has said: "*Those who strive to the utmost* (jáhadú) *for Our sake, We will guide them into Our ways*" (Kor. xxix, 69). And the Prophet said: "The (*mujáhid*) is he who struggles with all his might against himself (*jáhada nafsahu*) for God's sake." And he also said: "We have returned from the lesser war (*al-jihád al-aṣghar*) to the greater war (*al-jihád al-akbar*). On being asked, "What is the greater war?" he replied, "It is the struggle against one's self" (*mujáhadat al-nafs*). Thus the Apostle adjudged the mortification of the lower soul to be superior to the Holy War against unbelievers, because the former is more painful. You must know, then, that the way of mortification is plain and manifest, for it is approved by men of all religions and sects, and is observed and practised by the Ṣúfís in particular; and the term "mortification" (*mujáhadat*) is current among Ṣúfís of every class, and the Shaykhs have uttered many sayings on this topic. Sahl b. 'Abdalláh Tustarí carries the principle to an extreme point. It is related that he used to break his fast only once in fifteen days, and he ate but little food in the course of his long life. While all mystics have affirmed the need of mortification, and have declared it to be an indirect means (*asbáb*) of attaining contemplation (*musháhadat*), Sahl asserted that mortification is the direct cause (*'illat*) of the latter, and he attributed to search (*ṭalab*) a powerful effect on attainment (*yáft*), so that he even regarded the present life, spent in search, as superior to the future life of fruition. "If," he said, "you serve God in this world, you will attain proximity to Him in the next world: without that service there would not be this proximity: it follows that self-mortification, practised with the aid of God, is the direct cause of union with God." Others, on the contrary, hold that there is no direct cause of union with God, and whoever attains to God does so by Divine grace (*faḍl*), which is independent of human actions. Therefore, they argue, the object of mortification is to correct the vices of the lower soul, not to attain real proximity, and inasmuch as mortification is referred to Man, while contemplation is referred to God, it is impossible that one should be caused by the other. Sahl, however, cites in favour of his view the words of God: "*Those who strive to the utmost for Our sake, We will guide them into Our ways*" (Kor. xxix, 69), i.e. whoever mortifies himself will attain to contemplation. Furthermore, he contends that inasmuch as the books revealed to the Prophets, and the Sacred Law, and all the religious ordinances imposed on mankind involve mortification, they must all be false and vain if mortification were not the cause of contemplation. Again, both in this world and the next, everything is connected with principles and causes. If it is maintained that principles have no causes, there is an end of all law and order: neither can religious obligations be justified nor will food be the cause of repletion and clothes the cause of warmth. Accordingly, to regard actions as being caused is Unification (*tawḥíd*), and to rebut this is Nullification (*ta'ṭíl*). He who asserts it is proving the existence of contemplation, and he who denies it is denying the existence of contemplation. Does not training (*riyáḍat*) alter the animal qualities of a wild horse and substitute human qualities in their stead, so that he will pick up a whip from the ground and give it to his master, or will roll a ball with his foot? In the same way, a boy without sense and of foreign race is taught by training to speak Arabic, and take a new language in exchange for his mother tongue; and a savage beast is trained to go away when leave is given to it, and to come back when it is called, preferring captivity to freedom.[1] Therefore, Sahl and his followers argue, mortification is just as necessary for the attainment of union with God as diction and composition are necessary for the elucidation of ideas; and as one is led to knowledge of the Creator by assurance that the universe was created in time, so one is led to union with God by knowledge and mortification of the lower soul.

I will now state the arguments of the opposing party. They maintain that the verse of the Koran (xxix, 69) cited by Sahl is a *hysteron proteron*, and that the meaning of it is, "Those whom We guide into Our ways strive to the utmost for Our sake." And the Apostle said: "Not one of you shall be saved by his works." "O Apostle," they cried, "not even thou?" "Not even I," he said, "unless God encompass me with His mercy." Now, mortification is a man's act, and his act cannot possibly become the cause of his salvation, which depends on the Divine Will, as God hath said: "*Whomsoever God wishes to lead aright, He will open his breast to receive*

[1] Here follows an account of the mortification which the Prophet imposed on himself.

Islam, but whomsoever He wishes to lead astray, He will make his breast strait and narrow" (Kor. vi, 125). By affirming His will, He denies the (effect of the) religious ordinances which have been laid upon mankind. If mortification were the cause of union Iblís would not have been damned, or if neglect of mortification were the cause of damnation Adam would never have been blessed. The result hangs on predestined grace (*'ináyat*), not on abundance of mortification. It is not the case that he who most exerts himself is the most secure, but that he who has most grace is nearest to God. A monk worshipping in his cell may be far from God, and a sinner in the tavern may be near to Him. The noblest thing in the world is the faith of a child who is not subject to the religious law (*mukallaf*) and in this respect belongs to the same category as madmen: if, then, mortification is not the cause of the noblest of all gifts, no cause is necessary for anything that is inferior.

I, 'Alí b. 'Uthmán al-Jullábí, say that the difference between the two parties in this controversy lies in expression (*'ibárat*). One says, "He who seeks shall find," and the other says, "He who finds shall seek." Seeking is the cause of finding, but it is no less true that finding is the cause of seeking. The one party practises mortification for the purpose of attaining contemplation, and the other party practises contemplation for the purpose of attaining mortification. The fact is that mortification stands in the same relation to contemplation as Divine blessing (*tawfíq*), which is a gift from God, to obedience (*ṭá'at*): as it is absurd to seek obedience without Divine blessing, so it is absurd to seek Divine blessing without obedience, and as there can be no mortification without contemplation, so there can be no contemplation without mortification. Man is guided to mortification by a flash of the Divine Beauty, and inasmuch as that flash is the cause of the existence of mortification, Divine guidance (*hidáyat*) precedes mortification.

Now, as regards the argument of Sahl and his followers

that failure to affirm mortification involves the denial of all the religious ordinances which have come down in the books revealed to the Prophets, this statement requires correction. Religious obligations (*taklíf*) depend on Divine guidance (*hidáyat*), and acts of mortification only serve to affirm the proofs of God, not to effect real union with Him. God has said: "*And though We had sent down the angels unto them and the dead had spoken unto them and We had gathered before them all things together, they would not have believed unless God had so willed*" (Kor. vi, 111), for the cause of belief is Our will, not evidences or mortification. Accordingly, the revelations of the Prophets and the ordinances of religion are a means (*asbáb*) of attaining to union, but are not the cause (*'illat*) of union. So far as religious obligations are concerned, Abú Bakr was in the same position as Abú Jahl, but Abú Bakr, having justice and grace, attained, whereas Abú Jahl, having justice without grace, failed. Therefore the cause of attainment is attainment itself, not the act of seeking attainment, for if the seeker were one with the object sought the seeker would be one, and in that case he would not be a seeker, because he who has attained is at rest, which the seeker cannot be.

Again, in reference to their argument that the qualities of a horse are altered by mortification, you must know that mortification is only a means of bringing out qualities that are already latent in the horse but do not appear until he has been trained. Mortification will never turn a donkey into a horse or a horse into a donkey, because this involves a change of identity; and since mortification has not the power of transforming identity it cannot possibly be affirmed in the presence of God.

Over that spiritual director, namely, Sahl, there used to pass a mortification of which he was independent and which, while he was in the reality thereof, he was unable to express in words. He was not like some who have made it their religion to talk about mortification without practising it. How absurd that what ought to consist wholly in action should become nothing but words! In short, the Ṣúfís are unanimous in recognizing the existence of mortification and discipline, but hold that it is wrong to pay regard to them. Those who deny mortification do not mean to deny its reality, but only to deny that any regard should be paid to it or that anyone should be pleased with his own actions in the place of holiness, inasmuch as mortification is the act of Man, while contemplation is a state in which one is kept by God, and a man's actions do not begin to have value until God keeps him thus. The mortification of those whom God loves is the work of God in them without choice on their part: it overwhelms and melts them away; but the mortification of ignorant men is the work of themselves in themselves by their own choice: it perturbs and distresses them, and distress is due to evil. Therefore, do not speak of thine own actions while thou canst avoid it, and never in any circumstances follow thy lower soul, for it is thy phenomenal being that veils thee from God. If thou wert veiled by one act alone, thou mightest be unveiled by another, but since thy whole being is a veil thou wilt not become worthy of subsistence (*baqá*) until thou art wholly annihilated. It is related in a well-known anecdote that Ḥusayn b. Manṣúr (al-Ḥalláj) came to Kúfa and lodged in the house of Muḥammad b. al-Ḥusayn al-'Alawí. Ibráhím Khawwáṣ also came to Kúfa, and, having heard of al-Ḥalláj, went to see him. Al-Ḥalláj said: "O Ibráhím, during these forty years of your connexion with Ṣúfiism, what have you gained from it?" Ibráhím answered: "I have made the doctrine of trust in God (*tawakkul*) peculiarly my own." Al-Ḥalláj said: "You have wasted your life in cultivating your spiritual nature: what has become of annihilation in Unification (*al-faná fí 'l-tawḥíd*)?" i.e. "trust in God is a term denoting your conduct towards God and your spiritual excellence in regard to relying on Him: if a man spends his whole life in remedying his spiritual nature, he will need another life for remedying his material nature, and his life will be lost before he has found a trace or vestige of God". And a story is told of Shaykh Abú 'Alí Siyáh of Merv, that he said: "I saw my lower soul in a form resembling my own, and some one had seized it by its hair and gave it into my hands. I bound it to a tree and was about to destroy it, when it cried out, 'O Abú 'Alí, do not trouble yourself. I am God's army (*lashkar-i khudáyam*): you cannot reduce me to naught.'" And it is related concerning Muḥammad b. 'Ulyán of Nasá, an eminent companion of Junayd, that he said: "In my novitiate, when I had become aware of the corruptions of the lower soul and acquainted with its places of ambush, I always felt a violent hatred of it in my heart. One day something like a young fox came forth from my throat, and God caused me to know that it was my lower soul. I cast it under my feet, and at every kick that I gave it, it grew bigger. I said: 'Other things are destroyed by pain and blows: why dost thou increase?' It replied: 'Because I was created perverse: that which is pain to other things is pleasure to me, and their pleasure is my pain.'" Shaykh Abu 'l-'Abbás Shaqání, who was the Imám of his time, said: "One day I came into my house and found a yellow dog lying there, asleep. Thinking it had come in from the street, I was about to turn it out. It crept under my skirt and vanished." Shaykh Abu 'l-Qásim Gurgání, who to-day is the Quṭb—may God prolong his life!—relates, speaking of his novitiate, that he saw his lower soul in the form of a snake. A dervish said: "I saw my lower soul in the shape of a mouse. 'Who art thou?' I asked. It answered: 'I am the destruction of the heedless, for I urge them to evil, and the salvation of those who love God, for if I were not with them in my corruption they would be puffed up with pride in their purity.'"

All these stories prove that the lower soul is a real substance (*'ayní*), not a mere attribute, and that it has attributes which we clearly perceive. The Apostle said: "Thy worst enemy is thy lower soul, which is between thy two sides." When you have obtained knowledge of it you recognize that it can be mastered by discipline, but that its essence and substance do not perish. If it is rightly known and under control, the seeker need not care though it continues to exist in him.

Hence the purpose of mortifying the lower soul is to destroy its attributes, not to annihilate its reality. Now I will discuss the true nature of passion and the renunciation of lusts.

Discourse on the true nature of Passion (hawá).

You must know that, according to the opinion of some, passion is a term applied to the attributes of the lower soul, but, according to others, a term denoting the natural volition (*irádat-i ṭab'*) whereby the lower soul is controlled and directed, just as the spirit is controlled by the intelligence. Every spirit that is devoid of the faculty of intelligence is imperfect, and similarly every lower soul that is devoid of the faculty of passion is imperfect. Man is continually being called by intelligence and passion into contrary ways. If he obeys the call of intelligence he attains to faith, but if he obeys the call of passion he arrives at error and infidelity. Therefore passion is a veil and a false guide, and man is commanded to resist it. Passion is of two kinds: (1) desire of pleasure and lust, and (2) desire of worldly honour and authority. He who follows pleasure and lust haunts taverns, and mankind are safe from his mischief, but he who desires honour and authority lives in cells (*ṣawámi'*) and monasteries, and not only has lost the right way himself but also leads others into error. One whose every act depends on passion, and who finds satisfaction in following it, is far from God although he be with you in a mosque, but one who has renounced and abandoned it is near to God although he be in a church. Ibráhím Khawwáṣ relates this anecdote: "Once I heard that in Rúm there was a monk who had been seventy years in a monastery. I said to myself: 'Wonderful! Forty years is the term of monastic vows: what is the state of this man that he has remained there for seventy years?' I went to see him. When I approached, he opened a window and said to me: 'O Ibráhím, I know why you have come. I have not stayed here for seventy years because of monastic vows, but I have a dog foul with passion, and I have taken my abode in this monastery for the purpose of guarding the dog (*sagbání*), and preventing it from doing harm to others.' On hearing him say this I exclaimed: 'O Lord, Thou art able to bestow righteousness on a man even though he be involved in sheer error.' He said to me: 'O Ibráhím, how long will you seek men? Go and seek yourself, and when you have found yourself keep watch over yourself, for this passion clothes itself every day in three hundred and sixty diverse garments of godhead and leads men astray.'"

In short, the devil cannot enter a man's heart until he desires to commit a sin: but when a certain quantity of passion appears, the devil takes it and decks it out and displays it to the man's heart; and this is called diabolic suggestion (*waswás*). It begins from passion, and in reference to this fact God said to Iblís when he threatened to seduce all mankind: "*Verily, thou hast no power over My servants*" (Kor. xv, 42), for the devil in reality is a man's lower soul and passion. Hence the Apostle said: "There is no one whom his devil (i.e. his passion) has not subdued except 'Umar, for he has subdued his devil." Passion is mingled as an ingredient in the clay of Adam; whoever renounces it becomes a prince and whoever follows it becomes a captive. Junayd was asked: "What is union with God?" He replied: "To renounce passion," for of all the acts of devotion by which God's favour is sought none has greater value than resistance to passion, because it is easier for a man to destroy a mountain with his nails than to resist passion. I have read in the Anecdotes that Dhu 'l-Nún the Egyptian said: "I saw a man flying through the air, and asked him how he had attained to this degree. He answered: 'I set my feet on passion (*hawá*) in order that I might ascend into the air (*hawá*).'" It is related that Muḥammad b. Faḍl al-Balkhí said: "I marvel at one who goes with his passion into God's House and visits Him: why does not he trample on his passion that he may attain to Him?"

The most manifest attribute of the lower soul is lust (*shahwat*).

Lust is a thing that is dispersed in different parts of the human body, and is served by the senses. Man is bound to guard all his members from it, and he shall be questioned concerning the acts of each. The lust of the eye is sight, that of the ear is hearing, that of the nose is smell, that of the tongue is speech, that of the palate is taste, that of the body (*jasad*) is touch, and that of the mind is thought (*andíshídan*). It behoves the seeker of God to spend his whole life, day and night, in ridding himself of these incitements to passion which show themselves through the senses, and to pray God to make him such that this desire will be removed from his inward nature, since whoever is afflicted with lust is veiled from all spiritual things. If anyone should repel it by his own exertions, his task would be long and painful. The right way is resignation (*taslím*). It is related that Abú 'Alí Siyáh of Merv said: "I had gone to the bath and in accordance with the custom of the Prophet I was using a razor (*pubis tondendæ causâ*). I said to myself: 'O Abú 'Alí, amputate this member which is the source of all lusts and keeps thee afflicted with so much evil.' A voice in my heart whispered: 'O Abú 'Alí, wilt thou interfere in My kingdom? Are not all thy limbs equally at My disposal? If thou do this, I swear by My glory that I will put a hundredfold lust and passion in every hair in that place.'"

Although a man has no power over what is vicious in his constitution, he can get an attribute changed by Divine aid and by resigning himself to God's will and by divesting himself of his own power and strength. In reality, when he resigns himself, God protects him; and through God's protection he comes nearer to annihilating the evil than he does through self-mortification, since flies are more easily driven away with an umbrella (*mikanna*) than with a fly-whisk (*midhabba*). Unless Divine protection is predestined to a man, he cannot abstain from anything by his own exertion, and unless God exerts Himself towards a man, that man's exertion is of no use. All acts of exertion fall under two heads: their object is either to avert the predestination of God or to acquire something in spite of predestination; and both these objects are impossible. It is related that when Shiblí was ill, the physician advised him to be abstinent. "From what shall I abstain?" said he, "from that which God bestows upon me, or from that which He does not bestow? It is impossible to abstain from the former, and the latter is not in my hands." I will discuss this question carefully on another occasion.

7. The Ḥakímís.

They are the followers of Abú 'Abdalláh Muḥammad b. 'Alí al-Ḥakím al-Tirmidhí, who was one of the religious leaders of his time and the author of many works on every branch of exoteric and esoteric science. His doctrine was based on saintship (*wiláyat*), and he used to explain the true nature of saintship and the degrees of the saints and the observance of the proper arrangement of their ranks.

As the first step towards understanding his doctrine, you must know that God has saints (*awliyá*), whom He has chosen out of mankind, and whose thoughts He has withdrawn from worldly ties and delivered from sensual temptations; and He has stationed each of them in a particular degree, and has opened unto them the door of these mysteries. Much might be said on this topic, but I must briefly set forth several points of capital importance.

Discourse on the Affirmation of Saintship (wiláyat).

You must know that the principle and foundation of Ṣúfiism and knowledge of God rests on saintship, the reality of which is unanimously affirmed by all the Shaykhs, though every one has expressed himself in different language. The peculiarity of Muḥammad b. 'Alí (al-Ḥakím) lies in the fact that he applied this term to the theory of Ṣúfiism.

Waláyat means, etymologically, "power to dispose" (*taṣarruf*), and *wiláyat* means "possession of command" (*imárat*). *Waláyat* also means "lordship" (*rubúbiyyat*); hence God hath said: "*In this case the lordship* (al-waláyat) *belongs to God who is the*

Truth" (Kor. xviii, 42), because the unbelievers seek His protection and turn unto Him and renounce their idols. And *wiláyat* also means "love" (*maḥabbat*). *Walí* may be the form *fa'íl* with the meaning of *maf'úl*, as God hath said: "*And He takes charge of* (yatawallá) *the righteous*" (Kor. vii, 195), for God does not leave His servant to his own actions and attributes, but keeps him under His protection. And *walí* may be the form *fa'íl*, equivalent to *fá'il*, with an intensive force, because a man takes care (*tawallí kunad*) to obey God and constantly to fulfil the obligations that he owes to Him. Thus *walí* in the active meaning is "one who desires" (*muríd*), while in the passive meaning it denotes "one who is the object of God's desire" (*murád*). All these meanings, whether they signify the relation of God to Man or that of Man to God, are allowable, for God may be the protector of His friends, inasmuch as He promised His protection to the Companions of the Apostle, and declared that the unbelievers had no protector (*mawlá*).[1] And, moreover, He may distinguish them in an exclusive way by His friendship, as He hath said, "*He loves them and they love Him*" (Kor. v, 59), so that they turn away from the favour of mankind: He is their friend (*walí*) and they are His friends (*awliyá*). And He may confer on one a "friendship" (*wiláyat*) that enables him to persevere in obedience to Him, and keeps him free from sin, and on another a "friendship" that empowers him to loose and bind, and makes his prayers answered and his aspirations effectual, as the Apostle said: "There is many a one with dirty hair, dust-stained, clad in two old garments, whom men never heed; but if he were to swear by God, God would verify his oath." It is well known that in the Caliphate of 'Umar b. al-Khaṭṭáb, the Nile, in accordance with its usual habit, ceased to flow; for in the time of Paganism they used annually to adorn a maiden and throw her into the river to make it flow again. 'Umar therefore wrote on a piece of paper: "O river, if thou hast stopped of thy own will, thou

[1] Kor. xlvii, 12.

doest wrong, and if by command of God, 'Umar bids thee flow." When this paper was thrown in, the Nile resumed its course.

My purpose in discussing saintship and affirming its reality is to show you that the name of saint (*walí*) is properly applied to those in whom the above-mentioned qualities are actually present (*ḥál*) and not merely reputed (*qál*). Certain Shaykhs formerly composed books on this subject, but they became rare and soon disappeared. Now I will commend to you the explanation given by that venerable spiritual director who is the author of the doctrine—for my own belief in it is greater—in order that much instruction may be gained, not only by yourself, but also by every seeker of Ṣúfiism who may have the good fortune to read this book.

SECTION.

You must know that the word *walí* is current among the vulgar, and is to be found in the Koran and the Apostolic Traditions: e.g., God hath said, "*Verily, on the friends* (awliyá) *of God no fear shall come, and they shall not grieve*" (Kor. x, 63); and again, "*God is the friend* (walí) *of those who believe*" (Kor. ii, 258). And the Apostle said: "Among the servants of God there are some whom the prophets and martyrs deem happy." He was asked: "Who are they? Describe them to us that perchance we may love them." He replied: "Those who love one another, through God's mercy, without wealth and without seeking a livelihood: their faces are luminous, and they sit on thrones of light; they are not afraid when men are afraid, nor do they grieve when men grieve." Then he recited: "*Verily, on the friends of God no fear shall come, and they shall not grieve*" (Kor. x, 63). Furthermore, the Apostle said that God said: "He who hurts a saint (*walí*) has allowed himself to make war on Me."

These passages show that God has saints (*awliyá*) whom He has specially distinguished by His friendship and whom He has chosen to be the governors of His kingdom and has marked out to manifest His actions and has peculiarly favoured with diverse kinds of miracles (*karámát*) and has purged of natural corruptions and has delivered from subjection to their lower soul and passion, so that all their thoughts are of Him and their intimacy is with Him alone. Such have been in past ages, and are now, and shall be hereafter until the Day of Resurrection, because God has exalted this (Moslem) community above all others and has promised to preserve the religion of Muḥammad. Inasmuch as the traditional and intellectual proofs of this religion are to be found among the divines (*'ulamá*), it follows that the visible proof is to be found among the Saints and elect of God. Here we have two parties opposed to us, namely, the Mu'tazilites and the rank and file of the Anthropomorphists (*Ḥashwiyya*). The Mu'tazilites deny that one Moslem is specially privileged more than another; but if a saint is not specially privileged, neither is a prophet specially privileged; and this is infidelity. The vulgar Anthropomorphists allow that special privileges may be conferred, but assert that such privileged persons no longer exist, although they did exist in the past. It is all the same, however, whether they deny the past or the future, since one side of denial is no better than another.

God, then, has caused the prophetic evidence (*burhán-i nabawí*) to remain down to the present day, and has made the Saints the means whereby it is manifested, in order that the signs of the Truth and the proof of Muḥammad's veracity may continue to be clearly seen. He has made the Saints the governors of the universe; they have become entirely devoted to His business, and have ceased to follow their sensual affections. Through the blessing of their advent the rain falls from heaven, and through the purity of their lives the plants spring up from the earth, and through their spiritual influence the Moslems gain victories over the unbelievers. Among them there are four thousand who are concealed and do not know one another and are not aware of the excellence of their state, but in all circumstances are hidden from themselves and from mankind. Traditions have come down to this effect, and the sayings of the Saints proclaim the truth thereof, and I myself—God be praised!—have had ocular experience (*khabar-i 'iyán*) of this matter. But of those who have power to loose and to bind and are the officers of the Divine court there are three hundred, called *Akhyár*, and forty, called *Abdál*, and seven, called *Abrár*, and four, called *Awtád*, and three, called *Nuqabá*, and one, called *Quṭb* or *Ghawth*. All these know one another and cannot act save by mutual consent.

Here the vulgar may object to my assertion that they know one another to be saints, on the ground that, if such is the case, they must be secure as to their fate in the next world. I reply that it is absurd to suppose that knowledge of saintship involves security. A believer may have knowledge of his faith and yet not be secure: why should not the same hold good of a saint who has knowledge of his saintship? Nevertheless, it is possible that God should miraculously cause the saint to know his security in regard to the future life, while maintaining him in a state of spiritual soundness and preserving him from disobedience. The Shaykhs differ on this question for the reason which I have explained. Those belonging to the four thousand who are concealed do not admit that the saint can know himself to be such, whereas those of the other class take the contrary view. Each opinion is supported by many lawyers and scholastics. Abú Isḥáq Isfará'iní[1] and some of the ancients hold that a saint is ignorant of his saintship, while Abú Bakr b. Fúrak[2] and others of the past generation hold that he is conscious of it. I ask the former party, what loss or evil does a saint suffer by knowing himself? If they allege that he is conceited when he knows himself to be a saint, I answer that Divine protection is a necessary condition of saintship, and one who is protected from evil cannot fall into self-conceit. It is a very common notion (*sukhan-i sakht 'ámiyána*) that a saint, to whom extraordinary miracles (*karámát*) are continually vouchsafed, does not know himself to be a saint or these

[1] See Ibn Khallikán, No. 4.

[2] See Ibn Khallikán, No. 621; Brockelmann, i, 166.

miracles to be miracles. Both parties have adherents among the common people, but opinion is of no account.

The Mu'tazilites, however, deny special privileges and miracles, which constitute the essence of saintship. They affirm that all Moslems are friends (*awliyá*) of God when they are obedient to Him, and that anyone who fulfils the ordinances of the Faith and denies the attributes and vision of God and allows believers to be eternally damned in Hell and acknowledges only such obligations as are imposed by Reason, without regard to Revelation, is a "friend" (*walí*). All Moslems agree that such a person is a "friend", but a friend of the Devil. The Mu'tazilites also maintain that, if saintship involved miracles, all believers must have miracles vouchsafed to them, because they all share in faith (*ímán*), and if they share in what is fundamental they must likewise share in what is derivative. They say, further, that miracles may be vouchsafed both to believers and to infidels, e.g. when anyone is hungry or fatigued on a journey some person may appear in order to give him food or mount him on an animal for riding. If it were possible, they add, for anyone to traverse a great distance in one night, the Apostle must have been that man; yet, when he set out for Mecca, God said, "*And they* (the animals) *carry your burdens to a land which ye would not have reached save with sore trouble to yourselves*" (Kor. xvi, 7). I reply: "Your arguments are worthless, for God said, '*Glory to Him who transported His servant by night from the sacred mosque to the farther mosque*'" (Kor. xvii, 1). Miracles are special, not general; but it would have been a general instance if all the Companions had been miraculously conveyed to Mecca, and this would have destroyed all the principles of faith in the unseen. Faith is a general term, applicable to the righteous and the wicked alike, whereas saintship is special. The journey of the Companions to Mecca falls under the former category, but inasmuch as the case of the Apostle was a special one, God conveyed him in one night from Mecca to Jerusalem, and thence to a space of two bow-lengths from the Divine presence; and he returned ere the night was far spent. Again, to deny special privileges is manifestly unreasonable. As in a palace there are chamberlains, janitors, grooms, and viziers, who, although they are equally the king's servants, are not equal in rank, so all believers are equal in respect of their faith, but some are obedient, some wise, some pious, and some ignorant.

SECTION.

The Shaykhs, every one, have given hints as to the true meaning of saintship. Now I will bring together as many of these selected definitions as possible.

Abú 'Alí Júzajání says: "The saint is annihilated in his own state and subsistent in the contemplation of the Truth: he cannot tell anything concerning himself, nor can he rest with anyone except God," because a man has knowledge only of his own state, and when all his states are annihilated he cannot tell anything about himself; and he cannot rest with anyone else, to whom he might tell his state, because to communicate one's hidden state to another is to reveal the secret of the Beloved, which cannot be revealed except to the Beloved himself. Moreover, in contemplation it is impossible to regard aught except God: how, then, can he be at rest with mankind? Junayd said: "The saint hath no fear, because fear is the expectation either of some future calamity or of the eventual loss of some object of desire, whereas the saint is the son of his time (*ibn waqtihi*): he has no future that he should fear anything; and as he hath no fear so he hath no hope, since hope is the expectation either of gaining an object of desire or of being relieved from a misfortune, and this belongs to the future; nor does he grieve, because grief arises from the rigour of time, and how should he feel grief who is in the radiance of satisfaction (*riḍá*) and the garden of concord (*muwáfaqat*)?" The vulgar imagine this saying to imply that, inasmuch as the saint feels neither fear nor hope nor grief, he has security (*amn*) in their place; but he has not security, for security arises from not seeing that which is hidden, and from turning one's back on "time"; and this (absence of security) is characteristic of those who pay no regard to their humanity (*bashariyyat*) and are not content with attributes. Fear and hope and security and grief all refer to the interests of the lower soul, and when that is annihilated satisfaction (*riḍá*) becomes an attribute of Man, and when satisfaction has been attained his states become steadfast (*mustaqím*) in vision of the Author of states (*muḥawwil*), and his back is turned on all states. Then saintship is revealed to his heart and its meaning is made clear to his inmost thoughts. Abú 'Uthman Maghribí says: "The saint is sometimes celebrated (*mashhúr*), but he is not seduced (*maftún*)," and another says: "The saint is sometimes hidden (*mastúr*), but he is not celebrated." Seduction consists in falsehood: inasmuch as the saint must be veracious, and miracles cannot possibly be performed by a liar, it follows that the saint is incapable of being seduced. These two sayings refer to the controversy whether the saint knows himself to be such: if he knows, he is celebrated, and if he does not know, he is seduced; but the explanation of this is tedious. It is related that Ibráhím b. Adham asked a certain man whether he desired to be one of God's saints, and on his replying "Yes", said: "Do not covet anything in this world or the next, and devote thyself entirely to God, and turn to God with all thy heart." To covet this world is to turn away from God for the sake of that which is transitory, and to covet the next world is to turn away from God for the sake of that which is everlasting: that which is transitory perishes and its renunciation becomes naught, but that which is everlasting cannot perish, hence its renunciation also is imperishable. Abú Yazíd was asked: "Who is a saint?" He answered: "That one who is patient under the command and prohibition of God," because the more a man loves God the more does his heart revere what He commands and the farther is his body from what He forbids. It is related that Abú Yazíd said: "Once I was told that a saint of God was in such and such a town. I set out to visit him. When I arrived at his mosque he came forth from his chamber and spat on the floor of the mosque. I turned back without saluting him, and said to myself: 'A saint must keep the religious law in order that God may keep him in his spiritual state. Had this man been a saint his respect for the mosque would have prevented him from spitting on its floor, or God would have preserved him from marring the grace vouchsafed to him.' The same night I dreamed that the Apostle said to me, 'O Abú Yazíd, the blessing of that which thou hast done is come to thee.' Next day I attained to this degree which ye behold." And I have heard that a man who came to visit Shaykh Abú Sa'íd entered the mosque with his left foot foremost. The Shaykh gave orders that he should be dismissed, saying: "He who does not know how to enter the house of the Friend is not suitable for us." Some heretics who have adopted this perilous doctrine assert that service of God (*khidmat*) is necessary only while one is becoming a saint, but that after one has become a saint service is abolished. This is clearly wrong. There is no "station" on the way to the Truth where any obligation of service is abolished. I will explain this matter fully in its proper place.

Discourse on the Affirmation of Miracles (karámát).

You must know that miracles may be vouchsafed to a saint so long as he does not infringe the obligations of the religious law. Both parties of the orthodox Moslems agree on this point, nor is it intellectually impossible, because such miracles are a species of that which is predestined by God, and their manifestation does not contradict any principle of the religious law, nor, on the other hand, is it repugnant to the mind to conceive them as a genus. A miracle is a token of a saint's veracity, and it cannot be manifested to an impostor except as a sign that his pretensions are false. It is an extraordinary act (*fi'lí náqiḍ-i 'ádat*), performed while he is still subject to the obligations of religion; and whoever is able, through knowledge given him by God, to distinguish by the method of deduction what is true from what is false, he too is a saint. Some Sunnís maintain that miracles are established, but not to the degree of an evidentiary miracle (*mu'jizat*[1]): they do not admit, for example, that prayers may be answered and fulfilled, and so forth, contrary to custom. I ask in reply: "What do you consider wrong in the performance by a true saint, while he is subject to religious obligations, of an act which violates custom?" If they say that it is not a species of that which is predestined by God, this statement is erroneous; and if they say that it is a species of that which is predestined, but that its performance by a true saint involves the annulment of prophecy and the denial of special privileges to the prophets, this assertion also is inadmissible, since the saint is specially distinguished by miracles (*karámát*) and the prophet by evidentiary miracles (*mu'jizát*); and inasmuch as the saint is a saint and the prophet is a prophet, there is no likeness between them to justify such precaution. The pre-eminence of the prophets depends on their exalted rank and on their being preserved from the defilement of sin, not on miracles or evidentiary miracles or acts which violate custom. All the prophets are equal so far as they all have the power of working such miracles (*i'jáz*), but some are superior to others in degree. Since, then, notwithstanding this equality in regard to their actions, some prophets are superior to others, why should not miracles (*karámát*) which violate custom be vouchsafed also to the saints, although the prophets are superior to them? And since, in the case of the prophets, an act which violates custom does not cause one of them to be more exalted or more specially privileged than another, so, in the case of the saints, a similar act does not cause a saint to be more specially privileged than a prophet, i.e. the saints do not become like in kind (*hamsán*) to the prophets. This proof will clear away, for reasonable men, any difficulties that this matter may have

[1] The name *mu'jizat* is given to a miracle performed by a prophet, while one performed by a saint is called *karámat*.

presented to them. "But suppose," it may be said, "that a saint whose miracles violate custom should claim to be a prophet." I reply that this is impossible, because saintship involves veracity, and he who tells a falsehood is no saint. Moreover, a saint who pretends to prophesy casts an imputation on (the genuineness of) evidentiary miracles, which is infidelity. Miracles (*karámát*) are vouchsafed only to a pious believer, and falsehood is impiety. That being so, the miracles of the saint confirm the evidence of the prophet. There is no difficulty in reconciling the two classes of miracles. The apostle establishes his prophecy by establishing the reality of evidentiary miracles, while the saint, by the miracles which he performs, establishes both the prophecy of the apostle and his own saintship. Therefore the veracious saint says the same thing as the veracious prophet. The miracles of the former are identical with the evidentiary miracles of the latter. A believer, seeing the miracles of a saint, has more faith in the veracity of the prophet, not more doubt, because there is no contradiction between the claims made by them. Similarly, in law, when a number of heirs are agreed in their claim, if one of them establishes his claim the claim of the others is established; but not so if their claims are contradictory. Hence, when a prophet adduces evidentiary miracles as evidence that his prophecy is genuine, and when his claim is confirmed by a saint, it is impossible that any difficulty should arise.

Discourse on the difference between Evidentiary Miracles (mu'jizát) *and Miracles* (karámát).

Inasmuch as it has been shown that neither class of miracles can be wrought by an impostor, we must now distinguish more clearly between them. *Mu'jizát* involve publicity and *karámát* secrecy, because the result of the former is to affect others, while the latter are peculiar to the person by whom they are performed. Again, the doer of *mu'jizát* is quite sure that he has wrought an extraordinary miracle, whereas the doer of *karámát* cannot be sure whether he has really wrought a miracle or whether he is insensibly deceived (*istidráj*). He who performs *mu'jizát* has authority over the law, and in arranging it he denies or affirms, according as God commands him, that he is insensibly deceived.[1] On the other hand, he who performs *karámát* has no choice but to resign himself (to God's will) and to accept the ordinances that are laid upon him, because the *karámát* of a saint are never in any way incompatible with the law laid down by a prophet. It may be said: "If evidentiary miracles are the proof of a prophet's veracity, and if nevertheless you assert that miracles of the same kind may be performed by one who is not a prophet, then they become ordinary events (*mu'tád*): therefore your proof of the reality of *mu'jizát* annuls your argument establishing the reality of *karámát*." I reply: "This is not the case. The *karámat* of a saint is identical with, and displays the same evidence as, the *mu'jizat* of a prophet: the quality of *i'jáz* (inimitability) exhibited in the one instance does not impair the same quality in the other instance." When the infidels put Khubayb on the gallows at Mecca, the Apostle, who was then seated in the mosque at Medína, saw him and told the Companions what was being done to him. God also lifted the veil from the eyes of Khubayb, so that he saw the Apostle and cried, "Peace be with thee!" and God caused the Apostle to hear his salutation, and caused Khubayb to hear the Apostle's answer. Now, the fact that the Apostle at Medína saw Khubayb at Mecca was an evidentiary miracle, and the fact that Khubayb at Mecca saw the Apostle at Medína was likewise an extraordinary act. Accordingly there is no difference between absence in time and absence in space; for Khubayb's miracle (*karámat*) was wrought when he was absent from the Apostle in space, and the miracles of later days were wrought by those who were absent from the Apostle in time. This is a clear distinction and a manifest proof that *karámát* cannot possibly be in contradiction with *i'jáz* (miracles performed by a prophet). *Karámát* are not established unless they bear testimony to the truth of one who has performed a *mu'jizat*,

[1] B. omits the words "that he is insensibly deceived".

and they are not vouchsafed except to a pious believer who bears such testimony. *Karámát* of Moslems are an extraordinary miracle (*mu'jizat*) of the Apostle, for as his law is permanent so must his proof (*ḥujjat*) also be permanent. The saints are witnesses to the truth of the Apostle's mission, and it is impossible that a miracle (*karámat*) should be wrought by an unbeliever (*bégána*).

On this topic a story is related of Ibráhím Khawwáṣ, which is very apposite here. Ibráhím said: "I went down into the desert in my usual state of detachment from worldly things (*tajríd*). After I had gone some distance a man appeared and begged me to let him be my companion. I looked at him and was conscious of a feeling of repugnance. He said to me: 'O Ibráhím, do not be vexed. I am a Christian, and one of the Ṣábians among them. I have come from the confines of Rúm in the hope of being thy companion.' When I knew that he was an unbeliever, I regained my equanimity, and felt it more easy to take him as my companion and to fulfil my obligations towards him. I said: 'O monk, I fear that thou wilt suffer from want of meat and drink, for I have nothing with me.' 'O Ibráhím,' said he, 'is thy fame in the world so great, and art thou still concerned about meat and drink?' I marvelled at his boldness and accepted him as my companion in order to test his claim. After journeying seven days and nights we were overtaken by thirst. He stopped and cried: 'O Ibráhím, they trumpet thy praise throughout the world. Now let me see what privileges of intimacy (*gustákhíhá*) thou hast in this court (i.e. to what extent thou art a favourite with God), for I can endure no more.' I laid my head on the earth and cried: 'O Lord, do not shame me before this unbeliever, who thinks well of me!' When I raised my head I saw a dish on which were placed two loaves of bread and two cups of water. We ate and drank and went on our way. After seven days had passed I resolved to test him ere he should again put me to the proof. 'O monk,' I said, 'now it is thy turn. Let me see the fruits of thy mortification.' He laid his head on the earth and muttered something. Immediately a dish appeared containing four loaves and four cups of water. I was amazed and grieved, and I despaired of my state. 'This has appeared,' I said, 'for the sake of an unbeliever: how can I eat or drink thereof?' He bade me taste, but I refused, saying, 'Thou art not worthy of this, and it is not in harmony with thy spiritual condition. If I regard it as a miracle (*karámat*), miracles are not vouchsafed to unbelievers; and if I regard it as a contribution (*ma'únat*) from thee, I must suspect thee of being an impostor.' He said: 'Taste, O Ibráhím! I give thee joy of two things: firstly, of my conversion to Islam (here he uttered the profession of faith), and secondly, of the great honour in which thou art held by God.' 'How so?' I asked. He answered: 'I have no miraculous powers, but my shame on account of thee made me lay my head on the earth and beg God to give me two loaves and two cups of water if the religion of Muḥammad is true, and two more loaves and cups if Ibráhím Khawwáṣ is one of God's saints.'" Then Ibráhím ate and drank, and the man who had been a monk rose to eminence in Islam.

Now, this violation of custom, although attached to the *karámat* of a saint, is identical with the evidentiary miracles which are wrought by prophets, but it is rare that in a prophet's absence an evidence should be vouchsafed to another person, or that in the presence of a saint some portion of his miraculous powers should be transferred to another person. In fact, the end of saintship is only the beginning of prophecy. That monk was one of the hidden (saints), like Pharaoh's magicians. Ibráhím confirmed the Prophet's power to violate custom, and his companion also was endeavouring both to confirm prophecy and to glorify saintship; a purpose which God in His eternal providence fulfilled. This is a clear difference between *karámat* and *i'jáz*. The manifestation of miracles to the saints is a second miracle, for they ought to be kept secret, not intentionally divulged. My Shaykh used to say that if a saint reveals his saintship and claims to be a saint, the soundness of his spiritual state is not impaired thereby, but if he takes pains to obtain publicity he is led astray by self-conceit.

Discourse on the performance of miracles belonging to the evidentiary class by those who pretend to godship.

The Shaykhs of this sect and all orthodox Moslems are agreed that an extraordinary act resembling a prophetic miracle (*mu'jizat*) may be performed by an unbeliever, in order that by means of his performance he may be shown beyond doubt to be an impostor. Thus, for example, Pharaoh lived four hundred years without once falling ill; and when he climbed up to any high ground the water followed him, and stopped when he stopped, and moved when he moved. Nevertheless, intelligent men did not hesitate to deny his pretensions to godship, inasmuch as every intelligent person acknowledges that God is not incarnate (*mujassam*) and composite (*murakkab*). You will judge by analogy the wondrous acts related of Shaddád, who was the lord of Iram, and Nimrod. Similarly, we are told on trustworthy authority that in the last days Dajjál will come and will claim godship, and that two mountains will go with him, one on his right hand and the other on his left; and that the mountain on his right hand will be the place of felicity, and the mountain on his left hand will be the place of torment; and that he will call the people to himself and will punish those who refuse to join him. But though he should perform a hundredfold amount of such extraordinary acts, no intelligent person would doubt the falsity of his claim, for it is well known that God does not sit on an ass and is not blind. Such things fall under the principle of Divine deception (*istidráj*). So, again, one who falsely pretends to be an apostle may perform an extraordinary act, which proves him an impostor, just as a similar act performed by a true apostle proves him genuine. But no such act can be performed if there be any possibility of doubt or any difficulty in distinguishing the true claimant from the impostor, for in that case the principle of allegiance (*bay'at*) would be nullified. It is possible, moreover, that something of the same kind as a miracle (*karámat*) may be performed by a pretender to saintship who, although his conduct is bad, is blameless in his religion, inasmuch as by that miraculous act he confirms the truth of the Apostle and manifests the grace of God vouchsafed to him and does not attribute the act in question to his own power. One who speaks the truth, without evidence, in the fundamental matter of faith (*ímán*), will always speak the truth, with evidence and firm belief, in the matter of saintship, because his belief is of the same quality as the belief of the saint; and though his actions do not square with his belief, his claim of saintship is not demonstrably contradicted by his evil conduct, any more than his claim of faith could be. In fact, miracles (*karámát*) and saintship are Divine gifts, not things acquired by Man, so that human actions (*kasb*) cannot become the cause of Divine guidance.

I have already said that the saints are not preserved from sin (*ma'ṣúm*), for sinlessness belongs to the prophets, but they are protected (*maḥfúẓ*) from any evil that involves the denial of their saintship; and the denial of saintship, after it has come into being, depends on something inconsistent with faith, namely, apostasy (*riddat*): it does not depend on sin. This is the doctrine of Muḥammad b. 'Alí Ḥakím of Tirmidh, and also of Junayd, Abu 'l-Ḥasan Núrí, Ḥárith Muḥásibí, and many other mystics (*ahl-i ḥaqá'iq*). But those who attach importance to conduct (*ahl-i mu'ámalát*), like Sahl b. 'Abdalláh of Tustar, Abú Sulaymán Dáráni, Ḥamdún Qaṣṣár, and others, maintain that saintship involves unceasing obedience (*ṭá'at*), and that when a great sin (*kabíra*) occurs to the mind of a saint he is deposed from his saintship. Now, as I have stated before, there is a consensus of opinion (*ijmá'*) among Moslems that a great sin does not put anyone outside the pale of faith; and one saintship (*wiláyat*) is no better than another. Therefore, since the saintship of knowledge of God (*ma'rifat*), which is the foundation of all miracles vouchsafed by Divine grace (*karámathá*), is not lost through sin, it is impossible that what is inferior to that in

Q

excellence and grace (*karámat*) should disappear because of sin. The controversy among the Shaykhs on this matter has run to great length, and I do not intend to record it here.

It is most important, however, that you should know with certainty in what state this miraculous grace is manifested to the saint: in sobriety or intoxication, in rapture (*ghalabat*) or composure (*tamkín*). I have fully explained the meaning of intoxication and sobriety in my account of the doctrine of Abú Yazíd. He and Dhu 'l-Nún the Egyptian and Muḥammad b. Khafíf and Ḥusayn b. Manṣúr (al-Ḥalláj) and Yaḥyá b. Mu'ádh Rází and others hold that miracles are not vouchsafed to a saint except when he is in the state of intoxication, whereas the miracles of the prophets are wrought in the state of sobriety. Hence, according to their doctrine, this is a clear distinction between *mu'jizát* and *karámát*, for the saint, being enraptured, pays no heed to the people and does not call upon them to follow him, while the prophet, being sober, exerts himself to attain his object and challenges the people to rival what he has done. Moreover, the prophet may choose whether he will manifest or conceal his extraordinary powers, but the saints have no such choice; sometimes a miracle is not granted to them when they desire it, and sometimes it is bestowed when they do not desire it, for the saint has no propaganda, so that his attributes should be subsistent, but he is hidden and his proper state is to have his attributes annihilated. The prophet is a man of law (*ṣáḥib shar'*), and the saint is a man of inward feeling (*ṣáḥib sirr*). Accordingly, a miracle (*karámat*) will not be manifested to a saint unless he is in a state of absence from himself and bewilderment, and unless his faculties are entirely under the control of God. While saints are with themselves and maintain the state of humanity (*bashariyyat*), they are veiled; but when the veil is lifted they are bewildered and amazed through realizing the bounties of God. A miracle cannot be manifested except in the state of unveiledness (*kashf*), which is the rank of proximity (*qurb*); and whoever is in that state, to him worthless stones appear even as gold. This is the state of intoxication with which no human being, the prophets alone excepted, is permanently endowed. Thus, one day, Ḥáritha was transported from this world and had the next world revealed to him; he said: "I have cut myself loose from this world, so that its stones and its gold and its silver and its clay are all one to me." Next day he was seen tending asses, and on being asked what he was doing, he said: "I am trying to get the food that I need." Therefore, the saints, while they are sober, are as ordinary men, but while they are intoxicated their rank is the same as that of the prophets, and the whole universe becomes like gold unto them. Shiblí says—

"*Gold wherever we go, and pearls*
Wherever we turn, and silver in the waste."

I have heard the Master and Imám Abu 'l-Qásim Qushayrí say: "Once I asked Ṭábaráni about the beginning of his spiritual experience. He told me that on one occasion he wanted a stone from the river-bed at Sarakhs. Every stone that he touched turned into a gem, and he threw them all away." This was because stones and gems were the same to him, or rather, gems were of less value, since he had no desire for them. And I have heard Khwája Imám Khazá'iní at Sarakhs relate as follows: "In my boyhood I went to a certain place to get mulberry leaves for silkworms. When it was midday I climbed a tree and began to shake the branches. While I was thus employed Shaykh Abu 'l-Faḍl b. al-Ḥasan passed by, but he did not see me, and I had no doubt that he was beside himself and that his heart was with God. Suddenly he raised his head and cried with the boldness of intimacy: 'O Lord, it is more than a year since Thou hast given me a small piece of silver (*dángí*) that I might have my hair cut. Is this the way to treat Thy friends?' No sooner had he spoken than I saw all the leaves and boughs and roots of the trees turned to gold. Abu 'l-Faḍl exclaimed: 'How strange! The least hint that I utter is a backsliding (*hama ta'ríḍ-i má í'ráḍ ast*). One cannot say a word to Thee for the sake of relieving one's mind.'" It is related that Shiblí cast four hundred dínárs into the Tigris. When asked what he was doing, he replied: "Stones are better in the water." "But why," they said, "don't you give the money to the poor?" He answered: "Glory to God! what plea can I urge before Him if I remove the veil from my own heart only to place it on the hearts of my brother Moslems? It is not religious to wish them worse than myself." All these cases belong to the state of intoxication, which I have already explained.

On the other hand, Junayd and Abu 'l-'Abbás Sayyárí and Abú Bakr Wásiṭí and Muḥammad b. 'Alí of Tirmidh, the author of the doctrine, hold that miracles are manifested in the state of sobriety and composure (*ṣaḥw ú tamkín*), not in the state of intoxication. They argue that the saints of God are the governors of His kingdom and the overseers of the universe, which God has committed absolutely to their charge: therefore their judgments must be the soundest of all, and their hearts must be the most tenderly disposed of all towards the creatures of God. They are mature (*rasídagán*); and whereas agitation and intoxication are marks of inexperience, with maturity agitation is transmuted into composure. Then, and only then, is one a saint in reality, and only then are miracles genuine. It is well known among Ṣúfís that every night the *Awtád* must go round the whole universe, and if there should be any place on which their eyes have not fallen, next day some imperfection will appear in that place; and they must then inform the *Quṭb*, in order that he may fix his attention on the weak spot, and that by his blessing the imperfection may be removed. As regards the assertion that gold and earth are one to the saint, this indifference is a sign of intoxication and failure to see truly. More excellent is the man of true sight and sound perception, to whom gold is gold and earth is earth, but who recognizes the evil of the former and says: "O yellow ore! O white ore! beguile some one else, for I am aware of your corruptedness." He who sees the corruptedness of gold and silver perceives them to be a veil (between himself and God), and God will reward him for having renounced them. Contrariwise, he to whom gold is even as earth is not made perfect by renouncing earth. Ḥáritha, being intoxicated, declared that stones and gold were alike to him, but Abú Bakr, being sober, perceived the evil of laying hands on worldly wealth, and knew that God would reward him for rejecting it. Therefore he renounced it, and when the Apostle asked him what he had left for his family he answered, "God and His Apostle." And the following story is related by Abú Bakr Warráq of Tirmidh: "One day Muḥammad b. 'Alí (al-Ḥakím) said that he would take me somewhere. I replied: 'It is for the Shaykh to command.' Soon after we set out I saw an exceedingly dreadful wilderness, and in the midst thereof a golden throne placed under a green tree beside a fountain of running water. Seated on the throne was a person clad in beautiful raiment, who rose when Muḥammad b. 'Alí approached, and bade him sit on the throne. After a while, people came from every side until forty were gathered together. Then Muḥammad b. 'Alí waved his hand, and immediately food appeared from heaven, and we ate. Afterwards Muḥammad b. Alí asked a question of a man who was present, and he in reply made a long discourse of which I did not understand a single word. At last the Shaykh begged leave and took his departure, saying to me: 'Go, for thou art blest.' On our return to Tirmidh, I asked him what was that place and who was that man. He told me that the place was the Desert of the Israelites (*tíh-i Baní Isrá'íl*) and that the man was the *Quṭb* on whom the order of the universe depends. 'O Shaykh,' I said, 'how did we reach the Desert of the Israelites from Tirmidh in such a brief time?' He answered: 'O Abú Bakr, it is thy business to arrive (*rasídan*), not to ask questions (*pursídan*).'" This is a mark, not of intoxication, but of sanity.

Now I will mention some miracles and stories of the Ṣúfís,

and link thereto certain evidence which is to be found in the Book (the Koran).

Discourse concerning their Miracles.

The reality of miracles having been established by logical argument, you must now become acquainted with the evidence of the Koran and the genuine Traditions of the Apostle. Both Koran and Tradition proclaim the reality of miracles and extraordinary acts wrought by saints. To deny this is to deny the authority of the sacred texts. One example is the text, "*And We caused the clouds to overshadow you and the manna and the quails to descend upon you*" (Kor. ii, 54). If any sceptic should assert that this was an evidentiary miracle (*mu'jizat*) of Moses, I raise no objection, because all the miracles of the saints are an evidentiary miracle of Muḥammad; and if he says that this miracle was wrought in the absence of Moses, although it occurred in his time, and that therefore it was not necessarily wrought by him, I reply that the same principle holds good in the case of Moses, when he quitted his people and went to Mount Sinai, as in the case of Muḥammad; for there is no difference between being absent in time and being absent in space. We are also told of the miracle of Áṣaf b. Barkhiyá, who brought the throne of Bilqís to Solomon in the twinkling of an eye (Kor. xxvii, 40). This cannot have been a *mu'jizat*, for Áṣaf was not an apostle; had it been a *mu'jizat*, it must have been wrought by Solomon: therefore it was a *karámat*. We are told also of Mary that whenever Zacharias went into her chamber he found winter fruits in summer and summer fruits in winter, so that he said: "'*Whence hadst thou this?' She answered, 'It is from God'*" (Kor. iii, 32). Everyone admits that Mary was not an apostle. Furthermore, we have the story of the men of the cave (*aṣḥáb al-kahf*), how their dog spoke to them, and how they slept and turned about in the cave (Kor. xviii, 17). All these were extraordinary acts, and since they certainly were not a *mu'jizat*, they must have been a *karámat*. Such miracles (*karámát*) may be, for example, the answering of prayers through the accomplishment of wishes conceived by one who is subject to the religious law (*ba-ḥuṣúl-i umúr-i mawhúm andar zamán-i taklíf*), or the traversing of great distances in a short time, or the appearance of food from an unaccustomed place, or power to read the thoughts of others, etc.

Among the genuine Traditions is the story of the cave (*ḥadíth al-ghár*), which is told as follows. One day the Companions of the Apostle begged him to relate to them some marvellous tale of the ancient peoples. He said: "Once three persons were going to a certain place. At eventide they took shelter in a cave, and while they were asleep a rock fell from the mountain and blocked the mouth of the cave. They said to one another, 'We shall never escape from here unless we make our disinterested actions plead for us before God.' So one of them began: 'I had a father and mother and I had no worldly goods except a goat, whose milk I used to give to them; and every day I used to gather a bundle of firewood and sell it and spend the money in providing food for them and myself. One night I came home rather late, and before I milked the goat and steeped their food in the milk they had fallen asleep. I kept the bowl in my hand and stood there, without having eaten anything, until morning, when they awoke and ate; then I sat down.' 'O Lord' (he continued), 'if I speak the truth concerning this matter, send us deliverance and come to our aid!'" The Apostle said: "Thereupon the rock moved a little and a crevice appeared. The next man said: 'There was a beautiful blind girl, with whom I was deeply in love, but she would not listen to my suit. I managed to send to her a hundred and twenty dínárs with a promise that she should keep the money if she would be mine for one night. When she came the fear of God seized my heart. I turned from her and let her keep the money.' He added, 'O God, if I speak the truth, deliver us!'" The Apostle said: "Then the rock moved a little further and the crevice widened, but they could not yet go forth. The third man said: 'I had some labourers working for me. When the work was done they all received their wages except one, who disappeared. With his wages I bought a sheep. Next year there were two, and in the year after that there were four, and they soon became a large flock. After several years the labourer returned and asked me for his wages. I said to him, "Go and take all these sheep; they are your property." He thought I must be mocking him, but I assured him that it was true, and he went off with the whole flock.' The narrator added, 'O Lord, if I speak the truth, deliver us!'" "He had scarcely finished," said the Apostle, "when the rock moved away from the mouth of the cave and let the three men come forth."[1] It is related that Abú Sa'íd Kharráz said: "For a long time I used to eat only once in three days. I was journeying in the desert, and on the third day I felt weak through hunger. A voice from heaven cried to me, 'Dost thou prefer food that will quiet thy lower nature, or an expedient that will enable thee to overcome thy weakness without food?' I replied, 'O God, give me strength!' Then I rose and travelled twelve stages

[1] Here follow (1) a Tradition, related by Abú Hurayra, of three infants who were miraculously endowed with speech: (*a*) Jesus, (*b*) a child who exculpated the monk Jurayj (George) when he was falsely accused by a harlot, (*c*) a child who divined the characters of a horseman and a woman. (2) A story of Zá'ida, the handmaid of the Caliph 'Umar: how a knight descended from heaven and gave her a message from Riḍwán, the keeper of Paradise, to the Prophet; and how, when she could not lift a bundle of firewood from a rock on which she had laid it, the Prophet bade the rock go with her and carry the firewood to 'Umar's house. (3) A story of 'Alá b. al-Ḥaḍramí, who, having been sent on a warlike expedition by the Prophet, walked dry-shod across a river with his company. (4) A story of 'Abdalláh b. 'Umar, at whose bidding a lion decamped and left the way open for a party of travellers. (5) A story of a man who was seen sitting in the air, and when Abraham asked him by what means he had obtained such power, replied that he had renounced the world and that God had bestowed on him an aerial dwelling-place where he was not disturbed by any thought of mankind. (6) A story of the Caliph 'Umar, who was on the point of being killed by a Persian, when two lions suddenly appeared and caused the assassin to desist. (7) A story of Khálid b. Walíd, who said "Bismillah" and drank a deadly poison, which did him no harm. (8) A story, related by Ḥasan of Baṣra, of a negro who turned the walls of a tavern into gold. (9) A story, related by Ibráhím b. Adham, of a shepherd who smote a rock with his staff and caused water to gush forth. (10) A story of a cup which pronounced the words "Glory to God" in the hearing of Abú Dardá and Salmán Fárisí.

without meat or drink." It is well known that at the present day the house of Sahl b. 'Abdalláh at Tustar is called the House of the Wild Beasts (*bayt al-sibá'*), and the people of Tustar are agreed that many wild beasts used to come to him, and that he fed and tended them. Abu 'l-Qásim of Merv tells the following story: "As I was walking on the seashore with Abú Sa'íd Kharráz, I saw a youth clad in a patched frock and carrying a bucket (*rakwa*), to which an ink-bottle was fastened. Kharráz said: 'When I look at this youth he seems to be one of the adepts (*rasídagán*), but when I look at his ink-bottle I think he is a student. Let me question him.' So he accosted the youth and said, 'What is the way to God?' The youth answered: 'There are two ways to God: the way of the vulgar and the way of the elect. Thou hast no knowledge of the latter, but the way of the vulgar, which thou pursuest, is to regard thine own actions as the cause of attaining to God, and to suppose that an ink-bottle is one of the things that interfere with attainment.'" Dhu 'l-Nún the Egyptian says: "Once I embarked in a ship voyaging from Egypt to Jidda. Among the passengers was a youth wearing a patched frock. I was eager to be his companion, but he inspired me with such awe that I did not venture to address him, for his spiritual state was very exalted and he was constantly engaged in devotion. One day a certain man lost a purse of jewels, and suspicion fell on this youth. They were about to maltreat him, but I said, 'Let me question him courteously.' I told him that he was suspected of theft and that I had saved him from maltreatment. 'And now,' I said, 'what is to be done?' He looked towards Heaven and spoke a few words. The fishes came to the surface of the sea, each with a jewel in its mouth. He took a jewel and gave it to his accuser; then he set his foot on the water and walked away. Thereupon the real thief dropped the purse, and the people in the ship repented." Ibráhím Raqqí[1] is related to have said: "In my novitiate I set out to visit Muslim Maghribí. I found him in his mosque,

[1] Died in 326 A.H. See Abu 'l-Maḥásin, *Nujúm*, ii, 284, 13.

acting as precentor. He pronounced *al-ḥamd* incorrectly. I said to myself, 'My trouble has been wasted.' Next day, when I was going to the bank of the Euphrates to perform the religious ablution, I saw a lion asleep on the road. I turned back, and was faced by another lion which had been following me. Hearing my cry of despair, Muslim came forth from his cell. When the lions saw him they humbled themselves before him. He took the ear of each one and rubbed it, saying, 'O dogs of God, have not I told you that you must not interfere with my guests?' Then he said to me: 'O Abú Isḥáq, thou hast busied thyself with correcting thy exterior for the sake of God's creatures, hence thou art afraid of them; but it has been my business to correct my interior for God's sake, hence His creatures are afraid of me.'" One day my Shaykh set out from Bayt al-Jinn to Damascus. Heavy rain had begun to fall, and I was walking with difficulty in the mire. I noticed that the Shaykh's shoes and clothes were perfectly dry. On my pointing this out to him, he said: "Yes; God has preserved me from mud ever since I put unquestioning trust in Him and guarded my interior from the desolation of cupidity." Once an experience occurred to me which I could not unravel. I set out to visit Shaykh Abu 'l-Qásim Gurgání at Ṭús. I found him alone in his chamber in the mosque, and he was expounding precisely the same difficulty to a pillar, so that I was answered without having asked the question. "O Shaykh," I cried, "to whom art thou saying this?" He replied: "O son, God just now caused this pillar to speak and ask me this question." In Farghána, at a village called Ashlátak,[1] there was an old man, one of the *Awtád* of the earth. His name was Báb 'Umar[2]—all the dervishes in that country give the title of Báb to their great Shaykhs—and he had an old wife called Fáṭima. I went from Uzkand to see him. When I entered his presence he said: "Why have you come?" I replied: "In order that I might see the Shaykh in person and that he might look on me with kindness." He said: "I have been seeing you continually

[1] L. سلاتک. IJ. اسلاتک. [2] See *Nafaḥát*, No. 351.

since such and such a day, and I wish to see you as long as you are not removed from my sight." I computed the day and year: it was the very day on which my conversion began. The Shaykh said: "To traverse distance (*sipardan-i masáfat*) is child's play: henceforth pay visits by means of thought (*himmat*); it is not worth while to visit any person (*shakhṣ*), and there is no virtue in bodily presence (*ḥuḍúr-i ashbáḥ*)." Then he bade Fáṭima bring something to eat. She brought a dish of new grapes, although it was not the season for them, and some fresh ripe dates, which cannot possibly be procured in Farghána. On another occasion, while I was sitting alone, as is my custom, beside the tomb of Shaykh Abú Sa'íd at Mihna, I saw a white pigeon fly under the cloth (*fúṭa*) covering the sepulchre. I supposed that the bird had escaped from its owner, but when I looked under the cloth nothing was to be seen. This happened again next day, and also on the third day. I was at a loss to understand it, until one night I dreamed of the saint and asked him about my experience. He answered: "That pigeon is my good conduct (*ṣafá-yi mu'ámalat*), which comes every day to my tomb to feast with me (*ba-munádamat-i man*)."[1] I might adduce many more of these tales without exhausting them, but my purpose in this book is to establish the principles of Ṣúfiism. As regards derivatives and matters of conduct books have been compiled by the traditionists (*naqqálán*), and these topics are disseminated from the pulpit by preachers (*mudhakkirán*). Now I will give, in one or two sections, an adequate account of certain points bearing on the present discussion, in order that I may not have to return to it again.

Discourse on the Superiority of the Prophets to the Saints.

You must know that, by universal consent of the Ṣúfí Shaykhs, the saints are at all times and in all circumstances subordinate to the prophets, whose missions they confirm.

[1] Here the author tells the story, which has already been related (p. 142 *supra*), of Abú Bakr Warráq, who was commanded by Muḥammad b. 'Alí of Tirmidh to throw some of the latter's mystical writings into the Oxus.

The prophets are superior to the saints, because the end of saintship is only the beginning of prophecy. Every prophet is a saint, but some saints are not prophets. The prophets are constantly exempt from the attributes of humanity, while the saints are so only temporarily; the fleeting state (*ḥál*) of the saint is the permanent station (*maqám*) of the prophet; and that which to the saints is a station (*maqám*) is to the prophets a veil (*ḥijáb*). This view is held unanimously by the Sunní divines and the Ṣúfí mystics, but it is opposed by a sect of the Ḥashwiyya—the Anthropomorphists (*mujassima*) of Khurásán—who discourse in a self-contradictory manner concerning the principles of Unification (*tawḥíd*), and who, although they do not know the fundamental doctrine of Ṣúfiism, call themselves saints. Saints they are indeed, but saints of the Devil. They maintain that the saints are superior to the prophets, and it is a sufficient proof of their error that they declare an ignoramus to be more excellent than Muḥammad, the Chosen of God. The same vicious opinion is held by another sect of Anthropomorphists (*mushabbiha*), who pretend to be Ṣúfís, and admit the doctrines of the incarnation of God and His descent (into the human body) by transmigration (*intiqál*), and the division (*tajziya*) of His essence. I will treat fully of these matters when I give my promised account of the two reprobated sects (of Ṣúfís). The sects to which I am now referring claim to be Moslems, but they agree with the Brahmans in denying special privileges to the prophets; and whoever believes in this doctrine becomes an infidel. Moreover, the prophets are propagandists and Imáms, and the saints are their followers, and it is absurd to suppose that the follower of an Imám is superior to the Imám himself. In short, the lives, experiences, and spiritual powers of all the saints together appear as nothing compared with one act of a true prophet, because the saints are seekers and pilgrims, whereas the prophets have arrived and have found and have returned with the command to preach and to convert the people. If any one of the above-mentioned heretics should urge that an ambassador sent by a king is usually inferior to the person to whom he is sent, as e.g. Gabriel is inferior to the Apostles, and that this is against my argument, I reply that an ambassador sent to a single person should be inferior to him, but when an ambassador is sent to a large number of persons or to a people, he is superior to them, as the Apostles are superior to the nations. Therefore one moment of the prophets is better than the whole life of the saints, because when the saints reach their goal they tell of contemplation (*musháhadat*) and obtain release from the veil of humanity (*bashariyyat*), although they are essentially men. On the other hand, contemplation is the first step of the apostle; and since the apostle's starting-place is the saint's goal, they cannot be judged by the same standard. Do not you perceive that, according to the unanimous opinion of all the saints who seek God, the station of union (*jam'*) belongs to the perfection of saintship? Now, in this station, a man attains such a degree of rapturous love that his intelligence is enraptured in gazing upon the act of God (*fi'l*), and in his longing for the Divine Agent (*fá'il*) he regards the whole universe as that and sees nothing but that. Thus Abú 'Alí Rúdbárí says: "Were the vision of that which we serve to vanish from us, we should lose the name of servantship (*'ubúdiyyat*)," for we derive the glory of worship (*'ibádat*) solely from vision of Him. This is the beginning of the state of the prophets, inasmuch as separation (*tafriqa*) is inconceivable in relation to them. They are entirely in the essence of union, whether they affirm or deny, whether they approach or turn away, whether they are at the beginning or at the end. Abraham, in the beginning of his state, looked on the sun and said: "*This is my Lord*," and he looked on the moon and stars and said: "*This is my Lord*" (Kor. vi, 76–8), because his heart was overwhelmed by the Truth and he was united in the essence of union. Therefore he saw naught else, or if he saw aught else he did not see it with the eye of "otherness" (*ghayr*), but with the eye of union (*jam'*), and in the reality of that vision he disavowed his own and said: "*I love not those that set*" (Kor. vi, 76). As he began with union, so he ended with union. Saintship has a beginning and an end, but prophecy has not. The prophets were prophets from the first, and shall be to the last, and before they existed they were prophets in the knowledge and will of God. Abú Yazíd was asked about the state of the prophets. He replied: "Far be it from me to say! We have no power to judge of them, and in our notions of them we are wholly ourselves. God has placed their denial and affirmation in such an exalted degree that human vision cannot reach unto it." Accordingly, as the rank of the saints is hidden from the perception of mankind, so the rank of the prophets is hidden from the judgment of the saints. Abú Yazíd was the proof (*ḥujjat*) of his age, and he says: "I saw that my spirit (*sirr*) was borne to the heavens. It looked at nothing and gave no heed, though Paradise and Hell were displayed to it, for it was freed from phenomena and veils. Then I became a bird, whose body was of Oneness and whose wings were of Everlastingness, and I continued to fly in the air of the Absolute (*huwiyyat*), until I passed into the sphere of Purification (*tanzíh*), and gazed upon the field of Eternity (*azaliyyat*) and beheld there the tree of Oneness. When I looked I myself was all those. I cried: 'O Lord, with my egoism (*maní-yi man*) I cannot attain to Thee, and I cannot escape from my selfhood. What am I to do?' God spake: 'O Abú Yazíd, thou must win release from thy "thou-ness" by following My beloved i.e. (Muḥammad). Smear thine eyes with the dust of his feet and follow him continually.'" This is a long narrative. The Ṣúfís call it the Ascension (*mi'ráj*) of Báyazíd;[1] and the term "ascension" denotes proximity to God (*qurb*). The ascension of prophets takes place outwardly and in the body, whereas that of saints takes place inwardly and in the spirit. The body of an apostle resembles the heart

[1] A full account of Báyazíd's ascension is given in the *Tadhkirat al-Awliyá*, i, 172 ff.

and spirit of a saint in purity and nearness to God. This is a manifest superiority. When a saint is enraptured and intoxicated he is withdrawn from himself by means of a spiritual ladder and brought near to God; and as soon as he returns to the state of sobriety all those evidences have taken shape in his mind and he has gained knowledge of them. Accordingly, there is a great difference between one who is carried thither in person and one who is carried thither only in thought (*fikrat*), for thought involves duality.

Discourse on the Superiority of the Prophets and Saints to the Angels.

The whole community of orthodox Moslems and all the Ṣúfí Shaykhs agree that the prophets and such of the saints as are guarded from sin (*maḥfúẓ*) are superior to the angels. The opposite view is held by the Mu'tazilites, who declare that the angels are superior to the prophets, being of more exalted rank, of more subtle constitution, and more obedient to God. I reply that this is not as you imagine, for an obedient body, an exalted rank, and a subtle constitution cannot be causes of superiority, which belongs only to those on whom God has bestowed it. Iblís had all the qualities that you mention, yet he is universally acknowledged to have become accursed. The superiority of the prophets is indicated by the fact that God commanded the angels to worship Adam; for the state of one who is worshipped is higher than the state of the worshipper. If they argue that, just as a true believer is superior to the Ka'ba, an inanimate mass of stone, although he bows down before it, so the angels may be superior to Adam, although they bowed down before him, I reply: "No one says that a believer bows down to a house or an altar or a wall, but all say that he bows down to God, and it is admitted by all that the angels bowed down to Adam (Kor. ii, 32). How, then, can the Ka'ba be compared to Adam? A traveller may worship God on the back of the animal which he is riding, and he is excused if his face be not turned towards the Ka'ba; and, in like manner, one who has lost his bearings in a desert, so that he cannot tell the direction of the Ka'ba, will have done his duty in whatever direction he may turn to pray. The angels offered no excuse when they bowed down to Adam, and the one who made an excuse for himself became accursed." These are clear proofs to any person of insight.

Again, the angels are equal to the prophets in knowledge of God, but not in rank. The angels are without lust, covetousness, and evil; their nature is devoid of hypocrisy and guile, and they are instinctively obedient to God; whereas lust is an impediment in human nature; and men have a propensity to commit sins and to be impressed by the vanities of this world; and Satan has so much power over their bodies that he circulates with the blood in their veins; and closely attached to them is the lower soul (*nafs*), which incites them to all manner of wickedness. Therefore, one whose nature has all these characteristics and who, in spite of the violence of his lust, refrains from immorality, and notwithstanding his covetousness renounces this world, and, though his heart is still tempted by the Devil, turns back from sin and averts his face from sensual depravity in order to occupy himself with devotion and persevere in piety and mortify his lower soul and contend against the Devil, such a one is in reality superior to the angel who is not the battle-field of lust, and is naturally without desire of food and pleasures, and has no care for wife and child and kinsfolk, and need not have recourse to means and instruments, and is not absorbed in corrupt ambitions. A Gabriel, who worships God so many thousands of years in the hope of gaining a robe of honour, and the honour bestowed on him was that of acting as Muḥammad's groom on the night of the Ascension—how should he be superior to one who disciplines and mortifies his lower soul by day and night in this world, until God looks on him with favour and grants to him the grace of seeing Himself and delivers him from all distracting thoughts? When the pride of the angels passed all bounds, and every one of them vaunted the purity of his conduct and spoke with an unbridled tongue in blame of mankind, God resolved that He would show to them their real state. He therefore bade them choose three of the chief among them, in whom they had confidence, to go to the earth and be its governors and reform its people. So three angels were chosen, but before they came to the earth one of them perceived its corruption and begged God to let him return. When the other two arrived on the earth God changed their nature so that they felt a desire for food and drink and were inclined to lust, and God punished them on that account, and the angels were forced to recognize the superiority of mankind to themselves.[1] In short, the elect among the true believers are superior to the elect among the angels, and the ordinary believers are superior to the ordinary angels. Accordingly those men who are preserved (*ma'ṣúm*) and protected (*maḥfúẓ*) from sin are more excellent than Gabriel and Michael, and those who are not thus preserved are better than the Recording Angels (*ḥafaẓa*) and the noble Scribes (*kirám-i kátibín*).

Something has been said on this subject by every one of the Shaykhs. God awards superiority to whom He pleases, over whom He pleases. You must know that saintship is a Divine mystery which is revealed only through conduct (*rawish*). A saint is known only to a saint. If this matter could be made plain to all reasonable men it would be impossible to distinguish the friend from the foe or the spiritual adept from the careless worldling. Therefore God so willed that the pearl of His love should be set in the shell of popular contempt and be cast into the sea of affliction, in order that those who seek it may hazard their lives on account of its preciousness and dive to the bottom of this ocean of death, where they will either win their desire or bring their mortal state to an end.

8. THE KHARRÁZÍS.

They are the followers of Abú Sa'íd Kharráz, who wrote brilliant works on Ṣúfiism and attained a high degree in

[1] See Kor. ii, 96 ff.

detachment from the world. He was the first to explain the state of annihilation and subsistence (*faná ú baqá*), and he comprehended his whole doctrine in these two terms. Now I will declare their meaning and show the errors into which some have fallen in this respect, in order that you may know what his doctrine is and what the Ṣúfís intend when they employ these current expressions.

Discourse on Subsistence (baqá) *and Annihilation* (faná).

You must know that annihilation and subsistence have one meaning in science and another meaning in mysticism, and that formalists (*ẓáhiriyán*) are more puzzled by these words than by any other technical terms of the Ṣúfís. Subsistence in its scientific and etymological acceptation is of three kinds: (1) a subsistence that begins and ends in annihilation, e.g. this world, which had a beginning and will have an end, and is now subsistent; (2) a subsistence that came into being and will never be annihilated, viz. Paradise and Hell and the next world and its inhabitants; (3) a subsistence that always was and always will be, viz. the subsistence of God and His eternal attributes. Accordingly, knowledge of annihilation lies in your knowing that this world is perishable, and knowledge of subsistence lies in your knowledge that the next world is everlasting.

But the subsistence and annihilation of a state (*ḥál*) denotes, for example, that when ignorance is annihilated knowledge is necessarily subsistent, and that when sin is annihilated piety is subsistent, and that when a man acquires knowledge of his piety his forgetfulness (*ghaflat*) is annihilated by remembrance of God (*dhikr*), i.e., when anyone gains knowledge of God and becomes subsistent in knowledge of Him he is annihilated from (entirely loses) ignorance of Him, and when he is annihilated from forgetfulness he becomes subsistent in remembrance of Him, and this involves the discarding of blameworthy attributes and the substitution of praiseworthy attributes. A different signification, however, is attached to the terms in question by the elect among the Ṣúfís. They do not refer these expressions to "knowledge" (*'ilm*) or to "state" (*ḥál*), but apply them solely to the degree of perfection attained by the saints who have become free from the pains of mortification and have escaped from the prison of "stations" and the vicissitude of "states", and whose search has ended in discovery, so that they have seen all things visible, and have heard all things audible, and have discovered all the secrets of the heart; and who, recognizing the imperfection of their own discovery, have turned away from all things and have purposely become annihilated in the object of desire, and in the very essence of desire have lost all desires of their own, for when a man becomes annihilated from his attributes he attains to perfect subsistence, he is neither near nor far, neither stranger nor intimate, neither sober nor intoxicated, neither separated nor united; he has no name, or sign, or brand, or mark.

In short, real annihilation from anything involves consciousness of its imperfection and absence of desire for it, not merely that a man should say, when he likes a thing, "I am subsistent therein," or when he dislikes it, that he should say, "I am annihilated therefrom"; for these qualities are characteristic of one who is still seeking. In annihilation there is no love or hate, and in subsistence there is no consciousness of union or separation. Some wrongly imagine that annihilation signifies loss of essence and destruction of personality, and that subsistence indicates the subsistence of God in Man; both these notions are absurd. In India I had a dispute on this subject with a man who claimed to be versed in Koranic exegesis and theology. When I examined his pretensions I found that he knew nothing of annihilation and subsistence, and that he could not distinguish the eternal from the phenomenal. Many ignorant Ṣúfís consider that total annihilation (*faná-yi kulliyyat*) is possible, but this is a manifest error, for annihilation of the different parts of a material substance (*ṭínati*) can never take place. I ask these ignorant and mistaken men: "What do you mean by this kind of annihilation?" If they answer,

"Annihilation of substance" (*faná-yi 'ayn*), that is impossible; and if they answer, "Annihilation of attributes," that is only possible in so far as one attribute may be annihilated through the subsistence of another attribute, both attributes belonging to Man; but it is absurd to suppose that anyone can subsist through the attributes of another individual. The Nestorians of Rúm and the Christians hold that Mary annihilated by self-mortification all the attributes of humanity (*awṣáf-i násúti*) and that the Divine subsistence became attached to her, so that she was made subsistent through the subsistence of God, and that Jesus was the result thereof, and that he was not originally composed of the stuff of humanity, because his subsistence is produced by realization of the subsistence of God; and that, in consequence of this, he and his mother and God are all subsistent through one subsistence, which is eternal and an attribute of God. All this agrees with the doctrine of the anthropomorphistic sects of the Ḥashwiyya, who maintain that the Divine essence is a *locus* of phenomena (*maḥall-i ḥawádith*) and that the Eternal may have phenomenal attributes. I ask all who proclaim such tenets: "What difference is there between the view that the Eternal is the *locus* of the phenomenal and the view that the phenomenal is the *locus* of the Eternal, or between the assertion that the Eternal has phenomenal attributes and the assertion that the phenomenal has eternal attributes?" Such doctrines involve materialism (*dahr*) and destroy the proof of the phenomenal nature of the universe, and compel us to say that both the Creator and His creation are eternal or that both are phenomenal, or that what is created may be commingled with what is uncreated, and that what is uncreated may descend into what is created. If, as they cannot help admitting, the creation is phenomenal, then their Creator also must be phenomenal, because the *locus* of a thing is like its substance; if the *locus* (*maḥall*) is phenomenal, it follows that the contents of the *locus* (*ḥáll*) are phenomenal too. In fine, when one thing is linked and united and commingled with another, both things are in principle as one.

Accordingly, our subsistence and annihilation are attributes of ourselves, and resemble each other in respect of their being our attributes. Annihilation is the annihilation of one attribute through the subsistence of another attribute. One may speak, however, of an annihilation that is independent of subsistence, and also of a subsistence that is independent of annihilation: in that case annihilation means "annihilation of all remembrance of other", and subsistence means "subsistence of the remembrance of God" (*baqá-yi dhikr-i ḥaqq*). Whoever is annihilated from his own will subsists in the will of God, because thy will is perishable and the will of God is everlasting: when thou standest by thine own will thou standest by annihilation, but when thou art absolutely controlled by the will of God thou standest by subsistence. Similarly, the power of fire transmutes to its own quality anything that falls into it, and surely the power of God's will is greater than that of fire; but fire affects only the quality of iron without changing its substance, for iron can never become fire.

SECTION.

All the Shaykhs have given subtle indications on this subject. Abú Sa'íd Kharráz, the author of the doctrine, says: "Annihilation is annihilation of consciousness of manhood (*'ubúdiyyat*), and subsistence is subsistence in the contemplation of Godhead (*iláhiyyat*)," i.e., it is an imperfection to be conscious in one's actions that one is a man, and one attains to real manhood (*bandagí*) when one is not conscious of them, but is annihilated so as not to see them, and becomes subsistent through beholding the action of God. Hence all one's actions are referred to God, not to one's self, and whereas a man's actions that are connected with himself are imperfect, those which are attached to him by God are perfect. Therefore, when anyone becomes annihilated from things that depend on himself, he becomes subsistent through the beauty of Godhead. Abú Ya'qúb Nahrajúrí says: "A man's true servantship (*'ubúdiyyat*) lies in annihilation and subsistence," because no one is capable of serving God with sincerity until he renounces all self-interest: therefore to renounce humanity (*ádamiyyat*) is annihilation, and to be sincere in servantship is subsistence. And Ibráhím b. Shaybán says: "The science of annihilation and subsistence turns on sincerity (*ikhlás*) and unity (*wáḥidiyyat*) and true servantship; all else is error and heresy," i.e., when anyone acknowledges the unity of God he feels himself overpowered by the omnipotence of God, and one who is overpowered (*maghlúb*) is annihilated in the might of his vanquisher; and when his annihilation is rightly fulfilled on him, he confesses his weakness and sees no resource except to serve God, and tries to gain His satisfaction (*riḍá*). And whoever explains these terms otherwise, i.e. annihilation as meaning "annihilation of substance" and subsistence as meaning "subsistence of God (in Man)", is a heretic and a Christian, as has been stated above.

Now I, 'Alí b. 'Uthmán al-Jullábí, declare that all these sayings are near to each other in meaning, although they differ in expression; and their real gist is this, that annihilation comes to a man through vision of the majesty of God and through the revelation of Divine omnipotence to his heart, so that in the overwhelming sense of His majesty this world and the next world are obliterated from his mind, and "states" and "stations" appear contemptible in the sight of his aspiring thought, and what is shown to him of miraculous grace vanishes into nothing: he becomes dead to reason and passion alike, dead even to annihilation itself; and in that annihilation of annihilation his tongue proclaims God, and his mind and body are humble and abased, as in the beginning when Adam's posterity were drawn forth from his loins without admixture of evil and took the pledge of servantship to God (Kor. vii, 171).

Such are the principles of annihilation and subsistence. I have discussed a portion of the subject in the chapter on Poverty and Ṣúfiism, and wherever these terms occur in the present work they bear the meaning which I have explained.

9. THE KHAFÍFÍS.

They are the followers of Abú 'Abdalláh Muḥammad b. Khafíf of Shíráz, an eminent mystic in his time and the author of celebrated treatises on various branches of Ṣúfiism. He was a man of great spiritual influence, and was not led by his lusts. I have heard that he contracted four hundred marriages. This was due to the fact that he was of royal descent, and that after his conversion the people of Shíráz paid great court to him, and the daughters of kings and nobles desired to marry him for the sake of the blessing which would accrue to them. He used to comply with their wishes, and then divorce them before consummation of the marriage. But in the course of his life forty wives, who were strangers to him (*bégána*), two or three at a time, used to serve him as bed-makers (*khádimán-i firásh*), and one of them—she was the daughter of a vizier—lived with him for forty years. I have heard from Abu 'l-Ḥasan 'Alí b. Bakrán of Shíráz that one day several of his wives were gathered together, and each one was telling some story about him. They all agreed *sese nunquam eum vidisse libidini obsequentem.* Hitherto each of them had believed that she was peculiarly treated in this respect, and when they learned that the Shaykh's behaviour was the same towards them all, they were astonished and doubted whether such was truly the case. Accordingly, they sent two of their number to question the vizier's daughter, who was his favourite, as to his dealings with her. She replied: "When the Shaykh wedded me and I was informed that he would visit me that night, I prepared a fine repast and adorned myself assiduously. As soon as he came and the food was brought in, he called me to him and looked for a while first at me and then at the food. Then he took my hand and drew it into his sleeve. From his breast to his navel there were fifteen knots (*'aqd*) growing out of his belly. He said, 'Ask me what these are'; so I asked him and he replied, 'They are knots made by the tribulation and anguish of my abstinence in renouncing a face like this and viands like these.'

He said no more, but departed; and that is all my intimacy with him."

The form of his doctrine in Ṣúfiism is "absence" (*ghaybat*) and "presence" (*ḥuḍúr*). I will explain it as far as possible.

Discourse on Absence (ghaybat) *and Presence* (ḥuḍúr).

These terms, although apparently opposed to each other, express the same meaning from different points of view. "Presence" is "presence of the heart", as a proof of intuitive faith (*yaqín*), so that what is hidden from it has the same force as what is visible to it. "Absence" is "absence of the heart from all things except God" to such an extent that it becomes absent from itself and absent even from its absence, so that it no longer regards itself; and the sign of this state is withdrawal from all formal authority (*ḥukm-i rusúm*), as when a prophet is divinely preserved from what is unlawful. Accordingly, absence from one's self is presence with God, and *vice versâ*. God is the lord of the human heart: when a divine rapture (*jadhbat*) overpowers the heart of the seeker, the absence of his heart becomes equivalent to its presence (with God); partnership (*shirkat*) and division (*qismat*) disappear, and relationship to "self" comes to an end, as one of the Shaykhs has said in verse—

"*Thou art the Lord of my heart,*
Without any partner: how, then, can it be divided?"

Inasmuch as God is sole lord of the heart, He has absolute power to keep it absent or present as He will, and, in regard to the essence of the case, this is the whole argument for the doctrine of His favourites; but when a distinction is made, the Shaykhs hold various opinions on the subject, some preferring "presence" to "absence", while others declare that "absence" is superior to "presence". There is the same controversy as that concerning sobriety and intoxication, which I have explained above; but these terms indicate that the human attributes are still subsistent, whereas "absence" and "presence" indicate that the human attributes are annihilated: therefore the latter terms are in reality more sublime. "Absence" is preferred to "presence" by Ibn 'Aṭá, Ḥusayn b. Manṣúr (al-Ḥalláj), Abú Bakr Shiblí, Bundár b. al-Ḥusayn, Abú Ḥamza of Baghdád, Sumnún Muḥibb, and a number of the Shaykhs of 'Iráq. They say: "Thou thyself art the greatest of all veils between thee and God: when thou hast become absent from thyself, the evils implicit in thy being are annihilated in thee, and thy state undergoes a fundamental change: the 'stations' of novices become a veil to thee, and the 'states' of those who seek God become a source of mischief to thee; thine eye is closed to thyself and to all that is other than God, and thy human attributes are consumed by the flame of proximity to God (*qurbat*). This is the same state of 'absence' in which God drew thee forth from the loins of Adam, and caused thee to hear His exalted word, and distinguished thee by the honorary robe of Unification and the garment of contemplation; so long as thou wert absent from thyself, thou wert present with God face to face, but when thou becamest present with thine own attributes, thou becamest absent from thy proximity to God. Therefore thy 'presence' is thy perdition. This is the meaning of God's word, '*And now are ye come unto us alone, as We created you at first*'" (Kor, vi, 94). On the other hand, Ḥárith Muḥásibí, Junayd, Sahl b. 'Abdalláh, Abú Ja'far Ḥaddád,[1] Ḥamdún Qaṣṣár, Abú Muḥammad Jurayrí, Ḥuṣrí, Muḥammad b. Khafíf, who is the author of the doctrine, and others hold that "presence" is superior to "absence". They argue that inasmuch as all excellences are bound up with "presence", and as "absence" from one's self is a way leading to "presence" with God, the way becomes an imperfection after you have arrived at the goal. "Presence" is the fruit of "absence", but what light is to be found in "absence" without "presence"? A man must needs renounce heedlessness in order that, by means of this "absence", he may attain to "presence"; and

[1] *Nafaḥát*, No. 201.

when he has attained his object, the means by which he attained it has no longer any worth.

"*The 'absent' one is not he who is absent from his country,*
But he who is absent from all desire.
The 'present' one is not he who hath no desire,
But he who hath no heart (*no thought of worldly things*),
So that his desire is ever fixed on God."

It is a well-known story that one of the disciples of Dhu 'l-Nún set out to visit Abú Yazíd. When he came to Abú Yazíd's cell and knocked at the door Abú Yazíd said: "Who art thou, and whom dost thou wish to see?" He answered: "Abú Yazíd." Abú Yazíd said: "Who is Abú Yazíd, and where is he, and what thing is he? I have been seeking Abú Yazíd for a long while, but I have not found him." When the disciple returned to Dhu 'l-Nún and told him what had passed, Dhu 'l-Nún said: "My brother Abú Yazíd is lost with those who are lost in God." A certain man came to Junayd and said: "Be present with me for a moment that I may speak to thee." Junayd answered: "O young man, you demand of me something that I have long been seeking. For many years I have been wishing to become present with myself a moment, but I cannot; how, then, can I become present with you just now?" Therefore, "absence" involves the sorrow of being veiled, while "presence" involves the joy of revelation, and the former state can never be equal to the latter. Shaykh Abú Sa'íd says on this subject—

Taqashsha'a ghaymu 'l-hajri 'an qamari 'l-ḥubbi
Wa-asfara núru 'l-ṣubḥi 'an ẓulmati 'l-ghaybi.

"The clouds of separation have been cleared away from the moon of love,
And the light of morning has shone forth from the darkness of the Unseen."

The distinction made by the Shaykhs between these two terms is mystical, and on the surface merely verbal, for they seem to be approximately the same. To be present with God is to be absent from one's self—what is the difference?—and one who is not absent from himself is not present with God. Thus, forasmuch as the impatience of Job in his affliction did not proceed from himself, but on the contrary he was then absent from himself, God did not distinguish his impatience from patience, and when he cried, "*Evil hath befallen me*" (Kor. xxi, 83), God said, "*Verily, he was patient.*" This is evidently a judgment founded on the essential nature of the case (*ḥukm ba-'ayn*). It is related that Junayd said: "For a time I was such that the inhabitants of heaven and earth wept over my bewilderment (*ḥayrat*); then, again, I became such that I wept over their absence (*ghaybat*); and now my state is such that I have no knowledge either of them or of myself." This is an excellent indication of "presence".

I have briefly explained the meaning of "presence" and "absence" in order that you may be acquainted with the doctrine of the Khafífís, and may also know in what sense these terms are used by the Ṣúfís.

10. THE SAYYÁRÍS.

They are the followers of Abu 'l-'Abbás Sayyárí, the Imám of Merv. He was learned in all the sciences and associated with Abú Bakr Wásiṭí. At the present day he has numerous followers in Nasá and Merv. His school of Ṣúfiism is the only one that has kept its original doctrine unchanged, and the cause of this fact is that Nasá and Merv have never been without some person who acknowledged his authority and took care that his followers should maintain the doctrine of their founder. The Sayyárís of Nasá carried on a discussion with those of Merv by means of letters, and I have seen part of this correspondence at Merv; it is very fine. Their expositions are based on "union" (*jam'*) and "separation" (*tafriqa*). These words are common to all scientists and are employed by specialists in every branch of learning as a means of rendering their explanations intelligible, but they bear different meanings in each case. Thus, in arithmetic *jam'* denotes the addition and *tafriqa* the subtraction of numbers; in grammar *jam'* is the agreement of words in derivation, while *tafriqa* is the difference in meaning; in law *jam'* is analogy (*qiyás*) and *tafriqa* the characteristics of an authoritative text (*ṣifát-i nuṣṣ*), or *jam'* is the text and *tafriqa* the analogy; in divinity *jam* denotes the essential and *tafriqa* the formal attributes of God.[1] But the Ṣúfís do not use these terms in any of the significations which I have mentioned. Now, therefore, I will explain the meaning attached to them by the Ṣúfís and the various opinions of the Shaykhs on this subject.

Discourse on Union (jam') *and Separation* (tafriqa).

God united all mankind in His call, as He says, "*And God calls to the abode of peace*"; then He separated them in respect of Divine guidance, and said, "*and guides whom He willeth into the right way*" (Kor. x, 26). He called them all, and banished some in accordance with the manifestation of His will; He united them all and gave a command, and then separated them, rejecting some and leaving them without succour, but accepting others and granting to them Divine aid; then once more he united a certain number and separated them, giving to some immunity from sin and to others a propensity towards evil. Accordingly the real mystery of union is the knowledge and will of God, while separation is the manifestation of that which He commands and forbids: e.g., He commanded Abraham to behead Ishmael, but willed that he should not do so; and He commanded Iblís to worship Adam, but willed the contrary; and He commanded Adam not to eat the corn, but willed that he should eat it; and so forth. Union is that which He unites by His attributes, and separation is that which He separates by His acts. All this involves cessation of human volition and affirmation of the Divine will so as to exclude all personal initiative. As regards what has been said on the subject of union and separation, all the Sunnís, except the

[1] For the distinction between *ṣifát-i dhát* and *ṣifát-i fi'l* see Dozy, *Supplément*, ii, 810.

Mu'tazilites, are in agreement with the Ṣúfí Shaykhs, but at this point they begin to diverge, some applying the terms in question to the Divine Unity (*tawḥíd*), some to the Divine attributes, and some to the Divine acts. Those who refer to the Divine Unity say that there are two degrees of union, one in the attributes of God and the other in the attributes of Man. The former is the mystery of Unification (*tawḥíd*), in which human actions have no part whatever; the latter denotes acknowledgment of the Divine Unity with sincere conviction and unfailing resolution. This is the opinion of Abú 'Alí Rúdbárí. Those, again, who refer these terms to the Divine attributes say that union is an attribute of God, and separation an act of God in which Man does not co-operate, because God has no rival in Godhead. Therefore union can be referred only to His substance and attributes, for union is equality in the fundamental matter (*al-taswiyat fi 'l-aṣl*), and no two things are equal in respect of eternity except His substance and His attributes, which, when they are separated by expository analysis (*'ibárat ú tafṣíl*), are not united. This means that God has eternal attributes, which are peculiar to Him and subsist through Him; and that He and His attributes are not two, for His Unity does not admit difference and number. On this ground, union is impossible except in the sense indicated above.

Separation in predicament (*al-tafriqat fi 'l-ḥukm*) refers to the actions of God, all of which are separate in this respect. The predicament of one is being (*wujúd*); of another, not-being (*'adam*), but a not-being that is capable of being; of another, annihilation (*faná*), and of another subsistence (*baqá*). There are some, again, who refer these terms to knowledge (*'ilm*) and say that union is knowledge of the Divine Unity and separation knowledge of the Divine ordinances: hence theology is union and jurisprudence is separation. One of the Shaykhs has said, to the same effect: "Union is that on which theologians (*ahl al-'ilm*) are agreed, and separation is that on which they differ." Again, all the Ṣúfí mystics, whenever they use the term "separation" in the course of their expositions and indications, attach to it the meaning of "human actions" (*makásib*), e.g. self-mortification, and by "union" they signify "divine gifts" (*mawáhib*), e.g. contemplation. Whatever is gained by means of mortification is "separation", and whatever is solely the result of Divine favour and guidance is "union". It is Man's glory that, while his actions exist and mortification is possible, he should escape by God's goodness from the imperfection of his own actions, and should find them to be absorbed in the bounties of God, so that he depends entirely on God and commits all his attributes to His charge and refers all his actions to Him and none to himself, as Gabriel told the Apostle that God said: "My servant continually seeks access to Me by means of works of supererogation until I love him; and when I love him, I am his ear and his eye and his hand and his heart and his tongue: through Me he hears and sees and speaks and grasps," i.e., in remembering Me he is enraptured by the remembrance (*dhikr*) of Me, and his own "acquisition" (*kasb*) is annihilated so as to have no part in his remembrance, and My remembrance overpowers his remembrance, and the relationship of humanity (*ádamiyyat*) is entirely removed from his remembrance: then My remembrance is his remembrance, and in his rapture he becomes even as Abú Yazíd in the hour when he said: "Glory to me! how great is my majesty!" These words were the outward sign of his speech, but the speaker was God. Similarly, the Apostle said: "God speaks by the tongue of 'Umar." The fact is that when the Divine omnipotence manifests its dominion over humanity, it transports a man out of his own being, so that his speech becomes the speech of God. But it is impossible that God should be mingled (*imtizáj*) with created beings or made one (*ittiḥád*) with His works or become incarnate (*ḥáll*) in things: God is exalted far above that, and far above that which the heretics ascribe to Him.

It may happen, then, that God's love holds absolute sway over the heart of His servant, and that his reason and natural faculties are too weak to sustain its rapture and intensity, and that he loses all control of his power to act (*kasb*). This state is called "union".[1] Herewith are connected all extraordinary miracles (*i'jáz*) and acts of miraculous grace (*karámát*). All ordinary actions are "separation", and all acts which violate custom are "union". God bestows these miracles on His prophets and saints, and refers His actions to them and theirs to Himself, as He hath said: "*Verily, they who swear fealty unto thee, swear fealty unto God*" (Kor. xlviii, 10), and again: "*Whosoever obeys the Apostle has obeyed God*" (Kor. iv, 82). Accordingly, His saints are united (*mujtami'*) by their inward feelings (*asrár*) and separated (*muftariq*) by their outward behaviour, so that their love of God is strengthened by the internal union, and the right fulfilment of their duty as servants of God is assured by their external separation. A certain great Shaykh says—

"*I have realized that which is within me, and my tongue hath conversed with Thee in secret,*
And we are united in one respect, but we are separated in another.
Although awe has hidden Thee from the glances of mine eye,
Ecstasy has made Thee near to my inmost parts."[2]

The state of being inwardly united he calls "union", and the secret conversation of the tongue he calls "separation"; then he indicates that both union and separation are in himself, and attributes the basis (*qá'ida*) of them to himself. This is very subtle.

SECTION.

Here I must notice a matter of controversy between us and those who maintain that the manifestation of union is the denial of separation, because the two terms contradict each

[1] Here the author illustrates the meaning of "union" and "separation" by the action of Muḥammad when he threw gravel in the eyes of the unbelievers at Badr, and by that of David when he slew Goliath. See p. 185 *supra*.

[2] The last words are corrupt and unmetrical in all the texts. I have found the true reading, مـن الأحشاء دانى, in a MS. of the *Kitáb al-Luma'* by Abú Naṣr al-Sarráj, which has recently come into the possession of Mr. A. G. Ellis.

other, and that when anyone passes under the absolute sway of Divine guidance he ceases to act and to mortify himself. This is sheer nullification (*ta'ṭíl*), for a man must never cease to practise devotion and mortify himself as long as he has the possibility and power of doing so. Moreover, union is not apart from separation, as light is apart from the sun, and accident from substance, and attribute from object: therefore, neither is self-mortification apart from Divine guidance, nor the Truth from the Law, nor discovery from search. But mortification may precede or follow Divine guidance. In the former case a man's tribulation is increased, because he is in "absence" (*ghaybat*), while in the latter case he has no trouble or pain, because he is in "presence" (*ḥaḍrat*). Those to whom negation is the source (*mashrab*) of actions, and to whom it seems to be the substance (*'ayn*) of action, commit a grave error. A man, however, may attain such a degree that he regards all his qualities as faulty and defective, for when he sees that his praiseworthy qualities are vicious and imperfect, his blameworthy qualities will necessarily appear more vicious. I adduce these considerations because some ignorant persons, who have fallen into an error that is closely akin to infidelity, assert that no result whatever depends upon our exertion, and that inasmuch as our actions and devotions are faulty and our mortifications are imperfect a thing left undone is better than a thing done. To this argument I reply: "You are agreed in supposing that everything done by us has an energy (*fi'l*), and you declare that our energies are a centre of defect and a source of evil and corruption: consequently you must also suppose that things left undone by us have an energy; and since in both cases there is an energy involving defect, how can you regard that which we leave undone as better than that which we do?" This notion evidently is a noxious delusion. Here we have an excellent criterion to distinguish the believer from the infidel. Both agree that their energies are inherently defective, but the believer, in accordance with God's command, deems a thing done to be better than a thing left undone, while the infidel, in accordance with his denial of the Creator (*t'aṭíl*), deems a thing left undone to be better than a thing done.

Union, then, involves this—that, although the imperfection of separation is recognized, its authority (*ḥukm*) should not be let go; and separation involves this—that, although one is veiled from the sight of union, he nevertheless thinks that separation is union. Muzayyin the Elder[1] says in this sense: "Union is the state of privilege (*khuṣúṣiyyat*) and separation is the state of a servant (*'ubúdiyyat*), these states being indissolubly combined with each other," because it is a work of the privileged state to fulfil the duties of servantship; therefore, although the tediousness and painfulness of self-mortification and personal effort may be removed from one who performs all that is required of him in this respect, it is impossible that the substance (*'ayn*) of self-mortification and religious obligation should be removed from anyone, even though he be in the essence of union, unless he has an evident excuse that is generally acknowledged by the authority of the religious law. Now I will explain this matter in order that you may better understand it.

Union is of two kinds: (1) sound union (*jam'-i salámat*), and (2) broken union (*jam'-i taksír*). Sound union is that which God produces in a man when he is in the state of rapture and ecstasy, and when God causes him to receive and fulfil His commandments and to mortify himself. This was the state of Sahl b. 'Abdalláh and Abú Ḥafṣ Ḥaddád and Abu 'l-'Abbás Sayyárí, the author of the doctrine. Abú Yazíd of Bisṭám, Abú Bakr Shiblí, Abu 'l-Ḥasan Ḥuṣrí, and a number of great Shaykhs were continually in a state of rapture until the hour of prayer arrived; then they returned to consciousness, and after performing their prayers became enraptured again. While thou art in the state of separation, thou art thou, and thou fulfillest the command of God; but when God transports thee He has the best right to see that thou performest His command, for two reasons: firstly, in order that the token of servantship may

[1] *Nafaḥát*, No. 188.

not be removed from thee, and secondly, in order that He may keep His promise that He will never let the law of Muḥammad be abrogated. "Broken union" (*jam'-i taksír*) is this: that a man's judgment becomes distraught and bewildered, so that it is like the judgment of a lunatic: then he is either excused from performing his religious obligations or rewarded (*mashkúr*) for performing them; and the state of him who is rewarded is sounder than the state of him who is excused.

You must know, in short, that union does not involve any peculiar "station" (*maqám*) or any peculiar "state" (*ḥál*), for union is the concentration of one's thoughts (*jam'-i himmat*) upon the object of one's desire. According to some the revelation of this matter takes place in the "stations" (*maqámát*), according to others in the "states" (*aḥwál*), and in either case the desire of the "united" person (*ṣáḥib jam'*) is attained by negating his desire. This holds good in everything, e.g., Jacob concentrated his thoughts on Joseph, so that he had no thought but of him; and Majnún concentrated his thoughts on Laylá, so that he saw only her in the whole world, and all created things assumed the form of Laylá in his eyes. One day, when Abú Yazíd was in his cell, some one came and asked: "Is Abú Yazíd here?" He answered: "Is any-one here except God?" And a certain Shaykh relates that a dervish came to Mecca and remained in contemplation of the Ka'ba for a whole year, during which time he neither ate nor drank, nor slept, nor cleansed himself, because of the concentration of his thoughts upon the Ka'ba, which thereby became the food of his body and the drink of his soul. The principle in all these cases is the same, viz. that God divided the one substance of His love and bestows a particle thereof, as a peculiar gift, upon every one of His friends in proportion to their enravishment with Him; then He lets down upon that particle the shrouds of humanity and nature and temperament and spirit, in order that by its powerful working it may transmute to its own quality all the particles that are attached to it, until the lover's clay is wholly converted into love, and all his actions and looks become so many indispensable conditions of love. This state is named "union" alike by those who regard the inward meaning and those who regard the outward expression. Ḥusayn b. Manṣúr (al-Ḥalláj) says in this sense:

"*Thy will be done, O my Lord and Master!*
Thy will be done, O my purpose and meaning!
O essence of my being, O goal of my desire,
O my speech and my hints and my gestures!
O all of my all, O my hearing and my sight,
O my whole and my element and my particles!"

Therefore, to one whose qualities are only borrowed from God, it is a disgrace to affirm his own existence, and an act of dualism (*zunnár*) to pay any heed to the phenomenal universe; and all created objects are despicable to his soaring thought. Some have been led by their dialectical subtlety and their admiration of phraseology to speak of "the union of union" (*jam' al-jam'*). This is a good expression as phrases go, but if you consider the meaning, it is better not to predicate union of union, because the term "union" cannot properly be applied except to separation. Before union can be united it must first have been separated, whereas the fact is that union does not change its state. The expression, therefore, is liable to be misunderstood, because one who is "united" does not look forth from himself to what is above or to what is below him. Do not you perceive that when the two worlds were displayed to the Apostle on the night of the Ascension he paid no heed to anything? He was in "union", and one who is "united" does not behold "separation". Hence God said: "*His gaze swerved not, nor did it stray*" (Kor. liii, 17). In my early days I composed a book on this subject and entitled it *Kitáb 'al-bayán li-ahl al-'iyán*,[1] and I have also discussed the matter at length in the *Baḥr al-qulúb*[2] in the chapter on

[1] "The Book of Exposition for Persons of Intuition."
[2] "The Sea of Hearts."

"Union". I will not now burden my readers by adding to what I have said here.

This sketch of the doctrine of the Sayyárís concludes my account of those Ṣúfí sects which are approved and follow the path of true theosophy. I now turn to the opinions of those heretics who have connected themselves with the Ṣúfís and have adopted Ṣúfiistic phraseology as a means of promulgating their heresy. My aim is to expose their errors in order that novices may not be deceived by their pretensions and may guard themselves from mischief.

11. THE ḤULÚLÍS.

Of those two reprobate sects which profess to belong to Ṣúfiism and make the Ṣúfís partners in their error, one follows Abú Ḥulmán of Damascus.[1] The stories which his adherents relate of him do not agree with what is written about him in the books of the Shaykhs, for, while the Ṣúfís regard him as one of themselves, these sectaries impute to him the doctrines of incarnation (*ḥulúl*) and commixture (*imtizáj*) and transmigration of spirits (*naskh-i arwáḥ*). I have seen this statement in the book of Muqaddasí,[2] who attacks him; and the same notion of him has been formed by theologians, but God knows best what is the truth. The other sect refer their doctrine to Fáris,[3] who pretends to have derived it from Ḥusayn b. Manṣúr (al-Ḥalláj), but he is the only one of Ḥusayn's followers who holds such tenets. I saw Abú Ja'far Ṣaydalání[4] with four thousand men, dispersed throughout 'Iráq, who were Ḥallájís; and they all cursed Fáris on account of this doctrine. Moreover, in the compositions of al-Ḥalláj himself there is nothing but profound theosophy.

[1] See note, p. 131.

[2] The *nisba* Muqaddasí or Maqdisí belongs to a number of Moslem writers. I do not know which of them is intended here.

[3] See *Nafaḥát*, No. 178.

[4] This person, whom the author has already mentioned at the beginning of Chapter XIII, is not identical with the Ṣúfí of the same name who was a contemporary of Junayd (*Nafaḥát*, No. 197).

I, 'Alí b. 'Uthmán al-Jullábí, say that I do not know who Fáris and Abú Ḥulmán were or what they said, but anyone who holds a doctrine conflicting with Unification and true theosophy has no part in religion at all. If religion, which is the root, is not firmly based, Ṣúfiism, which is the branch and offspring of religion, must with more reason be unsound, for it is inconceivable that miracles and evidences should be manifested except to religious persons and Unitarians. All the errors of these sectaries are in regard to the spirit (*rúḥ*). Now, therefore, I will explain its nature and principles according to the Sunní canon, and in the course of my explanation I will notice the erroneous and delusive opinions of the heretics in order that your faith may be strengthened thereby.

Discourse on the Spirit (al-rúḥ).

You must know that knowledge concerning the existence of the spirit is intuitive (*ḍarúrí*), and the intelligence is unable to apprehend its (the spirit's) nature. Every Moslem divine and sage has expressed some conjectural opinion on this point, which has also been debated by unbelievers of various sorts. When the unbelievers of Quraysh, prompted by the Jews, sent Naḍr b. al-Ḥárith to question the Apostle concerning the nature and essence of the spirit, God in the first place affirmed its substance and said, "*And they will ask thee concerning the spirit*"; then He denied its eternity, saying, "*Answer, 'The spirit belongs to that which* (i.e. the creation of which) *my Lord commanded'*" (Kor. xvii, 87). And the Apostle said: "The spirits are hosts gathered together: those that know one another agree, and those that do not know one another disagree." There are many similar proofs of the existence of the spirit, but they contain no authoritative statement as to its nature. Some have said that the spirit is the life whereby the body lives, a view which is also held by a number of scholastic philosophers. According to this view the spirit is an accident (*'araḍ*), which at God's command keeps the body alive, and from which proceed conjunction, motion, cohesion.

and similar accidents by which the body is changed from one state to another. Others, again, declare that the spirit is not life, but that life does not exist without it, just as the spirit does not exist without the body, and that the two are never found apart, because they are inseparable, like pain and the knowledge of pain. According to this view also the spirit is an accident, like life. All the Ṣúfí Shaykhs, however, and most orthodox Moslems hold that the spirit is a substance, and not an attribute; for, so long as it is connected with the body, God continually creates life in the body, and the life of Man is an attribute and by it he lives, but the spirit is deposited in his body and may be separated from him while he is still living, as in sleep. But when it leaves him, intelligence and knowledge can no longer remain with him, for the Apostle has said that the spirits of martyrs are in the crops of birds: consequently it must be a substance; and the Apostle has said that the spirits are hosts (*junúd*), and hosts are subsistent (*báqí*), and no accident can subsist, for an accident does not stand by itself.

The spirit, then, is a subtle body (*jismí laṭíf*), which comes and goes by the command of God. On the night of the Ascension, when the Apostle saw in Heaven Adam, Joseph, Moses, Aaron, Jesus, and Abraham, it was their spirits that he saw; and if the spirit were an accident, it would not stand by itself so as to become visible, for it would need a *locus* in substances, and substances are gross (*kathíf*). Accordingly, it has been ascertained that the spirit is subtle and corporeal (*jasím*), and being corporeal, it is visible, but visible only to the eye of intelligence (*chashm-i dil*). And spirits may reside in the crops of birds or may be armies that move to and fro, as the Apostolic Traditions declare.

Here we are at variance with the heretics, who assert that the spirit is eternal (*qadím*), and worship it, and regard it as the sole agent and governor of things, and call it the uncreated spirit of God, and aver that it passes from one body to another. No popular error has obtained such wide acceptance as this doctrine, which is held by the Christians, although they express it in terms that appear to conflict with it, and by all the Indians, Tibetans, and Chinese, and is supported by the consensus of opinion among the Shí'ites, Carmathians, and Isma'ílís (*Báṭiniyán*), and is embraced by the two false sects above-mentioned. All these sectaries base their belief on certain propositions and bring forward proofs in defence of their assertion. I ask them this question: "What do you mean by 'eternity' (*qidam*)? Do you mean the pre-existence of a non-eternal thing, or an eternal thing that never came into being?" If they mean the pre-existence of a non-eternal thing, then there is no difference between us in principle, for we too say that the spirit is non-eternal (*muḥdath*), and that it existed before the body, as the Apostle said: "God created the spirits two thousand years before the bodies." Accordingly, the spirit is one sort of God's creatures, and He joins it to another sort of His creatures, and in joining them together He produces life through His predestination. But the spirit cannot pass from body to body, because, just as a body cannot have two lives, so a spirit cannot have two bodies. If these facts were not affirmed in Apostolic Traditions by an Apostle who speaks the truth, and if the matter were considered purely from the standpoint of a reasonable intelligence, then the spirit would be life and nothing else, and it would be an attribute, not a substance. Now suppose, on the other hand, they say that the spirit is an eternal thing that never came into being. In this case, I ask: "Does it stand by itself or by something else?" If they say, "By itself," I ask them, "Is God its world (*'álam*) or not?" If they answer that God is not its world, they affirm the existence of two eternal beings, which is contrary to reason, for the eternal is infinite, and the essence of one eternal being would limit the other. But if they answer that God is its world, then I say that God is eternal and His creatures are non-eternal: it is impossible that the eternal should be commingled with the non-eternal or made one with it, or become immanent in it, or that the non-eternal should be the place of the eternal or that the eternal should carry it; for whatever is joined to anything must be like that to which it is joined, and only homogeneous things are capable of being united and separated. And if they say that the spirit does not stand by itself, but by something else, then it must be either an attribute (*ṣifat*) or an accident (*'araḍ*). If it is an accident, it must either be in a *locus* or not. If it is in a *locus*, its *locus* must be like itself, and neither can be called eternal; and to say that it has no *locus* is absurd, for an accident cannot stand by itself. If, again, they say that the spirit is an eternal attribute—and this is the doctrine of the Ḥulúlís and those who believe in metempsychosis (*tanásukhiyán*)—and call it an attribute of God, I reply that an eternal attribute of God cannot possibly become an attribute of His creatures; for, if His life could become the life of His creatures, similarly His power could become their power; and inasmuch as an attribute stands by its object, how can an eternal attribute stand by a non-eternal object? Therefore, as I have shown, the eternal has no connexion with the non-eternal, and the doctrine of the heretics who affirm this is false. The spirit is created and is under God's command. Anyone who holds another belief is in flagrant error and cannot distinguish what is non-eternal from what is eternal. No saint, if his saintship be sound, can possibly be ignorant of the attributes of God. I give praise without end to God, who hath guarded us from heresies and dangers, and hath bestowed on us intelligence to examine and refute them by our arguments, and hath given us faith in order that we may know Him. When men who see only the exterior hear stories of this kind from theologians, they imagine that this is the doctrine of all aspirants to Ṣúfiism. They are grossly mistaken and utterly deceived, and the consequence is that they are blinded to the beauty of our mystic knowledge and to the loveliness of Divine saintship and to the flashes of spiritual illumination, because eminent Ṣúfís regard popular applause and popular censure with equal indifference.

SECTION.

One of the Shaykhs says: "The spirit in the body is like fire in fuel; the fire is created (*makhlúq*) and the coal is made (*maṣnú'*)." Nothing can be described as eternal except the essence and attributes of God. Abú Bakr Wásiṭí has discoursed on the spirit more than any of the Ṣúfí Shaykhs. It is related that he said: "There are ten stations (*maqámát*) of spirits: (1) the spirits of the sincere (*mukhliṣán*), which are imprisoned in a darkness and know not what will befall them; (2) the spirits of pious men (*pársá-mardán*), which in the heaven of this world rejoice in the fruits of their actions and take pleasure in devotions, and walk by the strength thereof; (3) the spirits of disciples (*murídán*), which are in the fourth heaven and dwell with the angels in the delights of veracity, and in the shadow of their good works; (4) the spirits of the beneficent (*ahl-i minan*), which are hung in lamps of light from the Throne of God, and their food is mercy, and their drink is favour and proximity; (5) the spirits of the faithful (*ahl-i wafá*), which thrill with joy in the veil of purity and the station of electness (*iṣṭifá*); (6) the spirits of martyrs (*shahídán*), which are in Paradise in the crops of birds, and go where they will in its gardens early and late; (7) the spirits of those who yearn (*mushtáqán*), which stand on the carpet of respect (*adab*) clad in the luminous veils of the Divine attributes; (8) the spirits of gnostics (*'árifán*), which, in the precincts of holiness, listen at morn and eve to the word of God and see their places in Paradise and in this world; (9) the spirits of lovers (*dústán*), which have become absorbed in contemplation of the Divine beauty and the station of revelation (*kashf*), and perceive nothing but God and rest content with no other thing; (10) the spirits of dervishes, which have found favour with God in the abode of annihilation, and have suffered a transformation of quality and a change of state."

It is related concerning the Shaykhs that they have seen the spirit in different shapes, and this may well be, because, as I have said, it is created, and a subtle body (*jismí laṭíf*) is necessarily visible. God shows it to every one of His servants, when and as it pleases Him.

I, 'Alí b. 'Uthmán al-Jullábí, declare that our life is wholly through God, and our stability is through Him, and our being kept alive is the act of God in us, and we live through His creation, not through His essence and attributes. The doctrine of the animists (*rúḥiyán*) is entirely false. Belief in the eternity of the spirit is one of the grave errors which prevail among the vulgar, and is expressed in different ways, e.g. they use the terms "soul" and "matter" (*nafs ú hayúlá*), or "light" and "darkness" (*núr ú ẓulmat*), and those Ṣúfí impostors speak of "annihilation" and "subsistence" (*faná ú baqá*), or "union" and "separation" (*jam' ú tafriqa*), or adopt similar phrases as a fair mask for their infidelity. But the Ṣúfís abjure these heretics, for the Ṣúfís hold that saintship and true love of God depend on knowledge of Him, and anyone who does not know the eternal from the non-eternal is ignorant in what he says, and the intelligent pay no attention to what is said by the ignorant. Now I will unveil the portals of the practice and theory of the Ṣúfís, furnishing my explanation with evident proofs, in order that you may the more easily comprehend my meaning, and that any sceptic possessed of insight may be led back into the right way, and that I may thereby gain a blessing and a Divine reward.

CHAPTER XV.

THE UNCOVERING OF THE FIRST VEIL: CONCERNING THE GNOSIS OF GOD (*ma'rifat Allah*).

The Apostle said: "If ye knew God as He ought to be known, ye would walk on the seas, and the mountains would move at your call." Gnosis of God is of two kinds: cognitional (*'ilmí*) and emotional (*ḥálí*). Cognitional gnosis is the foundation of all blessings in this world and in the next, for the most important thing for a man at all times and in all circumstances is knowledge of God, as God hath said: "*I only created the genii and mankind that they might serve Me*" (Kor. li, 56), i.e. that they might know Me. But the greater part of men neglect this duty, except those whom God hath chosen and whose hearts He hath vivified with Himself. Gnosis is the life of the heart through God, and the turning away of one's inmost thoughts from all that is not God. The worth of everyone is in proportion to gnosis, and he who is without gnosis is worth nothing. Theologians, lawyers, and other classes of men give the name of gnosis (*ma'rifat*) to right cognition (*'ilm*) of God, but the Ṣúfí Shaykhs call right feeling (*ḥál*) towards God by that name. Hence they have said that gnosis (*ma'rifat*) is more excellent than cognition (*'ilm*), for right feeling (*ḥál*) is the result of right cognition, but right cognition is not the same thing as right feeling, i.e. one who has not cognition of God is not a gnostic (*'árif*), but one may have cognition of God without being a gnostic. Those of either class who were ignorant of this distinction engaged in useless controversy, and the one party disbelieved in the other party. Now I will explain the matter in order that both may be instructed.

SECTION.

You must know that there is a great difference of opinion touching the gnosis and right cognition of God. The Mu'tazilites assert that gnosis is intellectual and that only a reasonable person (*'áqil*) can possibly have it. This doctrine is disproved by the fact that madmen, within Islam, are deemed to have gnosis, and that children, who are not reasonable, are deemed to have faith. Were the criterion of gnosis an intellectual one, such persons must be without gnosis, while unbelievers could not be charged with infidelity, provided only that they were reasonable beings. If reason were the cause of gnosis, it would follow that every reasonable person must know God, and that all who lack reason must be ignorant of Him; which is manifestly absurd. Others pretend that demonstration (*istidlál*) is the cause of knowledge of God, and that such knowledge is not gained except by those who deduce it in this manner. The futility of this doctrine is exemplified by Iblís, for he saw many evidences, such as Paradise, Hell, and the Throne of God, yet they did not cause him to have gnosis. God hath said that knowledge of Him depends on His will (Kor. vi, 111). According to the view of orthodox Moslems, soundness of reason and regard to evidences are a means (*sabab*) to gnosis, but not the cause (*'illat*) thereof: the sole cause is God's will and favour, for without His favour (*'ináyat*) reason is blind. Reason does not even know itself: how, then, can it know another? Heretics of all sorts use the demonstrative method, but the majority of them do not know God. On the other hand, whenever one enjoys the favour of God, all his actions are so many tokens of gnosis; his demonstration is search (*ṭalab*), and his neglect of demonstration is resignation to God's will (*taslím*); but, in reference to perfect gnosis, resignation is no better than search, for search is a principle that cannot be neglected, while resignation is a principle that excludes the possibility of agitation (*iḍṭiráb*), and these two principles do not essentially involve gnosis. In reality Man's only guide and enlightener is God. Reason and the proofs adduced by reason are unable to direct anyone into the right way. If the infidels were to return from the place of Judgment to this world, they would bring their infidelity back with them (cf. Kor. vi, 28). When the Commander of the Faithful, 'Alí, was asked concerning gnosis, he said: "I know God by God, and I know that which is not God by the light of God." God created the body and committed its life to the spirit (*ján*), and He created the soul (*dil*) and committed its life to Himself. Hence, inasmuch as reason and human faculties and evidences have no power to make the body live, they cannot make the soul live, as God hath said: "*Shall he who was dead and whom We have restored to life and to whom We have given a light whereby he may walk among men . . . ?*" (Kor. vi, 122), i.e. "I am the Creator of the light in which believers are illumined". It is God that opens and seals the hearts of men (Kor. xxxix, 23; ii, 6): therefore He alone is able to guide them. Everything except Him is a cause or a means, and causes and means cannot possibly indicate the right way without the favour of the Causer. He it is that imposes the obligation of piety, which is essentially gnosis; and those on whom that obligation is laid, so long as they are in the state of obligation, neither bring it upon themselves nor put it away from themselves by their own choice: therefore Man's share in gnosis, unless God makes him know, is mere helplessness. Abu 'l-Ḥasan Núrí says: "There is none to point out the way to God except God Himself: knowledge is sought only for due performance of His worship." No created being is capable of leading anyone to God. Those who rely on demonstration are not more reasonable than was Abú Ṭálib, and no guide is greater than was Muḥammad; yet, since Abú Ṭálib was preordained to misery, the guidance of Muḥammad did not avail him. The first step of demonstration is a turning away from God, because demonstration involves the consideration of some other thing, whereas gnosis is a turning away from all that is not God. Ordinary objects of search are found by means of demonstration, but knowledge of God is extraordinary. Therefore, knowledge of Him is attained only by unceasing bewilderment of the reason, and His favour is not procured by any act of human acquisition, but is miraculously revealed to men's hearts. What is not God is phenomenal (*muḥdath*), and although a phenomenal being may reach another like himself he cannot reach his Creator and acquire Him while he exists, for in every act of acquisition he who makes the acquisition is predominant and the thing acquired is under his power. Accordingly, the miracle is not that reason should be led by the act to affirm the existence of the Agent, but that a saint should be led by the light of the Truth to deny his own existence. The knowledge gained is in the one case a matter of logic, in the other it becomes an inward experience. Let those who deem reason to be the cause of gnosis consider what reason affirms in their minds concerning the substance of gnosis, for gnosis involves the negation of whatever is affirmed by reason, i.e. whatever notion of God can be formed by reason, God is in reality something different. How, then, is there any room for reason to arrive at gnosis by means of demonstration? Reason and imagination are homogeneous, and where *genus* is affirmed gnosis is denied. To infer the existence of God from intellectual proofs is assimilation (*tashbíh*), and to deny it on the same grounds is nullification (*ta'ṭíl*). Reason cannot pass beyond these two principles, which in regard to gnosis are agnosticism, since neither of the parties professing them is Unitarian (*muwaḥḥid*).

Therefore, when reason is gone as far as possible, and the souls of His lovers must needs search for Him, they rest helplessly without their faculties, and while they so rest they grow restless and stretch their hands in supplication and seek a relief for their souls; and when they have exhausted every manner of search in their power, the power of God becomes theirs, i.e. they find the way from Him to Him, and are eased of the anguish of absence and set foot in the garden of intimacy and win to rest. And reason, when it sees that the souls have attained their desire, tries to exert its control, but fails; and when it fails it becomes distraught; and when it becomes distraught it abdicates. Then God clothes it in the garment of service (*khidmat*) and says to it: "While thou wert independent thou wert veiled by thy faculties and their exercise, and when these were annihilated thou didst fail, and having failed thou didst attain." Thus it is the allotted portion of the soul to be near unto God, and that of the reason is to do His service. God causes Man to know Him through Himself with a knowledge that is not linked to any faculty, a knowledge in which the existence of Man is merely metaphorical. Hence to the gnostic egoism is utter perfidy; his remembrance of God is without forgetfulness, and his gnosis is not empty words but actual feeling.

Others, again, declare that gnosis is the result of inspiration (*ilhám*). This also is impossible, because gnosis supplies a criterion for distinguishing truth from falsehood, whereas the inspired have no such criterion. If one says, "I know by inspiration that God is in space," and another says, "I know by inspiration that He is not in space," one of these contradictory statements must be true, but a proof is necessary in order to decide where the truth lies. Consequently, this view, which is held by the Brahmans and the inspirationists (*ilhámiyán*), falls to the ground. In the present age I have met a number of persons who carried it to an extreme and who connected their own position with the doctrine of religious men, but they are altogether in error, and their assertion is repugnant to all reasonable Moslems and unbelievers. If it be said that whatever conflicts with the sacred law is not inspiration, I reply that this argument is fundamentally unsound, because, if inspiration is to be judged and verified by the standard of the sacred law, then gnosis does not depend on inspiration, but on law and prophecy and Divine guidance.

Others assert that knowledge of God is intuitive (*ḍarúrí*). This also is impossible. Everything that is known in this way must be known in common by all reasonable men, and inasmuch as we see that some reasonable men deny the existence of God and hold the doctrines of assimilation (*tashbíh*) and nullification (*ta'ṭíl*), it is proved that knowledge of God is not intuitive. Moreover, if it were so, the principle of religious obligation (*taklíf*) would be destroyed, for that principle cannot possibly be applied to objects of intuitive knowledge, such as one's self, the heaven and the earth, day and night, pleasure and pain, etc., concerning the existence of which no reasonable man can have any doubt, and which he must know even against his will. But some aspirants to Ṣúfiism, considering the absolute certainty (*yaqín*) which they feel, say: "We know God intuitively," giving the name of intuition to this certainty. Substantially they are right, but their expression is erroneous, because intuitive knowledge cannot be exclusively restricted to those who are perfect; on the contrary, it belongs to all reasonable men. Furthermore, it appears in the minds of living creatures without any means or evidence, whereas the knowledge of God is a means (*sababí*). But Master Abú 'Alí Daqqáq and Shaykh Abú Sahl Ṣu'lúkí[1] and his father, who was a leading religious authority at Níshápúr, maintain that the beginning of gnosis is demonstrative and that its end is intuitive, just as technical knowledge is first acquired and finally becomes instinctive. "Do not you perceive," they say, "that in Paradise knowledge of God becomes intuitive? Why should it not become intuitive in this world too? And the Apostles, when they heard the word of God, either immediately or from the mouth of an angel or by revelation, knew Him intuitively." I reply that the inhabitants of Paradise know God intuitively in Paradise, because in Paradise no religious obligation is imposed, and the Apostles have no fear of being separated from God at the last, but enjoy the same security as those who know Him intuitively. The excellence of gnosis and faith lies in their being hidden; when they are made visible, faith becomes compulsory (*jabr*), and there is no longer any free will in regard to its visible substance (*'ayn*), and the foundations of the religious law are shaken, and the principle of apostasy is annulled, so

[1] See *Nafaḥát*, No. 373.

that Bal'am [1] and Iblís and Barṣíṣá [2] cannot properly be described as infidels, for it is generally allowed that they had knowledge of God. The gnostic, while he remains a gnostic, has no fear of being separated from God; separation is produced by the loss of gnosis, but intuitive knowledge cannot conceivably be lost. This doctrine is full of danger to the vulgar. In order that you may avoid its evil consequences you must know that Man's knowledge and his gnosis of God depend entirely on the information and eternal guidance of the Truth. Man's certainty in gnosis may be now greater and now less, but the principle of gnosis is neither increased nor diminished, since in either case it would be impaired. You must not let blind conformity enter into your knowledge of God, and you must know Him through His attributes of perfection. This can be attained only through the providence and favour of God, who has absolute control of our minds. If He so will, He makes one of His actions a guide that shows us the way to Himself, and if He will otherwise, He makes that same action an obstacle that prevents us from reaching Him. Thus Jesus was to some a guide that led them to gnosis, but to others he was an obstacle that hindered them from gnosis; the former party said, "This is the servant of God," and the latter said, "This is the son of God." Similarly, some were led to God by idols and by the sun and moon, while others were led astray. Such guides are a means of gnosis, but not the immediate cause of it, and one means is no better than another in relation to Him who is the author of them all. The gnostic's affirmation of a means is a sign of dualism (*zunnár*), and regard to anything except the object of knowledge is polytheism (*shirk*). When a man is doomed to perdition in the Preserved Tablet, nay, in the will and knowledge of God, how can any proof and demonstration lead him aright? The most high God, as He pleases and by whatever means He pleases, shows His servant the way to Himself and opens to him the

[1] See Baydáwí on Kor. vii, 174.

[2] See Goldziher & Landberg, *Die Legende vom Mönch Barṣīṣā* (1896), and M. Hartmann, *Der heilige Barṣīṣā* in *Der Islamische Orient* (1905), i, 23–8.

door of gnosis, so that he attains to a degree where the very essence of gnosis appears alien (*ghayr*) and its attributes become noxious to him, and he is veiled by his gnosis from the object known and realizes that his gnosis is a pretension (*da'wá*). Dhu 'l-Nún the Egyptian says: "Beware lest thou make pretensions to gnosis," and it has been said in verse—

"*The gnostics pretend to knowledge,*
But I avow ignorance: that is my knowledge."

Therefore do not claim gnosis, lest thou perish in thy pretension, but cleave to the reality thereof, that thou mayest be saved. When anyone is honoured by the revelation of the Divine majesty, his existence becomes a plague to him and all his attributes a source of corruption. He who belongs to God and to whom God belongs is not connected with anything in the universe. The real gist of gnosis is to recognize that to God is the kingdom. When a man knows that all possessions are in the absolute control of God, what further business has he with mankind, that he should be veiled from God by them or by himself? All such veils are the result of ignorance. As soon as ignorance is annihilated, they vanish, and this life is made equal in rank to the life hereafter.

SECTION.

Now, for instruction's sake, I will mention some of the numerous sayings which the Shaykhs have uttered on this subject.

'Abdalláh b. Mubárak says: "Gnosis consists in not being astonished by anything," because astonishment arises from an act exceeding the power of the doer, and inasmuch as God is omnipotent it is impossible that a gnostic should be astonished by His acts. If there be any room for astonishment, one must needs marvel that God exalts a handful of earth to such a degree that it receives His commands, and a drop of blood to such an eminence that it discourses of love and knowledge of Him, and seeks vision of Him, and desires union with Him.

Dhu 'l-Nún the Egyptian says: "Gnosis is in reality God's providential communication of the spiritual light to our inmost hearts," i.e., until God, in His providence, illuminates the heart of Man and keeps it from contamination, so that all created things have not even the worth of a mustard-seed in his heart, the contemplation of Divine mysteries, both inward and outward, does not overwhelm him with rapture; but when God has done this, his every look becomes an act of contemplation (*mushāhadat*). Shiblí says: "Gnosis is continual amazement (*ḥayrat*)." Amazement is of two kinds: (1) amazement at the essence and (2) amazement at the quality. The former is polytheism and infidelity, because no gnostic can possibly be in doubt concerning the essential nature of God; but the latter is gnosis, because the quality of God lies beyond reason's scope. Hence a certain one said: "O Guide of the amazed, increase my amazement!" In the first place, he affirmed the existence of God and the perfection of His attributes, and recognized that He is the object of men's search and the accomplisher of their prayers and the author of their amazement; then he asked for increase of amazement and recognized that in seeking God the reason has no alternative between amazement and polytheism. This sentiment is very fine. It may be, again, that knowledge of God's being involves amazement at one's own being, because when a man knows God he sees himself entirely subdued by the Divine omnipotence; and since his existence depends on God and his non-existence proceeds from God, and his rest and motion are produced by the power of God, he becomes amazed, saying: "Who and what am I?" In this sense the Apostle said: "He who knows himself has come to know his Lord," i.e. he who knows himself to be annihilated knows God to be eternally subsistent. Annihilation destroys reason and all human attributes, and when the substance of a thing is not accessible to reason it cannot possibly be known without amazement. Abú Yazíd said: "Gnosis consists in knowing that the motion and rest of mankind depend on God," and that without His permission no one has the least control of His kingdom, and that no one can perform any action until He creates the ability to act and puts the will to act in his heart, and that human actions are metaphorical and that God is the real agent. Muḥammad b. Wásiʻ says, describing the gnostic: "His words are few and his amazement perpetual," because only finite things admit of being expressed in words, and since the infinite cannot be expressed it leaves no resource except perpetual amazement. Shiblí says: "Real gnosis is the inability to attain gnosis," i.e. inability to know a thing, to the real nature of which a man has no clue except the impossibility of attaining it. Therefore, in attaining it, he will rightly take no credit to himself, because inability (*ʻajz*) is search, and so long as he depends on his own faculties and attributes, he cannot properly be described by that term; and when these faculties and attributes depart, then his state is not inability, but annihilation. Some pretenders, while affirming the attributes of humanity and the subsistence of the obligation to decide with sound judgment (*taklíf ba-ṣiḥḥat-i khiṭáb*) and the authority maintained over them by God's proof, declare that gnosis is impotence, and that they are impotent and unable to attain anything. I reply: "In search of what thing have you become so helpless?" Impotence (*ʻajz*) has two signs, which are not to be found in you: firstly, the annihilation of the faculties of search, and secondly, the manifestation of the glory of God (*tajallí*). Where the annihilation of the faculties takes place, there is no outward expression (*ʻibárat*); and where the glory of God is revealed, no clue can be given and no discrimination is conceivable. Hence one who is impotent does not know that he is so, or that the state attributed to him is called impotence. How should he know this? Impotence is other than God, and the affirmation of knowledge of other than God is not gnosis; and so long as there is room in the heart for aught except God, or the possibility of expressing aught except God, true gnosis has not been attained. The gnostic is not a gnostic until he turns aside from all that is not God. Abú Ḥafṣ Ḥaddád says: "Since I have known God, neither truth nor falsehood has entered my heart." When a man feels desire and passion he turns to the soul (*dil*) in order that it may guide him to the lower soul (*nafs*), which is the seat of falsehood; and when he finds the evidence of gnosis, he also turns to the soul in order that it may guide him to the spirit, which is the source of truth and reality. But when aught except God enters the soul, the gnostic, if he turns to it, commits an act of agnosticism. There is a great difference between one who turns to the soul and one who turns to God. Abú Bakr Wásiṭí says: "He who knows God is cut off from all things, nay, he is dumb and abject (*kharisa wa-'nqama'a*)," i.e. he is unable to express anything and all his attributes are annihilated. So the Apostle, while he was in the state of absence, said: "I am the most eloquent of the Arabs and non-Arabs"; but when he was borne to the presence of God, he said: "I know not how to utter Thy praise." Answer came: "O Muḥammad, if thou speakest not, I will speak; if thou deemest thyself unworthy to praise Me, I will make the universe thy deputy, that all its atoms may praise Me in thy name."

CHAPTER XVI.

The Uncovering of the Second Veil: Concerning Unification (*tawḥíd*).

God said, "*Your God is one*" (Kor. xvi, 23); and again, "*Say, 'God is one'*" (Kor. cxii, 1). And the Apostle said: "Long ago there was a man who did no good work except that he pronounced God to be one. When he was dying he said to his folk: 'After my death burn me and gather my ashes and on a windy day throw half of them into the sea, and scatter half of them to the winds of the earth, that no trace of me may be left.' As soon as he died and this was done, God bade the air and the water keep the ashes which they had received until the Resurrection; and when He raises that man from the dead, He will ask him why he caused himself to be burnt, and he will reply: 'O Lord, from shame of Thee, for I was a great sinner,' and God will pardon him."

Real unification (*tawḥíd*) consists in asserting the unity of a thing and in having a perfect knowledge of its unity. Inasmuch as God is one, without any sharer in His essence and attributes, without any substitute, without any partner in His actions, and inasmuch as Unitarians (*muwaḥḥidán*) have acknowledged that He is such, their knowledge of unity is called unification.

Unification is of three kinds: (1) God's unification of God, i.e. His knowledge of His unity; (2) God's unification of His creatures, i.e. His decree that a man shall pronounce Him to be one, and the creation of unification in his heart; (3) men's unification of God, i.e. their knowledge of the unity of God. Therefore, when a man knows God he can declare His unity and pronounce that He is one, incapable of union and separation, not admitting duality; that His unity is not a number so as to be made two by the predication of another number; that He is not finite so as to have six directions; that He has no space, and that He is not in space, so as to require the predication of space; that He is not an accident, so as to need a substance, nor a substance, which cannot exist without another like itself, nor a natural constitution (*ṭab'í*), in which motion and rest originate, nor a spirit so as to need a frame, nor a body so as to be composed of limbs; and that He does not become immanent (*ḥáll*) in things, for then He must be homogeneous with them; and that He is not joined to anything, for then that thing must be a part of Him; and that He is free from all imperfections and exalted above all defects; and that He has no like, so that He and His creature should make two; and that He has no child whose begetting would necessarily cause Him to be a stock (*aṣl*); and that His essence and attributes are unchangeable; and that He is endowed with those attributes of perfection which believers and Unitarians affirm, and which He has described Himself as possessing; and that He is exempt from those attributes which heretics arbitrarily impute to Him; and that He is Living, Knowing, Forgiving, Merciful, Willing, Powerful, Hearing, Seeing, Speaking, and Subsistent; and that His knowledge is not a state (*ḥál*) in Him, nor His power solidly planted (*ṣalábat*) in Him, nor His hearing and sight detached (*mutajarrid*) in Him, nor His speech divided in Him; and that He together with His attributes exists from eternity; and that objects of cognition are not outside of His knowledge, and that entities are entirely dependent on His will; and that He does that which He has willed, and wills that which He has known, and no creature has cognisance thereof; and that His decree is an absolute fact, and that His friends have no resource except resignation; and that He is the sole predestinator of good and evil, and the only being that is worthy of hope or fear; and that He creates all benefit and injury; and that He alone gives judgment, and His judgment is all wisdom; and that no one has any possibility of attaining unto Him; and that the inhabitants of Paradise shall behold Him; and that assimilation (*tashbíh*) is inadmissible; and that such terms as "confronting" and "seeing face to face" (*muqábalat ú muwájahat*) cannot be applied to His being; and that His saints may enjoy the contemplation (*musháhadat*) of Him in this world.

Those who do not acknowledge Him to be such are guilty of impiety. I, 'Alí b. 'Uthmán al-Jullábí, said at the beginning of this chapter that unification consists in declaring the unity of a thing, and that such a declaration cannot be made without knowledge. The Sunnís have declared the unity of God with true comprehension, because, seeing a subtle work and a unique act, they recognized that it could not possibly exist by itself, and finding manifest evidences of origination (*ḥudúth*) in every thing, they perceived that there must be an Agent who brought the universe into being—the earth and heaven and sun and moon and land and sea and all that moves and rests and their knowledge and speech and life and death. For all these an artificer was indispensable. Accordingly, the Sunnís, rejecting the notion that there are two or three artificers, declared themselves satisfied with a single artificer who is perfect, living, knowing, almighty, and unpartnered. And inasmuch as an act requires at least one agent, and the existence of two agents for one act involves the dependence of one on the other, it follows that the Agent is unquestionably and certainly one. Here we are at variance with the dualists, who affirm light and darkness, and with the Magians, who affirm Yazdán and Ahriman, and with the natural philosophers (*ṭabá'i'iyán*), who affirm nature and potentiality (*quwwat*), and with the astronomers (*falakiyán*), who affirm the seven planets, and with the Mu'tazilites, who affirm creators and artificers without end. I have briefly refuted all these vain opinions in a book, entitled *Al-Ri'áyat li-ḥuqúq Allah*,[1] to which or to the works of the ancient theologians I must refer anyone who desires further information. Now I will turn to the indications which the Shaykhs have given on this subject.

[1] "The Observance of what is due to God."

SECTION.

It is related that Junayd said: "Unification is the separation of the eternal from that which was originated in time," i.e. you must not regard the eternal as a *locus* of phenomena, or phenomena as a *locus* of the eternal; and you must know that God is eternal and that you are phenomenal, and that nothing of your *genus* is connected with Him, and that nothing of His attributes is mingled in you, and that there is no homogeneity between the eternal and the phenomenal. This is contrary to the above-mentioned doctrine of those who hold the spirit to be eternal. When the eternal is believed to descend into phenomena, or phenomena to be attached to the eternal, no proof remains of the eternity of God and the origination of the universe; and this leads to materialism (*madhhab-i dahriyán*). In all the actions of phenomena there are proofs of unification and evidences of the Divine omnipotence and signs which establish the eternity of God, but men are too heedless to desire only Him or to be content only with keeping Him in remembrance. Ḥusayn b. Manṣúr (al-Ḥalláj) says: "The first step in unification is the annihilation of separation (*tafríd*)," because separation is the pronouncement that one has become separated from imperfections (*áfát*), while unification is the declaration of a thing's unity: therefore in isolation (*fardániyyat*) it is possible to affirm that which is other than God, and this quality may be ascribed to others besides God; but in unity (*waḥdániyyat*) it is not possible to affirm other than God, and unity may not be ascribed to anything except Him. Accordingly, the first step in unification is to deny (that God has) a partner (*sharík*) and to put admixture (*mizáj*) aside, for admixture on the way (to God) is like seeking the highway with a lamp (*mizáj andar minháj chún ṭalab-i minháj báshad ba-siráj*). And Ḥuṣrí says: "Our principles in unification are five: the removal of phenomenality, and the affirmation of eternity, and departure from familiar haunts, and separation from brethren, and forgetfulness of what is known and unknown." The removal of phenomenality consists in denying that phenomena have any connexion with unification or that they can possibly attain to His holy essence; and the affirmation of eternity consists in being convinced that God always existed, as I have already explained in discussing the saying of Junayd; and departure from familiar haunts means, for the novice, departure from the habitual pleasures of the lower soul and the forms of this world, and for the adept, departure from lofty stations and glorious states and exalted miracles (*karámát*); and separation from brethren means turning away from the society of mankind and turning towards the society of God, since any thought of other than God is a veil and an imperfection, and the more a man's thoughts are associated with other than God the more is he veiled from God, because it is universally agreed that unification is the concentration of thoughts (*jam'-i himam*), whereas to be content with other than God is a sign of dispersion of thought (*tafriqa-i himmat*); and forgetfulness of a thing which is known or unknown means the unification of that thing, for unification denies whatever the knowledge of mankind affirms about it; and whatever their ignorance affirms about it is merely contrary to their knowledge, for ignorance is not unification, and knowledge of the reality of unification cannot be attained without denying the personal initiative (*taṣarruf*) in which knowledge and ignorance consist. A certain Shaykh relates: "While Ḥuṣrí was speaking to an audience, I fell asleep and dreamed that two angels came down from Heaven and listened for some time to his discourse. Then one said to the other, 'What this man says is the theory (*'ilm*) of unification, not unification itself (*'ayn*).' When I awoke he was explaining unification. He looked at me and said, 'O So-and-so, it is impossible to speak of unification except theoretically.'" It is related that Junayd said: "Unification is this, that one should be a figure (*shakhṣ*) in the hands of God, a figure over which His decrees pass according as He in His omnipotence determines, and that one should be sunk in the seas of His unity, self-annihilated and dead alike to the call of mankind to him and his answer to them, absorbed by the reality of the Divine unity in true proximity, and lost to sense and action, because God fulfils in him what He hath willed of him, namely, that his last state should become his first state, and that he should be as he was before he existed." All this means that the Unitarian in the will of God has no more a will of his own, and in the unity of God no regard to himself, so that he becomes like an atom as he was in the eternal past when the covenant of unification was made, and God answered the question which He Himself had asked, and that atom was only the object of His speech.[1] Mankind have no joy in such a one that they should call him to anything, and he has no friendship with anyone that he should respond to their call. This saying indicates the annihilation of human attributes and perfect resignation to God in the state when a man is overpowered by the revelation of His majesty, so that he becomes a passive instrument and a subtle substance that feels nothing, and his body is a repository for the mysteries of God, to whom his speech and actions are attributed; but, unconscious of all as he is, he remains subject to the ordinances of the religious law, to the end that the proof of God may be established. Such was the Apostle when on the night of the Ascension he was borne to the station of proximity; he desired that his body should be destroyed and his personality be dissolved, but God's purpose was to establish His proof. He bade the Apostle remain in the state that he was in; whereupon he gained strength and displayed the existence of God from out of his own non-existence and said, "I am not as one of you. Verily, I pass the night with my Lord, and he gives me food and drink"; and he also said, "I am with God in a state in which none of the cherubim nor any prophet is capable of being contained with me." It is related that Sahl b. 'Abdalláh said: "Unification is this, that you should recognize that the essence of God is endowed with knowledge, that it is not comprehensible nor visible to the eye in this world, but that

[1] Kor. vii, 171.

it exists in the reality of faith, infinite, incomprehensible, non-incarnate; and that He will be seen in the next world, outwardly and inwardly in His kingdom and His power; and that mankind are veiled from knowledge of the ultimate nature of His essence; and that their hearts know Him, but their intellects cannot reach unto Him; and that believers shall behold Him with their (spiritual) eyes, without comprehending His infinity." This saying includes all the principles of unification. And Junayd said: "The noblest saying concerning unification is that of Abú Bakr: 'Glory to God, who has not vouchsafed to His creatures any means of attaining unto knowledge of Him except through impotence to attain unto knowledge of Him.'" Many have mistaken the meaning of these words of Abú Bakr and suppose that impotence to attain to gnosis is the same thing as agnosticism. This is absurd, because impotence refers only to an existing state, not to a state that is non-existent. For example, a dead man is not incapable of life, but he cannot be alive while he is dead; and a blind man is not incapable of seeing, but he cannot see while he is blind. Therefore, a gnostic is not incapable of gnosis so long as gnosis is existent, for in that case his gnosis resembles intuition. The saying of Abú Bakr may be brought into connexion with the doctrine of Abú Sahl Ṣu'lúkí and Master Abú 'Alí Daqqáq, who assert that gnosis is acquired in the first instance, but finally becomes intuitive. The possessor of intuitive knowledge is compelled and incapable of putting it away or drawing it to himself. Hence, according to what Abú Bakr says, unification is the act of God in the heart of His creature. Shiblí says: "Unification veils the Unitarian from the beauty of Oneness," because unification is said to be the act of Man, and an act of Man does not cause the revelation of God, and in the reality of revelation that which does not cause revelation is a veil. Man with all his attributes is other than God, for if his attributes are accounted Divine, then he himself must be accounted Divine, and then Unitarian, unification, and the

One become, all three, causes of the existence of one another; and this is precisely the Christian Trinity. If any attribute prevents the seeker of God from annihilating himself in unification, he is still veiled by that attribute, and while he is veiled he is not a Unitarian, for all except God is vanity. This is the interpretation of "There is no god but God".[1]

The Shaykhs have discussed at large the terms by which unification is denoted. Some say that it is an annihilation that cannot properly be attained unless the attributes subsist, while others say that it has no attribute whatever except annihilation. The analogy of union and separation (*jam' ú tafriqa*) must be applied to this question in order that it may be understood. I, 'Alí b. 'Uthmán al-Jullábí, declare that unification is a mystery revealed by God to His servants, and that it cannot be expressed in language at all, much less in high-sounding phrases. The explanatory terms and those who use them are other than God, and to affirm what is other than God in unification is to affirm polytheism.

[1] Here the author cites an anecdote of Ibráhím al-Khawwáṣ and al-Ḥalláj which has been related above. See p. 205.

CHAPTER XVII.

THE UNCOVERING OF THE THIRD VEIL: CONCERNING FAITH (*ímán*).

The Apostle said: "Faith is belief in God and His angels and His (revealed) books." Etymologically, faith (*ímán*) means verification (*taṣdíq*). Concerning its principles in their application to the religious law there is great discussion and controversy. The Mu'tazilites hold that faith includes all acts of devotion, theoretical as well as practical: hence they say that sin puts a man outside the pale of faith. The Khárijites, who call a man an infidel because he commits a sin, are of the same opinion. Some declare that faith is simply a verbal profession, while others say it is only knowledge of God, and a party of Sunní scholastics assert that it is mere verification. I have written a separate work explaining this subject, but my present purpose is to establish what the Ṣúfí Shaykhs believe. They are divided on this question in the same way as the lawyers of the two opposite sects. Some of them, e.g. Fuḍayl b. 'Iyáḍ and Bishr Ḥáfí and Khayr al-Nassáj and Sumnún al-Muḥibb and Abú Ḥamza of Baghdád and Muḥammad Jurayrí and a great number of others, hold that faith is verbal profession and verification and practice; but others, e.g. Ibráhím b. Adham and Dhu 'l-Nún the Egyptian and Abú Yazíd of Bisṭám and Abú Sulaymán Dárání and Ḥárith Muḥásibí and Junayd and Sahl b. 'Abdalláh of Tustar and Shaqíq of Balkh and Ḥátim Aṣamm and Muḥammad b. al-Faḍl of Balkh and a number besides, hold that faith is verbal profession and verification. Some lawyers, i.e. Málik and Sháfi'í and Aḥmad b. Ḥanbal, maintain the former view, while the latter opinion is supported by Abú Ḥanífa and Ḥusayn b. Faḍl of Balkh and the followers of Abú Ḥanífa, such as Muḥammad b. al-Ḥasan, Dáwud Ṭá'í, and Abú Yúsuf. The difference between them is entirely one of expression and is devoid of substance, as I will now briefly explain, in order that no one may be charged with contradicting the principle of faith because he takes the one view or the other in this dispute.

SECTION.

You must know that the orthodox Moslems and the Ṣúfís are agreed that faith has a principle (*aṣl*) and a derivative (*far'*), the principle being verification in the heart, and the derivative being observance of the (Divine) command. Now the Arabs commonly and customarily transfer the name of a principle to a derivative by way of metaphor, e.g. they call the light of the sun "the sun". In this sense the former of the two parties mentioned above apply the name of faith to that obedience (*tá'at*) by which alone a man is made secure from future punishment. Mere verification (i.e. belief), without performance of the Divine commands, does not involve security. Therefore, since security is in proportion to obedience, and obedience together with verification and verbal profession is the cause of security, they bestowed on obedience the name of faith. The other party, however, asserted that gnosis, not obedience, is the cause of security. Obedience, they said, is of no avail without gnosis, whereas one who has gnosis but lacks obedience will be saved at the last, although it depends on the will of God whether he shall be pardoned by Divine grace or through the intercession of the Apostle, or whether he shall be punished according to the measure of his sin and then be delivered from Hell and transported to Paradise. Therefore, since those who have gnosis, although they are sinners, by reason of their gnosis do not remain for ever in Hell, while those who have only works without gnosis do not enter Paradise, it follows that here obedience is not the cause of security. The Apostle said: "None of you shall be saved by his works." Hence in reality, without any controversy among Moslems, faith is gnosis and acknowledgment and acceptance of works. Whoever knows God knows Him by one of His attributes, and the most elect of His attributes are of three kinds: those connected with His beauty (*jamál*) and with His majesty (*jalál*) and with His perfection (*kamál*). His perfection is not attainable except by those whose perfection is established and whose imperfection is banished. There remain beauty and majesty. Those whose evidence in gnosis is the beauty of God are always longing for vision, and those whose evidence is His majesty are always abhorring their own attributes and their hearts are stricken with awe. Now longing is an effect of love, and so is abhorrence of human attributes, because the lifting of the veil of human attributes is the very essence of love. Therefore faith and gnosis are love, and obedience is a sign of love. Whoever denies this neglects the command of God and knows nothing of gnosis. This evil is manifest among the aspirants to Ṣúfiism at the present day. Some heretics, seeing their excellence and persuaded of their high degree, imitate them and say: "Trouble only lasts while you do not know God: as soon as you know Him, all the labour of obedience is removed from the body." But they are wrong. I reply that when you know Him, the heart is filled with longing and His command is held in greater veneration than before. I admit that a pious man may reach a point where he is relieved from the irksomeness of obedience through the increase of Divine aid (*tawfíq*), so that he performs without trouble what is troublesome to others; but this result cannot be achieved without a longing that produces violent agitation. Some, again, say that faith comes entirely from God, while others say that it springs entirely from Man. This has long been a matter of controversy among the people in Transoxania. To assert that faith comes entirely from God is sheer compulsion (*jabr*), because Man must then have no choice; and to assert that it springs entirely from Man is pure free-will, for Man does not know God except through the knowledge that God gives him. The doctrine of unification is less than compulsion and more than free-will. Similarly, faith is really the act of Man joined to the guidance of God, as God hath said: "*Whomsoever God wishes to lead aright, He will open his breast to receive Islam; and whomsoever He wishes to lead astray, He will make his breast strait and narrow*" (Kor. vi, 125). On this principle, inclination to believe (*girawish*) is the guidance of God, while belief (*girawídan*) is the act of Man. The signs of belief are these: in the heart, holding firmly to unification; in the eye, refraining from forbidden sights and looking heedfully on evidences; in the ear, listening to His word; in the belly, being empty of what is unlawful; in the tongue, veracity. Hence those persons (who assert that faith comes entirely from God) maintain that gnosis and faith may increase and diminish, which is generally admitted to be false, for if it were true, then the object of gnosis must also be liable to increase and diminution. Accordingly, the increase and diminution must be in the derivative, which is the act; and it is generally agreed that obedience may diminish and increase. This does not please the anthropomorphists (*ḥashwiyán*) who imitate the two parties mentioned above, for some of them hold that obedience is an element of faith, while others declare that faith is a verbal profession and nothing else. Both these doctrines are unjust.

In short, faith is really the absorption of all human attributes in the search of God. This must be unanimously acknowledged by all believers. The might of gnosis overwhelms the attributes of agnosticism, and where faith exists agnosticism is banished, for, as it is said: "A lamp is of no use when the dawn rises." God hath said: "*Kings, when they enter a city, ruin it*" (Kor. xxvii, 34). When gnosis is established in the heart of the gnostic, the empire of doubt and scepticism and agnosticism is utterly destroyed, and the sovereignty of gnosis subdues his senses and passions so that in all his looks and acts and words he remains within the circle of its authority. I have read that when Ibráhím Khawwáṣ was asked concerning the reality of faith, he replied: "I have no answer to this question just now, because whatever I say is a mere expression, and it behoves me to answer by my actions; but I am setting out for Mecca: do thou accompany me that thou mayest be answered." The narrator continues: "I consented. As we journeyed through the desert, every day two loaves and two cups of water appeared. He gave one to me and took the other for himself. One day an old man rode up to us and dismounted and conversed with Ibráhím for a while; then he left us. I asked Ibráhím to tell me who he was. He replied: 'This is the answer to thy question.' 'How so?' I asked. He said: 'This was Khiḍr, who begged me to let him accompany me, but I refused, for I feared that in his company I might put confidence in him instead of in God, and then my trust in God (*tawakkul*) would have been vitiated. Real faith is trust in God.'" And Muḥammad b. Khafíf says: "Faith is the belief of the heart in that knowledge which comes from the Unseen," because faith is in that which is hidden, and it can be attained only through Divine strengthening of one's certainty, which is the result of knowledge bestowed by God.

Now I will come to matters of practice and will explain their difficulties.

CHAPTER XVIII.

The Uncovering of the Fourth Veil: Concerning Purification from Foulness.

After faith, the first thing incumbent on everyone is purification (*ṭahárat*) and the performance of prayer, i.e. to cleanse the body from filth and pollution, and to wash the three members,[1] and to wipe the head with water as the law prescribes, or to use sand in the absence of water or in severe illness. Purification is of two kinds: outward and inward. Thus prayer requires purification of the body, and gnosis requires purification of the heart. As, in the former case, the water must be clean, so in the latter case unification must be pure and belief undefiled. The Ṣúfís are always engaged in purification outwardly and in unification inwardly. The Apostle said to one of his Companions: "Be constant in ablution, that thy two guardian angels may love thee," and God hath said: "*God loves those who often repent and those who purify themselves*" (Kor. ii, 222). And the Apostle used to say in his invocations: "O God, purify my heart from hypocrisy." Even consciousness of the miraculous grace (*karámát*) vouchsafed to him he regarded as an affirmation of other than God, for in unification it is hypocrisy (*nifáq*) to affirm other than God. So long as a disciple's eye is obscured by a single atom of the miracles of the Shaykhs, from the standpoint of perfection that atom is a potential veil (between him and God). Hence Abú Yazíd said: "The hypocrisy of gnostics is better than the sincerity of disciples," i.e. that which is a "station" (*maqám*) to the novice is a veil to the adept. The novice desires to gain miracles, but the adept desires to gain the

[1] The face, hands, and feet.

Giver of miracles. In short, the affirmation of miracles, or of anything that involves the sight of other than God, appears hypocrisy to the people of the Truth (the Ṣúfís). Accordingly, what is noxious to the friends of God is a means of deliverance for all sinners, and what is noxious to sinners is a means of salvation for all infidels, because, if infidels knew, as sinners know, that their sins are displeasing to God, they would all be saved from infidelity; and if sinners knew, as the friends of God know, that all their actions are defective, they would all be saved from sin and purged of contamination. Therefore, outward and inward purification must go together; e.g., when a man washes his hands he must wash his heart clean of worldliness, and when he puts water in his mouth he must purify his mouth from the mention of other than God, and when he washes his face he must turn away from all familiar objects and turn towards God, and when he wipes his head he must resign his affairs to God, and when he washes his feet he must not form the intention of taking his stand on anything except according to the command of God. Thus he will be doubly purified. In all religious ordinances the external is combined with the internal; e.g. in faith, the tongue's profession with the heart's belief. The method of spiritual purification is to reflect and meditate on the evil of this world and to perceive that it is false and fleeting, and to make the heart empty of it. This result can be attained only by much self-mortification (*mujáhadat*), and the most important act of mortification is to observe the external rules of discipline (*ádáb-i ẓáhir*) assiduously in all circumstances. It is related that Ibráhím Khawwáṣ said: "I desire God to give me an everlasting life in this world, in order that, while mankind are engrossed in the pleasures of the world and forget God, I may observe the rules of religion amidst the affliction of the world and remember God." And it is related that Abú Ṭáhir Ḥaramí lived forty years at Mecca, and went outside of the sacred territory whenever he purified himself, because he would not pour the water which he had used for that purpose on ground that God had called His.

When Ibráhím Khawwáṣ was ill of dysentery in the congregational mosque at Rayy, he performed sixty complete ablutions in the course of a day and night, and he died in the water. Abú 'Alí Rúdbárí was for some time afflicted with distracting thoughts (*waswás*) in purification. "One day," he said, "I went into the sea at dawn and stayed there till sunrise. During that interval my mind was troubled. I cried out: 'O God, restore me to spiritual health!' A voice answered from the sea: 'Health consists in knowledge.'" It is related that when Sufyán Thawrí was dying, he purified himself sixty times for one prayer and said: "I shall at least be clean when I leave this world." They relate of Shiblí that one day he purified himself with the intention of entering the mosque. He heard a voice cry: "Thou hast washed thy outward self, but where is thy inward purity?" He turned back and gave away all that he possessed, and during a year he put on no more clothes than were necessary for prayer. Then he came to Junayd, who said to him: "O Abú Bakr, that was a very beneficial purification which you have performed; may God always keep you purified!" After that, Shiblí engaged in continual purification. When he was dying and could no longer purify himself, he made a sign to one of his disciples that he should purify him. The disciple did so, but forgot to let the water flow through his beard (*takhlíl-i maḥásin*). Shiblí was unable to speak. He seized the disciple's hand and pointed to his beard, whereupon the rite was duly performed. And it is also related of him that he said: "Whenever I have neglected any rule of purification, some vain conceit has always arisen in my heart." And Abú Yazíd said: "Whenever a thought of this world occurs to my mind, I perform a purification (*ṭahárati*); and whenever a thought of the next world occurs to me, I perform a complete ablution (*ghuslí*)," because this world is non-eternal (*muḥdath*), and the result of thinking of it is legal impurity (*ḥadath*), whereas the next world is the place of absence and repose (*ghaybat ú árám*), and the result of thinking of it is pollution (*janábat*): hence legal impurity involves purification and pollution involves total ablution. One day Shiblí purified himself. When he came to the door of the mosque a voice whispered in his heart: "Art thou so pure that thou enterest My house with this boldness?" He turned back, but the voice asked: "Dost thou turn back from My door? Whither wilt thou go?" He uttered a loud cry. The voice said: "Dost thou revile me?" He stood silent. The voice said: "Dost thou pretend to endure My affliction?" Shiblí exclaimed: "O God, I implore Thee to help me against Thyself."

The Ṣúfí Shaykhs have fully discussed the true meaning of purification, and have commanded their disciples not to cease from purifying themselves both outwardly and inwardly. He who would serve God must purify himself outwardly with water, and he who would come nigh unto God must purify himself inwardly with repentance. Now I will explain the principles of repentance (*tawbat*) and its corollaries.

Chapter concerning Repentance and its Corollaries.

You must know that repentance (*tawbat*) is the first station of pilgrims on the way to the Truth, just as purification (*ṭahárat*) is the first step of those who desire to serve God. Hence God hath said: "*O believers, repent unto God with a sincere repentance*" (Kor. lxvi, 8). And the Apostle said, "There is nothing that God loves more than a youth who repents"; and he also said, "He who repents of sin is even as one who has no sin"; then he added, "When God loves a man, sin shall not hurt him," i.e. he will not become an infidel on account of sin, and his faith will not be impaired. Etymologically *tawbat* means "return", and *tawbat* really involves the turning back from what God has forbidden through fear of what He has commanded. The Apostle said: "Penitence is the act of returning" (*al-nadam al-tawbat*). This saying comprises three things which are involved in *tawbat*, namely, (1) remorse for disobedience, (2) immediate abandonment of sin, and (3) determination not to sin again.

As repentance (*tawbat*) involves these three conditions, so contrition (*nadámat*) may be due to three causes: (1) fear of Divine chastisement and sorrow for evil actions, (2) desire of Divine favour and certainty that it cannot be gained by evil conduct and disobedience, (3) shame before God. In the first case the penitent is *tá'ib*, in the second case he is *muníb*, in the third case he is *awwáb*. Similarly, *tawbat* has three stations, viz., *tawbat*, through fear of Divine punishment; *inábat*, through desire of Divine reward; and *awbat*, for the sake of keeping the Divine command. *Tawbat* is the station of the mass of believers, and implies repentance from great sins (*kabírat*);[1] and *inábat* is the station of the saints and favourites of God (*awliyá ú muqarrabán*);[2] and *awbat* is the station of the prophets and apostles.[3] *Tawbat* is to return from great sins to obedience; *inábat* is to return from minor sins to love; and *awbat* is to return from one's self to God. Repentance (*tawbat*) has its origin in the stern prohibitions of God and in the heart's being aroused from the slumber of heedlessness. When a man considers his evil conduct and abominable deeds he seeks deliverance therefrom, and God makes it easy for him to repent and leads him back to the sweetness of obedience. According to the opinion of orthodox Moslems and all the Ṣúfí Shaykhs, a man who has repented of one sin may continue to commit other sins and nevertheless receive Divine recompense for having abstained from that one sin; and it may be that through the blessing of that recompense he will abstain from other sins. But the Bahshamí[4] sect of the Mu'tazilites hold that no one can properly be called repentant unless he avoids all great sins, a doctrine which is absurd, because a man is not punished for the sins that he does not commit, but if he renounces a certain kind of sin he has no fear of being punished for sins of that particular kind: consequently, he is repentant. Similarly, if he performs some

[1] Cf. Kor. lxvi, 8. [2] Cf. Kor. l, 32. [3] Cf. Kor. xxxviii, 44.
[4] Text, تهشمیان. See Shahristání, Haarbrücker's translation, i, 80.

religious duties and neglects others, he will be rewarded for those which he performed and will be punished for those which he neglected. Moreover, if anyone should have repented of a sin which he has not the means of committing at the moment, he is repentant, because through that past repentance he has gained contrition (*nadámat*), which is a fundamental part of repentance (*tawbat*), and at the moment he has turned his back on that kind of sin and is resolved not to commit it again, even though he should have the power and means of doing so at some future time. As regards the nature and property of repentance, the Ṣúfí Shaykhs hold diverse opinions. Sahl b. 'Abdalláh (al-Tustarí) and others believe that repentance consists in not forgetting your sins, but always regretting them, so that, although you have many good works to your credit, you will not be pleased with yourself on that account; since remorse for an evil action is superior to good works, and one who never forgets his sins will never become conceited. Junayd and others take the opposite view, that repentance consists in forgetting the sin. They argue that the penitent is a lover of God, and the lover of God is in contemplation of God, and in contemplation it is wrong to remember sin, for remembrance of sin is a veil between God and those who contemplate Him. This controversy goes back to the difference of opinion concerning mortification (*mujáhadat*) and contemplation (*musháhadat*), which has been discussed in my account of the doctrine of the Sahlís. Those who hold the penitent to be self-dependent regard his forgetfulness of sin as heedlessness, while those who hold that he is dependent on God deem his remembrance of sin to be polytheism. Moses, while his attributes were subsistent, said, "*I repent towards Thee*" (Kor. vii, 140), but the Apostle, while his attributes were annihilated, said, "I cannot tell Thy praise." Inasmuch as it behoves the penitent not to remember his own selfhood, how should he remember his sin? Indeed, remembrance of sin is a sin, for sin is an occasion of turning away from God, and so is the remembrance of it or the forgetting of it, since both remembrance and forgetfulness are connected with one's self. Junayd says: "I have read many books, but I have never found anything so instructive as this verse:—

'Idhá qultu má adhnabtu qálat mujíbat[an]
ḥayátuka dhanb[un] *lá yuqásu bihi dhanbu.'*

When I say: 'What is my sin?' she says in reply:
'Thy existence is a sin with which no other sin can be compared.'"

In short, repentance is a Divine strengthening and sin is a corporeal act: when contrition (*nadámat*) enters the heart the body has no means of expelling it; and as in the beginning no human act can expel repentance, so in the end no human act can maintain it. God hath said: "*And He turned* (tába) *unto him* (Adam), *for He is the Disposer towards repentance* (al-tawwáb), *the Merciful*" (Kor. ii, 35). The Koran contains many texts to the same effect, which are too well known to require citation.

Repentance is of three kinds: (1) from what is wrong to what is right, (2) from what is right to what is more right, (3) from selfhood to God. The first kind is the repentance of ordinary men; the second kind is the repentance of the elect; and the third kind of repentance belongs to the degree of Divine love (*maḥabbat*). As regards the elect, it is impossible that they should repent of sin. Do not you perceive that all the world feel regret for having lost the vision of God? Moses desired that vision and repented (Kor. vii, 140), because he asked for it with his own volition (*ikhtiyár*), for in love personal volition is a taint. The people thought he had renounced the vision of God, but what he really renounced was his personal volition. As regards those who love God, they repent not only of the imperfection of a station below the station to which they have attained, but also of being conscious of any "station" or "state" whatsoever.

SECTION.

Repentance does not necessarily continue after the resolution not to return to sin has been duly made. A penitent who in those circumstances returns to sin has in principle earned the Divine reward for repentance. Many novices of this sect (the Ṣúfís) have repented and gone back to wickedness and then once more, in consequence of an admonition, have returned to God. A certain Shaykh relates that he repented seventy times and went back to sin on every occasion, until at the seventy-first time he became steadfast. And Abú 'Amr b. Nujayd[1] tells the following story: "As a novice, I repented in the assembly-room of Abú 'Uthmán Ḥírí and persevered in my repentance for some while. Then I fell into sin and left the society of that spiritual director, and whenever I saw him from afar my remorse caused me to flee from his sight. One day I met him unexpectedly. He said to me: 'O son, do not associate with your enemies unless you are sinless (*ma'ṣúm*), for an enemy will see your faults and rejoice. If you must sin, come to us, that we may bear your affliction.' On hearing his words, I felt surfeited with sin and my repentance was established." A certain man, having repented of sin, returned to it and then repented once more. "How will it be," he said, "if I now turn to God?" A heavenly voice answered, saying: "Thou didst obey Me and I recompensed thee, then thou didst abandon Me and I showed indulgence towards thee; and if thou wilt return to Me, I will receive thee."

SECTION.

Dhu 'l-Nún the Egyptian says: "Ordinary men repent of their sins, but the elect repent of their heedlessness," because ordinary men shall be questioned concerning their outward behaviour, but the elect shall be questioned concerning the real nature of their conduct. Heedlessness, which to ordinary men is a pleasure, is a veil to the elect. Abú Ḥafṣ Ḥaddád says:

[1] *Nafaḥát*, No. 281.

"Man has no part in repentance, because repentance is from God to Man, not from Man to God." According to this saying, repentance is not acquired by Man, but is one of God's gifts, a doctrine which is closely akin to that of Junayd. Abu 'l-Ḥasan Búshanjí says: "When you feel no delight in remembering a sin, that is repentance," because the recollection of a sin is accompanied either by regret or by desire: one who regrets that he has committed a sin is repentant, whereas one who desires to commit a sin is a sinner. The actual sin is not so evil as the desire of it, for the act is momentary, but the desire is perpetual. Dhu 'l-Nún the Egyptian says: "There are two kinds of repentance, the repentance of return (*tawbat al-inábat*) and the repentance of shame (*tawbat al-istiḥyá*): the former is repentance through fear of Divine punishment, the latter is repentance through shame of Divine clemency." The repentance of fear is caused by revelation of God's majesty, while the repentance of shame is caused by vision of God's beauty. Those who feel shame are intoxicated, and those who feel fear are sober.

CHAPTER XIX.

The Uncovering of the Fifth Veil: Concerning Prayer (*al-ṣalát*).

Etymologically, prayer (*namáz*) means remembrance (of God) and submissiveness (*dhikr ú inqiyád*), but in the correct usage of lawyers the term is specially applied to the five prayers which God has ordered to be performed at five different times, and which involve certain preliminary conditions, viz.: (1) purification outwardly from filth and inwardly from lust; (2) that one's outward garment should be clean and one's inner garment undefiled by anything unlawful; (3) that the place where one purifies one's self should be outwardly free from contamination and inwardly free from corruptness and sin; (4) turning towards the *qibla*, the outward *qibla* being the Ka'ba and the inward *qibla* being the Throne of God, by which is meant the mystery of Divine contemplation; (5) standing outwardly in the state of power (*qudrat*) and inwardly in the garden of proximity to God (*qurbat*); (6) sincere intention to approach unto God; (7) saying "*Allah akbar*" in the station of awe and annihilation, and standing in the abode of union, and reciting the Koran distinctly and reverently, and bowing the head with humility, and prostrating one's self with abasement, and making the profession of faith with concentration, and saluting with annihilation of one's attributes. It is recorded in the Traditions that when the Apostle prayed, there was heard within him a sound like the boiling of a kettle. And when 'Alí was about to pray, his hair stood on end and he trembled and said: "The hour has come to fulfil a trust which the heavens and the earth were unable to bear."[1]

[1] Here the author cites a description given by Ḥátim al-Aṣamm of his manner of praying.

SECTION.

Prayer is a term in which novices find the whole way to God, from beginning to end, and in which their stations (*maqámát*) are revealed. Thus, for novices, purification takes the place of repentance, and dependence on a spiritual director takes the place of ascertaining the *qibla*, and standing in prayer takes the place of self-mortification, and reciting the Koran takes the place of inward meditation (*dhikr*), and bowing the head takes the place of humility, and prostration takes the place of self-knowledge, and profession of faith takes the place of intimacy (*uns*), and salutation takes the place of detachment from the world and escape from the bondage of "stations". Hence, when the Apostle became divested of all feelings of delight (*mashárib*) in complete bewilderment, he used to say: "O Bilál, comfort us by the call to prayer." The Ṣúfí Shaykhs have discussed this matter and each of them occupies a position of his own. Some hold that prayer is a means of obtaining "presence" with God (*ḥudúr*), and others regard it as a means of obtaining "absence" (*ghaybat*); some who have been "absent" become "present" in prayer, while others who have been "present" become "absent". Similarly, in the next world where God is seen, some, who are "absent", when they see God shall become "present", and *vice versâ*. I, 'Alí b. 'Uthmán al-Jullábí, assert that prayer is a Divine command and is not a means of obtaining either "presence" or "absence", because a Divine command is not a means to anything. The cause of "presence" is "presence" itself, and the cause of "absence" is "absence" itself. If prayer were the cause or means of "presence", it could be performed only by one who was "present", and if it were the cause of "absence", one who was "absent" would necessarily become "present" by neglecting to perform it. But inasmuch as it must be performed by all, whether they be "present" or "absent", prayer is sovereign in its essence and independent.

Prayer is mostly performed and prescribed by those who are engaged in self-mortification or who have attained to steadfastness (*istiqámat*). Thus the Shaykhs order their disciples to perform four hundred bowings in prayer during a day and night, that their bodies may be habituated to devotion; and the steadfast likewise perform many prayers in thanksgiving for the favour which God has bestowed upon them. As regards those who possess "states" (*arbáb-i aḥwál*), their prayers, in the perfection of ecstasy, correspond to the "station" of union, so that through their prayers they become united; or again, when ecstasy is withdrawn, their prayers correspond to the "station" of separation, so that thereby they become separated. The former, who are united in their prayers, pray by day and night and add supererogatory prayers to those which are incumbent on them, but the latter, who are separated, perform no more prayers than they need. The Apostle said: "In prayer lies my delight," because prayer is a source of joy to the steadfast. When the Apostle was brought nigh unto God on the night of the Ascension, and his soul was loosed from the fetters of phenomenal being, and his spirit lost consciousness of all degrees and stations, and his natural powers were annihilated, he said, not of his own will, but inspired by longing: "O God, do not transport me to yonder world of affliction! Do not throw me under the sway of nature and passion!" God answered: "It is My decree that thou shalt return to the world for the sake of establishing the religious law, in order that I may give thee there what I have given thee here." When he returned to this world, he used to say as often as he felt a longing for that exalted station: "O Bilál, comfort us by the call to prayer!" Thus to him every time of prayer was an Ascension and a new nearness to God. Sahl b. 'Abdalláh says: "It is a sign of a man's sincerity that he has an attendant angel who urges him to pray when the hour of prayer is come, and wakes him if he be asleep." This mark (of sincerity) was apparent in Sahl himself, for although he had become palsied in his old age he used to recover the use of his limbs whenever the hour of prayer arrived; and after having performed his prayers he was unable to move from his place. One of the Shaykhs says: "Four things are necessary to him who prays:

annihilation of the lower soul (*nafs*), loss of the natural powers, purity of the inmost heart, and perfect contemplation." Annihilation of the lower soul is to be attained only by concentration of thought; loss of the natural powers only by affirmation of the Divine majesty, which involves the destruction of all that is other than God; purity of the inmost heart only by love; and perfect contemplation only by purity of the inmost heart. It is related that Ḥusayn b. Manṣúr (al-Ḥalláj) used to lay upon himself the obligation of performing four hundred bowings of prayer in a day and a night. On being asked why he took so much trouble in the high degree which he enjoyed, he answered: "Pain and pleasure indicate your feelings, but those whose attributes are annihilated feel no effect either of pleasure or of pain. Beware lest you call remissness maturity and desire of the world search for God." A certain man relates: "I was praying behind Dhu 'l-Nún. When he began to pronounce the *takbír*, he cried '*Allah akbar*' and fell in a swoon like a lifeless body." Junayd, after he had grown old, did not omit any item of the litanies (*awrád*) of his youth. When he was urged to refrain from some of these supererogatory acts of devotion to which his strength was unequal, he replied that he could not abandon at the last those exercises which had been the means of his acquiring spiritual welfare at the first. It is well known that the angels are ceaselessly engaged in worship, because they are spiritual and have no lower soul (*nafs*). The lower soul deters men from obedience, and the more it is subdued the more easy does the performance of worship become; and when it is entirely annihilated, worship becomes the food and drink of Man, even as it is the food and drink of the angels. 'Abdalláh b. Mubárak says: "In my boyhood I remember seeing a female ascetic who was bitten by a scorpion in forty places while she was praying, but no change of expression was visible in her countenance. When she had finished, I said: 'O mother, why didst not thou fling the scorpion away from thee?' She answered: 'Ignorant boy! dost thou deem it right that while I am engaged in God's business I should attend to my own?'"

Abu 'l-Khayr Aqṭa'[1] had a gangrene in his foot. The physicians declared that his foot must be amputated, but he would not allow this to be done. His disciples said: "Cut it off while he is praying, for at that time he is unconscious." The physicians acted on this advice. When Abu 'l-Khayr finished his prayers he found that his foot had been amputated.[2]

Some Ṣúfís perform obligatory acts of devotion openly, but conceal those which are supererogatory in order that they may escape from ostentation (*riyá*). Anyone (they say) who desires that others should take notice of his religious practices becomes a hypocrite; and if he says that although other people see his devotions he himself is unconscious of them, that too is hypocrisy. Other Ṣúfís, however, exhibit both their obligatory and supererogatory acts of devotion, on the ground that ostentation is unreal and piety real: therefore, it is absurd to hide reality for the sake of unreality. "Do not let any thought of ostentation (they say) enter your heart, and worship God wherever you will." The Shaykhs have observed the true spirit of the rules of devotional practice, and have enjoined their disciples to do the same. One of them says: "I travelled for forty years, and during that time I did not miss a single public service of prayer, but was in some town every Friday."

The corollaries of prayer belong to the stations of love, of which I will now set forth the principles in full.

Chapter concerning Love and matters connected therewith.

God hath said, "*O believers, whosoever among you apostatize from their religion, God will assuredly bring in their stead a people whom He will love and who will love Him*" (Kor. v, 59); and He hath also said, "*Some men take idols beside God and love them as they love God, but the believers love God best*" (Kor. ii, 160). And the Apostle said: "I heard Gabriel say

[1] *Nafaḥát*, No. 259.

[2] Here follows a story, already related in the notice of Abú Bakr (p. 70), concerning the different manner in which Abú Bakr and 'Umar recited the Koran when they performed their prayers.

that God said, 'Whoever despises any of My friends has declared war against Me. I do not hesitate in anything as I hesitate to seize the soul of My faithful servant who dislikes death and whom I dislike to hurt, but he cannot escape therefrom; and no means whereby My servant seeks My favour is more pleasing to Me than the performance of the obligations which I have laid upon him; and My servant continuously seeks My favour by works of supererogation until I love him, and when I love him I am his hearing and his sight and his hand and his helper.'" And the Apostle also said, "God loves to meet those who love to meet Him, and dislikes to meet those who dislike to meet Him"; and again, "When God loves a man He says to Gabriel, 'O Gabriel, I love such and such a one, so do thou love him'; then Gabriel loves him and says to the dwellers in Heaven, 'God loves such and such a one,' and they love him too; then he bestows on him favour in the earth, so that he is loved by the inhabitants of the earth; and as it happens with regard to love, so does it happen with regard to hate."

Maḥabbat (love) is said to be derived from *ḥibbat*, which are seeds that fall to the earth in the desert. The name *ḥubb* (love) was given to such desert seeds (*ḥibb*), because love is the source of life just as seeds are the origin of plants. As, when the seeds are scattered in the desert, they become hidden in the earth, and rain falls upon them and the sun shines upon them and cold and heat pass over them, yet they are not corrupted by the changing seasons, but grow up and bear flowers and give fruit, so love, when it takes its dwelling in the heart, is not corrupted by presence or absence, by pleasure or pain, by separation or union. Others say that *maḥabbat* is derived from *ḥubb*, meaning "a jar full of stagnant water", because when love is collected in the heart and fills it, there is no room there for any thought except of the beloved, as Shiblí says: "Love is called *maḥabbat* because it obliterates (*tamḥú*) from the heart everything except the beloved." Others say that *maḥabbat* is derived from *ḥubb*, meaning "the four conjoined pieces of wood on which a water-jug is placed, because a lover lightly bears whatever his beloved metes out to him—honour or disgrace, pain or pleasure, fair treatment or foul". According to others, *maḥabbat* is derived from *ḥabb*, the plural of *ḥabbat*, and *ḥabbat* is the core of the heart, where love resides. In this case, *maḥabbat* is called by the name of its dwelling-place, a principle of which there are numerous examples in Arabic. Others derive it from *ḥabáb*, "bubbles of water and the effervescence thereof in a heavy rainfall," because love is the effervescence of the heart in longing for union with the beloved. As the body subsists through the spirit, so the heart subsists through love, and love subsists through vision of, and union with, the beloved. Others, again, declare that *ḥubb* is a name applied to pure love, because the Arabs call the pure white of the human eye *ḥabbat al-insán*, just as they call the pure black (core) of the heart *ḥabbat al-qalb*: the latter is the seat of love, the former of vision. Hence the heart and the eye are rivals in love, as the poet says:

"*My heart envies mine eye the pleasure of seeing,*
And mine eye envies my heart the pleasure of meditating."

SECTION.

You must know that the term "love" (*maḥabbat*) is used by theologians in three significations. Firstly, as meaning restless desire for the object of love, and inclination and passion, in which sense it refers only to created beings and their mutual affection towards one another, but cannot be applied to God, who is exalted far above anything of this sort. Secondly, as meaning God's beneficence and His conferment of special privileges on those whom He chooses and causes to attain the perfection of saintship and peculiarly distinguishes by diverse kinds of His miraculous grace. Thirdly, as meaning praise which God bestows on a man for a good action (*thaná-yi jamíl*).[1]

Some scholastic philosophers say that God's love, which He has made known to us, belongs to those traditional attributes,

[1] Cf. Qushayrí (Cairo, 1318 A.H.), 170, 14 sqq.

like His face and His hand and His settling Himself firmly on His throne (*istiwá*), of which the existence from the standpoint of reason would appear to be impossible if they had not been proclaimed as Divine attributes in the Koran and the Sunna. Therefore we affirm them and believe in them, but suspend our own judgment concerning them. These scholastics mean to deny that the term "love" can be applied to God in all the senses which I have mentioned. I will now explain to you the truth of this matter.

God's love of Man is His good will towards him and His having mercy on him. Love is one of the names of His will (*irádat*), like "satisfaction", "anger", "mercy", etc., and His will is an eternal attribute whereby He wills His actions. In short, God's love towards Man consists in showing much favour to him, and giving him a recompense in this world and the next, and making him secure from punishment and keeping him safe from sin, and bestowing on him lofty "states" and exalted "stations" and causing him to turn his thoughts away from all that is other than God. When God peculiarly distinguishes anyone in this way, that specialization of His will is called love. This is the doctrine of Ḥárith Muḥásibí and Junayd and a large number of the Ṣúfí Shaykhs as well as of the lawyers belonging to both the sects; and most of the Sunní scholastics hold the same opinion. As regards their assertion that Divine love is "praise given to a man for a good action" (*thaná-yi jamíl bar banda*), God's praise is His word (*kalám*), which is uncreated; and as regards their assertion that Divine love means "beneficence", His beneficence consists in His actions. Hence the different views are substantially in close relation to each other.

Man's love towards God is a quality which manifests itself in the heart of the pious believer, in the form of veneration and magnification, so that he seeks to satisfy his Beloved and becomes impatient and restless in his desire for vision of Him, and cannot rest with anyone except Him, and grows familiar with the remembrance (*dhikr*) of Him, and abjures the remembrance of everything besides. Repose becomes unlawful to him and rest flees from him. He is cut off from all habits and associations, and renounces sensual passion and turns towards the court of love and submits to the law of love and knows God by His attributes of perfection. It is impossible that Man's love of God should be similar in kind to the love of His creatures towards one another, for the former is desire to comprehend and attain the beloved object, while the latter is a property of bodies. The lovers of God are those who devote themselves to death in nearness to Him, not those who seek His nature (*kayfiyyat*), because the seeker stands by himself, but he who devotes himself to death (*mustahlik*) stands by his Beloved; and the truest lovers are they who would fain die thus, and are overpowered, because a phenomenal being has no means of approaching the Eternal save through the omnipotence of the Eternal. He who knows what is real love feels no more difficulties, and all his doubts depart. Love, then, is of two kinds—(1) the love of like towards like, which is a desire instigated by the lower soul and which seeks the essence (*dhát*) of the beloved object by means of sexual intercourse; (2) the love of one who is unlike the object of his love and who seeks to become intimately attached to an attribute of that object, e.g. hearing without speech or seeing without eye. And believers who love God are of two kinds—(1) those who regard the favour and beneficence of God towards them, and are led by that regard to love the Benefactor; (2) those who are so enraptured by love that they reckon all favours as a veil (between themselves and God) and by regarding the Benefactor are led to (consciousness of) His favours. The latter way is the more exalted of the two.

SECTION.

Among the Ṣúfí Shaykhs Sumnún al-Muḥibb holds a peculiar doctrine concerning love. He asserts that love is the foundation and principle of the way to God, that all "states" and "stations" are stages of love, and that every stage and abode in which the seeker may be admits of destruction, except the abode of love, which is not destructible in any circumstances so long as the way itself remains in existence. All the other Shaykhs agree with him in this matter, but since the term "love" is current and well known, and they wished the doctrine of Divine love to remain hidden, instead of calling it "love" they gave it the name of "purity" (*ṣafwat*), and the lover they called "Ṣúfí"; or they used the word "poverty" (*faqr*) to denote the renunciation of the lover's personal will in his affirmation of the Beloved's will, and they called the lover "poor" (*faqír*). I have explained the theory of "purity" and "poverty" in the beginning of this book.

'Amr b. 'Uthmán Makkí says in the *Kitáb-i Maḥabbat*[1] that God created the souls (*dilhá*) seven thousand years before the bodies and kept them in the station of proximity (*qurb*), and that he created the spirits (*jánhá*) seven thousand years before the souls and kept them in the degree of intimacy (*uns*), and that he created the hearts (*sirrhá*) seven thousand years before the spirits and kept them in the degree of union (*waṣl*), and revealed the epiphany of His beauty to the heart three hundred and sixty times every day and bestowed on it three hundred and sixty looks of grace, and He caused the spirits to hear the word of love and manifested three hundred and sixty exquisite favours of intimacy to the soul, so that they all surveyed the phenomenal universe and saw nothing more precious than themselves and were filled with vanity and pride. Therefore God subjected them to probation: He imprisoned the heart in the spirit and the spirit in the soul and the soul in the body; then He mingled reason (*'aql*) with them, and sent prophets and gave commands; then each of them began to seek its original station. God ordered them to pray. The body betook itself to prayer, the soul attained to love, the spirit arrived at proximity to God, and the heart found rest in union with Him. The explanation of love is not love, because love is a feeling (*ḥál*), and feelings are never mere words (*qál*). If the whole world

[1] "The Book of Love."

wished to attract love, they could not; and if they made the utmost efforts to repel it, they could not. Love is a Divine gift, not anything that can be acquired.

SECTION.

Concerning excessive love (*'ishq*) there is much controversy among the Shaykhs. Some Ṣúfís hold that excessive love towards God is allowable, but that it does not proceed from God. Such love, they say, is the attribute of one who is debarred from his beloved, and Man is debarred from God, but God is not debarred from Man: therefore Man may love God excessively, but the term is not applicable to God. Others, again, take the view that God cannot be the object of Man's excessive love, because such love involves a passing beyond limits, whereas God is not limited. The moderns assert that excessive love, in this world and the next, is properly applied only to the desire of attaining the essence, and inasmuch as the essence of God is not attainable, the term (*'ishq*) is not rightly used in reference to Man's love towards God, although the terms "love" (*maḥabbat*) and "pure love" (*ṣafwat*) are correct. They say, moreover, that while love (*maḥabbat*) may be produced by hearing, excessive love (*'ishq*) cannot possibly arise without actual vision: therefore it cannot be felt towards God, who is not seen in this world. The essence of God is not attainable or perceptible, that Man should be able to feel excessive love towards Him; but Man feels love (*maḥabbat*) towards God, because God, through His attributes and actions, is a gracious benefactor to His friends. Since Jacob was absorbed in love (*maḥabbat*) for Joseph, from whom he was separated, his eyes became bright and clear as soon as he smelt Joseph's shirt; but since Zulaykhá was ready to die on account of her excessive love (*'ishq*) for Joseph, her eyes were not opened until she was united with him. It has also been said that excessive love is applicable to God, on the ground that neither God nor excessive love has any opposite.

SECTION.

I will now mention a few of the innumerable indications which the Ṣúfí Shaykhs have given as to the true nature of love. Master Abu 'l-Qásim Qushayrí says: "Love is the effacement of the lover's attributes and the establishment of the Beloved's essence," i.e. since the Beloved is subsistent (*báqí*) and the lover is annihilated (*fání*) the jealousy of love requires that the lover should make the subsistence of the Beloved absolute by negating himself, and he cannot negate his own attributes except by affirming the essence of the Beloved. No lover can stand by his own attributes, for in that case he would not need the Beloved's beauty; but when he knows that his life depends on the Beloved's beauty, he necessarily seeks to annihilate his own attributes, which veil him from his Beloved; and thus in love for his Friend he becomes an enemy to himself. It is well known that the last words of Ḥusayn b. Manṣúr (al-Ḥalláj) on the scaffold were *Ḥasb al-wájid ifrád al-wáḥid*, "It is enough for the lover that he should make the One single," i.e. that his existence should be cleared away from the path of love and that the dominion of his lower soul should be utterly destroyed. Abú Yazíd Bisṭámí says: "Love consists in regarding your own much as little and your Beloved's little as much." This is how God Himself deals with His servants, for He calls "little" that which He has given to them in this world (Kor. iv, 79), but calls their praise of Him "much"—"*the men and women who praise God much*" (Kor. xxxiii, 35)—in order that all His creatures may know that He is the real Beloved, because nothing is little that God bestows on Man, and all is little that Man offers to God. Sahl b. 'Abdalláh al-Tustarí says: "Love consists in embracing acts of obedience (*mu'ánaqat al-ṭá'át*) and in avoiding acts of disobedience," because a man performs the command of his beloved more easily in proportion to the strength of love in his heart. This is a refutation of those heretics who declare that a man may attain to such a degree of love that obedience is no longer required of him, a doctrine which is sheer heresy. It is impossible that any person, while his understanding is sound, should be relieved of his religious obligations, because the law of Muḥammad will never be abrogated, and if one such person may be thus relieved why not all? The case of persons overcome with rapture (*maghlúb*) and idiots (*ma'túh*) is different. It is possible, however, that God in His love should bring a man to such a degree that it costs him no trouble to perform his religious duties, because the more one loves Him who gives the command the less trouble will he have in executing it. When the Apostle abandoned himself entirely to devotion both by day and night, so that his blessed feet became swollen, God said: "*We have not sent down the Koran to thee in order that thou shouldst be miserable*" (Kor. xx, 1). And it is also possible that one should be relieved of the consciousness of performing the Divine command, as the Apostle said: "Verily, a veil is drawn over my heart, and I ask forgiveness of God seventy times daily," i.e. he asked to be forgiven for his actions, because he was not regarding himself and his actions, that he should be pleased with his obedience, but was paying regard to the majesty of God's command and was thinking that his actions were not worthy of God's acceptance. Sumnún Muḥibb says: "The lovers of God have borne away the glory of this world and the next, for the Prophet said, 'A man is with the object of his love.'" Therefore they are with God in both worlds, and those who are with God can do no wrong. The glory of this world is God's being with them, and the glory of the next world is their being with God. Yaḥyá b. Mu'ádh al-Rází says: "Real love is neither diminished by unkindness nor increased by kindness and bounty," because in love both kindness and unkindness are causes, and the cause of a thing is reduced to nothing when the thing itself actually exists. A lover delights in the affliction that his beloved makes him suffer, and having love he regards kindness and unkindness with the same indifference. The story is well known how Shiblí was supposed to be insane and was confined in a madhouse. Some persons came to visit him. "Who are you?" he asked. They answered: "Thy friends," whereupon he pelted them with stones and put them to flight. Then he said: "Had you been my friends, you would not have fled from my affliction."

CHAPTER XX.

The Uncovering of the Sixth Veil: Concerning Alms (*al-zakát*).

Alms is one of the obligatory ordinances of the faith. It becomes due on the completion of a benefit; e.g., two hundred dirhems constitute a complete benefit (*ni'mati tamám*), and anyone who is in possession of that sum ought to pay five dirhems; or if he possesses twenty dínárs he ought to pay half a dínár; or if he possesses five camels he ought to pay one sheep, and so forth. Alms is also due on account of dignity (*jáh*), because that too is a complete benefit. The Apostle said: "Verily, God has made it incumbent upon you to pay the alms of your dignity, even as He has made it incumbent upon you to pay the alms of your property"; and he said also: "Everything has its alms, and the alms of a house is the guest-room."

Alms is really thanksgiving for a benefit received, the thanks being similar in kind to the benefit. Thus health is a great blessing, for which every limb owes alms. Therefore healthy persons ought to occupy all their limbs with devotion and not yield them to pleasure and pastime, in order that the alms due for the blessing of health may be fully paid. Moreover, there is an alms for every spiritual blessing, namely, outward and inward acknowledgment of that blessing in proportion to its worth. Thus, when a man knows that the blessings bestowed upon him by God are infinite, he should render infinite thanks by way of alms. The Ṣúfís do not consider it praiseworthy to give alms on account of worldly blessings, because they disapprove of avarice, and a man must needs be extremely avaricious to keep two hundred dirhems in his possession for a whole year and then give away five dirhems in alms. Since it is the custom of the generous to lavish their wealth, and since they are disposed to be liberal, how should almsgiving be incumbent upon them?

I have read in the Anecdotes that a certain formal theologian, wishing to make trial of Shiblí, asked him what sum ought to be given in alms. Shiblí replied: "Where avarice is present and property exists, five dirhems out of every two hundred dirhems, and half a dínár out of every twenty dínárs. That is according to thy doctrine; but according to mine, a man ought not to possess anything, in which case he will be saved from the trouble of giving alms." The divine asked: "Whose authority do you follow in this matter?" Shiblí said: "The authority of Abú Bakr the Veracious, who gave away all that he possessed, and on being asked by the Apostle what he had left behind for his family, answered, 'God and His Apostle.'" And it is related that 'Alí said in an ode—

"*Almsgiving is not incumbent on me,*
For how can a generous man be required to give alms?"

But it is absurd for anyone to cultivate ignorance and to say that because he has no property he need not be acquainted with the theory of almsgiving. To learn and obtain knowledge is an essential obligation, and to profess one's self independent of knowledge is mere infidelity. It is one of the evils of the present age that many who pretend to be pious dervishes reject knowledge in favour of ignorance. The author says: "Once I was giving devotional instruction to some novices in Ṣúfiism and was discussing the chapter on the poor-rate of camels (*ṣadaqat al-ibil*) and explaining the rules in regard to she-camels that have entered on their third or second or fourth year (*bint-i labún ú bint-i makhád̤ ú ḥiqqa*). An ignorant fellow, tired of listening to my discourse, rose and said: 'I have no camels: what use is this knowledge to me?' I answered: 'Knowledge is necessary in taking alms no less than in giving alms: if anyone should give you a she-camel in her third year and you should accept her, you ought to be informed on this point; and even though one has no property and does not want to have any property, he is not thereby relieved from the obligation of knowledge.'"

SECTION.

Some of the Ṣúfí Shaykhs have accepted alms, while others have declined to do so. Those whose poverty is voluntary (*ba-ikhtiyár*) belong to the latter class. "We do not amass property," they say, "therefore we need not give alms; nor will we accept alms from worldlings, lest they should have the upper hand (*yad-i 'ulyá*) and we the lower (*yad-i suflá*)." But those who in their poverty are under Divine compulsion (*muḍtarr*) accept alms, not for their own wants but with the purpose of relieving a brother Moslem of his obligation. In this case the receiver of alms, not the giver, has the upper hand; otherwise, the words of God, "*And He accepteth the alms*" (Kor. ix, 105), are meaningless, and the giver of alms must be superior to the receiver, a belief which is utterly false. No; the upper hand belongs to him who takes something from a brother Moslem in order that the latter may escape from a heavy responsibility. Dervishes are not of this world (*dunyá'í*), but of the next world (*'uqbá'í*), and if a dervish fails to relieve a worldling of his responsibility, the worldling will be held accountable and punished at the Resurrection for having neglected to fulfil his obligation. Therefore God afflicts the dervish with a slight want in order that worldlings may be able to perform what is incumbent upon them. The upper hand is necessarily the hand of the dervish who receives alms in accordance with the requirement of the law, because it behoves him to take that which is due to God. If the hand of the recipient were the lower hand, as some anthropomorphists (*ahl-i ḥashw*) declare, then the hands of the Apostles, who often received alms due to God and delivered it to the proper authority, must have been lower (than the hands of those who gave the alms to them). This view is erroneous; its adherents do not see that the

Apostles received alms in consequence of the Divine command. The religious Imáms have acted in the same manner as the Apostles, for they have always received payments due to the public treasury. Those are in the wrong who assert that the hand of the receiver is the lower and that of the giver is the higher.

Chapter on Liberality and Generosity.

In the opinion of theologians liberality (*júd*) and generosity (*sakhá*), when regarded as human attributes, are synonymous; but God, although He is called liberal (*jawád*), is not called generous (*sakhí*), because He has not called Himself by the latter name, nor is He so called in any Apostolic Tradition. All orthodox Moslems are agreed that it is not allowable to apply to God any name that is not proclaimed in the Koran and the Sunna: thus He may be called knowing (*'álim*), but not intelligent (*'áqil*) or wise (*faqíh*), although the three terms bear the same signification. Hence God is called liberal, since that name is accompanied by His blessing; and He is not called generous, since that name lacks His blessing. Men have made a distinction between liberality (*júd*) and generosity (*sakhá*), and have said that the generous man discriminates in his liberality, and that his actions are connected with a selfish motive (*gharaḍ*) and a cause (*sabab*). This is a rudimentary stage in liberality, for the liberal man does not discriminate, and his actions are devoid of self-interest and without any secondary cause. These two qualities were exhibited by two Apostles, viz., Abraham, the Friend of God (*Khalíl*), and Muḥammad, the Beloved of God (*Ḥabíb*). It is related in the genuine Traditions that Abraham was accustomed not to eat anything until a guest came to him. Once, after three days had passed without the arrival of a guest, a fire-worshipper appeared at the door, but Abraham, on hearing who he was, refused to give him entertainment. God reproached him on this account, saying: "Wilt not thou give a piece of bread to one whom I have nourished for seventy years?"

But Muḥammad, when the son of Ḥátim visited him, spread his own mantle on the ground for him and said: "Honour the noble chieftain of a people when he comes to you." Abraham's position was generosity, but our Apostle's was liberality.

The best rule in this matter is set forth in the maxim that liberality consists in following one's first thought, and that it is a sign of avarice when the second thought prevails over the first; for the first thought is unquestionably from God. I have read that at Níshápúr there was a merchant who used regularly to attend the meetings held by Shaykh Abú Sa'íd. One day a dervish who was present begged the Shaykh to give him something. The merchant had a dínár and a small piece of clipped money (*quráḍa*). His first thought was: "I will give the dínár," but on second thoughts he gave the clipped piece. When the Shaykh finished his discourse the merchant asked: "Is it right for anyone to contend with God?" The Shaykh answered: "You contended with Him: He bade you give the dínár, but you gave the clipping." I have also read that Shaykh Abú 'Abdalláh Rúdbárí came to the house of a disciple in his absence, and ordered that all the effects in the house should be taken to the bazaar. When the disciple returned he was delighted that the Shaykh had behaved with such freedom, but he said nothing. His wife, however, tore off her dress and flung it down, saying: "This belongs to the effects of the house." The husband exclaimed: "You are doing more than is necessary and showing self-will." "O husband," said she, "what the Shaykh did was the result of his liberality: we too must exert ourselves (*takalluf kuním*) to display liberality." "Yes," replied the husband, "but if we allow the Shaykh to be liberal, that is real liberality in us, whereas liberality, regarded as a human quality, is forced and unreal." A disciple ought always to sacrifice his property and himself in obedience to the command of God. Hence Sahl b. 'Abdalláh (al-Tustarí) said: "The Ṣúfí's blood may be shed with impunity, and his property may be seized." I have heard the following story of Shaykh Abú Muslim Fárisí: "Once (he said) I set out with a number of people for the Ḥijáz. In the neighbourhood of Ḥulwán we were attacked by Kurds, who stripped us of our patched frocks. We offered no resistance. One man, however, became greatly excited, whereupon a Kurd drew his scimitar and killed him, notwithstanding our entreaties that his life might be spared. On our asking why he had killed him he answered: 'Because he is no Ṣúfí and acts disloyally in the company of saints: such a one is better dead.' We said: 'How so?' He replied: 'The first step in Ṣúfiism is liberality. This fellow, who was so desperately attached to these rags that he quarrelled with his own friends, how should he be a Ṣúfí? His own friends, I say, for it is a long time since we have been doing as you do, and plundering you and stripping you of worldly encumbrances.'"[1] A man came to the house of Ḥasan b. 'Alí and said that he owed four hundred dirhems. Ḥasan gave him four hundred dínárs and went into the house, weeping. They asked him why he wept. He answered: "I have been remiss in making inquiry into the circumstances of this man, and have reduced him to the humiliation of begging." Abú Sahl Ṣu'lúkí never put alms into the hand of a dervish, and always used to lay on the ground anything that he gave. "Worldly goods," he said, "are too worthless to be placed in the hand of a Moslem, so that my hand should be the upper and his the lower."[2] I once met a dervish to whom a Sultan had sent three hundred drachms of pure gold. He went to a bath-house, and gave the whole sum to the superintendent and immediately departed. I have already discussed the subject of liberality in the chapter on preference (*íthár*), where I have dealt with the doctrine of the Núrís.

1 Here follows a story of 'Abdalláh b. Ja'far and an Abyssinian slave, who let a dog eat the whole of his daily portion of food.

2 Here the author relates three short anecdotes illustrating the liberality of Muḥammad.

CHAPTER XXI.

THE UNCOVERING OF THE SEVENTH VEIL: ON FASTING (*al-ṣawm*).

God hath said: "*O believers, fasting is prescribed unto you*" (Kor. ii, 179). And the Apostle said that he was informed by Gabriel that God said: "Fasting is mine, and I have the best right to give recompense for it" (*al-ṣawm lí wa-ana ajzá bihi*),[1] because the religious practice of fasting is a mystery unconnected with any external thing, a mystery in which none other than God participates: hence its recompense is infinite. It has been said that mankind enter Paradise through God's mercy, and that their rank therein depends on their religious devotion, and that their abiding therein for ever is the recompense of their fasting, because God said: "I have the best right to give recompense for it." Junayd said: "Fasting is half of the Way." I have seen Shaykhs who fasted without intermission, and others who fasted only during the month of Ramaḍán: the former were seeking recompense, and the latter were renouncing self-will and ostentation. Again, I have seen others who fasted and were not conscious of anyone and ate only when food was set before them. This is more in accordance with the Sunna. It is related that the Apostle came to 'Á'isha and Ḥafṣa, who said to him: "We have kept some dates and butter (*ḥays*) for thee." "Bring it," said he; "I was intending to fast, but I will fast another day instead." I have seen others who fasted on the "white days" (from the 13th to the 15th of every month), and on the ten (last nights) of the blessed month (Ramaḍán), and also during Rajab, Sha'bán, and Ramaḍán. Others I have seen who observed the fast of David, which the

[1] The usual reading is *ajzí*, "I give recompense," but the Persian translation, *ba-jazá-yi án man awlátaram*, is equivalent to *ana ajzá bihi*.

Apostle called the best of fasts, i.e. they fasted one day and broke their fast the next day. Once I came into the presence of Shaykh Aḥmad Bukhárí. He had a dish of sweetmeat (*ḥalwá*) before him, from which he was eating, and he made a sign to me that I should do the same. As is the way of young men, I answered (without consideration) that I was fasting. He asked why. I said: "In conformity with such and such a one." He said: "It is not right for human beings to conform with human beings." I was about to break my fast, but he said: "Since you wish to be quit of conformity with him, do not conform with me, for I too am a human being." Fasting is really abstinence, and this includes the whole method of Ṣúfiism (*ṭaríqat*). The least degree in fasting is hunger, which is God's food on earth, and is universally commended in the eye of the law and of reason. One month's continual fasting is incumbent on every reasonable Moslem who has attained to manhood. The fast begins on the appearance of the moon of Ramaḍán, and continues until the appearance of the moon of Shawwál, and for every day a sincere intention and firm obligation are necessary. Abstinence involves many obligations, e.g., keeping the belly without food and drink, and guarding the eye from lustful looks, and the ear from listening to evil speech about anyone in his absence, and the tongue from vain or foul words, and the body from following after worldly things and disobedience to God. One who acts in this manner is truly keeping his fast, for the Apostle said to a certain man, "When you fast, let your ear fast and your eye and your tongue and your hand and every limb;" and he also said, "Many a one has no good of his fasting except hunger and thirst."

I dreamed that I saw the Apostle and asked him to give me a word of counsel, and that he replied: "Imprison thy tongue and thy senses." To imprison the senses is complete self-mortification, because all kinds of knowledge are acquired through the five senses: sight, hearing, taste, smell, and touch. Four of the senses have a particular *locus*, but the fifth, namely touch, is spread over the whole body. Everything that becomes known to human beings passes through these five doors, except intuitive knowledge and Divine inspiration, and in each sense there is a purity and an impurity ; for, just as they are open to knowledge, reason, and spirit, so they are open to imagination and passion, being organs which partake of piety and sin and of felicity and misery. Therefore it behoves him who is keeping a fast to imprison all the senses in order that they may return from disobedience to obedience. To abstain only from food and drink is child's play. One must abstain from idle pleasures and unlawful acts, not from eating lawful food. I marvel at those who say that they are keeping a voluntary fast and yet fail to perform an obligatory duty. Not to commit sin is obligatory, whereas continual fasting is an apostolic custom (which may be observed or neglected). When a man is divinely protected from sin all his circumstances are a fast. It is related by Abú Ṭalḥa al-Málikí that Sahl b. 'Abdalláh of Tustar was fasting on the day of his birth and also on the day of his death, because he was born in the forenoon and tasted no milk until the evening prayer, and on the day of his decease he was keeping a fast. But continual fasting (*rúza-i wiṣál*) has been forbidden by the Apostle, for when he fasted continually, and his Companions conformed with him in that respect, he forbade them, saying: "I am not as one of you: I pass the night with my Lord, who gives me food and drink." The votaries of self-mortification assert that this prohibition was an act of indulgence, not a veto declaring such fasts to be unlawful, and others regard them as being contrary to the Sunna, but the fact is that continuance (*wiṣál*) is impossible, because the day's fast is interrupted by night or, at any rate, does not continue beyond a certain period. It is related that Sahl b. 'Abdalláh of Tustar used to eat only once in fifteen days, and when the month of Ramaḍán arrived he ate nothing until the Feast, and performed four hundred bowings in prayer every night. This exceeds the limit of human endurance, and cannot be accomplished by anyone without Divine aid, which itself becomes his nourishment. It is well known that Shaykh

Abú Naṣr Sarráj,[1] the author of the *Luma'*,[2] who was surnamed the Peacock of the Poor (*Ṭá'ús al-fuqará*), came to Baghdád in the month of Ramaḍán, and was given a private chamber in the Shúníziyya mosque, and was appointed to preside over the dervishes until the Feast. During the nightly prayers of Ramaḍán (*taráwíḥ*) he recited the whole Koran five times. Every night a servant brought a loaf of bread to his room. When he departed, on the day of the Feast, the servant found all the thirty loaves untouched. 'Alí b. Bakkár relates that Ḥafṣ Miṣṣísí ate nothing in Ramaḍán except on the fifteenth day of that month. We are told that Ibráhím Adham fasted from the beginning to the end of Ramaḍán, and, although it was the month of Tammúz (July), worked every day as a harvester and gave his wages to the dervishes, and prayed from nightfall to daybreak; they watched him closely and saw that he neither ate nor slept. It is said that Shaykh Abú 'Abdalláh Khafíf during his life kept forty uninterrupted fasts of forty days, and I have met with an old man who used annually to keep two fasts of forty days in the desert. I was present at the death-bed of Dánishmand Abú Muḥammad Bánghari; he had tasted no food for eighty days and had not missed a single occasion of public worship. At Merv there were two spiritual directors; one was called Mas'úd and the other was Shaykh Abú 'Alí Siyáh. Mas'úd sent a message to Abú 'Alí, saying: "How long shall we make empty pretensions? Come, let us sit fasting for forty days." Abú 'Alí replied: "No; let us eat three times a day and nevertheless require only one purification during these forty days." The difficulties of this question are not yet removed. Ignorant persons conclude that continuance in fasting is possible, while physicians allege that such a theory is entirely baseless. I will now explain the matter in full. To fast continuously, without infringing the Divine command, is a miracle (*karámat*). Miracles have a special, not a general, application: if they were vouchsafed to all, faith would be an act of necessity

[1] *Nafaḥát*, No. 353. [2] "Brilliancies." *Naf.* entitles it لمعة.

(*jabr*) and gnostics would not be recompensed on account of gnosis. The Apostle wrought evidentiary miracles (*mu'jizát*) and therefore divulged his continuance in fasting; but he forbade the saints (*ahl-i karámat*) to divulge it, because a *karámat* involves concealment, whereas a *mu'jizat* involves revelation. This is a clear distinction between the miracles performed by Apostles and those performed by saints, and will be sufficient for anyone who is divinely guided. The forty days' fasts (*chilla*) of the saints are derived from the fast of Moses (Kor. vii, 138). When the saints desire to hear the word of God spiritually, they remain fasting for forty days. After thirty days have passed they rub their teeth; then they fast ten days more, and God speaks to their hearts, because whatever the prophets enjoy openly the saints may enjoy secretly. Now, hearing the word of God is not compatible with the subsistence of the natural temperament: therefore the four humours must be deprived of food and drink for forty days in order that they may be utterly subdued, and that the purity of love and the subtlety of the spirit may hold absolute sway.

Chapter on Hunger and matters connected with it.

Hunger sharpens the intelligence and improves the mind and health. The Apostle said: "Make your bellies hungry and your livers thirsty and your bodies naked, that perchance your hearts may see God in this world." Although hunger is an affliction to the body, it illumines the heart and purifies the soul, and leads the spirit into the presence of God. To eat one's fill is an act worthy of a beast. One who cultivates his spiritual nature by means of hunger, in order to devote himself entirely to God and detach himself from worldly ties, is not on the same level with one who cultivates his body by means of gluttony, and serves his lusts. "The men of old ate to live, but ye live to eat." For the sake of a morsel of food Adam fell from Paradise, and was banished far from the neighbourhood of God.

He whose hunger is compulsory is not really hungry, because

one who desires to eat after God has decreed the contrary is virtually eating; the merit of hunger belongs to him who abstains from eating, not to him who is debarred from eating. Kattání[1] says: "The novice shall sleep only when he is overpowered by slumber, and speak only when he must, and eat only when he is starving." According to some, starvation (*fáqa*) involves abstention from food for two days and nights; others say three days and nights, or a week, or forty days, because true mystics believe that a sincere man (*ṣádiq*) is only once hungry in forty days; his hunger merely serves to keep him alive, and all hunger besides is natural appetite and vanity. You must know that all the veins in the bodies of gnostics are evidences of the Divine mysteries, and that their hearts are tenanted by visions of the Most High. Their hearts are doors opened in their breasts, and at these doors are stationed reason and passion: reason is reinforced by the spirit, and passion by the lower soul. The more the natural humours are nourished by food, the stronger does the lower soul become, and the more impetuously is passion diffused through the members of the body; and in every vein a different kind of veil (*ḥijábí*) is produced. But when food is withheld from the lower soul it grows weak, and the reason gains strength, and the mysteries and evidences of God become more visible, until, when the lower soul is unable to work and passion is annihilated, every vain desire is effaced in the manifestation of the Truth, and the seeker of God attains to the whole of his desire. It is related that Abu 'l-'Abbás Qaṣṣáb said: "My obedience and disobedience depend on two cakes of bread: when I eat I find in myself the stuff of every sin, but when I abstain from eating I find in myself the foundation of every act of piety." The fruit of hunger is contemplation of God (*mushāhadat*), of which the forerunner is mortification (*mujáhadat*). Repletion combined with contemplation is better than hunger combined with mortification, because contemplation is the battle-field of men, whereas mortification is the playground of children.

[1] *Nafaḥát*, No. 215.

CHAPTER XXII.

THE UNCOVERING OF THE EIGHTH VEIL: CONCERNING THE PILGRIMAGE.

The pilgrimage (*ḥajj*) is binding on every Moslem of sound mind who is able to perform it and has reached manhood. It consists in putting on the pilgrim's garb at the proper place, in standing on 'Arafát, in circumambulating the Ka'ba, and in running between Ṣafá and Marwa. One must not enter the sacred territory without being clad as a pilgrim (*bé iḥrám*). The sacred territory (*ḥaram*) is so called because it contains the Station of Abraham (*Maqám-i Ibráhím*). Abraham had two stations: the station of his body, namely, Mecca, and the station of his sóul, namely, friendship (*khullat*). Whoever seeks his bodily station must renounce all lusts and pleasures and put on the pilgrim's garb and clothe himself in a winding-sheet (*kafan*) and refrain from hunting lawful game, and keep all his senses under strict control, and be present at 'Arafát and go thence to Muzdalifa and Mash'ar al-Ḥarám, and pick up stones and circumambulate the Ka'ba and visit Miná and stay there three days and throw stones in the prescribed manner and cut his hair and perform the sacrifice and put on his (ordinary) clothes. But whoever seeks his spiritual station must renounce familiar associations and bid farewell to pleasures and take no thought of other than God (for his looking towards the phenomenal world is interdicted); then he must stand on the 'Arafát of gnosis (*ma'rifat*) and from there set out for the Muzdalifa of amity (*ulfat*) and from there send his heart to circumambulate the temple of Divine purification (*tanzíh*), and throw away the stones of passion and corrupt thoughts in the Miná of faith, and sacrifice his lower soul on the altar of mortification and arrive at the station of friendship (*khullat*).

To enter the bodily station is to be secure from enemies and their swords, but to enter the spiritual station is to be secure from separation (from God) and its consequences.[1]

Muḥammad b. al-Faḍl says: "I wonder at those who seek His temple in this world: why do not they seek contemplation of Him in their hearts? The temple they sometimes attain and sometimes miss, but contemplation they might enjoy always. If they are bound to visit a stone, which is looked at only once a year, surely they are more bound to visit the temple of the heart, where He may be seen three hundred and sixty times in a day and night. But the mystic's every step is a symbol of the journey to Mecca, and when he reaches the sanctuary he wins a robe of honour for every step." Abú Yazíd says: "If anyone's recompense for worshipping God is deferred until to-morrow he has not worshipped God aright to-day," for the recompense of every moment of worship and mortification is immediate. And Abú Yazíd also says: "On my first pilgrimage I saw only the temple; the second time, I saw both the temple and the Lord of the temple; and the third time I saw the Lord alone." In short, where mortification is, there is no sanctuary: the sanctuary is where contemplation is. Unless the whole universe is a man's trysting-place where he comes nigh unto God and a retired chamber where he enjoys intimacy with God, he is still a stranger to Divine love; but when he has vision the whole universe is his sanctuary.

"*The darkest thing in the world is the Beloved's house without the Beloved.*"

Accordingly, what is truly valuable is not the Ka'ba, but contemplation and annihilation in the abode of friendship, of which things the sight of the Ka'ba is indirectly a cause. But we must recognize that every cause depends on the author of causes (*musabbib*), from whatever hidden place the providence of God may appear, and whencesoever the desire of the seeker may be fulfilled. The object of mystics (*mardán*) in

[1] Here follows the story of Abraham and Nimrod which has occurred before, p. 73.

traversing wildernesses and deserts is not the sanctuary itself, for to a lover of God it is unlawful to look upon His sanctuary. No; their object is mortification in a longing that leaves them no rest, and eager dissolution in a love that has no end. A certain man came to Junayd. Junayd asked him whence he came. He replied: "I have been on the pilgrimage." Junayd said: "From the time when you first journeyed from your home have you also journeyed away from all sins?" He said: "No." "Then," said Junayd, "you have made no journey. At every stage where you halted for the night did you traverse a station on the way to God?" He said: "No." "Then," said Junayd, "you have not trodden the road stage by stage. When you put on the pilgrim's garb at the proper place did you discard the attributes of humanity as you cast off your ordinary clothes?" "No." "Then you have not put on the pilgrim's garb. When you stood on 'Arafát did you stand one instant in contemplation of God?" "No." "Then you have not stood on 'Arafát. When you went to Muzdalifa and achieved your desire did you renounce all sensual desires?" "No." "Then you have not gone to Muzdalifa. When you circumambulated the Temple did you behold the immaterial beauty of God in the abode of purification?" "No." "Then you have not circumambulated the Temple. When you ran between Ṣafá and Marwa did you attain to the rank of purity (*ṣafá*) and virtue (*muruwwat*)?" "No." "Then you have not run. When you came to Miná did all your wishes (*munyathá*) cease?" "No." "Then you have not yet visited Miná. When you reached the slaughter-place and offered sacrifice did you sacrifice the objects of sensual desire?" "No." "Then you have not sacrificed. When you threw the stones did you throw away whatever sensual thoughts were accompanying you?" "No." "Then you have not yet thrown the stones, and you have not yet performed the pilgrimage. Return and perform the pilgrimage in the manner which I have described in order that you may arrive at the station of Abraham." Fuḍayl b. 'Iyáḍ says: "I saw at Mount 'Arafát a youth who stood silent with bowed head while all the people were praying aloud, and I asked him why he did not pray like them. He answered that he was in great distress, having lost the spiritual state (*waqtí*) which he formerly enjoyed, and that he could by no means cry aloud unto God. I said: 'Pray, in order that through the blessings of this multitude God may accomplish thy desire.' He was about to lift up his hands and pray, when suddenly he uttered a shriek and died on the spot." Dhu 'l-Nún the Egyptian says: "At Miná I saw a young man sitting quietly while the people were engaged in the sacrifices. I looked at him to see what he was doing. He cried: 'O God, all the people are offering sacrifice. I wish to sacrifice my lower soul to Thee; do Thou accept it.' Having spoken, he pointed with his forefinger to his throat and fell dead—may God have mercy on him!"

Pilgrimages, then, are of two kinds: (1) in absence (from God) and (2) in presence (of God). Anyone who is absent from God at Mecca is in the same position as if he were absent from God in his own house, and anyone who is present with God in his own house is in the same position as if he were present with God at Mecca. Pilgrimage is an act of mortification (*mujáhadat*) for the sake of obtaining contemplation (*mushláhadat*), and mortification does not become the direct cause of contemplation, but is only a means to it. Therefore, inasmuch as a means has no further effect on the reality of things, the true object of pilgrimage is not to visit the Ka'ba, but to obtain contemplation of God.

Chapter on Contemplation.

The Apostle said: "Make your bellies hungry and your livers thirsty and leave the world alone, that perchance ye may see God with your hearts"; and he also said, "Worship God as though thou sawest Him, for if thou dost not see Him, yet He sees thee." God said to David: "Dost thou know what is knowledge of Me? It is the life of the heart in contemplation of Me." By "contemplation" the Ṣúfís mean spiritual vision of

God in public and private, without asking how or in what manner. Abu 'l-'Abbás b. 'Aṭá says in reference to the words of God: "*As to those who say, 'Our Lord is God,' and who become steadfast*" (Kor. xli, 30), i.e. "they say 'Our Lord is God' in self-mortification and they 'become steadfast' on the carpet of contemplation".

There are really two kinds of contemplation. The former is the result of perfect faith (*ṣiḥḥat-i yaqín*), the latter of rapturous love, for in the rapture of love a man attains to such a degree that his whole being is absorbed in the thought of his Beloved and he sees nothing else. Muḥammad b. Wási' says: "I never saw anything without seeing God therein," i.e. through perfect faith. This vision is from God to His creatures. Shiblí says: "I never saw anything except God," i.e. in the rapture of love and the fervour of contemplation. One sees the act with his bodily eye and, as he looks, beholds the Agent with his spiritual eye; another is rapt by love of the Agent from all things else, so that he sees only the Agent. The one method is demonstrative (*istidlálí*), the other is ecstatic (*jadhbí*). In the former case, a manifest proof is derived from the evidences of God; in the latter case, the seer is enraptured and transported by desire: evidences and verities are a veil to him, because he who knows a thing does not reverence aught besides, and he who loves a thing does not regard aught besides, but renounces contention with God and interference with Him in His decrees and His acts. God hath said of the Apostle at the time of his Ascension: "*His eyes did not swerve or transgress*" (Kor. liii, 17), on account of the intensity of his longing for God. When the lover turns his eye away from created things, he will inevitably see the Creator with his heart. God hath said: "*Tell the believers to close their eyes*" (Kor. xxiv, 30), i.e. to close their bodily eyes to lusts and their spiritual eyes to created things. He who is most sincere in self-mortification is most firmly grounded in contemplation for inward contemplation is connected with outward mortification. Sahl b. 'Abdalláh of Tustar says: "If anyone shuts his eye to God for a single moment, he will never be rightly guided all his life long," because to regard other than God is to be handed over to other than God, and one who is left at the mercy of other than God is lost. Therefore the life of contemplatives is the time during which they enjoy contemplation (*musháhadat*): time spent in seeing ocularly (*mu'áyanat*) they do not reckon as life, for that to them is really death. Thus, when Abú Yazíd was asked how old he was, he replied: "Four years." They said: "How can that be?" He answered: "I have been veiled (from God) by this world for seventy years, but I have seen Him during the last four years: the period in which one is veiled does not belong to one's life." Shiblí cried in his prayers: "O God, hide Paradise and Hell in Thy unseen places, that Thou mayest be worshipped disinterestedly." One who is forgetful of God nevertheless worships Him, through faith, because human nature has an interest in Paradise; but inasmuch as the heart has no interest in loving God, one who is forgetful of God is debarred from contemplating Him. The Apostle told 'Á'isha that he did not see God on the night of the Ascension, but Ibn 'Abbás relates that the Apostle told him that he saw God on that occasion. Accordingly, this remains a matter of controversy; but in saying that he did not see God the Apostle was referring to his bodily eye, whereas in saying the contrary he was referring to his spiritual eye. Since 'Á'isha was a formalist and Ibn 'Abbás a spiritualist, the Apostle spoke with each of them according to their insight. Junayd said: "If God should say to me, 'Behold Me,' I should reply, 'I will not behold Thee,' because in love the eye is other (than God) and alien: the jealousy of other-ness would prevent me from beholding Him. Since in this world I was wont to behold Him without the mediation of the eye, how should I use such mediation in the next world?"

"*Truly, I envy mine eye the sight of Thee,*
And I close mine eye when I look on Thee."

Junayd was asked: "Do you wish to see God?" He said:

"No." They asked why. He answered: "When Moses wished, he did not see Him, and when Muḥammad did not wish, he saw Him." Our wishing is the greatest of the veils that hinder us from seeing God, because in love the existence of self-will is disobedience, and disobedience is a veil. When self-will vanishes in this world, contemplation is attained, and when contemplation is firmly established, there is no difference between this world and the next. Abú Yazíd says: "God has servants who would apostatize if they were veiled from Him in this world or in the next," i.e. He sustains them with perpetual contemplation and keeps them alive with the life of love; and when one who enjoys revelation is deprived of it, he necessarily becomes an apostate. Dhu 'l-Nún says: "One day, when I was journeying in Egypt, I saw some boys who were throwing stones at a young man. I asked them what they wanted of him. They said: 'He is mad.' I asked how his madness showed itself, and they told me that he pretended to see God. I turned to the young man and inquired whether he had really said this. He answered: 'I say that if I should not see God for one moment, I should remain veiled and should not be obedient towards Him.'" Some Ṣúfís have fallen into the mistake of supposing that spiritual vision and contemplation represent such an idea (*ṣúratí*) of God as is formed in the mind by the imagination either from memory or reflection. This is utter anthropomorphism (*tashbíh*) and manifest error. God is not finite that the imagination should be able to define Him or that the intellect should comprehend His nature. Whatever can be imagined is homogeneous with the intellect, but God is not homogeneous with any *genus*, although in relation to the Eternal all phenomenal objects—subtle and gross alike—are homogeneous with each other notwithstanding their mutual contrariety. Therefore contemplation in this world resembles vision of God in the next world, and since the Companions of the Apostle (*aṣḥáb*) are unanimously agreed that vision is possible hereafter, contemplation is possible here. Those who tell of contemplation either in this or the other world only say that it is possible, not that they have enjoyed or now enjoy it, because contemplation is an attribute of the heart (*sirr*) and cannot be expressed by the tongue except metaphorically. Hence silence ranks higher than speech, for silence is a sign of contemplation (*mushâhadat*), whereas speech is a sign of ocular testimony (*shahâdat*). Accordingly the Apostle, when he attained proximity to God, said: "I cannot tell Thy praise," because he was in contemplation, and contemplation in the degree of love is perfect unity (*yagânagí*), and any outward expression in unity is other-ness (*bégânagí*). Then he said: "Thou hast praised Thyself," i.e. Thy words are mine, and Thy praise is mine, and I do not deem my tongue capable of expressing what I feel. As the poet says:

"*I desired my beloved, but when I saw him*
I was dumbfounded and possessed neither tongue nor eye."

CHAPTER XXIII.

The Uncovering of the Ninth Veil: Concerning Companionship, together with its Rules and Principles.

The Apostle said: "Good manners (*ḥusn al-adab*) are a part of faith." And he also said: "My Lord corrected me (*addabaní*) and gave me an excellent correction." You must know that the seemliness and decorum of all religious and temporal affairs depends on rules of discipline (*ádáb*), and that every station in which the various classes of mankind are placed has its own particular rule. Among men good manners consist in the observance of virtue (*muruwwat*); as regards religion they consist in the observance of the Apostolic custom (*sunna*); and as regards love they consist in the observance of respect (*ḥurmat*). These three categories are connected with each other, because one who is without virtue does not comply with the custom of the Apostle, and whoever fails to comply with the custom of the Apostle does not observe due respect. In matters of conduct the observance of discipline is the result of reverence for the object of desire; and reverence for God and His ordinances springs from fear of God (*taqwá*). Anyone who disrespectfully tramples on the reverence that is due to the evidences of God has no part or lot in the Path of Ṣúfiism; and in no case are rules of discipline neglected by seekers of God, because they are habituated to such rules, and habit is second nature. It is impossible that a living creature should be divested of its natural humours: therefore, so long as the human body remains in existence men are bound to keep the rules of obedience to God, sometimes with effort (*takalluf*) and sometimes without effort: with effort when they are 'sober', but when they are 'intoxicated' God sees that they keep the rules. A person who neglects the rules cannot possibly be a saint, for "good manners are characteristic of those whom God loves". When God vouchsafes a miracle to anyone, it is a proof that He causes him to fulfil the duties of religion. This is opposed to the view of some heretics, who assert that when a man is overpowered by love he is no longer subject to obedience. I will set forth this matter more lucidly in another place.

Rules of discipline are of three kinds. Firstly, those which are observed towards God in unification (*tawḥíd*). Here the rule is that one must guard one's self in public and private from any disrespectful act, and behave as though one were in the presence of a king. It is related in the genuine Traditions that one day the Apostle was sitting with his legs drawn in (*páy gird*). Gabriel came and said: "O Muḥammad, sit as servants do in their master's presence." Ḥárith Muḥásibí is said never to have leaned his back against a wall, by day or night, for forty years, and never to have sat except on his knees. On being asked why he gave himself so much trouble he replied: "I am ashamed to sit otherwise than as a servant while I am contemplating God." I, 'Alí b. 'Uthmán al-Jullábí, was once in a village called Kamand,[1] at the extremity of Khurásán. There I saw a well-known and very excellent man, whose name is Adíb-i Kamandí. For twenty years he had never sat down except in his prayers, when he was pronouncing the profession of faith. I inquired the reason of this, and he answered that he had not yet attained such a degree that he should sit while contemplating God. Abú Yazíd was asked by what means he had gained so high spiritual rank. He answered: "By good companionship with God," i.e. by keeping the rules of discipline and behaving in private as in public. All human beings ought to learn from Zulaykhá how to observe good manners in contemplating the object of their adoration, for when she was alone with Joseph and besought him to consent to her wishes, she first

[1] Kumand, according to *Nafaḥát*, No. 379.

covered up the face of her idol in order that it might not witness her want of propriety. And when the Apostle was borne to Heaven at the Ascension, his observance of discipline restrained him from paying any regard either to this world or to the next.

The second kind of discipline is that which is observed towards one's self in one's conduct, and which consists in avoiding, when one is in one's own company, any act that would be improper in the company of one's fellow-creatures or of God, e.g., one must not utter an untruth by declaring one's self to be what one is not, and one must eat little in order that one may seldom go to the lavatory, and one must not look at anything which it is not decent for others to see. It is related that 'Alí never beheld his own nakedness, because he was ashamed to see in himself what he was forbidden to see in others.

The third kind of discipline is that which is observed in social intercourse with one's fellow-creatures. The most important rule for such intercourse is to act well, and to observe the custom of the Apostle at home and abroad.

These three sorts of discipline cannot be separated from one another. Now I will set them forth in detail as far as possible, in order that you and all my readers may follow them more easily.

Chapter on Companionship and matters connected therewith.

God hath said: "*Verily, the merciful God will bestow love on those who believe and do good works*" (Kor. xix, 96), i.e., He will love them and cause them to be loved, because they do their duty towards their brethren and prefer them to themselves. And the Apostle said: "Three things render thy brother's love toward thee sincere: that thou shouldst salute him when thou meetest him, and that thou shouldst make room for him when he sits beside thee, and that thou shouldst call him by the name that he likes best." And God said, "*The believers are brethren: therefore reconcile your two brethren*"

(Kor. xlix, 10); and the Apostle said, "Get many brethren, for your Lord is bashful (*ḥayí*) and kind: He will be ashamed to punish His servant in the presence of his brethren on the Day of Resurrection."

But companionship must be for God's sake, not for the purpose of gratifying the lower soul or any selfish interest, in order that a man may be divinely rewarded for observing the rules of companionship. Málik b. Dínár said to his son-in-law, Mughíra b. Shu'ba: "If you derive no religious benefit from a brother and friend, abandon his society, that you may be saved," i.e. associate either with one who is superior or with one who is inferior to yourself. In the former case you will derive benefit from him, and in the latter case the benefit will be mutual, since each will learn something from the other. Hence the Apostle said, "It is the whole of piety to instruct one who is ignorant;" and Yaḥyá b. Mu'ádh (al-Rází) said, "He is a bad friend to whom you need to say, 'Remember me in thy prayers'" (because a man ought always to pray for anyone with whom he has associated even for a moment); and he is a bad friend with whom you cannot live except on condition of flattering him (because candour is involved in the principle of companionship); and he is a bad friend to whom you need to apologize for a fault that you have committed (because apologies are made by strangers, and in companionship it is wrong to be on such terms). The Apostle said: "A man follows the religion of his friend: take heed, therefore, with whom you form a friendship." If he associates with the good, their society will make him good, although he is bad; and if he associates with the wicked, he will be wicked, although he is good, because he will be consenting to their wickedness. It is related that a man said, while he was circumambulating the Ka'ba, "O God, make my brethren good!" On being asked why he did not implore a boon for himself in such a place, he replied: "I have brethren to whom I shall return; if they are good, I shall be good with them, and if they are wicked, I shall be wicked with them."

The Ṣúfí Shaykhs demand from each other the fulfilment of the duties of companionship and enjoin their disciples to require the same, so that amongst them companionship has become like a religious obligation. The Shaykhs have written many books explaining the rules of Ṣúfí companionship; e.g., Junayd composed a work entitled *Taṣḥíḥ al-irádat*,[1] and Aḥmad b. Khaḍrúya of Balkh another, entitled *Al-Ri'áyat bi-ḥuqúq*[2] *Allah*,[3] and Muḥammad b. 'Alí of Tirmidh another, entitled *Ádáb al-murídín*.[4] Other exhaustive treatises on this subject have been written by Abu 'l-Qásim al-Ḥakím,[5] Abú Bakr al-Warráq, Sahl b. 'Abdalláh (al-Tustarí), Abú 'Abd al-Raḥmán al-Sulamí, and Master Abu 'l-Qásim Qushayrí. All those writers are great authorities on Ṣúfiism, but I desire that my book should enable anyone who possesses it to dispense with other books and, as I said in the preface, be sufficient in itself for you and for all students of the Ṣúfí doctrine. I will now classify in separate chapters their various rules of discipline relating to conduct.

Chapter concerning the Rules of Companionship.

Since you have perceived that the most important thing for the novice is companionship, the fulfilment of its obligations is necessarily incumbent on him. Solitude is fatal to the novice, for the Apostle said, "Satan is with the solitary, but he is farther away from two who are together;" and God hath said, "*There is no private discourse among three persons but God is the fourth of them*" (Kor. lviii, 8). I have read in the Anecdotes that a disciple of Junayd imagined that he had attained to the degree of perfection, and that it was better for him to be alone. Accordingly he went into retirement and withdrew from the society of his brethren. At nightfall a camel used to appear, and he was told that it would take him to Paradise; on

[1] "The Rectification of Discipleship."
[2] So all the texts, instead of the correct *li-ḥuqúq*.
[3] "The Observance of what is due to God."
[4] "Rules of Conduct for Disciples.
[5] *Nafaḥát*, No. 129.

mounting it, he was conveyed to a pleasant demesne, with beautiful inhabitants and delicious viands and flowing streams, where he stayed till dawn ; then he fell asleep, and on waking found himself at the door of his cell. These experiences filled him with pride and he could not refrain from boasting of them. When Junayd heard the story he hastened to the disciple's cell, and having received from him a full account of what had passed, said to him : "To-night, when you come to that place, remember to say thrice, 'There is no strength or power but in God, the High, the Great.'" The same night he was carried off as usual, and though in his heart he did not believe Junayd, by way of trial he repeated those words thrice. The crew around him shrieked and vanished, and he found himself seated on a dunghill in the midst of rotten bones. He acknowledged his fault and repented and returned to companionship.

The principle of the Ṣúfís in companionship is that they should treat everyone according to his degree. Thus they treat old men with respect, like fathers ; those of their own sort with agreeable familiarity, like brothers ; and young men with affection, like sons. They renounce hate, envy, and malice, and do not withhold sincere admonition from anyone. In companionship it is not permissible to speak evil of the absent, or to behave dishonestly, or to deny one another on account of any word or deed, because a companionship which is begun for God's sake should not be cut short by human words or acts. The author says : "I asked the Grand Shaykh Abu 'l-Qásim Gurgání what obligations were involved in companionship. He replied : 'It involves this, that you should not seek your own interest ; all the evils of companionship arise from selfishness. Solitude is better for a selfish man. He who neglects his own interests and looks after the interests of his companion hits the mark in companionship.'" A certain dervish relates as follows : "Once I set out from Kúfa to visit Mecca. On the way I met Ibráhím Khawwáṣ and begged him to let me accompany him. He said : 'In companionship it is necessary that one should command and the other should obey : which do you choose?' I answered: 'You be the commander.' He said: 'Now do not fail to comply with my orders.' When we arrived at the halting-place, he bade me sit down, and himself drew water from the well and, since the weather was cold, he gathered sticks and kindled a fire, and whenever I attempted to do anything he told me to sit down. At nightfall it began to rain heavily. He took off his patched frock and held it over my head all night. I was ashamed, but could not say a word on account of the condition imposed on me. When morning came, I said: 'To-day it is my turn to be commander.' He said: 'Very well.' As soon as we reached the halting-place, he began to perform the same menial offices as before, and on my telling him not to disobey my orders he retorted that it was an act of disobedience to let one's self be served by one's commander. He continued to behave in this way until we arrived at Mecca; then I felt so ashamed that I fled from him. He espied me, however, at Miná and said to me: 'O son, when you associate with dervishes see that you treat them in the same fashion as I treated you.'"

Dervishes are divided into two classes: residents (*muqímán*) and travellers (*musáfirán*). According to the custom of the Shaykhs, the travelling dervishes should regard the resident ones as superior to themselves, because they go to and fro in their own interest, while the resident dervishes have settled down in the service of God: in the former is the sign of search, in the latter is the token of attainment; hence those who have found and settled down are superior to those who are still seeking. Similarly, the resident dervishes ought to regard the travelling ones as superior to themselves, because they are laden with worldly encumbrances, while the travelling dervishes are unencumbered and detached from the world. Again, old men should prefer to themselves the young, who are newer to the world and whose sins are less numerous; and young men should prefer to themselves the old, who have outstripped them in devotion and service.

Section.

Culture (*adab*) really means "the collection of virtuous qualities", though in ordinary language anyone is called "cultured" (*adíb*) who is acquainted with Arabic philology and grammar. But the Ṣúfís define culture as "dwelling with praiseworthy qualities", and say that it means "to act with propriety towards God in public and private"; if you act thus, you are "cultured", even if you are a foreigner (i.e. a non-Arab), and if not, you are the opposite. Those who have knowledge are in every case more honoured than those who have intelligence. A certain Shaykh was asked: "What does culture involve?" He said: "I will answer you by quoting a definition which I have heard, 'If you speak, your speech will be sincere, and if you act, your actions will be true.'" An excellent distinction has been made by Shaykh Abú Naṣr Sarráj, the author of the *Luma'*, who says: "As regards culture (*adab*), there are three classes of mankind. Firstly, worldlings, whose culture mainly consists in eloquence and rhetoric and learning and knowledge of the nightly conversations (*asmár* [1]) of kings and Arabic poetry. Secondly, the religious, whose culture chiefly consists in disciplining the lower soul and correcting the limbs and observing the legal ordinances and renouncing lusts. Thirdly, the elect (i.e. the Ṣúfís), whose culture consists for the most part in spiritual purity and keeping watch over their hearts and fulfilling their promises and guarding the 'state' in which they are and paying no heed to extraneous suggestions and behaving with propriety in the positions of search (for God), in the states of presence (with God), and in the stations of proximity (to God)." This saying is comprehensive. The different matters which it includes are discussed in several places in this book.

Chapter on the Rules of Companionship affecting Residents.

Dervishes who choose to reside, and not to travel, are bound to observe the following rules of discipline. When a traveller

[1] Another reading is *asmá*, "names," but I find *asmár* in the MS. of the *Kitáb al-Luma'* belonging to Mr. A. G. Ellis, where this passage occurs on f. 63*a*.

comes to them, they must meet him joyfully and receive him with respect and treat him like an honoured guest and freely set before him whatever food they have, modelling their behaviour upon that of Abraham. They must not inquire whence he has come or whither he is going or what is his name, but must deem that he has come from God and is going to God and that his name is "servant of God"; then they must see whether he desires to be alone or in company: if he prefers to be alone, they must give him an empty room, and if he prefers company, they must consort with him unceremoniously in a friendly and sociable manner. When he lays his head on his pillow at night the resident dervish ought to offer to wash his feet, but if the traveller should not allow him to do this and should say that he is not accustomed to it, the resident must not insist, for fear of causing him annoyance. Next day, he must offer him a bath and take him to the cleanest bath available and save his clothes from (becoming dirty in) the latrines of the bath, and not permit a strange attendant to wait upon him, but wait upon him zealously in order to make him clean of all stains, and scrape (*bikhárad*) his back and rub his knees and the soles of his feet and his hands: more than this he is not obliged to do. And if the resident dervish has sufficient means, he should provide a new garment for his guest; otherwise, he need not trouble himself, but he should clean his guest's clothes so that he may put them on when he comes out of the bath. If the traveller remains two or three days, he should be invited to visit any spiritual director or Imám who may be in the town, but he must not be compelled to pay such visits against his inclination, because those who seek God are not always masters of their own feelings; e.g., Ibráhím Khawwáṣ on one occasion refused to accompany Khiḍr, who desired his society, for he was unwilling that his feelings should be engaged by anyone except God. Certainly it is not right that a resident dervish should take a traveller to salute worldly men or to attend their entertainments, sick-beds, and funerals; and if a resident hopes to make travellers an instrument of mendicancy (*álat-i gadá'í*) and conduct them from house to house, it would be better for him to refrain from serving them instead of subjecting them to humiliation. Among all the troubles and inconveniences that I have suffered when travelling none was worse than to be carried off time after time by ignorant servants and impudent dervishes of this sort and conducted from the house of such and such a Khwája to the house of such and such a Dihqán, while, though apparently complaisant, I felt a great dislike to go with them. I then vowed that, if ever I became resident, I would not behave towards travellers with this impropriety. Nothing derived from associating with ill-mannered persons is more useful than the lesson that you must endure their disagreeable behaviour and must not imitate it. On the other hand, if a travelling dervish becomes at his ease (*munbasiṭ*) with a resident and stays for some time and makes a worldly demand, the resident is bound immediately to give him what he wants; but if the traveller is an impostor and low-minded, the resident must not act meanly in order to comply with his impossible requirements, for this is not the way of those who are devoted to God. What business has a dervish to associate with devotees if he needs worldly things? Let him go to the market and buy and sell, or let him be a soldier at the sultan's court. It is related that, while Junayd and his pupils were sitting occupied in some ascetic discipline, a travelling dervish came in. They exerted themselves to entertain him and placed food before him. He said: "I want such and such a thing besides this." Junayd said to him: "You must go to the bazaar, for you are a man of the market, not of the mosque and the cell." Once I set out from Damascus with two dervishes to visit Ibn al-Mu'allá,[1] who was living in the country near Ramla. On the way we arranged that each of us should think of the matter concerning which we were in doubt, in order that that venerable director might tell us our secret thoughts and solve our difficulties. I said to myself: "I will desire of him the

[1] I. Ibn al-'Alá.

poems and intimate supplications (*munáját*) of Ḥusayn b. Manṣúr (al-Ḥalláj)." One of my companions said, "I will desire him to pray that my disease of the spleen (*ṭiḥál*) may become better;" and the other said, "I will wish for sweetmeat of different colours" (*ḥalwá-yi ṣábúní*). As soon as we arrived, Ibn al-Mu'allá commanded that a manuscript of the poems and supplications of Ḥusayn should be presented to me, and laid his hand on the belly of the invalid so that his illness was assuaged, and said to the other dervish: "Parti-coloured sweetmeat is eaten by soldiers (*'awánán*); you are dressed as a saint, and the dress of a saint does not accord with the appetite of a soldier. Choose one or the other."

In short, the resident is not obliged to pay attention to the travelling dervish unless the latter's attention is paid entirely to God. If he is devoted to his own interests, it is impossible that another should help him to gratify his selfishness, for dervishes are guides (*ráhbarán*), not brigands (*ráhburán*), to each other. So long as anyone perseveres in a selfish demand, his friend ought to resist it, but when he renounces it, then his friend ought to satisfy it. In the Traditions of the Apostle it is related that he made a brotherhood between Salmán (al-Fárisí) and Abú Dharr Ghifárí, both of whom were leading men among the People of the Veranda (*ahl-i ṣuffa*) and eminent spiritualists. One day, when Salmán came to visit Abú Dharr at his house, Abú Dharr's wife complained to him that her husband neither ate by day nor slept by night. Salmán told her to fetch some food, and said to Abú Dharr: "O brother, I desire thee to eat, since this fasting is not incumbent on thee." Abú Dharr complied. And at night Salmán said: "O brother, I beg thee to sleep: thy body and thy wife have a claim upon thee, as well as thy Lord." Next day Abú Dharr went to the Apostle, who said: "I say the same thing as Salmán said yesterday: verily, thy body has a claim upon thee." Inasmuch as Abú Dharr had renounced his selfish pleasures, Salmán persuaded him to gratify them. Whatever you do on this principle is sound and impregnable. Once, in the territories of 'Iráq, I was restlessly occupied (*tápákí míkardam*) in seeking wealth and squandering it, and I had run largely into debt. Everyone who wanted anything turned to me, and I was troubled and at a loss to know how I could accomplish their desires. An eminent person wrote to me as follows: "Beware lest you distract your mind from God by satisfying the wishes of those whose minds are engrossed in vanity. If you find anyone whose mind is nobler than your own, you may justly distract your mind in order to give peace to his. Otherwise, do not distract yourself, since God is sufficient for His servants." These words brought me instant relief.

Chapter concerning their Rules in Travel.

When a dervish chooses to travel, not to reside, he ought to observe the following rules. In the first place, he must travel for God's sake, not for pleasure, and as he journeys outwardly, so he should flee inwardly from his sensual affections; and he must always keep himself in a state of purity and not neglect his devotions; and his object in travelling must be either pilgrimage or war (against infidels) or to see a (holy) site or to derive instruction or to seek knowledge or to visit a venerable person, a Shaykh, or the tomb of a saint; otherwise his journey will be faulty. And he cannot do without a patched frock and a prayer-rug and a bucket and a rope and a pair of shoes (*kafsh*) or clogs (*na'layn*) and a staff: the patched frock to cover his nakedness, the prayer-rug to pray on, the bucket to cleanse himself with, and the staff to protect him from attacks and for other purposes. Before stepping on the prayer-rug he must put on his shoes or clogs in a state of purity. If anyone carries other articles, for the sake of keeping the Sunna (Apostolic custom), such as a comb and nail-scissors and a needle and a little box of antimony (*mukḥula*), he does right. If, however, anyone provides himself with more utensils than those which have been mentioned, we have to consider in what station he is: if he is a novice every article will be a shackle and a stumbling-block and a veil to him, and will afford him the means of showing self-conceit, but if he is a firmly grounded adept he may carry all these articles and more. I heard the following story from Shaykh Abú Muslim Fáris b. Ghálib al-Fárisí. "One day (he said) I paid a visit to Shaykh Abú Sa'íd b. Abi 'l-Khayr Fadlalláh b. Muhammad. I found him sleeping on a couch with four cushions (*takhtí chahár-bálish*), one of his legs thrown across the other; and he was dressed in fine Egyptian linen (*diqqí Miṣrí*). My garment was so dirty that it resembled leather, and my body was emaciated by austerities. On looking at Abú Sa'íd a feeling of scepticism overcame me. I said to myself: 'He is a dervish, and so am I, yet he is in all this luxury and I in this sore tribulation.' He immediately divined my thoughts and was aware of my vainglory. 'O Abú Muslim,' said he, 'in what díwán have you read that a self-conceited man is a dervish? Since I see God in all things, God sets me on a throne, and since you see yourself in everything, God keeps you in affliction: my lot is contemplation, while yours is mortification. These are two stations on the Way to God, but God is far aloof from them both, and a dervish is dead to all stations and free from all states.' On hearing these words my senses forsook me, and the whole world grew dark in my eyes. When I came to myself I repented, and he accepted my repentance. Then I said: 'O Shaykh, give me leave to depart, for I cannot bear the sight of thee.' He answered, 'O Abú Muslim, you speak the truth;' then he quoted this verse:—

> '*That which my ear was unable to hear by report*
> *My eye beheld actually all at once.*'"

The travelling dervish must always observe the custom of the Apostle, and when he comes to the house of a resident he should enter his presence respectfully and greet him; and he should first take off the shoe on his left foot, as the Apostle did; and when he puts his shoes on, he should first put on the shoe belonging to his right foot; and he should wash his right foot before his left; and he should perform two bowings of the head by way of salutation (in prayer) and then occupy himself with attending to the (religious) duties incumbent on dervishes. He must not in any case interfere with the residents, or behave immoderately towards anyone, or talk of the hardships which he may have suffered in travelling, or discourse on theology, or tell anecdotes, or recite traditions in company, for all this is a sign of self-conceit. He must be patient when he is vexed by fools and must tolerate their irksomeness for God's sake, for in patience there are many blessings. If residents or their servants bid him go with them to salute or visit the townspeople, he must acquiesce if he can, but in his heart he ought to dislike paying such marks of respect to worldlings, although he should excuse the behaviour of his brethren who act thus. He must take care not to trouble them by making any unreasonable demand, and he must not drag them to the court of high officials with the purpose of seeking an idle pleasure for himself. Travelling, as well as resident, dervishes must always, in companionship, endeavour to please God, and must have a good belief in each other, and not speak ill of any comrade face to face with him or behind his back, because true mystics in regarding the act see the Agent, and inasmuch as every human being, of whatever description he may be—faulty or faultless, veiled or illuminated—belongs to God and is His creature, to quarrel with a human act is to quarrel with the Divine Agent.

Chapter concerning their Rules in Eating.

Men cannot dispense with nourishment, but moral virtue requires that they should not eat or drink in excess. Sháfi'í says: "He who thinks about that which goes into his belly is worth only that which comes out of it." Nothing is more hurtful to a novice in Ṣúfiism than eating too much. I have read in the Anecdotes that Abú Yazíd was asked why he praised hunger so highly. He answered: "Because if Pharaoh had been hungry he would not have said, 'I am your Supreme Lord,' and if Qárún (Korah) had been hungry he would not have been rebellious." Tha'laba[1] was praised by all so long as he was hungry, but when he ate his fill he displayed hypocrisy. Sahl b. 'Abdalláh (al-Tustarí) said: "In my judgment, a belly full of wine is better than one full of lawful food." On being asked the reason of this he said: "When a man's belly is filled with wine, his intellect is stupefied and the flame of lust is quenched, and people are secure from his hand and tongue; but when his belly is filled with lawful food he desires foolishness, and his lust waxes great and his lower soul rises to seek her pleasures." The Shaykhs have said, describing the Ṣúfís: "They eat like sick men, and sleep like shipwrecked men, and speak like one whose children have died."

It is an obligatory rule that they should not eat alone, but should unselfishly share their food with one another; and when seated at table they should not be silent, and should begin by saying "In God's name"; and they should not put anything down or lift anything up in such a way as to offend their comrades, and they should dip the first mouthful in salt, and should deal fairly by their friends. Sahl b. 'Abdalláh (al-Tustarí) was asked about the meaning of the verse: "*Verily God enjoins justice and beneficence*" (Kor. xvi, 92). He replied: "Justice consists in dealing fairly with one's friend in regard to a morsel of food, and beneficence consists in deeming him to have a better claim to that morsel than yourself." My Shaykh used to say: "I am astonished at the impostor who declares that he has renounced the world, and is anxious about a morsel of food." Furthermore, the Ṣúfí should eat with his right hand and should look only at his own morsel, and while eating he should not drink unless he is extremely thirsty, and if he drinks he should drink only as much as will moisten his liver. He should not eat large mouthfuls, and should chew his food well and not make haste; otherwise he will be acting contrary to the custom of the Apostle, and

[1] See Bayḍáwí on Kor. ix, 76.

will probably suffer from indigestion (*tukhama*). When he has finished eating, he should give praise to God and wash his hands. If two or three or more persons belonging to a community of dervishes go to a dinner and eat something without informing their brethren, according to some Shaykhs this is unlawful and constitutes a breach of companionship, but some hold it to be allowable when a number of persons act thus in union with each other, and some allow it in the case of a single person, on the ground that he is not obliged to deal fairly when he is alone but when he is in company; consequently, being alone, he is relieved of the obligations of companionship and is not responsible for his act. Now, the most important principle in this matter is that the invitation of a dervish should not be refused, and that the invitation of a rich man should not be accepted. Dervishes ought not to go to the houses of rich men or beg anything of them: such conduct is demoralizing for Ṣúfís, because worldlings are not on confidential terms (*maḥram*) with the dervish. Much wealth, however, does not make a man "rich" (*dunyá-dár*), nor does little wealth make him "poor". No one who acknowledges that poverty is better than riches is "rich", even though he be a king; and anyone who disbelieves in poverty is "rich", even though he be reduced to want. When a dervish attends a party he should not constrain himself either to eat or not to eat, but should behave in accordance with his feelings at the time (*bar ḥukm-i waqt*). If the host is a congenial person (*maḥram*), it is right that a married man (*muta'ahhil*) should condone a fault; and if the host is uncongenial, it is not allowable to go to his house. But in any case it is better not to commit a fault, for Sahl b. 'Abdalláh (al-Tustarí) says: "Backsliding is abasement" (*al-zillat dhillat*).

Chapter concerning their Rules in Walking.

God hath said: "*And the servants of the Merciful are they who walk on the earth meekly*" (Kor. xxv, 64). The seeker of God, as he walks, should know at each step he makes whether that step is against God or of God: if it is against God, he must ask for pardon, and if it is of God, he must persevere in it, that it may be increased. One day Dáwud Ṭá'í had taken some medicine. They said to him: "Go into the court of this house for a little while, in order that the good result of the medicine may become apparent." He replied: "I am ashamed that on the Day of Judgment God should ask me why I made a few steps for my own selfish pleasure. God Almighty hath said: '*And their feet shall bear witness of that which they used to commit*'" (Kor. xxxvi, 65). Therefore the dervish should walk circumspectly, with his head bowed in meditation (*muráqabat*), and not look in any direction but in front. If any person meets him on the way, he must not draw himself back from him for the sake of saving his dress, for all Moslems are clean, and their clothes too; such an act is mere conceit and self-ostentation. If, however, the person who meets him is an unbeliever, or manifestly filthy, he may turn from him unobtrusively. And when he walks with a number of people, he must not attempt to go in front of them, since that is an excess of pride; nor must he attempt to go behind them, since that is an excess of humility, and humility of which one is conscious is essentially pride. He must keep his clogs and shoes as clean as he can by day in order that God, through the blessings thereof, may keep his clothes (clean) by night. And when one or more dervishes are with anyone, he should not stop on the way (to talk) with any person, nor should he tell that person to wait for him. He should walk quietly and should not hurry, else his walk will resemble that of the covetous; nor should he walk slowly, for then his walk will resemble that of the proud; and he should take steps of the full length (*gám-i tamám nihad*). In fine, the walk of the seeker of God should always be of such a description that if anyone should ask him whither he is going he should be able to answer decisively: "*Verily, I am going to my Lord: He will direct me*" (Kor. xxxvii, 97). Otherwise his walking is a curse to him, because right steps (*khaṭawát*) proceed from right thoughts (*khaṭarát*): accordingly if a man's thoughts are concentrated on God, his feet will follow his thoughts. It is related that Abú Yazíd said: "The inconsiderate walk (*rawish-i bé murāqabat*) of a dervish is a sign that he is heedless (of God), because all that exists is attained in two steps: one step away from self-interest and the other step firmly planted on the commandments of God." The walk of the seeker is a sign that he is traversing a certain distance, and since proximity to God is not a matter of distance, what can the seeker do but cut off his feet in the abode of rest?

Chapter concerning their Rules of Sleeping in travel and at home.

There is a great difference of opinion among the Shaykhs on this subject. Some hold that it is not permissible for a novice to sleep except when he is overpowered by slumber, for the Apostle said: "Sleep is the brother of Death," and inasmuch as life is a benefit conferred by God, whereas death is an affliction, the former must be more excellent than the latter. And it is related that Shiblí said: "God looked upon me and said, 'He who sleeps is heedless, and he who is heedless is veiled.'" Others, again, hold that a novice may sleep at will and even constrain himself to sleep after having performed the Divine commands, for the Apostle said: "The Pen does not record (evil actions) against the sleeper until he awakes, or against the boy until he reaches puberty, or against the madman until he recovers his wits." When a man is asleep, people are secure from his mischief and he is deprived of his personal volition and his lower soul is prevented from gaining its desires and the Recording Angels cease to write; his tongue makes no false assertion and speaks no evil of the absent, and his will places no hope in conceit and ostentation; "he does not possess for himself either bane or boon or death or life or resurrection." Hence Ibn 'Abbás says: "Nothing is more grievous to Iblís than a sinner's sleep; whenever the sinner sleeps, Iblís says, 'When will he wake and rise up that he may disobey God?'" This was a point of controversy between Junayd and 'Alí b.

Sahl al-Iṣfahání. The latter wrote to Junayd a very fine epistle, which I have heard, to the effect that sleep is heedlessness and rest is a turning away from God: the lover must not sleep or rest by day or by night, otherwise he will lose the object of his desire and will forget himself and his state and will fail to attain to God, as God said to David, "O David, he who pretends to love Me and sleeps when night covers him is a liar." Junayd said in his reply to that letter: "Our wakefulness consists in our acts of devotion to God, whereas our sleep is God's act towards us: that which proceeds from God to us without our will is more perfect than that which proceeds from us to God with our will. Sleep is a gift which God bestows on those who love Him." This question depends on the doctrine of sobriety and intoxication, which has been fully discussed above. It is remarkable that Junayd, who was himself a "sober" man, here supports intoxication. Seemingly, he was enraptured at the time when he wrote and his temporary state may have expressed itself by his tongue; or, again, it may be that the opposite is the case and that sleep is actually sobriety, while wakefulness is actually intoxication, because sleep is an attribute of humanity, and a man is "sober" so long as he is in the shadow of his attributes: wakefulness, on the other hand, is an attribute of God, and when a man transcends his own attribute he is enraptured. I have met with a number of Shaykhs who agree with Junayd in preferring sleep to wakefulness, because the visions of the saints and of most of the apostles occurred during sleep. And the Apostle said: "Verily, God takes pride in the servant who sleeps while he prostrates himself in prayer; and He says to His angels, 'Behold My servant, whose spirit is in the abode of secret conversation (*najwá*) while his body is on the carpet of worship.'" The Apostle also said: "Whoever sleeps in a state of purification, his spirit is permitted to circumambulate the Throne and prostrate itself before God." I have read in the Anecdotes that Sháh Shujá' of Kirmán kept awake for forty years. One night he fell asleep and saw God, and afterwards he used always to sleep in hope of seeing the same vision. This is the meaning of the verse of Qays of the Banú 'Ámir [1]—

"Truly I wish to sleep, although I am not drowsy,
That perchance thy beloved image may encounter mine."

Other Shaykhs whom I have seen agree with 'Alí b. Sahl in preferring wakefulness to sleep, because the apostles received their revelations and the saints their miracles while they were awake. One of the Shaykhs says: "If there were any good in sleep there would be sleep in Paradise," i.e., if sleep were the cause of love and proximity to God, it would follow that there must be sleep in Paradise, which is the dwelling-place of proximity; since neither sleep nor any veil is in Paradise, we know that sleep is a veil. Those who are fond of subtleties (*arbáb-i láṭá'if*) say that when Adam fell asleep in Paradise Eve came forth from his left side, and Eve was the source of all his afflictions. They say also that when Abraham told Ishmael that he had been ordered in a dream to sacrifice him, Ishmael replied: "This is the punishment due to one who sleeps and forgets his beloved. If you had not fallen asleep you would not have been commanded to sacrifice your son." It is related that Shiblí every night used to place in front of him a bowl of salt water and a needle for applying collyrium, and whenever he was about to fall asleep he would dip the needle in the salt water and draw it along his eyelids. I, 'Alí b. 'Uthmán al-Jullábí, have met with a spiritual director who used to sleep after finishing the performance of his obligatory acts of devotion; and I have seen Shaykh Aḥmad Samarqandí, who was living at Bukhárá: during forty years he had never slept at night, but he used to sleep a little in the daytime. This question turns on the view taken of life and death. Those who prefer death to life must prefer sleep to waking, while those who prefer life to death must prefer waking to sleep. Merit belongs, not to the man who forces himself to keep awake, but to the man who is kept awake. The Apostle, whom God chose and whom He raised to the highest rank,

[1] Generally known as Majnún, the lover of Laylá. See Brockelmann, i, 48.

did not force himself either to sleep or to wake. God commanded him, saying: "*Rise and pray during the night, except a small part: half thereof or less*" (Kor. lxxiii, 2–3). Similarly, merit does not belong to the man who forces himself to sleep, but only to the man who is put to sleep. The Men of the Cave did not constrain themselves to sleep or to wake, but God threw slumber upon them and nourished them without their will. When a man attains to such a degree that his will no longer exists, and his hand is withdrawn from everything, and his thoughts are averted from all except God, it matters not whether he is asleep or awake: in either case he is full of honour. Now, as regards the sleep of the novice, he ought to deem that his first sleep is his last, and repent of his sins and satisfy all who have a claim against him; and he ought to perform a comely purification and sleep on his right side, facing the *qibla*; and having set his worldly affairs in order, he ought to give thanks for the blessing of Islam, and make a vow that if he should wake again he will not return to sin. One who has set his affairs in order while he is awake has no fear of sleep or of death. A well-known story is told of a certain spiritual director, that he used to visit an Imám who was engrossed in maintaining his dignity and was a prey to self-conceit, and that he used to say to him: "O So-and-so, you must die." This offended the Imám, for "why (he said) should this beggar be always repeating these words to me?" One day he answered: "I will begin to-morrow." Next day when the spiritual director came in the Imám said to him: "O So-and-so, you must die." He put down his prayer-rug and spread it out, and laid his head on it and exclaimed, "I am dead," and immediately yielded up his soul. The Imám took warning, and perceived that this spiritual director had been bidding him prepare for death, as he himself had done. My Shaykh used to enjoin his disciples not to sleep unless overpowered by slumber, and when they had once awaked not to fall asleep again, since a second sleep is unlawful and unprofitable to those who seek God.

Chapter concerning their Rules in Speech and Silence.

God hath commanded His servants to speak well, e.g. to acknowledge His lordship and to praise Him and to call mankind to His court. Speech is a great blessing conferred on Man by God, and thereby is Man distinguished from all other things. Some interpreters of the text, "*We have honoured the sons of Adam*" (Kor. xvii, 72), explain it as meaning "by the gift of speech". Nevertheless, in speech there are also great evils, for the Apostle said: "The worst that I fear for my people is the tongue." In short, speech is like wine: it intoxicates the mind, and those who begin to have a taste for it cannot abstain from it. Accordingly, the Ṣúfís, knowing that speech is harmful, never spoke except when it was necessary, i.e. they considered the beginning and end of their discourse; if the whole was for God's sake, they spoke; otherwise they kept silence, because they firmly believed that God knows our secret thoughts (cf. Kor. xliii, 80). The Apostle said: "He who keeps silence is saved." In silence there are many advantages and spiritual favours (*futúḥ*), and in speech there are many evils. Some Shaykhs have preferred silence to speech, while others have set speech above silence. Among the former is Junayd, who said: "Expressions are wholly pretensions, and where realities are established pretensions are idle." Sometimes it is excusable not to speak although one has the will to do so, i.e. fear becomes an excuse for not speaking in spite of one's having the will and the power to speak; and refusal to speak of God does not impair the essence of gnosis. But at no time is a man excused for mere pretension devoid of reality, which is the principle of hypocrites. Pretension without reality is hypocrisy, and reality without pretension is sincerity, because "he who is grounded in eloquence needs no tongue to communicate with his Lord" Expressions only serve to inform another than God, for God Himself requires no explanation of our circumstances, and others than God are not worth so much that we should occupy ourselves with them. This is corroborated by the saying of

Junayd, "He who knows God is dumb," for in actual vision (*'iyán*) exposition (*bayán*) is a veil. It is related that Shiblí rose up in Junayd's meeting-place and cried aloud, "O my object of desire!" and pointed to God. Junayd said: "O Abú Bakr, if God is the object of your desire, why do you point to Him, who is independent of this? And if the object of your desire is another, God knows what you say: why do you speak falsely?" Shiblí asked God to pardon him for having uttered those words.

Those who put speech above silence argue that we are commanded by God to set forth our circumstances, for the pretension subsists in the reality, and *vice versâ*. If a man continues for a thousand years to know God in his heart and soul, but has not confessed that he knows God, he is virtually an infidel unless his silence has been due to compulsion. God has bidden all believers give Him thanks and praise and rehearse His bounties, and He has promised to answer the prayers of those who invoke Him. One of the Shaykhs has said that whoever does not declare his spiritual state is without any spiritual state, since the state proclaims itself.

"*The tongue of the state* (lisán al-ḥál) *is more eloquent than my tongue,*
And my silence is the interpreter of my question."

I have read in the Anecdotes that one day when Abú Bakr Shiblí was walking in the Karkh quarter of Baghdád he heard an impostor saying: "Silence is better than speech." Shiblí replied: "Thy silence is better than thy speech, but my speech is better than my silence, because thy speech is vanity and thy silence is an idle jest, whereas my silence is modesty and my speech is knowledge." I, 'Alí b. 'Uthmán al-Jullábí, declare that there are two kinds of speech and two kinds of silence: speech is either real or unreal, and silence is either fruition or forgetfulness. If one speaks truth, his speech is better than his silence, but if one speaks falsehood, his silence is better than his speech. "He who speaks hits the mark or misses it, but he who is made to speak is preserved from transgression." Thus Iblís said, "*I am better than he*" (Kor. xxxviii, 77), but Adam was made to say, "*O Lord, we have done wrong unto ourselves*" (Kor. vii, 22). The missionaries (*dá'iyán*) of this sect are permitted or compelled to speak, and shame or helplessness strikes them dumb: "he whose silence is shame, his speech is life." Their speech is the result of vision, and speech without vision appears to them despicable. They prefer silence to speech so long as they are with themselves, but when they are beside themselves their words are written on the hearts of men. Hence that spiritual director said: "He whose silence to God is gold, his speech to another than God is gilt." The seeker of God, who is absorbed in servantship, must be silent, in order that the adept, who proclaims Lordship, may speak, and by his utterances may captivate the hearts of his disciples. The rule in speaking is not to speak unless bidden, and then only of the thing that is bidden; and the rule in silence is not to be ignorant or satisfied with ignorance or forgetful. The disciple must not interrupt the speech of spiritual directors, or let his personal judgment intrude therein, or use far-fetched expressions in answering them. He must never tell a lie, or speak ill of the absent, or offend any Moslem with that tongue which has made the profession of faith and acknowledged the unity of God. He must not address dervishes by their bare names or speak to them until they ask a question. It behoves the dervish, when he is silent, not to be silent in falsehood, and when he speaks, to speak only the truth. This principle has many derivatives and innumerable refinements, but I will not pursue the subject, lest my book should become too long.

Chapter concerning their Rules in Asking.

God hath said: "*They ask not men with importunity*" (Kor. ii, 274). Any one of them who asks should not be repulsed, for God said to the Apostle: "*Do not drive away the beggar*" (Kor. xciii, 10). As far as possible they should beg of God only, for begging involves turning away from God to another, and when a man turns away from God there is danger that God may leave him in that predicament. I have read that a certain worldling said to Rábi'a 'Adawiyya[1]: "O Rábi'a, ask something of me that I may procure what you wish." "O sir," she replied, "I am ashamed to ask anything of the Creator of the world; how, then, should I not be ashamed to ask anything of a fellow-creature?" It is related that in the time of Abú Muslim, the head of the ('Abbásid) propaganda, an innocent dervish was seized on suspicion of theft, and was imprisoned at Chahár Ṭáq.[2] On the same night Abú Muslim dreamed that the Apostle came to him and said: "God has sent me to tell you that one of His friends is in your prison. Arise and set him free." Abú Muslim leapt from his bed, and ran with bare head and feet to the prison gate, and gave orders to release the dervish, and begged his pardon and bade him ask a boon. "O prince," he replied, "one whose Master rouses Abú Muslim at midnight, and sends him to deliver a poor dervish from affliction—how should that one ask a boon of others?" Abú Muslim began to weep, and the dervish went on his way. Some, however, hold that a dervish may beg of his fellow-creatures, since God says: "*They ask not men with importunity*," i.e. they may ask but not importune. The Apostle begged for the sake of providing for his companions, and he said to us: "Seek your wants from those whose faces are comely."

The Ṣúfí Shaykhs consider begging to be permissible in three cases. Firstly, with the object of freeing one's mind from preoccupation, for, as they have said, we should not attach so much importance to two cakes of bread that we should spend the whole day and night in expecting them; and when we are starving we want nothing else of God, because no anxiety is so engrossing as anxiety on account of food. Therefore, when the disciple of Shaqíq visited

[1] *Nafaḥát*, No. 578; Ibn Khallikán, No. 230.

[2] A village, mentioned by Ibn al-Athír (x, 428, 24), in the vicinity of Baghdád.

Báyazíd, and in answer to Báyazíd's question as to the state of Shaqíq informed him that he was entirely disengaged from mankind, and was putting all his trust in God, Báyazíd said: "When you return to Shaqíq, tell him to beware of again testing God with two loaves: if he is hungry, let him beg of his fellow-creatures and have done with the cant of trust in God." Secondly, it is permissible to beg with the object of training the lower soul. The Ṣúfís beg in order that they may endure the humiliation of begging, and may perceive what is their worth in the eyes of other men, and may not be proud. When Shiblí came to Junayd, Junayd said to him: "O Abú Bakr, your head is full of conceit, because you are the son of the Caliph's principal chamberlain and the governor of Sámarrá. No good will come from you until you go to the market and beg of everyone whom you see, that you may know your true worth." Shiblí obeyed. He begged in the market for three years, with ever decreasing success. One day, having gone through the whole market and got nothing, he returned to Junayd and told him. Junayd said: "Now, Abú Bakr, you see that you have no worth in the eyes of men: do not fix your heart on them. This matter (i.e. begging) is for the sake of discipline, not for the sake of profit." It is related that Dhu 'l-Nún the Egyptian said: "I had a friend who was in accord with God. After his death I saw him in a dream, and asked him how God had dealt with him. He answered that God had forgiven him. I asked him: 'On account of what virtue?' He replied that God raised him to his feet and said: 'My servant, you suffered with patience much contumely and tribulation from base and avaricious men, to whom you stretched out your hands: therefore I forgive you.'" Thirdly, they beg from mankind because of their reverence for God. They recognize that all worldly possessions belong to God, and they regard all mankind as His agents, from whom—not from God Himself—they beg anything that is for the benefit of the lower soul; and in the eyes of one who beholds his own want, the servant that makes a petition to an agent is more reverent and obedient than he that makes a petition to God. Therefore, their begging from another is a sign of presence and of turning towards God, not a sign of absence and of turning away from Him. I have read that Yaḥyá b. Mu'ádh (al-Rází) had a daughter, who one day asked her mother for something. "Ask it of God," said the mother. "I am ashamed," the girl replied, "to ask a material want from Him. What you give me is His too and is my allotted portion." The rules of begging are as follows: If you beg unsuccessfully you should be more cheerful than when you succeed, and you should not regard any human creature as coming between God and yourself. You should not beg of women or market-folk (*aṣḥáb-i aswáq*), and you should not tell your secret to anyone unless you are sure that his money is lawful. As far as possible you should beg unselfishly, and should not use the proceeds for worldly show and for housekeeping, or convert them into property. You should live in the present, and let no thought of the morrow enter your mind, else you will incur everlasting perdition. You should not make God a springe to catch alms, and you should not display piety in order that more alms may be given to you on account of your piety. I once met an old and venerable Ṣúfí, who had lost his way in the desert and came, hunger-stricken, into the market-place at Kúfa with a sparrow perched on his hand, crying: "Give me something for the sake of this sparrow!" The people asked him why he said this. He replied: "It is impossible that I should say 'Give me something for God's sake!' One must employ the intercession of an insignificant creature to obtain worldly goods."

This is but a small part of the obligations involved in begging. I have abridged the topic for fear of being tedious.

Chapter concerning their Rules in Marriage and Celibacy and matters connected therewith.

God hath said: "*They* (women) *are a garment unto you and ye are a garment unto them*" (Kor. ii, 183). And the Apostle said: "Marry, that ye may multiply; for I will vaunt you against all other nations on the Day of Resurrection, even in respect of the still-born." And he said also: "The women who bring the greatest blessing are they who cost least to maintain, whose faces are comeliest, and whose dowries are cheapest." Marriage is permitted to all men and women, and is obligatory on those who cannot abstain from what is unlawful, and is a *sunna* (i.e. sanctioned by the custom of the Apostle) for those who are able to support a family. Some of the Ṣúfí Shaykhs hold marriage to be desirable as a means of quelling lust, and acquisition (of sustenance) to be desirable as a means of freeing the mind from anxiety. Others hold that the object of marriage is procreation; for, if the child dies before its father, it will intercede for him (before God), and if the father dies first, the child will remain to pray for him.[1] The Apostle said: "Women are married for four things: wealth, nobility, beauty, and religion. Do ye take one that is religious, for, after Islam, there is nothing that profits a man so much as a believing and obedient wife who gladdens him whenever he looks on her." And the Apostle said: "Satan is with the solitary," because Satan decks out lust and presents it to their minds. No companionship is equal in reverence and security to marriage, when husband and wife are congenial and well-suited to each other, and no torment and anxiety is so great as an uncongenial wife. Therefore the dervish must, in the first place, consider what he is doing and picture in his mind the evils of celibacy and of marriage, in order that he may choose the state of which he can more easily overcome the evils. The evils of celibacy are two: (1) the neglect of an Apostolic custom, (2) the fostering of lust in the heart and the danger of falling into unlawful ways. The evils of marriage are also two: (1) the preoccupation of the mind with other than God, (2) the distraction of the body for the sake of sensual pleasure. The root of this matter lies in retirement and companionship. Marriage is proper for those who

[1] Here a story is told of the Caliph 'Umar, who asked Umm Kulthúm, the Prophet's granddaughter, in marriage from her father 'Alí.

prefer to associate with mankind, and celibacy is an ornament to those who seek retirement from mankind. The Apostle said: "Go: the recluses (*al-mufarridún*) have preceded you." And Ḥasan of Baṣra says: "The lightly burdened shall be saved and the heavily laden shall perish." Ibráhím Khawwáṣ relates the following story: "I went to a certain village to visit a reverend man who lived there. When I entered his house I saw that it was clean, like a saint's place of worship. In its two corners two niches (*miḥráb*) had been made; the old man was seated in one of them, and in the other niche an old woman was sitting, clean and bright: both had become weak through much devotion. They showed great joy at my coming, and I stayed with them for three days. When I was about to depart I asked the old man, 'What relation is this chaste woman to you?' He answered, 'She is my cousin and my wife.' I said, 'During these three days your intercourse with one another has been very like that of strangers.' 'Yes,' said he, 'it has been so for five and sixty years.' I asked him the cause of this. He replied: 'When we were young we fell in love, but her father would not give her to me, for he had discovered our fondness for each other. I bore this sorrow for a long while, but on her father's death my father, who was her uncle, gave me her hand. On the wedding-night she said to me: "You know what happiness God has bestowed upon us in bringing us together and taking all fear away from our hearts. Let us therefore to-night refrain from sensual passion and trample on our desires and worship God in thanksgiving for this happiness." I said, "It is well." Next night she bade me do the same. On the third night I said, "Now we have given thanks for two nights for your sake; to-night let us worship God for my sake." Five and sixty years have passed since then, and we have never touched one another, but spend all our lives in giving thanks for our happiness.'" Accordingly, when a dervish chooses companionship, it behoves him to provide his wife with lawful food and pay her dowry out of lawful property, and not indulge in sensual pleasure so long as any obligation towards God, or any part of

His commandments, is unfulfilled. And when he performs his devotions and is about to go to bed, let him say, as in secret converse with God: "O Lord God, Thou hast mingled lust with Adam's clay in order that the world may be populated, and Thou in Thy knowledge hast willed that I should have this intercourse. Cause it to be for the sake of two things: firstly, to guard that which is unlawful by means of that which is lawful; and secondly, vouchsafe to me a child, saintly and acceptable, not one who will divert my thoughts from Thee." It is related that a son was born to Sahl b. 'Abdalláh al-Tustarí. Whenever the child asked his mother for food, she used to bid him ask God, and while he went to the niche (*miḥráb*) and bowed himself in prayer, she used secretly to give him what he wanted, without letting him know that his mother had given it to him. Thus he grew accustomed to turn unto God. One day he came back from school when his mother was absent, and bowed himself in prayer. God caused the thing that he sought to appear before him. When his mother came in she asked, "Where did you get this?" He answered, "From the place whence it comes always."

The practice of an Apostolic rule of life must not lead the dervish to seek worldly wealth and unlawful gain or preoccupy his heart, for the dervish is ruined by the destruction of his heart, just as the rich man is ruined by the destruction of his house and furniture; but the rich man can repair his loss, while the dervish cannot. In our time it is impossible for anyone to have a suitable wife, whose wants are not excessive and whose demands are not unreasonable. Therefore many persons have adopted celibacy and observe the Apostolic Tradition: "The best of men in latter days will be those who are light of back," i.e. who have neither wife nor child. It is the unanimous opinion of the Shaykhs of this sect that the best and most excellent Ṣúfís are the celibates, if their hearts are uncontaminated and if their natures are not inclined to sins and lusts. The vulgar, in gratifying their lusts, appeal to the Apostle's saying, that the three things he loved in the world were scent, women, and prayer, and argue that since he loved women marriage must be more excellent than celibacy. I reply: "The Apostle also said that he had two trades, namely, poverty (*faqr*) and the spiritual combat (*jihád*): why, then, do ye shun these things? If he loved that (viz. marriage), this (viz. celibacy) was his trade. Your desires have a greater propensity to the former, but it is absurd, on that ground, to say that he loves what you desire. Anyone who follows his desires for fifty years and supposes that he is following the practice of the Apostle is in grave error." A woman was the cause of the first calamity that overtook Adam in Paradise, and also of the first quarrel that happened in this world, i.e. the quarrel of Abel and Cain. A woman was the cause of the punishment inflicted on the two angels (Hárút and Márút); and down to the present day all mischiefs, worldly and religious have been caused by women. After God had preserved me for eleven years from the dangers of matrimony, it was my destiny to fall in love with the description of a woman whom I had never seen, and during a whole year my passion so absorbed me that my religion was near being ruined, until at last God in His bounty gave protection to my wretched heart and mercifully delivered me. In short, Ṣúfiism was founded on celibacy; the introduction of marriage brought about a change. There is no flame of lust that cannot be extinguished by strenuous effort, because, whatever vice proceeds from yourself, you possess the instrument that will remove it: another is not necessary for that purpose. Now the removal of lust may be effected by two things, one of which involves self-constraint (*takalluf*), while the other lies outside the sphere of human action and mortification. The former is hunger, the latter is an agitating fear or a true love, which is collected by the dispersion of (sensual) thoughts: a love which extends its empire over the different parts of the body and divests all the senses of their sensual quality. Aḥmad Ḥammádí of Sarakhs, who went to Transoxania and lived there, was a venerable man. On being asked whether he desired to marry, he answered: "No, because I am either absent from myself or present with myself: when I am absent, I have no consciousness of the two worlds; and when I am present, I keep my lower soul in such wise that when it gets a loaf of bread it thinks that it has got a thousand houris. It is a great thing to occupy the mind: let it be anxious about whatsoever you will." Others, again, recommend that neither state (marriage or celibacy) should be regarded with predilection, in order that we may see what the decree of Divine providence will bring to light: if celibacy be our lot, we should strive to be chaste, and if marriage be our destiny, we should comply with the custom of the Apostle and strive to clear our hearts (of worldly anxieties). When God ordains celibacy unto a man, his celibacy should be like that of Joseph, who, although he was able to satisfy his desire for Zulaykhá, turned away from her and busied himself with subduing his passion and considering the vices of his lower soul at the moment when Zulaykhá was alone with him. And if God ordains marriage unto a man, his marriage should be like that of Abraham, who by reason of his absolute confidence in God put aside all care for his wife; and when Sarah became jealous he took Hagar and brought her to a barren valley and committed her to the care of God. Accordingly, a man is not ruined by marriage or by celibacy, but the mischief consists in asserting one's will and in yielding to one's desires. The married man ought to observe the following rules. He should not leave any act of devotion undone, or let any "state" be lost or any "time" be wasted. He should be kind to his wife and should provide her with lawful expenses, and he should not pay court to tyrants and governors with the object of meeting her expenses. He should behave thus, in order that, if a child is born, it may be such as it ought to be. A well-known story is told of Aḥmad b. Ḥarb of Níshápúr, that one day, when he was sitting with the chiefs and nobles of Níshápúr who had come to offer their respects to him, his son entered the room, drunk, playing a guitar, and singing, and passed by insolently without heeding them. Aḥmad, perceiving that they were put out of countenance, said: "What is the matter?" They replied: "We are ashamed that this lad should pass by you in such a state." Aḥmad said: "He is excusable. One night my wife and I partook of some food that was brought to us from a neighbour's house. That same night this son was begotten, and we fell asleep and let our devotions go. Next morning we inquired of our neighbour as to the source of the food that he had sent to us, and we found that it came from a wedding-feast in the house of a government official." The following rules should be observed by the celibate. He must not see what is improper to see or think what is improper to think, and he must quench the flames of lust by hunger and guard his heart from this world and from preoccupation with phenomena, and he must not call the desire of his lower soul "knowledge" or "inspiration", and he must not make the wiles (*bu 'l-'ajabí*) of Satan a pretext (for sin). If he acts thus he will be approved in Ṣúfiism.

CHAPTER XXIV.

The Uncovering of the Tenth Veil: explaining their phraseology and the definitions of their terms and the verities of the ideas which are signified.

Those employed in every craft and business, while discussing its mysteries with one another, make use of certain words and expressions of which the meaning is known only to themselves. Such expressions are invented for a double purpose: firstly, in order to facilitate the understanding of difficulties and bring them nearer to the comprehension of the novice; and secondly, in order to conceal the mysteries of that science from the uninitiated. The Ṣúfís also have technical terms for the purpose of expressing the matter of their discourse and in order that they may reveal or disguise their meaning as they please. I will now explain some of these terms and distinguish between the significations attached to various pairs of words.

Ḥál and *Waqt*.

Waqt (time) is a term with which Ṣúfís are familiar, and concerning which much has been said by the Shaykhs, but my object is to establish the truth, not to give long explanations. *Waqt* is that whereby a man becomes independent of the past and the future, as, for example, when an influence from God descends into his soul and makes his heart collected (*mujtami'*) he has no memory of the past and no thought of that which is not yet come. All people fail in this, and do not know what our past has been or what our future will be, except the possessors of *waqt*, who say: "Our knowledge cannot apprehend the future and the past, and we are happy with God in the present (*andar waqt*). If we occupy ourselves with to-morrow, or let any thought of it enter our minds, we shall be veiled (from God), and a veil is a great distraction (*parágandagí*)." It is absurd to think of the unattainable. Thus Abú Sa'íd Kharráz says: "Do not occupy your precious time except with the most precious of things, and the most precious of human things is the state of being occupied between the past and the future." And the Apostle said: "I have a time (*waqt*) with God, in which none of the cherubim nor any prophet rivals me," that is to say, "in which the eighteen thousand worlds do not occur to my mind and have no worth in my eyes." Therefore, on the night of the Ascension, when the kingdom of earth and heaven was arrayed before him in all its beauty, he did not look at anything (Kor. liii, 17), for Muṣṭafá was noble (*'azíz*), and the noble are not engrossed save by that which is noble. The "times" (*awqát*) of the Unitarian are two: one in the state of loss (*faqd*) and one in the state of gain (*wajd*), one in the place of union and one in the place of separation. At both these times he is overpowered (*maqhúr*), because both his union and his separation are effected by God without such volition or acquisition on his part as would make it possible to invest him with any attribute. When a man's power of volition is cut off from him, whatever he does or experiences is the result of "time" (*waqt*). It is related that Junayd said: "I saw a dervish in the desert, sitting under a mimosa-tree in a hard and uncomfortable spot, and asked him what made him sit there so still. He answered: 'I had a "time" and lost it here; now I am sitting and mourning.' I inquired how long he had been there. He answered: 'Twelve years. Will not the Shaykh offer up a prayer (*himmatí kunad*) on my behalf, that perchance I may find my "time" again?' I left him," said Junayd, "and performed the pilgrimage and prayed for him. My prayer was granted. On my return I found him seated in the same place. 'Why,' I said, 'do you not go from here, since you have obtained your wish?' He replied: 'O Shaykh, I settled myself in this place of desolation where I lost my capital: is it right that I should leave the place where I have found my capital once more and where I enjoy the society of God? Let the Shaykh go in peace, for I will mix my dust with the dust of this spot, that I may rise at the Resurrection from this dust which is the abode of my delight.'" No man can attain to the reality of "time" by exerting his choice, for "time" is a thing that does not come within the scope of human acquisition, that it should be gained by effort, nor is it sold in the market, that anyone should give his life in exchange for it, and the will has no power either to attract or to repel it. The Shaykhs have said, "Time is a cutting sword," because it is characteristic of a sword to cut, and "time" cuts the root of the future and the past, and obliterates care of yesterday and to-morrow from the heart. The sword is a dangerous companion: either it makes its master a king or it destroys him. Although one should pay homage to the sword and carry it on one's own shoulder for a thousand years, in the moment of cutting it does not discriminate between its master's neck and the neck of another. Violence (*qahr*) is its characteristic, and violence will not depart from it at the wish of its master.

Ḥál (state) is that which descends upon "time" (*waqt*) and adorns it, as the spirit adorns the body. *Waqt* has need of *ḥál*, for *waqt* is beautified by *ḥál* and subsists thereby. When the owner of *waqt* comes into possession of *ḥál*, he is no more subject to change and is made steadfast (*mustaqím*) in his state; for, when he has *waqt* without *ḥál*, he may lose it, but when *ḥál* attaches itself to him, all his state (*rúzgár*) becomes *waqt*, and that cannot be lost: what seems to be coming and going (*ámad shud*) is really the result of becoming and manifestation (*takawwun ú ẓuhúr*), just as, before this, *waqt* descended on him who has it. He who is in the state of becoming (*muta-kawwin*) may be forgetful, and on him who is thus forgetful *ḥál* descends and *waqt* is made stable (*mutamakkin*); for the possessor of *waqt* may become forgetful, but the possessor of *ḥál* cannot possibly be so. The tongue of the possessor of *ḥál* is silent concerning his *ḥál*, but his actions proclaim the reality of his *ḥál*. Hence that spiritual director said: "To ask about *ḥál* is absurd," because *ḥál* is the annihilation of speech (*maqál*). Master Abú 'Alí Daqqáq says: "If there is joy or woe in this world or the next world, the portion of *waqt* is that (feeling) in which thou art." But *ḥál* is not like this; when *ḥál* comes on a man from God, it banishes all these feelings from his heart. Thus Jacob was a possessor of *waqt*: now he was blinded by separation, now he was restored to sight by union, now he was mourning and wailing, now he was calm and joyful. But Abraham was a possessor of *ḥál*: he was not conscious of separation, that he should be stricken with grief, nor of union, that he should be filled with joy. The sun and moon and stars contributed to his *ḥál*, but he, while he gazed, was independent of them: whatever he looked on, he saw only God, and he said: "*I love not them that set*" (Kor. vi, 76). Accordingly, the world sometimes becomes a hell to the possessor of *waqt*, because he is contemplating absence (*ghaybat*) and his heart is distressed by the loss of his beloved; and sometimes his heart is like a Paradise in the blessedness of contemplation, and every moment brings to him a gift and a glad message from God. On the other hand, it makes no difference to the possessor of *ḥál* whether he is veiled by affliction or unveiled by happiness; for he is always in the place of actual vision (*'iyán*). *Ḥál* is an attribute of the object desired (*murád*), while *waqt* is the rank of the desirer (*muríd*). The latter is with himself in the pleasure of *waqt*, the former with God in the delight of *ḥál*. How far apart are the two degrees!

Maqám and *Tamkín*, and the difference between them.

Maqám (station) denotes the perseverance of the seeker in fulfilling his obligations towards the object of his search with strenuous exertion and flawless intention. Everyone who desires God has a station (*maqám*), which, in the beginning of his search, is a means whereby he seeks God. Although the seeker derives some benefit from every station through which he passes, he finally rests in one, because a station and the quest thereof involve contrivance and design (*tarkíb. ú ḥíla*), not conduct and practice (*rawish ú mu'ámalat*). God hath said: "*None of us but hath a certain station*" (Kor. xxxvii, 164). The station of Adam was repentance (*tawbat*), that of Noah was renunciation (*zuhd*), that of Abraham was resignation (*taslím*), that of Moses was contrition (*inábat*), that of David was sorrow (*ḥuzn*), that of Jesus was hope (*rajá*), that of John (the Baptist) was fear (*khawf*), and that of our Apostle was praise (*dhikr*). They drew something from other sources by which they abode, but each of them returned at last to his original station. In discussing the doctrine of the Muḥásibís, I gave a partial explanation of the stations and distinguished between *ḥál* and *maqám*. Here, however, it is necessary to make some further remarks on this subject. You must know that the Way to God is of three kinds: (1) *maqám*, (2) *ḥál*, (3) *tamkín*. God sent all the prophets to explain the Way and to elucidate the principle of the different stations. One hundred and twenty-four thousand apostles, and a few over that number, came with as many stations. On the advent of our Apostle a *ḥál* appeared to those in each station and attained a pitch where all human acquisition was left behind, until religion was made perfect unto men, as God hath said: "*To-day I have perfected your religion for you and have completed My bounty unto you*" (Kor. v, 5); then the *tamkín* (steadfastness) of the steadfast appeared; but if I were to enumerate every *ḥál* and explain every *maqám*, my purpose would be defeated.

Tamkín denotes the residence of spiritual adepts in the abode of perfection and in the highest grade. Those in stations can pass on from their stations, but it is impossible to pass beyond the grade of *tamkín*, because *maqám* is the grade of beginners, whereas *tamkín* is the resting-place of adepts, and *maqámát* (stations) are stages on the way, whereas *tamkín* is repose within the shrine. The friends of God are absent (from themselves) on the way and are strangers (to themselves) in the stages: their hearts are in the presence (of God), and in the presence every instrument is evil and every tool is (a token of) absence (from God) and infirmity. In the epoch of Paganism the poets used to praise men for noble deeds, but they did not recite their panegyric until some time had elapsed. When a poet came into the presence of the person whom he had celebrated, he used to draw his sword and hamstring his camel and then break his sword, as though to say: "I needed a camel to bring me from a far distance to thy presence, and a sword to repel the envious who would have hindered me from paying homage to thee: now that I have reached thee, I kill my camel, for I will never depart from thee again; and I break my sword, for I will not admit into my mind the thought of being severed from thy court." Then, after a few days, he used to recite his poem. Similarly, when Moses attained to *tamkín*, God bade him put off his shoes and cast away his staff (Kor. xx, 12), these being articles of travel and Moses being in the presence of God. The beginning of love is search, but the end is rest: water flows in the river-bed, but when it reaches the ocean it ceases to flow and changes its taste, so that those who desire water avoid it, but those who desire pearls devote themselves to death and fasten the plummet of search to their feet and plunge headlong into the sea, that they may either gain the hidden pearl or lose their dear lives. And one of the Shaykhs says: "*Tamkín* is the removal of *talwín*." *Talwín* also is a technical term of the Ṣúfís, and is closely connected in meaning with *tamkín*, just as *ḥál* is connected with *maqám*. The signification of *talwín* is change and turning from one state to another, and the above-mentioned saying means that he who is steadfast (*mutamakkin*) is not vacillating (*mutaraddid*), for he has carried all that belongs to him into the presence of God and has erased every thought of other than God from his mind, so that no act that passes over him alters his outward predicament and no state changes his inward predicament. Thus Moses was subject to *talwín*: he fell in a swoon (Kor. vii, 139) when God revealed His glory to Mount Sinai; but Muḥammad was steadfast: he suffered no change, although he was in the very revelation of glory from Mecca to a space of two bow-lengths from God; and this is the highest grade. Now *tamkín* is of two kinds—one referring to the dominant influence of God (*sháhid-i ḥaqq*), and the other referring to the dominant influence of one's self (*sháhid-i khud*). He whose *tamkín* is of the latter kind retains his attributes unimpaired, but he whose *tamkín* is of the former kind has no attributes; and the terms effacement (*maḥw*), sobriety (*ṣaḥw*), attainment (*laḥq*), destruction (*maḥq*),[1] annihilation (*faná*), subsistence (*baqá*), being (*wujúd*), and not-being (*'adam*) are not properly applied to one whose attributes are annihilated, because a subject is necessary for the maintenance of these qualities, and when the subject is absorbed (*mustaghriq*) he loses the capacity for maintaining them.

Muḥáḍarat and *Mukáshafat*, and the difference between them.

Muḥáḍarat denotes the presence of the heart in the subtleties of demonstration (*bayán*), while *mukáshafat* denotes the presence of the spirit (*sirr*) in the domain of actual vision (*'iyán*). *Muḥáḍarat* refers to the evidences of God's signs (*áyát*), and *mukáshafat* to the evidences of contemplation (*musháhadát*). The mark of *muḥáḍarat* is continual meditation upon God's signs, while the mark of *mukáshafat* is continual amazement at God's infinite greatness. There is a difference between one who meditates upon the Divine acts and one who is amazed at the Divine majesty: the one is a follower of friendship, the other is a companion of love. When the Friend of God (Abraham) looked on the kingdom of heaven and meditated on the reality of its existence, his heart was made "present" (*ḥáḍir*) thereby: through beholding the act he became a seeker of the Agent; his "presence" (*ḥuḍúr*) made the act a proof of the Agent, and in perfect gnosis he exclaimed: "*I turn my face with true belief unto Him who created the heavens and the earth*" (Kor. vi, 79). But when the Beloved of God (Muḥammad) was borne to Heaven he shut his eyes from the sight of all things; he saw neither God's act nor created beings

[1] *Maḥq* denotes annihilation of a man's being in the essence of God, while *maḥw* denotes annihilation of his actions in the action of God (Jurjání, *Ta'rífát*).

nor himself, but the Agent was revealed to him, and in that revelation (*kashf*) his desire increased: in vain he sought vision, proximity, union; in proportion as the exemption (*tanzíh*) of his Beloved (from all such conceptions) became more manifest to him the more did his desire increase; he could neither turn back nor go forward, hence he fell into amazement. Where friendship was, amazement seemed infidelity, but where love was, union was polytheism, and amazement became the sole resource, because in friendship the object of amazement was being (*hastí*), and such amazement is polytheism, but in love the object of amazement was nature and quality (*chigúnagí*), and this amazement is unification (*tawḥíd*). In this sense Shiblí used always to say: "O Guide of the amazed, increase my amazement!" for in contemplation (of God) the greater one's amazement the higher one's degree. The story of Abú Sa'íd Kharráz and Ibráhím b. Sa'd 'Alawí[1] is well known—how they saw a friend of God on the seashore and asked him "What is the Way to God?" and how he answered that there are two ways to God, one for the vulgar and one for the elect. When they desired him to explain this he said: "The way of the vulgar is that on which you are going: you accept for some cause and you decline for some cause; but the way of the elect is to see only the Causer, and not to see the cause." The true meaning of these anecdotes has already been set forth.

Qabḍ and *Basṭ*, and the difference between them.

Qabḍ (contraction) and *basṭ* (expansion) are two involuntary states which cannot be induced by any human act or banished by any human exertion. God hath said: "*God contracts and expands*" (Kor. ii, 246). *Qabḍ* denotes the contraction of the heart in the state of being veiled (*ḥijáb*), and *basṭ* denotes the expansion of the heart in the state of revelation (*kashf*). Both states proceed from God without effort on the part of Man. The *qabḍ* of gnostics is like the fear of novices, and the *basṭ* of gnostics is like the hope of novices. This is the sense in

[1] *Nafaḥát*, No. 15.

which the Ṣúfís use the terms *qabḍ* and *basṭ*. Some Shaykhs hold that *qabḍ* is superior in degree to *basṭ*, for two reasons: (1) it is mentioned before *basṭ* in the Koran, (2) *qabḍ* involves dissolution and oppression, whereas *basṭ* involves nutrition and favour: it is undoubtedly better to dissolve one's humanity and oppress one's lower soul than to foster and favour them, since they are the greatest veil (between Man and God). Others, again, hold that *basṭ* is superior to *qabḍ*. The fact, they say, that *qabḍ* is mentioned before *basṭ* in the Koran shows the superiority of *basṭ*, for the Arabs are accustomed to mention in the first place that which is inferior in merit, e.g. God hath said: "*There is one of them who injures his own soul, and one who keeps the middle way, and one who outstrips the others in good works by the permission of God*" (Kor. xxxv, 29). Moreover, they argue that in *basṭ* there is joy and in *qabḍ* grief; gnostics feel joy only in union with the object of knowledge, and grief only in separation from the object of desire, therefore rest in the abode of union is better than rest in the abode of separation. My Shaykh used to say that both *qabḍ* and *basṭ* are the result of one spiritual influence, which descends from God on Man, and either fills the heart with joy and subdues the lower soul or subdues the heart and fills the lower soul with joy; in the latter case contraction (*qabḍ*) of the heart is expansion (*basṭ*) of the lower soul, and in the former case expansion of the heart is contraction of the lower soul. He who interprets this matter otherwise is wasting his breath. Hence Báyazíd said: "The contraction of hearts consists in the expansion of souls, and the expansion of hearts in the contraction of souls." The contracted soul is guarded from injury, and the expanded heart is restrained from falling into defect, because jealousy is the rule in love, and contraction is a sign of God's jealousy; and it is necessary that lovers should reproach one another, and expansion is a sign of mutual reproach. It is a well-known tradition that John wept ever since he was born, while Jesus smiled ever since he was born, because John was in contraction and Jesus in expansion. When they met John used to say,

"O Jesus, hast thou no fear of being cut off (from God)?" and Jesus used to say, "O John, hast thou no hope of God's mercy? Neither thy tears nor my smiles will change the eternal decree of God."

Uns and *Haybat*, and the difference between them.

Uns (intimacy) and *haybat* (awe) are two states of the dervishes who travel on the Way to God. When God manifests His glory to a man's heart so that His majesty (*jalál*) predominates, he feels awe (*haybat*), but when God's beauty (*jamál*) predominates he feels intimacy (*uns*): those who feel awe are distressed, while those who feel intimacy are rejoiced. There is a difference between one who is burned by His majesty in the fire of love and one who is illuminated by His beauty in the light of contemplation. Some Shaykhs have said that *haybat* is the degree of gnostics and *uns* the degree of novices, because the farther one has advanced in the presence of God and in divesting Him of attributes the more his heart is overwhelmed with awe and the more averse he is to intimacy, for one is intimate with those of one's own kind, and intimacy with God is inconceivable, since no homogeneity or resemblance can possibly exist between God and Man. If intimacy is possible, it is possible only with the praise (*dhikr*) of Him, which is something different from Himself, because that is an attribute of Man; and in love, to be satisfied with another than the Beloved is falsehood and pretension and self-conceit. *Haybat*, on the other hand, arises from contemplating greatness, which is an attribute of God, and there is a vast difference between one whose experience proceeds from himself through himself and one whose experience proceeds from the annihilation of himself through the subsistence of God. It is related that Shiblí said: "For a long time I used to think that I was rejoicing in the love of God and was intimate with contemplation of Him: now I know that intimacy is impossible except with a congener." Some, however, allege that *haybat* is a corollary of separation and punishment, while *uns* is the result of union and mercy; therefore the friends of God must be guarded from the consequences of *haybat* and be attached to *uns*, for *uns* involves love, and as homogeneity is impossible in love (of God), so it is impossible in *uns*. My Shaykh used to say: "I wonder at those who declare intimacy with God to be impossible, after God has said, '*Verily My servants*,' and '*Say to My servants*', and '*When My servants shall ask thee*', and '*O My servants, no fear shall come on you this day, and ye shall not grieve*' (Kor. xliii, 68). A servant of God, seeing this favour, cannot fail to love Him, and when he has loved he will become intimate, because awe of one's beloved is estrangement (*bégánagí*), whereas intimacy is oneness (*yagánagí*). It is characteristic of men to become intimate with their benefactors, and inasmuch as God has conferred on us so great benefits and we have knowledge of Him, it is impossible that we should talk of awe." I, 'Alí b. 'Uthmán al-Jullábí, say that both parties in this controversy are right, because the power of *haybat* is exerted upon the lower soul and its desires, and tends to annihilate human nature, while the power of *uns* is exerted upon the heart and tends to foster gnosis in the heart. Therefore God annihilates the souls of those who love Him by revealing His majesty and endows their hearts with everlasting life by revealing His beauty. The followers of annihilation (*faná*) regard *haybat* as superior, but the followers of subsistence (*baqá*) prefer *uns*.

Qahr and *Luṭf*, and the difference between them.

These two expressions are used by the Ṣúfís in reference to their own state. By *qahr* (violence) they signify the reinforcement given to them by God in annihilating their desires and in restraining the lower soul from its concupiscence; and by *luṭf* (kindness) they signify God's help towards the subsistence of their hearts and towards the continuance of contemplation and towards the permanence of ecstasy in the degree of steadfastness (*istiqámat*). The adherents of *luṭf* say Divine grace (*karámat*) is the attainment of one's desire, but the others say that Divine grace is this—that God through His will should restrain a man from his own will and should overpower him with will-lessness (*bémurádí*), so that if he were thirsty and plunged into a river, the river would become dry. It is related that in Baghdád were two eminent dervishes, the one a believer in *qahr* and the other a believer in *luṭf*, who were always quarrelling and each preferring his own state to that of his neighbour. The dervish who preferred *luṭf* set out for Mecca and entered the desert, but never reached his destination. No news of him was heard for many years, but at last he was seen by a traveller on the road between Mecca and Baghdád. "O my brother," he said, "when you return to 'Iráq tell my friend at Karkh that if he wishes to see a desert, with all its hardships, like Karkh of Baghdád, with all its marvels, let him come here, for this desert is Karkh to me!" When the traveller arrived at Karkh he delivered this message to the other dervish, who said: "On your return, tell him that there is no superiority in the fact that the desert has been made like Karkh to him, in order that he may not flee from the court (of God); the superiority lies in the fact that Karkh, with all its wondrous opulence, has been made to me like a painful desert, and that nevertheless I am happy here." And it is related that Shiblí said, in his secret converse with God: "O Lord, I will not turn from Thee, although Thou shouldst make the heaven a collar for my neck and the earth a shackle for my foot and the whole universe athirst for my blood." My Shaykh used to say: "One year a meeting of the saints of God took place in the midst of the desert, and I accompanied my spiritual director, Ḥuṣrí, to that spot. I saw some of them approaching on camels, some borne on thrones, and some flying, but Ḥuṣrí paid no heed to them. Then I saw a youth with torn shoes and a broken staff. His feet could scarcely support him, and his head was bare and his body emaciated. As soon as he appeared Ḥuṣrí sprang up and ran to meet him and led him to a lofty seat. This astonished me, and afterwards I questioned the Shaykh about the youth. He replied: 'He is one of God's saints who does not follow saintship, but saintship follows him; and he pays no attention to miracles (*karámát*).'" In short, what we choose for ourselves is noxious to us. I desire only that God should desire for me, and therein preserve me from the evil thereof and save me from the wickedness of my soul. If He keep me in *qahr* I do not wish for *lutf*, and if He keep me in *lutf* I do not wish for *qahr*. I have no choice beyond His choice.

Nafy and *Ithbát*, and the difference between them.

The Shaykhs of this Path give the names of *nafy* (negation) and *ithbát* (affirmation) to the effacement of the attributes of humanity by the affirmation of Divine aid (*ta'yíd*). By negation they signify the negation of the attributes of humanity, and by affirmation they mean the affirmation of the power of the Truth, because effacement (*maḥw*) is total loss, and total negation is applicable only to the attributes; for negation of the essence is impossible while the Universal (*kulliyyat*) subsists. It is necessary, therefore, that blameworthy attributes should be negated by the affirmation of praiseworthy qualities, i.e. the pretension to love of God is negated by affirmation of the reality, for pretension is one of the vanities of the lower soul. But the Ṣúfís, when their attributes are overpowered by the might of the Truth, habitually say that the attributes of humanity are negated by affirming the subsistence of God. This matter has already been discussed in the chapter on poverty and purity and in that on annihilation and subsistence. They say also that the words in question signify the negation of Man's choice by the affirmation of God's choice. Hence that blessed one said: "God's choice for His servant with His knowledge of His servant is better than His servant's choice for himself with his ignorance of his Lord," because love, as all agree, is the negation of the lover's choice by affirmation of the Beloved's choice. I have read in the Anecdotes that a dervish was drowning in the sea, when some one cried: "Brother, do you wish to be saved?" He said: "No." "Then do you wish to be drowned?" "No." "It is a wonder that you will not choose either to die or to be saved." "What have I to do with safety," said the dervish, "that I should choose it? My choice is that God should choose for me." The Shaykhs have said that negation of one's own choice is the least grade in love. Now, God's choice has no beginning in time and cannot possibly be negated, but Man's choice is accidental (*'araḍí*) and admits of negation, and must be trodden under foot, that the eternal choice of God may subsist for ever.[1] There has been much debate on this matter, but my sole aim is that you should know the significa-tion of the terms used by the Ṣúfís. I have mentioned some of these, e.g., *jam'* and *tafriqa*, and *faná* and *baqá*, and *ghaybat* and *ḥuḍúr*, and *sukr* and *ṣaḥw*, in the chapter treating of the doctrines of the Ṣúfís, and you must look there for the explanation of them.

Musámarat and *Muḥádathat*, and the difference between them.

These terms denote two states of the perfect Ṣúfí. *Muḥádathat* (conversation) is really spiritual talk conjoined with silence of the tongue, and *musámarat* (nocturnal discourse) is really continuance of unrestraint (*inbisáṭ*) combined with concealment of the most secret thoughts (*kitmán-i sirr*). The outward meaning of *musámarat* is a spiritual state (*waqtí*) existing between God and Man at night, and *muḥádathat* is a similar state, existing by day, in which there is exoteric and esoteric conversation. Hence secret prayers (*munáját*) by night are called *musámarat*, while invocations made by day are called *muḥádathat*. The daily state is based on revelation (*kashf*), and the nightly state on occultation (*satr*). In love *musámarat* is more perfect than *muḥádathat*, and is connected with the state of the Apostle, when God sent Gabriel to him with Buráq and conveyed him by night from Mecca to a space of

[1] Here the author refers to the example of Moses, whose prayer for vision of God was refused (Kor. vii, 139), because he was exercising his own choice.

two bow-lengths from His presence. The Apostle conversed secretly with God, and when he reached the goal his tongue became dumb before the revelation of God's majesty, and his heart was amazed at His infinite greatness, and he said: "I cannot tell Thy praise." *Muḥádathat* is connected with the state of Moses, who, seeking communion with God, after forty days came to Mount Sinai and heard the speech of God and asked for vision of Him, and failed of his desire. There is a plain difference between one who was conducted (Kor. xvii, 1) and one who came (Kor. vii, 139). Night is the time when lovers are alone with each other, and day is the time when servants wait upon their masters. When a servant transgresses he is reprimanded, but a lover has no law by the transgression of which he should incur blame, for lovers cannot do anything displeasing to each other.

'Ilm al-Yaqín and *'Ayn al-Yaqín* and *Ḥaqq al-Yaqín*, and the difference between them.

According to the principles of theology, all these expressions denote knowledge (*'ilm*). Knowledge without certain faith (*yaqín*) in the reality of the object known is not knowledge, but when knowledge is gained that which is hidden is as that which is actually seen. The believers who shall see God on the Day of Judgment shall see Him then in the same wise as they know Him now: if they shall see Him otherwise, either their vision will be imperfect then or their knowledge is faulty now. Both these alternatives are in contradiction with unification (*tawḥíd*), which requires that men's knowledge of God should be sound to-day and their vision of God should be sound to-morrow. Therefore certain knowledge (*'ilm-i yaqín*) is like certain sight (*'ayn-i yaqín*), and certain truth (*ḥaqq-i yaqín*) is like certain knowledge. Some have said that *'ayn al-yaqín* is the complete absorption (*istighráq*) of knowledge in vision, but this is impossible, because vision is an instrument for the attainment of knowledge, like hearing, etc.: since knowledge cannot be absorbed in hearing, its absorption in vision is equally impossible. By *'ilm al-yaqín* the Ṣúfís mean knowledge of (religious) practice in this world according to the Divine commandments; by *'ayn al-yaqín* they mean knowledge of the state of dying (*naz'*) and the time of departure from this world; and by *ḥaqq al-yaqín* they mean intuitive knowledge of the vision (of God) that will be revealed in Paradise, and of its nature. Therefore *'ilm al-yaqín* is the rank of theologians (*'ulamá*) on account of their correct observance of the Divine commands, and *'ayn al-yaqín* is the station of gnostics (*'árifán*) on account of their readiness for death, and *ḥaqq al-yaqín* is the annihilation-point of lovers (*dústán*) on account of their rejection of all created things. Hence *'ilm al-yaqín* is obtained by self-mortification (*mujáhadat*), and *'ayn al-yaqín* by intimate familiarity (*mu'ánasat*), and *ḥaqq al-yaqín* by contemplation (*musháhadat*). The first is vulgar, the second is elect, and the third is super-elect (*kháṣṣ al-kháṣṣ*).

'Ilm and *Ma'rifat*, and the difference between them.

Theologians have made no distinction between *'ilm* and *ma'rifat*, except when they say that God may be called *'álim* (knowing), but not *'árif* (gnostic), inasmuch as the latter epithet lacks Divine blessing. But the Ṣúfí Shaykhs give the name of *ma'rifat* (gnosis) to every knowledge that is allied with (religious) practice and feeling (*ḥál*), and the knower of which expresses his feeling; and the knower thereof they call *'árif*. On the other hand, they give the name of *'ilm* to every knowledge that is stripped of spiritual meaning and devoid of religious practice, and one who has such knowledge they call *'álim*. One, then, who knows the meaning and reality of a thing they call *'árif* (gnostic), and one who knows merely the verbal expression and keeps it in his memory without keeping the spiritual reality they call *'álim*. For this reason, when the Ṣúfís wish to disparage a rival they call him *dánishmand* (possessing knowledge). To the vulgar this seems objectionable, but the Ṣúfís do not intend to blame the man for having acquired knowledge, they blame him for neglecting the practice of religion, because the *'álim* depends on himself, but the *'árif* depends on his Lord. This question has been discussed at length in the chapter entitled "The Removal of the Veil of Gnosis", and I need not say any more now.

Sharí'at and *Ḥaqíqat*, and the difference between them.

These terms are used by the Ṣúfís to denote soundness of the outward state and maintenance of the inward state. Two parties err in this matter: firstly, the formal theologians, who assert that there is no distinction between *sharí'at* (law) and *ḥaqíqat* (truth), since the Law is the Truth and the Truth is the Law; secondly, some heretics, who hold that it is possible for one of these things to subsist without the other, and declare that when the Truth is revealed the Law is abolished. This is the doctrine of the Carmathians (*Qarámiṭa*) and the Shí'ites and their satanically inspired followers (*muwaswisán*). The proof that the Law is virtually separate from the Truth lies in the fact that in faith belief is separate from profession; and the proof that the Law and the Truth are not fundamentally separate, but are one, lies in the fact that belief without profession is not faith, and conversely profession without belief is not faith; and there is a manifest difference between profession and belief. *Ḥaqíqat*, then, signifies a reality which does not admit of abrogation and remains in equal force from the time of Adam to the end of the world, like knowledge of God and like religious practice, which is made perfect by sincere intention; and *sharí'at* signifies a reality which admits of abrogation and alteration, like ordinances and commandments. Therefore *sharí'at* is Man's act, while *ḥaqíqat* is God's keeping and preservation and protection, whence it follows that *sharí'at* cannot possibly be maintained without the existence of *ḥaqíqat*, and *ḥaqíqat* cannot be maintained without observance of *sharí'at*. Their mutual relation may be compared to that of body and spirit: when the spirit departs from the body the living body becomes a corpse and the spirit vanishes like wind, for their value depends on their conjunction with one another.

Similarly, the Law without the Truth is ostentation, and the Truth without the Law is hypocrisy. God hath said: "*Whosoever mortify themselves for Our sake, We will assuredly guide them in Our ways*" (Kor. xxix, 69): mortification is Law, guidance is Truth; the former consists in a man's observance of the external ordinances, while the latter consists in God's maintenance of a man's spiritual feelings. Hence the Law is one of the acts acquired by Man, but the Truth is one of the gifts bestowed by God.

Another class of terms and expressions are used by the Ṣúfís metaphorically. These metaphorical terms are more difficult to analyse and interpret, but I will explain them concisely.

Ḥaqq. By *ḥaqq* (truth) the Ṣúfís mean God, for *ḥaqq* is one of the names of God, as He hath said: "*This is because God is the Truth*" (Kor. xxii, 6).

Ḥaqíqat. By this word they mean a man's dwelling in the place of union with God, and the standing of his heart in the place of abstraction (*tanzíh*).

Khaṭarát. Any judgments of separation (*aḥkám-i tafríq*) that occur to the mind.

Waṭanát. Any Divine meanings that make their abode in the heart.

Ṭams. Negation of a substance of which some trace is left.

Rams. Negation of a substance, together with every trace thereof, from the heart.

'Alá'iq. Secondary causes to which seekers of God attach themselves and thereby fail to gain the object of their desire.

Wasá'iṭ. Secondary causes to which seekers of God attach themselves and thereby gain the object of their desire.

Zawá'id. Excess of lights (spiritual illumination) in the heart.

Fawá'id. The apprehension by the spirit of what it cannot do without.

Malja'. The heart's confidence in the attainment of its desire.

Manjá. The heart's escape from the place of imperfection.

Kulliyyat. The absorption (*istighráq*) of the attributes of humanity in the Universal (*kulliyyat*).

Lawá'iḥ. Affirmation of the object of desire, notwithstanding the advent of the negation thereof (*ithbát-i murád bá wurúd-i nafy-i án*).

Lawámi'. The manifestation of (spiritual) light to the heart while its acquirements (*fawá'id*) continue to subsist.

Ṭawáli'. The appearance of the splendours of (mystical) knowledge to the heart.

Ṭawáriq. That which comes into the heart, either with glad tidings or with rebuke, in secret converse (with God) at night.

Laṭá'if. A symbol (*ishárat*), presented to the heart, of subtleties of feeling.

Sirr. Concealment of feelings of love.

Najwá. Concealment of imperfections from the knowledge of other (than God).

Ishárat. Giving information to another of the object of desire, without uttering it on the tongue.

Ímá. Addressing anyone allusively, without spoken or unspoken explanation (*bé 'ibárat ú ishárat*).

Wárid. The descent of spiritual meanings upon the heart.

Intibáh. The departure of heedlessness from the heart.

Ishtibáh. Perplexity felt in deciding between truth and falsehood.

Qarár. The departure of vacillation from the reality of one's feeling.

Inzi'áj. The agitation of the heart in the state of ecstasy (*wajd*).

Another class of technical terms are those which the Ṣúfís employ, without metaphor, in unification (*tawḥíd*) and in setting forth their firm belief in spiritual realities.

'Álam. The term *'álam* (world) denotes the creatures of God. It is said that there are 18,000 or 50,000 worlds. Philosophers say there are two worlds, an upper and a lower,

while theologians say that *'álam* is whatever exists between the Throne of God and the earth. In short, *'álam* is the collective mass of created things. The Ṣúfís speak of the world of spirits (*arwáḥ*) and the world of souls (*nufús*), but they do not mean the same thing as the philosophers. What they mean is "the collective mass of spirits and souls".

Muḥdath. Posterior in existence, i.e. it was not and afterwards was.

Qadím. Anterior in existence, i.e. it always was, and its being was anterior to all beings. This is nothing but God.

Azal. That which has no beginning.

Abad. That which has no end.

Dhát. The being and reality of a thing.

Ṣifat. That which does not admit of qualification (*na't*), because it is not self-subsistent.

Ism. That which is not the object named (*ghayr-i musammá*).

Tasmiyat. Information concerning the object named.

Nafy. That which entails the non-existence of every object of negation.

Ithbát. That which entails the existence of every object of affirmation.

Siyyán. The possibility of the existence of one thing with another.

Ḍiddán. The impossibility of the existence of one thing simultaneously with the existence of another.

Ghayrán. The possibility of the existence of either of two things, notwithstanding the annihilation of the other.

Jawhar. The basis (*aṣl*) of a thing; that which is self-subsistent.

'Araḍ. That which subsists in *jawhar* (substance).

Jism. That which is composed of separate parts.

Su'ál. Seeking a reality.

Jawáb. Giving information concerning the subject-matter of a question (*su'ál*).

Ḥusn. That which is conformable to the (Divine) command.

Qubḥ. That which is not conformable to the (Divine) command.

Safah. Neglect of the (Divine) command.

Ẓulm. Putting a thing in a place that is not worthy of it.

'Adl. Putting everything in its proper place.

Malik. He with whose actions it is impossible to interfere.

Another class of terms requiring explanation are those which are commonly used by the Ṣúfís in a mystical sense that is not familiar to philologists.

Kháṭir. By *kháṭir* (passing thought) the Ṣúfís signify the occurrence in the mind of something which is quickly removed by another thought, and which its owner is able to repel from his mind. Those who have such thoughts follow the first thought in matters which come directly from God to Man. It is said that the thought occurred to Khayr Nassáj that Junayd was waiting at his door, but he wished to repel it. The same thought returned twice and thrice, whereupon he went out and discovered Junayd, who said to him: "If you had followed the first thought it would not have been necessary for me to stand here all this time." How was Junayd acquainted with the thought which occurred to Khayr? This question has been asked, and has been answered by the remark that Junayd was Khayr's spiritual director, and a spiritual director cannot fail to be acquainted with all that happens to one of his disciples.

Wáqi'a. By *wáqi'a* they signify a thought which appears in the mind and remains there, unlike *kháṭir*, and which the seeker has no means whatever of repelling: thus they say, *khaṭara 'alá qalbí*, "it occurred to my mind," but *waqa'a fí qalbí*, "it sank into my mind." All minds are subject to *kháṭir* (passing thought), but *wáqi'a* is possible only in a mind that is entirely filled with the notion of God. Hence, when any obstacle appears to the novice on the Way to God, they call it "a fetter" (*qayd*) and say: "A *wáqi'a* has befallen him." Philologists also use the term *wáqi'a* to signify any difficult question, and when it is answered satisfactorily they say, *wáqi'a ḥall shud*, "the difficulty is solved." But the mystics say that *wáqi'a* is that which is insoluble, and that whatever is solved is a *khátir*, not a *wáqi'a*, since the obstacles which confront mystics are not unimportant matters on which varying judgments are continually being formed.

Ikhtiyár. By *ikhtiyár* they signify their preference of God's choice to their own, i.e. they are content with the good and evil which God has chosen for them. A man's preference of God's choice is itself the result of God's choice, for unless God had caused him to have no choice, he would never have let his own choice go. When Abú Yazíd was asked, "Who is the prince (*amír*)?" he replied, "He to whom no choice is left, and to whom God's choice has become the only choice." It is related that Junayd, having caught fever, implored God to give him health. A voice spoke in his heart: "Who art thou to plead in My kingdom and make a choice? I can manage My kingdom better than thou. Do thou choose My choice instead of coming forward with thine."

Imtiḥán. By this expression they signify the probation of the hearts of the saints by diverse afflictions which come to them from God, such as fear, grief, contraction, awe, etc. God hath said: "*They whose hearts God hath proved for piety's sake: they shall win pardon and a great reward*" (Kor. xlix, 3). This is a lofty grade.

Balá. By *balá* (affliction) they signify the probation of the bodies of God's friends by diverse troubles and sicknesses and tribulations. The more severely a man is afflicted the nearer does he approach unto God, for affliction is the vesture of the saints and the cradle of the pure and the nourishment of the prophets. The Apostle said, "We prophets are the most afflicted of mankind;" and he also said, "The prophets are the most afflicted of mankind, then the saints, and then other men according to their respective ranks." *Balá* is the name of a tribulation, which descends on the heart and body of a true believer and which is really a blessing; and inasmuch as the mystery thereof is concealed from him, he is divinely recompensed for supporting the pains thereof. Tribulation that befalls unbelievers is not affliction (*balá*), but misery (*shaqáwat*), and unbelievers never obtain relief from misery. The degree of *balá* is more honourable than that of *imtiḥán*, for *imtiḥán* affects the heart only, whereas *balá* affects both the heart and the body and is thus more powerful.

Taḥallí. Imitation of praiseworthy people in word and deed. The Apostle said: "Faith is not acquired by *taḥallí* (adorning one's self with the qualities of others) and *tamanní* (wishing), but it is that which sinks deep into the heart and is verified by action." *Taḥallí*, then, is to imitate people without really acting like them. Those who seem to be what they are not will soon be put to shame, and their secret character will be revealed. In the view of spiritualists, however, they are already disgraced and their secret character is clear.

Tajallí. The blessed effect of Divine illumination on the hearts of the blest, whereby they are made capable of seeing God with their hearts. The difference between spiritual vision (*ru'yat ba-dil*) and actual vision (*ru'yat-i 'iyán*) is this, that those who experience *tajallí* (manifestation of God) see or do not see, according as they wish, or see at one time and do not see at another time, while those who experience actual vision in Paradise cannot but see, even though they wish not to see; for it is possible that *tajallí* should be hidden, whereas *ru'yat* (vision) cannot possibly be veiled.

Takhallí. Turning away from distractions which prevent a man from attaining to God. One of these is the present world, of which he should empty his hands; another is desire for the next world, of which he should empty his heart; a third is indulgence in vanity, of which he should empty his spirit; and a fourth is association with created beings, of which he should empty himself and from the thought of which he should disengage his mind.

Shurúd. The meaning of *shurúd* is "seeking restlessly to escape from (worldly) corruptions and veils"; for all the misfortunes of the seeker arise from his being veiled, and when the veil is lifted he becomes united with God. The Ṣúfís apply the term *shurúd* to his becoming unveiled (*isfár*) and his using every resource for that purpose; for in the beginning, i.e. in search, he is more restless; in the end, i e. in union, he becomes more steadfast.

Quṣúd. By *quṣúd* (aims) they signify perfect resolution to seek the reality of the object of search. The aims of the Ṣúfís do not depend on motion and rest, because the lover, although he be at rest in love, is still pursuing an aim (*qáṣid*). In this respect the Ṣúfís differ from ordinary men, whose aims produce in them some effect outwardly or inwardly; whereas the lovers of God seek Him without any cause and pursue their aim without movement of their own, and all their qualities are directed towards that goal. Where love exists, all is an aim.

Iṣṭiná'. By this term they mean that God makes a man faultless through the annihilation of all his selfish interests and sensual pleasures, and transforms in him the attributes of his lower soul, so that he becomes selfless. This degree belongs exclusively to the prophets, but some Shaykhs hold that it may be attained by the saints also.

Iṣṭifá. This signifies that God makes a man's heart empty to receive the knowledge of Himself, so that His knowledge (*ma'rifat*) diffuses its purity through his heart. In this degree all believers, the vulgar as well as the elect, are alike, whether they are sinful or pious or saints or prophets, for God hath said: "*We have given the Book as a heritage unto those of our servants whom We have chosen* (iṣṭafayná): *some of them are they who injure their own souls; some are they who keep the mean; and some are they who excel in good works*" (Kor. xxxv, 29).

Iṣṭilám. The manifestations (*tajalliyát*) of God which cause a man to be entirely overpowered by a merciful probation (*imtiḥán*), while his will is reduced to naught. *Qalb-i mumtaḥan*, "a proved heart," and *qalb-i muṣṭalam*, "a destroyed heart," bear the same meaning, although in the current usage of Ṣúfí phraseology *iṣṭilám* is more particular and exquisite than *imtiḥán*.

Rayn. A veil on the heart, i.e. the veil of infidelity and error, which cannot be removed except by faith. God hath said, describing the hearts of the unbelievers (Kor. lxxxiii, 14): "*By no means, but what they used to do hath covered their hearts*" (rána 'alá qulúbihim). Some have said that *rayn* cannot possibly be removed in any manner, since the hearts of unbelievers are not capable of receiving Islam, and those who do receive it must have been, in the foreknowledge of God, true believers.

Ghayn. A veil on the heart which is removed by asking pardon of God. It may be either thin or dense. The latter is for those who forget (God) and commit great sins; the former is for all, not excepting saint or prophet. Did not the Apostle say, "Verily, my heart is obscured (*yughánu 'alá qalbí*), and verily I ask pardon of God a hundred times every day." For removing the dense veil a proper repentance is necessary, and for removing the thin veil a sincere return to God. Repentance (*tawbat*) is a turning back from disobedience to obedience, and return (*rujú'*) is a turning back from self to God. Repentance is repentance from sin: the sin of common men is opposition to God's command, while the sin of lovers (of God) is opposition to God's will: therefore, the sin of common men is disobedience, and that of lovers is consciousness of their own existence. If anyone turns back from wrong to right, they say, "He is repentant (*tá'ib*);" but if anyone turns back from what is right to what is more right, they say, "He is returning (*á'ib*)." All this I have set forth in the chapter on repentance.

Talbís. They denote by *talbís* the appearance of a thing when its appearance is contrary to its reality, as God hath said: "*We should assuredly have deceived them* (lalabasná 'alayhim) *as they deceive others*" (Kor. vi, 9). This quality of deception cannot possibly belong to anyone except God, who shows the unbeliever in the guise of a believer and the believer in the guise of an unbeliever, until the time shall come for the manifestation of His decree and of the reality in every case. When a Ṣúfí conceals good qualities under a mask of bad, they say: "He is practising deception (*talbís*)," but they use this term in such instances only, and do not apply it to ostentation and hypocrisy, which are fundamentally *talbís*, because *talbís* is not used except in reference to an act performed by God.

Shurb. The Ṣúfís call the sweetness of piety and the delight of miraculous grace and the pleasure of intimacy *shurb* (drinking); and they can do nothing without the delight of *shurb*. As the body's drink is of water, so the heart's drink is of (spiritual) pleasure and sweetness. My Shaykh used to say that a novice without *shurb* is a stranger to (i.e. unacquainted with the duties of) the novitiate, and that a gnostic with *shurb* is a stranger to gnosis, because the novice must derive some pleasure (*shurbí*) from his actions in order that he may fulfil the obligations of a novice who is seeking God; but the gnostic ought not to feel such pleasure, lest he should be transported with that pleasure instead of with God: if he turn back to his lower soul he will not rest (with God).

Dhawq. Dhawq resembles *shurb*, but *shurb* is used solely in reference to pleasures, whereas *dhawq* is applied to pleasure and pain alike. One says *dhuqtu 'l-ḥaláwat*, "I tasted sweetness," and *dhuqtu 'l-balá*, "I tasted affliction;" but of *shurb* they say, *sharibtu bi-ka'si 'l-waṣl*, "I drank the cup of union," and *sharibtu bi-ka'si 'l-wudd*, "I drank the cup of love," and so forth.[1]

[1] This distinction between *shurb* and *dhawq* is illustrated by citations from the Koran, viz., lii, 19; xliv, 49; and liv, 48.

CHAPTER XXV.

The Uncovering of the Eleventh Veil: Concerning Audition (*samá'*).

The means of acquiring knowledge are five: hearing, sight, taste, smell, and touch. God has created for the mind these five avenues, and has made every kind of knowledge depend on one of them. Four of the five senses are situated in a special organ, but one, namely touch, is diffused over the whole body. It is possible, however, that this diffusion, which is characteristic of touch, may be shared by any of the other senses. The Mu'tazilites hold that no sense can exist but in a special organ (*maḥall-i makhṣúṣ*), a theory which is controverted by the fact that the sense of touch has no such organ. Since one of the five senses has no special organ, it follows that, if the sense of touch is generally diffused, the other senses may be capable of the same diffusion. Although it is not my purpose to discuss this question here, I thought a brief explanation necessary. God has sent Apostles with true evidences, but belief in His Apostles does not become obligatory until the obligatoriness of knowing God is ascertained by means of hearing. It is hearing, then, that makes religion obligatory; and for this reason the Sunnís regard hearing as superior to sight in the domain of religious obligation (*taklíf*). If it be said that vision of God is better than hearing His word, I reply that our knowledge of God's visibility to the faithful in Paradise is derived from hearing: it is a matter of indifference whether the understanding allows that God shall be visible or not, inasmuch as we are assured of the fact by oral tradition. Hence hearing is superior to sight. Moreover, all religious ordinances are based on hearing and could not be established without it; and all the prophets on their appearance first spoke in order that those who heard them might believe, then in the second place they showed miracles (*mu'jiza*), which also were corroborated by hearing. What has been said proves that anyone who denies audition denies the entire religious law.

Chapter on the Audition of the Koran and kindred matters.

The most beneficial audition to the mind and the most delightful to the ear is that of the Word of God, which all believers and unbelievers, human beings and perís alike, are commanded to hear. It is a miraculous quality of the Koran that one never grows weary of reading and hearing it, so that the Quraysh used to come secretly by night and listen to the Apostle while he was praying and marvel at his recitation, e.g., Naḍr b. al-Ḥárith, who was the most elegant of them in speech, and 'Utba b. Rabí'a, who was bewitchingly eloquent, and Abú Jahl b. Hishám, who was a wondrous orator. One night 'Utba swooned on hearing the Apostle recite a chapter of the Koran, and he said to Abú Jahl: "I am sure that these are not the words of any created being." The perís also came and listened to the Word of God, and said: "*Verily, we heard a marvellous recitation, which guides to the right way; and we shall not associate anyone with our Lord*" (Kor. lxxii, 1-2).[1] It is related that a man recited in the presence of 'Abdalláh b. Ḥanẓala: "*They shall have a couch of Hell-fire, and above them shall be quilts thereof*" (Kor. vii, 39). 'Abdalláh began to weep so violently that, to quote the narrator's words, "I thought life would depart from him." Then he rose to his feet. They bade him sit down, but he cried: "Awe of this verse prevents me from sitting down." It is related that the following verse was read in the presence of Junayd: "*O believers, why say ye that which ye do not?*" (Kor. lxi, 2). Junayd said: "O Lord, if we say, we say because of Thee, and if we do, we do because of Thy blessing: where, then, is our saying and doing?" It is related that Shiblí said, on hearing the verse "*And remember*

[1] After a further eulogy of the inimitable style of the Koran, the author relates the story of 'Umar's conversion.

thy Lord when thou forgettest" (Kor. xviii, 23), "Remembrance (of God) involves forgetfulness (of self), and all the world have stopped short at the remembrance of Him;" then he shrieked and fell senseless. When he came to himself, he said: "I wonder at the sinner who can hear God's Word and remain unmoved." A certain Shaykh says: "Once I was reading the Word of God, '*Beware of a day on which ye shall be returned unto God*' (Kor. ii, 281). A heavenly voice called to me, 'Do not read so loud; four perís have died from the terror inspired in them by this verse'." A dervish said: "For the last ten years I have not read nor heard the Koran except that small portion thereof which is used in prayer." On being asked why, he answered: "For fear lest it should be cited as an argument against me." One day I came into the presence of Shaykh Abu 'l-'Abbás Shaqání and found him reading: "*God propoundeth as a parable an owned slave who hath naught in his power*" (Kor. xvi, 77), and weeping and shrieking, so that he swooned and I thought he was dead. "O Shaykh," I cried, "what ails thee?" He said: "After eleven years I have reached this point in my set portion of the Koran and am unable to proceed farther." Abu 'l-'Abbás b. 'Aṭá was asked how much of the Koran he read daily. He answered: "Formerly I used to read the whole Koran twice in a day and night, but now after reading for fourteen years I have only reached the *Súrat al-Anfál*."[1] It is related that Abu 'l-'Abbás Qaṣṣáb said to a Koran-reader, "Recite," whereupon he recited: "*O noble one, famine hath befallen us and our people, and we are come with a petty merchandise*" (Kor. xii, 88). He said once more, "Recite," whereupon the reader recited: "*If he stole, a brother of his hath stolen heretofore*" (Kor. xii, 77). Abu 'l-'Abbás bade him recite a third time, so he recited: "*No blame shall be laid upon you this day: God forgiveth you*," etc. (Kor. xii, 92). Abu 'l-'Abbás cried: "O Lord, I am more unjust than Joseph's brethren, and Thou art more kind than Joseph: deal with me as he dealt with his wicked brethren."

[1] The chapter of the Spoils, a title given to the eighth chapter of the Koran.

All Moslems, pious and disobedient alike, are commanded to listen to the Koran, for God hath said: "*When the Koran is recited hearken thereto and be silent that perchance ye may win mercy*" (Kor. vii, 203).[1] And it is related that the Apostle said to Ibn Mas'úd: "Recite the Koran to me." Ibn Mas'úd said: "Shall I recite it to thee, to whom it was revealed?" The Apostle answered: "I wish to hear it from another." This is a clear proof that the hearer is more perfect in state than the reader, for the reader may recite with or without true feeling, whereas the hearer feels truly, because speech is a sort of pride and hearing is a sort of humility. The Apostle also said that the chapter of Húd had whitened his hair. It is explained that he said this because of the verse at the end of that chapter: "*Be thou steadfast, therefore, as thou hast been commanded*" (Kor. xi, 114), for Man is unable to be really steadfast in fulfilling the Divine commandments, inasmuch as he can do nothing without God's help.[2]

SECTION.

Zurára b. Abí Awfá, one of the chief Companions of the Apostle, while he was presiding over the public worship, recited a verse of the Koran, uttered a cry, and died. Abú Ja'far Juhaní,[3] an eminent Follower, on hearing a verse which Ṣáliḥ Murrí[4] read to him, gave a loud moan and departed from this world. Ibráhím Nakha'í[5] relates that while he was passing through a village in the neighbourhood of Kúfa he saw an old woman standing in prayer. As the marks of holiness were manifest on her countenance, he waited until she finished

[1] Here the author quotes a number of Koranic verses in which the faithful are enjoined to listen heedfully to the recitation of the sacred volume, or are rebuked for their want of attention.

[2] I have omitted here a story related by Abú Sa'íd al-Khudrí concerning Muḥammad's interview with a party of destitute refugees (*muhájirún*), to whom the Koran was being read.

[3] Bl. Abú Juhayn, J. Abú Juhaní.

[4] Sha'rání, *Ṭabaqát al-Kubrá*, i, 60.

[5] Ibn Khallikán, No. 1.

praying and then saluted her in hope of gaining a blessing thereby. She said to him, "Dost thou know the Koran?" He said, "Yes." She said, "Recite a verse." He did so, whereupon she cried aloud and sent her soul forth to meet the vision of God. Aḥmad b. Abi 'l-Ḥawárí relates the following tale. "I saw in the desert a youth, clad in a coarse frock, standing at the mouth of a well. He said to me: 'O Aḥmad, thou art come in good time, for I must needs hear the Koran, that I may give up my soul. Read me a verse.' God inspired me to read, '*Verily, those who say, "God is our Lord," and then are steadfast*' (Kor. xli, 30). 'O Aḥmad,' said he, 'by the Lord of the Ka'ba thou hast read the same verse which an angel was reading to me just now,' and with these words he gave up his soul."

Chapter on the Audition of Poetry, etc.

It is permissible to hear poetry. The Apostle heard it, and the Companions not only heard it but also spoke it. The Apostle said, "Some poetry is wisdom;" and he said, "Wisdom is the believer's lost she-camel: wherever he finds her, he has the best right to her;" and he said too, "The truest word ever spoken by the Arabs is the verse of Labíd,

'*Everything except God is vain,*
And all fortune is inevitably fleeting.'"

'Amr b. al-Sharíd[1] relates that his father said: "The Apostle asked me whether I could recite any poetry of Umayya b. Abi 'l-Salt, so I recited a hundred verses, and at the end of each verse he cried, 'Go on!' He said that Umayya almost became a Moslem in his poetry." Many such stories are told of the Apostle and the Companions. Erroneous views are prevalent on this subject. Some declare that it is unlawful to listen to any poetry whatever, and pass their lives in defaming their brother Moslems. Some, on the contrary, hold that all poetry is lawful, and spend their time in listening to love-songs and descriptions

[1] B. al-Rashíd.

of the face and hair and mole of the beloved. I do not intend to discuss the arguments which both parties in this controversy bring forward against each other. The Ṣúfí Shaykhs follow the example of the Apostle, who, on being asked about poetry, said: "What is good thereof is good and what is bad thereof is bad," i.e., whatever is unlawful, like backbiting and calumny and foul abuse and blame of any person and utterance of infidelity, is equally unlawful whether it be expressed in prose or in verse; and whatever is lawful in prose, like morality and exhortations and inferences drawn from the signs of God and contemplation of the evidences of the Truth, is no less lawful in verse. In fine, just as it is unlawful and forbidden to look at or touch a beautiful object which is a source of evil, so it is unlawful and forbidden to listen to that object or, similarly, to hear the description of it. Those who regard such hearing as absolutely lawful must also regard looking and touching as lawful, which is infidelity and heresy. If one says, "I hear only God and seek only God in eye and cheek and mole and curl," it follows that another may look at a cheek and mole and say that he sees and seeks God alone, because both the eye and the ear are sources of admonition and knowledge; then another may say that in touching a person, whose description it is thought allowable to hear and whom it is thought allowable to behold, he, too, is only seeking God, since one sense is no better adapted than another to apprehend a reality; then the whole religious law is made null and void, and the Apostle's saying that the eyes commit fornication loses all its force, and the blame of touching persons with whom marriage may legally be contracted is removed, and the ordinances of religion fall to the ground. Foolish aspirants to Ṣúfiism, seeing the adepts absorbed in ecstasy during audition (*samá'*), imagined that they were acting from a sensual impulse and said, "It is lawful, else they would not have done so," and imitated them, taking up the form but neglecting the spirit, until they perished themselves and led others into perdition. This is one of the great evils of our time. I will set it forth completely in the proper place.

Chapter on the Audition of Voices and Melodies.

The Apostle said, "Beautify your voices by reading the Koran aloud;" and God hath said, "*God addeth unto His creatures what He pleaseth*" (Kor. xxxv, 1), meaning, as the commentators think, a beautiful voice; and the Apostle said, "Whoso wishes to hear the voice of David, let him listen to the voice of Abú Músá al-Ash'arí." It is stated in well-known traditions that the inhabitants of Paradise enjoy audition, for there comes forth from every tree a different voice and melody. When diverse sounds are mingled together, the natural temperament experiences a great delight. This sort of audition is common to all living creatures, because the spirit is subtle, and there is a subtlety in sounds, so that when they are heard the spirit inclines to that which is homogeneous with itself. Physicians and those philosophers who claim to possess a profound knowledge of the truth have discussed this subject at large and have written books on musical harmony. The results of their invention are manifest to-day in the musical instruments which have been contrived for the sake of exciting passion and procuring amusement and pleasure, in accord with Satan, and so skilfully that (as the story is told) one day, when Isḥáq of Mawṣil[1] was playing in a garden, a nightingale, enraptured with the music, broke off its song in order to listen, and dropped dead from the bough. I have heard many tales of this kind, but my only purpose is to mention the theory that the temperaments of all living creatures are composed of sounds and melodies blended and harmonized. Ibráhím Khawwáṣ says: "Once I came to an Arab tribe and alighted at the hospitable abode of one of their chiefs. I saw a negro lying, shackled and chained, at the tent door in the heat of the sun. I felt pity for him and resolved to intercede with the chief on his behalf. When food was brought for my entertainment I refused to eat, knowing that nothing grieves an Arab more than this. The

[1] *Aghání*, 5, 52–131.

chief asked me why I refused, and I answered that I hoped his generosity would grant me a boon. He begged me to eat, assuring me that all he possessed was mine. 'I do not want your wealth,' I said, 'but pardon this slave for my sake.' 'First hear what his offence was,' the chief replied, 'then remove his chains. This slave is a camel-driver, and he has a sweet voice. I sent him with a few camels to my estates, to fetch me some corn. He put a double load on every camel and chanted so sweetly on the way that the camels ran at full speed. They returned hither in a short time, and as soon as he unloaded them they died one after another.' 'O prince,' I cried in astonishment, 'a nobleman like you does not speak falsely, but I wish for some evidence of this tale.' While we talked a number of camels were brought from the desert to the wells, that they might drink. The chief inquired how long they had gone without water. 'Three days,' was the reply. He then commanded the slave to chant. The camels became so occupied in listening to his song that they would not drink a mouthful of water, and suddenly they turned and fled, one by one, and dispersed in the desert. The chieftain released the slave and pardoned him for my sake."

We often see, for example, how camels and asses are affected with delight when their drivers trill an air. In Khurásán and 'Iráq it is the custom for hunters, when hunting deer (*áhú*) at night, to beat on a basin of brass (*ṭashtí*) in order that the deer may stand still, listening to the sound, and thus be caught. And in India, as is well known, some people go out to the open country and sing and make a tinkling sound, on hearing which the deer approach; then the hunters encircle them and sing, until the deer are lulled to sleep by the delightful melody and are easily captured. The same effect is manifest in young children who cease crying in the cradle when a tune is sung to them, and listen to the tune. Physicians say of such a child that he is sensible and will be clever when he grows up. On the death of one of the ancient kings of Persia his ministers wished to enthrone his son, who was a child two years old.

Buzurjmihr,[1] on being consulted, said: "Very good, but we must make trial whether he is sensible," and ordered singers to sing to him. The child was stirred with emotion and began to shake his arms and legs. Buzurjmihr declared that this was a hopeful sign and consented to his succession. Anyone who says that he finds no pleasure in sounds and melodies and music is either a liar and a hypocrite or he is not in his right senses, and is outside of the category of men and beasts. Those who prohibit music do so in order that they may keep the Divine commandment, but theologians are agreed that it is permissible to hear musical instruments if they are not used for diversion, and if the mind is not led to wickedness through hearing them. Many traditions are cited in support of this view. Thus, it is related that 'Á'isha said: "A slave-girl was singing in my house when 'Umar asked leave to enter. As soon as she heard his step she ran away. He came in and the Apostle smiled: 'O Apostle of God,' cried 'Umar, 'what hath made thee smile?' The Apostle answered, 'A slave-girl was singing here, but she ran away as soon as she heard thy step.' 'I will not depart,' said 'Umar, 'until I hear what the Apostle heard.' So the Apostle called the girl back and she began to sing, the Apostle listening to her." Many of the Companions have related similar traditions, which Abú 'Abd al-Raḥmán al-Sulamí has collected in his *Kitáb al-Samá'*[2]; and he has pronounced such audition to be permissible. In practising audition, however, the Ṣúfí Shaykhs desire, not permissibility as the vulgar do, but spiritual advantages. Licence is proper for beasts, but men who are subject to the obligations of religion ought to seek spiritual benefit from their actions. Once, when I was at Merv, one of the leaders of the *Ahl-i ḥadíth*[3] and the most celebrated of them all said to me: "I have composed a work on the permissibility of audition." I replied: "It is

[1] The vizier of Khusraw Núshírwán, the great Sásánian king of Persia (531–78 A.D.).

[2] *The Book of Audition.*

[3] "The followers of Tradition" as opposed to "the followers of Opinion" (*ahl-i ra'y*).

a great calamity to religion that the Imám should have made lawful an amusement which is the root of all immorality." "If you do not hold it to be lawful," said he, "why do you practise it?" I answered: "Its lawfulness depends on circumstances and cannot be asserted absolutely: if audition produces a lawful effect on the mind, then it is lawful; it is unlawful if the effect is unlawful, and permissible if the effect is permissible."

Chapter on the Principles of Audition.

You must know that the principles of audition vary with the variety of temperaments, just as there are different desires in various hearts, and it is tyranny to lay down one law for all. Auditors (*mustami'án*) may be divided into two classes: (1) those who hear the spiritual meaning, (2) those who hear the material sound. There are good and evil results in each case. Listening to sweet sounds produces an effervescence (*ghalayán*) of the substance moulded in Man: true (*ḥaqq*) if the substance be true, false (*báṭil*) if the substance be false. When the stuff of a man's temperament is evil, that which he hears will be evil too. The whole of this topic is illustrated by the story of David, whom God made His vicegerent and gave him a sweet voice and caused his throat to be a melodious pipe, so that wild beasts and birds came from mountain and plain to hear him, and the water ceased to flow and the birds fell from the air. It is related that during a month's space the people who were gathered round him in the desert ate no food, and the children neither wept nor asked for milk; and whenever the folk departed it was found that many had died of the rapture that seized them as they listened to his voice: one time, it is said, the tale of the dead amounted to seven hundred maidens and twelve thousand old men. Then God, wishing to separate those who listened to the voice and followed their temperament from the followers of the truth (*ahl-i ḥaqq*) who listened to the spiritual reality, permitted Iblís to work his will and display his wiles. Iblís fashioned a mandoline and a flute and took up a station opposite to the place where David was singing.

David's audience became divided into two parties: the blest and the damned. Those who were destined to damnation lent ear to the music of Iblís, while those who were destined to felicity remained listening to the voice of David. The spiritualists (*ahl-i ma'ní*) were conscious of nothing except David's voice, for they saw God alone; if they heard the Devil's music, they regarded it as a temptation proceeding from God, and if they heard David's voice, they recognized it as being a direction from God; wherefore they abandoned all things that are merely subsidiary and saw both right and wrong as they really are. When a man has audition of this kind, whatever he hears is lawful to him. Some impostors, however, say that their audition is contrary to the reality. This is absurd, for the perfection of saintship consists in seeing everything as it really is, that the vision may be right; if you see otherwise, the vision is wrong. The Apostle said: "O God, let us see things as they are." Similarly, right audition consists in hearing everything as it is in quality and predicament. The reason why men are seduced and their passions excited by musical instruments is that they hear unreally: if their audition corresponded with the reality, they would escape from all evil consequences. The people of error heard the word of God, and their error waxed greater than before. Some of them quoted "*The eyes attain not unto Him*" (Kor. vi, 103) as a demonstration that there shall be no vision of God; some cited "*Then He settled Himself on the throne*" (Kor. vii, 52) to prove that position and direction may be affirmed of Him; and some argued that God actually "comes", since He has said, "*And thy Lord shall come and the angels rank by rank*" (Kor. lxxxix, 23). Inasmuch as error was implanted in their minds, it profited them nothing to hear the Word of God. The Unitarian, on the other hand, when he peruses a poem, regards the Creator of the poet's nature and the Disposer of his thoughts, and drawing an admonition therefrom, sees in the act an evidence of the Agent. Thus he finds the right way even in falsehood, while those whom we have mentioned above lose the way in the midst of truth.

SECTION.

The Shaykhs have uttered many sayings on this subject. Dhu 'l-Nún the Egyptian says: "Audition is a Divine influence (*wárid al-ḥaqq*) which stirs the heart to seek God: those who listen to it spiritually (*ba-ḥaqq*) attain unto God (*taḥaqqaqa*), and those who listen to it sensually (*ba-nafs*) fall into heresy (*tazandaqa*)." This venerable Ṣúfí does not mean that audition is the cause of attaining unto God, but he means that the auditor ought to hear the spiritual reality, not the mere sound, and that the Divine influence ought to sink into his heart and stir it up. One who in that audition follows the truth will experience a revelation, whereas one who follows his lower soul (*nafs*) will be veiled and will have recourse to interpretation (*ta'wíl*). *Zandaqa* (heresy) is a Persian word which has been Arabicized. In the Arabic tongue it signifies "interpretation". Accordingly, the Persians call the commentary on their Book *Zand ú Pázand*.[1] The philologists, wishing to give a name to the descendants of the Magians, called them *zindíq* on the ground of their assertion that everything stated by the Moslems has an esoteric interpretation, which destroys its external sense. At the present day the Shí'ites of Egypt, who are the remnant of these Magians, make the same assertion. Hence the word *zindíq* came to be applied to them as a proper name. Dhu'l-Nún, by using this term, intended to declare that spiritualists in audition penetrate to the reality, while sensualists make a far-fetched interpretation and thereby fall into wickedness. Shiblí says: "Audition is outwardly a temptation (*fitnat*) and inwardly an admonition (*'ibrat*): he who knows the mystic sign (*ishárat*) may lawfully hear the admonition; otherwise, he has invited temptation and exposed himself to calamity," i.e. audition is calamitous and a source of evil to anyone whose whole heart is not absorbed in the thought of God. Abú 'Alí Rúdbárí said, in answer to a man who questioned him concerning audition: "Would that I were rid of it entirely!" because Man

[1] See Professor Browne's *Literary History of Persia*, i, 81.

is unable to do everything as it ought to be done, and when he fails to do a thing duly he perceives that he has failed and wishes to be rid of it altogether. One of the Shaykhs says: "Audition is that which makes the heart aware of the things in it that produce absence" (*má fíhá mina 'l-mughayyibát*), so that the effect thereof is to make the heart present with God. Absence (*ghaybat*) is a most blameworthy quality of the heart. The lover, though absent from his Beloved, must be present with him in heart; if he be absent in heart, his love is gone. My Shaykh said: "Audition is the viaticum of the indigent: one who has reached his journey's end hath no need of it," because hearing can perform no function where union is; news is heard of the absent, but hearing is naught when two are face to face. Ḥuṣrí says: "What avails an audition that ceases whenever the person whom thou hearest becomes silent? It is necessary that thy audition should be continuous and uninterrupted." This saying is a token of the concentration of his thoughts in the field of love. When a man attains so high a degree as this he hears (spiritual truths) from every object in the universe.

Chapter on the various opinions respecting Audition.

The Shaykhs and spiritualists hold different views as to audition. Some say that it is a faculty appertaining to absence, for in contemplation (of God) audition is impossible, inasmuch as the lover who is united with his Beloved fixes his gaze on Him and does not need to listen to him; therefore, audition is a faculty of beginners which they employ, when distracted by forgetfulness, in order to obtain concentration; but one who is already concentrated will inevitably be distracted thereby. Others, again, say that audition is a faculty appertaining to presence (with God), because love demands all; until the whole of the lover is absorbed in the whole of the Beloved, he is deficient in love: therefore, as in union the heart (*dil*) has love and the soul (*sirr*) has contemplation and the spirit has union and the body has service, so the ear also must have such a pleasure as the eye derives from seeing. How excellent, though on a frivolous topic, are the words of the poet who declared his love for wine!

> "*Give me wine to drink and tell me it is wine.*
> *Do not give it me in secret, when it can be given openly*,"[1]

i.e., let my eye see it and my hand touch it and my palate taste it and my nose smell it: there yet remains one sense to be gratified, viz. my hearing: tell me, therefore, this is wine, that my ear may feel the same delight as my other senses. And they say that audition appertains to presence with God, because he who is absent from God is a disbeliever (*munkir*), and those who disbelieve are not worthy to enjoy audition. Accordingly, there are two kinds of audition: mediate and immediate. Audition of which a reciter (*qárí*) is the source is a faculty of absence, but audition of which the Beloved (*yárí*) is the source is a faculty of presence. It was on this account that a well-known spiritual director said: "I will not put any created beings, except the chosen men of God, in a place where I can hear their talk or converse with them."

Chapter concerning their different grades in the reality of Audition.

You must know that each Ṣúfí has a particular grade in audition and that the feelings which he gains therefrom are proportionate to his grade. Thus, whatever is heard by penitents augments their contrition and remorse; whatever is heard by longing lovers increases their longing for vision; whatever is heard by those who have certain faith confirms their certainty; whatever is heard by novices verifies their elucidation (of matters which perplex them); whatever is heard by lovers impels them to cut off all worldly connexions; and whatever is heard by the spiritually poor forms a foundation for hopelessness. Audition is like the sun, which shines on all things but affects

[1] Abú Nuwás, *Die Weinlieder*, ed. by Ahlwardt, No. 29, verse 1.

them differently according to their degree: it burns or illumines or dissolves or nurtures. All the classes that I have mentioned are included in the three following grades: beginners (*mubtadiyán*), middlemen (*mutawassiṭán*), and adepts (*kámilán*). I will now insert a section treating of the state of each of these three grades in regard to audition, that you may understand this matter more easily.

SECTION.

Audition is an influence (*wárid*) proceeding from God, and inasmuch as this body is moulded of folly and diversion the temperament of the beginner is nowise capable of (enduring) the word of God, but is overpoweringly impressed by the descent of that spiritual reality, so that some lose their senses in audition and some die, and there is no one whose temperament retains its equilibrium. It is well known that in the hospitals of Rúm they have invented a wonderful thing which they call *angalyún*;[1] the Greeks call anything that is very marvellous by this name, e.g. the Gospel and the books (*waḍ'*) of Mání (Manes). The word signifies "promulgation of a decree" (*iẓhár-i ḥukm*). This *angalyún* resembles a stringed musical instrument (*rúdí az rúdha*). The sick are brought to it two days in the week and are forced to listen, while it is being played on, for a length of time proportionate to the malady from which they suffer; then they are taken away. If it is desired to kill anyone, he is kept there for a longer period, until he dies. Everyone's term of life is really written (in the tablets of destiny), but death is caused indirectly by various circumstances. Physicians and others may listen continually to the *angalyún* without being affected in any way, because it is consonant with their temperaments. I have seen in India a worm which appeared in a deadly poison and lived by it, because that poison was its whole being. In a town of Turkistán, on the frontiers of Islam, I saw a burning mountain, from the rocks of which sal-ammoniac fumes (*nawshádur*) were

[1] εὐαγγέλιον.

boiling forth;[1] and in the midst of that fire was a mouse, which died when it came out of the glowing heat. My object in citing these examples is to show that all the agitation of beginners, when the Divine influence descends upon them, is due to the fact that their bodies are opposed to it; but when it becomes continual the beginner receives it quietly. At first the Apostle could not bear the vision of Gabriel, but in the end he used to be distressed if Gabriel ever failed to come, even for a brief space. Similarly, the stories which I have related above show that beginners are agitated and that adepts are tranquil in audition. Junayd had a disciple who was wont to be greatly agitated in audition, so that the other dervishes were distracted. They complained to Junayd, and he told the disciple that he would not associate with him if he displayed such agitation in future. "I watched that dervish," says Abú Muhammad Jurayrí, "during audition: he kept his lips shut and was silent until every pore in his body opened; then he lost consciousness, and remained in that state for a whole day. I know not whether his audition or his reverence for his spiritual director was more perfect." It is related that a man cried out during audition. His spiritual director bade him be quiet. He laid his head on his knee, and when they looked he was dead. I heard Shaykh Abú Muslim Fáris b. Ghálib al-Fárisí say that some one laid his hand on the head of a dervish who was agitated during audition and told him to sit down: he sat down and died on the spot. Raqqí[2] relates that Darráj[3] said: "While Ibn al-Qúṭí[4] and I were walking on the bank of the Tigris between Baṣra and Ubulla, we came to a pavilion and saw a handsome man seated on the roof, and beside him a girl who was singing this verse:—

[1] The mountains referred to are the Jabal al-Buttam, to the east of Ṣamarcand. See G. Le Strange, *The Lands of the Eastern Caliphate*, p. 467.

[2] IJ. Duqqí. Qushayrí, who relates this story (184, 22), has "al-Raqqí". The *nisba* Duqqí refers to Abú Bakr Muḥammad al-Dínawarí (*Nafaḥát*, No. 229), while Raqqí probably denotes Ibráhím b. Dáwud al-Raqqí (ibid., No. 194).

[3] *Nafaḥát*, No. 207.

[4] So Qushayrí. The Persian texts have القرطى or القرظى. In the commentary on Qushayrí by Zakariyyá al-Anṣárí the name is written al-Fúṭí.

> *'My love was bestowed on thee in the way of God;*
> *Thou changest every day: it would beseem thee better not to do this.'*

A young man with a jug and a patched frock was standing beneath the pavilion. He exclaimed: 'O damsel, for God's sake chant that verse again, for I have only a moment to live; let me hear it and die!' The girl repeated her song, whereupon the youth uttered a cry and gave up his soul. The owner of the girl said to her, 'Thou art free,' and came down from the roof and busied himself with preparations for the young man's funeral. When he was buried all the people of Baṣra said prayers over him. Then the girl's master rose and said: 'O people of Baṣra, I, who am so-and-so, the son of so-and-so, have devoted all my wealth to pious works and have set free my slaves.' With these words he departed, and no one ever learned what became of him." The moral of this tale is that the novice should be transported by audition to such an extent that his audition shall deliver the wicked from their wickedness. But in the present age some persons attend meetings where the wicked listen to music, yet they say, "We are listening to God;" and the wicked join with them in this audition and are encouraged in their wickedness, so that both parties are destroyed. Junayd was asked: "May we go to a church for the purpose of admonishing ourselves and beholding the indignity of their unbelief and giving thanks for the gift of Islam?" He replied: "If you can go to a church and bring some of the worshippers back with you to the Court of God, then go, but not otherwise." When an anchorite goes into a tavern, the tavern becomes his cell, and when a haunter of taverns goes into a cell, that cell becomes his tavern. An eminent Shaykh relates that when he was walking in Baghdád with a dervish, he heard a singer chanting—

> *"If it be true, it is the best of all objects of desire,*
> *And if not, we have lived a pleasant life in it."*

The dervish uttered a cry and died. Abú 'Alí Rúdbárí says;

"I saw a dervish listening attentively to the voice of a singer. I too inclined my ear, for I wished to know what he was chanting. The words, which he sang in mournful accents, were these:—

'*I humbly stretch my hand to him who gives food liberally.*'

Then the dervish uttered a loud cry and fell. When we came near him we found that he was dead." A certain man says: "I was walking on a mountain road with Ibráhím Khawwáṣ. A sudden thrill of emotion seized my heart, and I chanted—

'*All men are sure that I am in love,*
But they know not whom I love.
There is in Man no beauty
That is not surpassed in beauty by a beautiful voice.'

Ibráhím begged me to repeat the verses, and I did so. In sympathetic ecstasy (*tawájud*) he danced a few steps on the stony ground. I observed that his feet sank into the rock as though it were wax. Then he fell in a swoon. On coming to himself he said to me: 'I have been in Paradise, and you were unaware.'" I once saw with my own eyes a dervish walking in meditation among the mountains of Ádharbáyaján and rapidly singing to himself these verses, with many tears and moans:—

"*By God, sun never rose or set but thou wert my heart's desire and my dream.*
And I never sat conversing with any people but thou wert the subject of my conversation in the midst of my comrades.
And I never mentioned thee in joy or sorrow but love for thee was mingled with my breath.
And I never resolved to drink water, when I was athirst, but I saw an image of thee in the cup.
And were I able to come I would have visited thee, crawling on my face or walking on my head."

On hearing these verses he changed countenance and sat down for a while, leaning his back against a crag, and gave up his soul.

SECTION.

Some of the Ṣúfí Shaykhs have objected to the hearing of odes and poems and to the recitation of the Koran in such a way that its words are intoned with undue emphasis, and they have warned their disciples against these practices and have themselves eschewed them and have displayed the utmost zeal in this matter. Of such objectors there are several classes, and each class has a different reason. Some have found traditions declaring the practices in question to be unlawful and have followed the pious Moslems of old in condemning them. They cite, for example, the Apostle's rebuke to Shírín, the handmaid of Ḥassán b. Thábit, whom he forbade to sing; and 'Umar's flogging the Companions who used to hear music; and 'Alí's finding fault with Mu'áwiya for keeping singing-girls, and his not allowing Ḥasan to look at the Abyssinian woman who used to sing and his calling her "the Devil's mate". They say, moreover, that their chief argument for the objectionableness of music is the fact that the Moslem community, both now and in past times, are generally agreed in regarding it with disapproval. Some go so far as to pronounce it absolutely unlawful, quoting Abu 'l-Ḥárith Bunání, who relates as follows: "I was very assiduous in audition. One night a certain person came to my cell and told me that a number of seekers of God had assembled and were desirous to see me. I went out with him and soon arrived at the place. They received me with extraordinary marks of honour. An old man, round whom they had formed a circle, said to me: 'With thy leave, some poetry will be recited.' I assented, whereupon one of them began to chant verses which the poets had composed on the subject of separation (from the beloved). They all rose in sympathetic ecstasy, uttering melodious cries and making exquisite gestures, while I remained lost in amazement at their behaviour. They continued in this enthusiasm until near daybreak, then the old man said, 'O Shaykh, art not thou curious to learn who am I and who are my companions?' I answered that the reverence which I felt towards him prevented me from asking that question. 'I myself,' said he, 'was once 'Azrá'íl and am now Iblís, and all the rest are my children. Two benefits accrue to me from such concerts as this: firstly, I bewail my own separation (from God) and remember the days of my prosperity, and secondly, I lead holy men astray and cast them into error.' From that time (said the narrator) I have never had the least desire to practise audition."

I, 'Alí b. 'Uthmán al-Jullábí, have heard the Shaykh and Imám Abu 'l-'Abbás al-Ashqání relate that one day, being in an assembly where audition was going on, he saw naked demons dancing among the members of the party and breathing upon them, so that they waxed hot.

Others, again, refuse to practise audition on the ground that, if they indulged in it, their disciples would conform with them and thereby run a grave risk of falling into mischief and of returning from penitence to sin and of having their passions violently roused and their virtue corrupted. It is related that Junayd said to a recently converted disciple: "If you wish to keep your religion safe and to maintain your penitence, do not indulge, while you are young, in the audition which the Ṣúfís practise; and when you grow old, do not let yourself be the cause of guilt in others."

Others say that there are two classes of auditors: those who are frivolous (*láhí*) and those who are divine (*iláhí*). The former are in the very centre of mischief and do not shrink from it, while the latter keep themselves remote from mischief by means of self-mortification and austerities and spiritual renunciation of all created things. "Since we" (so say the persons of whom I am now speaking) "belong to neither of these two classes, it is better for us to abstain from audition and to occupy ourselves with something that is suitable to our state."

Others say: "Inasmuch as audition is dangerous to the vulgar and their belief is disturbed by our taking part in it, and inasmuch as they are unable to attain to our degree therein and incur guilt through us, we have pity on the vulgar and give sincere advice to the elect and from altruistic motives decline to indulge in audition." This is a laudable course of action.

Others say: "The Apostle has said, 'It contributes to the excellence of a man's Islam if he leaves alone that which does not concern him.' Accordingly, we renounce audition as being unnecessary, for it is a waste of time to busy one's self with irrelevant things, and time is precious between lovers and the Beloved."

Others of the elect argue that audition is hearsay and its pleasure consists in gratification of a desire, and this is mere child's play. What value has hearsay when one is face to face? The act of real worth is contemplation (of God).

Such, in brief, are the principles of audition.

Chapter on Wajd *and* Wujúd *and* Tawájud.

Wajd and *wujúd* are verbal nouns, the former meaning "grief" and the latter "finding". These terms are used by Ṣúfís to denote two states which manifest themselves in audition: one state is connected with grief, and the other with gaining the object of desire. The real sense of "grief" is "loss of the Beloved and failure to gain the object of desire", while the real sense of "finding" is "attainment of the desired object". The difference between *ḥazan* (sorrow) and *wajd* is this, that the term *ḥazan* is applied to a selfish grief, whereas the term *wajd* is applied to grief for another in the way of love, albeit the relation of otherness belongs only to the seeker of God, for God Himself is never other than He is. It is impossible to explain the nature of *wajd*, because *wajd* is pain in actual vision, and pain (*alam*) cannot be described by pen (*qalam*). *Wajd* is a mystery between the seeker and the Sought, which only a revelation can expound. Nor is it possible to indicate the nature of *wujúd*, because *wujúd* is a thrill of emotion in contemplation of God, and emotion (*ṭarab*) cannot be reached by investigation (*ṭalab*). *Wujúd* is a grace bestowed by the Beloved on the lover, a grace of which no symbol can suggest the real nature. In my opinion, *wajd* is a painful affection of the heart, arising either from jest or earnest, either from sadness or gladness; and *wujúd* is the removal of a grief from the heart and the discovery of the object that was its cause. He who feels *wajd* is either agitated by ardent longing in the state of occultation (*ḥijáb*), or calmed by contemplation in the state of revelation (*kashf*). The Shaykhs hold different views on the question whether *wajd* or *wujúd* is more perfect. Some argue that, *wujúd* being characteristic of novices (*murídán*), and *wajd* of gnostics (*'árifán*), and gnostics being more exalted in degree than novices, it follows that *wajd* is higher and more perfect than *wujúd*; for (they say) everything that is capable of being found is apprehensible, and apprehensibility is characteristic of that which is homogeneous with something else: it involves finiteness, whereas God is infinite; therefore, what a man finds is naught but a feeling (*mashrabí*), but what he has not found, and in despair has ceased to seek, is the Truth of which the only finder is God. Some, again, declare that *wajd* is the glowing passion of novices, while *wujúd* is a gift bestowed on lovers, and, since lovers are more exalted than novices, quiet enjoyment of the gift must be more perfect than passionate seeking. This problem cannot be solved without a story, which I will now relate. One day Shiblí came in rapturous ecstasy to Junayd. Seeing that Junayd was sorrowful, he asked what ailed him. Junayd said, "He who seeks shall find." Shiblí cried, "No; he who finds shall seek." This anecdote has been discussed by the Shaykhs, because Junayd was referring to *wajd* and Shiblí to *wujúd*. I think Junayd's view is authoritative, for, when a man knows that his object of worship is not of the same *genus* as himself, his grief has no end. This topic has been handled in the present work. The Shaykhs agree that the power of knowledge should be greater than the power of *wajd*, since, if *wajd* be more powerful, the person affected by it is in a dangerous position, whereas one in whom knowledge preponderates is secure. It behoves the seeker in all circumstances to be a follower of knowledge and of the religious law, for when he is overcome by *wajd* he is deprived of discrimination (*khiṭáb*), and is not liable to recompense for good actions or punishment for evil, and is exempt from honour and disgrace alike: therefore he is in the predicament of madmen, not in that of the saints and favourites of God. A person in whom knowledge (*'ilm*) preponderates over feeling (*ḥál*) remains in the bosom of the Divine commands and prohibitions, and is always praised and rewarded in the palace of glory; but a person in whom feeling preponderates over knowledge is outside of the ordinances, and dwells, having lost the faculty of discrimination, in his own imperfection. This is precisely the meaning of Junayd's words. There are two ways: one of knowledge and one of action. Action without knowledge, although it may be good, is ignorant and imperfect, but knowledge, even if it be unaccompanied by action, is glorious and noble. Hence Abú Yazíd said, "The unbelief of the magnanimous is nobler than the Islam of the covetous;" and Junayd said, "Shiblí is intoxicated; if he became sober he would be an Imám from whom people would benefit." It is a well-known story that Junayd and Muḥammad[1] b. Masrúq and Abu 'l-'Abbás b. 'Aṭá were together, and the singer (*qawwál*) was chanting a verse. Junayd remained calm while his two friends fell into a forced ecstasy (*tawájud*), and on their asking him why he did not participate in the audition (*samá'*) he recited the word of God: "*Thou shalt think them* (the mountains) *motionless, but they shall pass like the clouds*" (Kor. xxvii, 90). *Tawájud* is "taking pains to produce *wajd*", by representing to one's mind, for example, the bounties and evidences of God, and thinking of union (*ittiṣál*) and wishing for the practices of holy men. Some do this *tawájud* in a formal manner, and imitate them by outward motions and methodical dancing and grace of gesture: such *tawájud* is absolutely unlawful. Others do it in a spiritual manner, with the desire of attaining to their condition and degree. The Apostle said, "He who makes himself like unto a people is one of them," and he said, "When ye recite the Koran, weep, or if ye weep not, then endeavour to

[1] Apparently a mistake for Aḥmad b. Muḥammad. See *Nafaḥát*, No. 83.

weep." This tradition proclaims that *tawájud* is permissible. Hence that spiritual director said: "I will go a thousand leagues in falsehood, that one step of the journey may be true."

Chapter on Dancing, etc.

You must know that dancing (*raqṣ*) has no foundation either in the religious law (of Islam) or in the path (of Ṣúfiism), because all reasonable men agree that it is a diversion when it is in earnest, and an impropriety (*laghwí*) when it is in jest. None of the Shaykhs has commended it or exceeded due bounds therein, and all the traditions cited in its favour by anthropomorphists (*ahl-i ḥashw*) are worthless. But since ecstatic movements and the practices of those who endeavour to induce ecstasy (*ahl-i tawájud*) resemble it, some frivolous imitators have indulged in it immoderately and have made it a religion. I have met with a number of common people who adopted Ṣúfiism in the belief that it is this (dancing) and nothing more. Others have condemned it altogether. In short, all foot-play (*páy-bází*) is bad in law and reason, by whomsoever it is practised, and the best of mankind cannot possibly practise it; but when the heart throbs with exhilaration and rapture becomes intense and the agitation of ecstasy is manifested and conventional forms are gone, that agitation (*iḍtiráb*) is neither dancing nor foot-play nor bodily indulgence, but a dissolution of the soul. Those who call it "dancing" are utterly wrong. It is a state that cannot be explained in words: "without experience no knowledge."

Looking at youths (aḥdáth). Looking at youths and associating with them are forbidden practices, and anyone who declares this to be allowable is an unbeliever. The traditions brought forward in this matter are vain and foolish. I have seen ignorant persons who suspected the Ṣúfís of the crime in question and regarded them with abhorrence, and I observed that some have made it a religious rule (*madhhabí*). All the Ṣúfí Shaykhs, however, have recognized the wickedness of such practices, which the adherents of incarnation (*ḥulúliyán*)—may

God curse them!—have left as a stigma on the saints of God and the aspirants to Ṣúfiism. But God knows best what is the truth.

Chapter on the Rending of Garments (fí 'l-kharq).

It is a custom of the Ṣúfís to rend their garments, and they have commonly done this in great assemblies where eminent Shaykhs were present. I have met with some theologians who objected to this practice and said that it is not right to tear an intact garment to pieces, and that this is an evil. I reply that an evil of which the purpose is good must itself be good. Anyone may cut an intact garment to pieces and sew it together again, e.g. detach the sleeves and body (*tana*) and gusset (*tiríz*) and collar from one another, and then restore the garment to its original condition; and there is no difference between tearing a garment into five pieces and tearing it into a hundred pieces. Besides, every piece gladdens the heart of a believer, when he sews it on his patched frock, and brings about the satisfaction of his desire. Although the rending of garments has no foundation in Ṣúfiism and certainly ought not to be practised in audition by anyone whose senses are perfectly controlled—for, in that case, it is mere extravagance—nevertheless, if the auditor be so overpowered that his sense of discrimination is lost and he becomes unconscious, then he may be excused (for tearing his garment to pieces); and it is allowable that all the persons present should rend their garments in sympathy with him. There are three circumstances in which Ṣúfís rend their garments: firstly, when a dervish tears his own garment to pieces through rapture caused by audition; secondly, when a number of his friends tear his garment to pieces at the command of a spiritual director on the occasion of asking God to pardon an offence; and thirdly, when they do the same in the intoxication of ecstasy. The most difficult case is that of the garment thrown off or torn in audition. It may be injured or intact. If it be injured, it should either be sewed together and given back to its owner or bestowed on another dervish or torn to pieces, for the sake of gaining a blessing, and divided among the members of the party. If it be intact, we have to consider what was the intention of the dervish who cast it off. If he meant it for the singer, let the singer take it; and if he meant it for the members of the party, let them have it; and if he threw it off without any intention, the spiritual director must determine whether it shall be given to those present and divided among them, or be conferred on one of them, or handed to the singer. If the dervish meant it for the singer, his companions need not throw off their garments in sympathy, because the cast-off garment will not go to his fellows and he will have given it voluntarily or involuntarily without their participation. But if the garment was thrown off with the intention that it should fall to the members of the party, or without any intention, they should all throw off their garments in sympathy; and when they have done this, the spiritual director ought not to bestow the garment on the singer, but it is allowable that any lover of God among them should sacrifice something that belongs to him and return the garment to the dervishes, in order that it may be torn to pieces and distributed. If a garment drops off while its owner is in a state of rapture, the Shaykhs hold various opinions as to what ought to be done, but the majority say that it should be given to the singer, in accordance with the Apostolic tradition: "The spoils belong to the slayer;" and that not to give it to the singer is to violate the obligations imposed by Ṣúfiism. Others contend—and I prefer this view—that, just as some theologians are of opinion that the dress of a slain man should not be given to his slayer except by permission of the Imám, so, here, this garment should not be given to the singer except by command of the spiritual director. But if its owner should not wish the spiritual director to bestow it, let no one be angry with him.

Chapter on the Rules of Audition.

The rules of audition prescribe that it should not be practised until it comes (of its own accord), and that you must not make a habit of it, but practise it seldom, in order that you may not cease to hold it in reverence. It is necessary that a spiritual director should be present during the performance, and that the place should be cleared of common people, and that the singer should be a respectable person, and that the heart should be emptied of worldly thoughts, and that the disposition should not be inclined to amusement, and that every artificial effort (*takalluf*) should be put aside. You must not exceed the proper bounds until audition manifests its power, and when it has become powerful you must not repel it but must follow it as it requires: if it agitates, you must be agitated, and if it calms, you must be calm; and you must be able to distinguish a strong natural impulse from the ardour of ecstasy (*wajd*). The auditor must have enough perception to be capable of receiving the Divine influence and of doing justice to it. When its might is manifested on his heart he must not endeavour to repel it, and when its force is broken he must not endeavour to attract it. While he is in a state of emotion, he must neither expect anyone to help him nor refuse anyone's help if it be offered. And he must not disturb anyone who is engaged in audition or interfere with him, or ponder what he means by the verse (to which he is listening),[1] because such behaviour is very distressing and disappointing to the person who is trying (to hear). He must not say to the singer, "You chant sweetly;" and if he chants unmelodiously or distresses his hearer by reciting poetry unmetrically, he must not say to him, "Chant better!" or bear malice towards him, but he must be unconscious of the singer's presence and commit him to God, who hears correctly. And if he have no part in the audition which is being enjoyed by others, it is not proper that he should look soberly on their intoxication, but he must keep quiet with his own "time" (*waqt*) and establish its dominion, that the blessings thereof may come to him. I, 'Alí

[1] The text of this clause is uncertain. I have followed B.'s reading, *ú murád-i úrá badán bayt-i ú bi-na-sanjad*, but I am not sure that it will bear the translation given above. L. has *badán niyyat-i ú*, and J. *badán nisbat-i ú*.

b. 'Uthmán al-Jullábí, think it more desirable that beginners should not be allowed to attend musical concerts (*samá'há*), lest their natures become depraved. These concerts are extremely dangerous and corrupting, because women on the roofs or elsewhere look at the dervishes who are engaged in audition; and in consequence of this the auditors have great obstacles to encounter. Or it may happen that a young reprobate is one of the party, since some ignorant Ṣúfís have made a religion (*madhhab*) of all this and have flung truth to the winds. I ask pardon of God for my sins of this kind in the past, and I implore His help, that He may preserve me both outwardly and inwardly from contamination, and I enjoin the readers of this book to hold it in due regard and to pray that the author may believe to the end and be vouchsafed the vision of God (in Paradise).

INDEX.

I.

Names of Persons, Peoples, Tribes, Sects, and Places.

A.

Aaron, 262.
'Abbás, uncle of the Prophet, 99.
'Abdalláh Anṣárí, 26.
—— b. Badr al-Juhaní, 81.
—— b. Ḥanẓala, 394.
—— b. Ja'far, 319.
—— b. Khubayq. *See* Abú Muḥammad 'Abdalláh b. Khubayq.
—— b. Mas'úd al-Hudhalí, 81.
—— b. Mubárak, 95–7, 274, 303.
—— b. Rabáḥ, 73.
—— b. 'Umar, 81, 191, 232.
—— b. Unays, 82.
'Abd al-Razzáq Ṣan'ání, 98.
Abel, 364.
Abraham, 40, 73, 74, 91, 115, 161, 232, 237, 252, 262, 317, 318, 326, 327, 328, 342, 353, 365, 370, 371, 373.
—— the Station of, 326, 328.
Abu 'l-'Abbás, 173.
—— Aḥmad b. Masrúq, 146–7.
—— Aḥmad b. Muḥammad al-Ashqání, 150, 168, 206, 395, 412.
—— Aḥmad b. Muḥammad al-Qaṣṣáb, 161, 325, 395.
—— Aḥmad b. Muḥammad b. Sahl al-Ámulí, 149–50.
—— b. 'Alí, 191.
—— b. 'Aṭá, 21, 23, 150, 158, 180, 249, 330, 395, 415.
—— Qásim b. al-Mahdí al-Sayyárí, 157–8, 228, 251–60.
Abu 'l-'Abbás Qaṣṣáb. *See* Abu 'l-'Abbás Aḥmad b. Muḥammad al-Qaṣṣáb.
—— Sayyárí. *See* Abu 'l-'Abbás Qásim b. al-Mahdí al-Sayyárí.
—— Shaqání. *See* Abu 'l-'Abbás Aḥmad b. Muḥammad al-Ashqání.
Abú 'Abdalláh al-Abíwardí (Báwardí), 123, 124.
—— Aḥmad b. 'Áṣim al-Anṭákí, 127.
—— Aḥmad b. Yaḥyá al-Jallá, 37, 134–5.
—— al-Ḥárith b. Asad al-Muḥásibí, 21, 108–9, 127, 154, 176–83, 225, 249, 286, 307, 335.
—— Junaydí, 173.
—— Khafíf. *See* Abú 'Abdalláh Muḥammad b. Khafíf.
—— Khayyáṭí, 161.
—— Muḥammad b. 'Alí al-Dástání, 164.
—— Muḥammad b. 'Alí al-Tirmidhí, 46, 141–2, 147, 200, 210–41, 338.
—— Muḥammad b. al-Faḍl al-Balkhí, 16, 134, 140–1, 208, 327.
—— Muḥammad b. al-Ḥakím, known as Muríd, 175.
—— Muḥammad b. Ismá'íl al-Maghribí, 147.
—— Muḥammad b. Khafíf, 50, 51, 150, 151, 158, 226, 247–51, 290, 323.
—— Rúdbárí, 318.
Abú 'Abd al-Raḥmán Ḥátim b. 'Ulwán al-Aṣamm, 13, 115, 286, 300.
—— Muḥammad b. al-Ḥusayn al-Sulamí, 81, 108, 401.

122, 150, 160, 166, 249, 257, 281, 282, 378, 405.
Abu'l-Ḥasan 'Alí b. Muḥammad al-Iṣfahání, 142-4, 150, 351, 353.
—— Búshanjí (Fúshanja), 44, 299.
—— al-Khurqání. *See* Abu 'l-Ḥasan 'Alí b. Aḥmad al-Khurqání.
—— Muḥammad b. Ismá'íl Khayr al-Nassáj, 144-5, 154, 155, 286, 387.
—— al-Núrí. *See* Abu 'l-Ḥasan Aḥmad b. Muḥammad al-Núrí.
—— b. Sáliba, 104, 166, 172.
—— Sarí b. Mughallis al-Saqaṭí, 110-11, 114, 117, 127, 128, 129, 131, 143, 144, 154.
—— b. Sim'ún, 21.
—— Sumnún b. 'Abdalláh al-Khawwáṣ, 59, 136-8, 249, 286, 308, 312.
Abú Ḥázim al-Madaní, 91.
Abú Ḥulmán, 131, 260, 261.
Abú Hurayra, 82, 232.
Abú 'Ísá 'Uwaym b. Sá'ida, 82.
Abú Isḥáq Ibráhím b. Adham b. Manṣúr, 12, 46, 68, 93, 103-5, 109, 111, 217, 232, 286, 323.
—— Ibráhím b. Aḥmad al-Khawwáṣ, 147, 153-4, 205, 207, 222, 223, 285, 289, 292, 293, 339, 342, 362, 399, 410.
—— Isfará'iní, 214.
—— b. Shahriyár, 172, 173.
Abú Ja'far Ḥaddád, 249.
—— Juhaní, 396.
—— Muḥammad b. 'Alí al-Ḥawárí, 173.
—— Muḥammad b. 'Alí b. Ḥusayn al-Báqir, 77-8.
—— Muḥammad b. al-Ḥusayn al-Ḥaramí, 174.
—— Muḥammad b. al-Miṣbáḥ al-Ṣaydalání, 172, 260.
—— Turshízí, 173.
Abú Jahl, 204, 394.
Abú Kabsha, 81.
Abu 'l-Khayr Aqṭa', 304.
Abú Lubába b 'Abd al-Mundhir, 81.
Abu 'l-Maḥásin, 137, 233.
Abú Maḥfúẓ Ma'rúf b. Fírúz al-Karkhí, 110, 113-15, 117.
Abú Ma'mar, of Iṣfahán, 56.
Abu 'l-Marthad Kinána b. al-Ḥusayn al-'Adawí, 81.
Abú Muḥammad 'Abdalláh b. Khubayq, 128.
—— Aḥmad b. al-Ḥusayn al-Jurayrí, 148-9, 150, 158, 249, 286, 408.
—— Bángharí, 174, 323.
—— Ja'far b. Muḥammad Ṣádiq, 78-80.
—— Ja'far b. Nuṣayr al-Khuldí, 155, 156-7, 193.
—— Murta'ish, 39, 42, 43, 53, 54, 155
—— Ruwaym b. Aḥmad, 21, 25, 134, 135-6, 194.
—— Sahl b. 'Abdalláh al-Tustarí, 13, 139-40, 148, 151, 189, 195-210, 225, 233, 249, 257, 283, 286, 296, 302, 311, 318, 322, 330, 338, 348, 349, 363.
Abú Músá al-Ash'arí, 399.
Abú Muslim, 358.
—— Fáris b. Ghálib al-Fárisí, 165, 172, 319, 346, 408.
Abú Naṣr al-Sarráj, 255, 323, 341.
Abú Nuwás, 8, 406.
Abu 'l-Qásim, of Merv, 233.
—— 'Abd al-Karím b. Hawázin al-Qushayrí, 24, 114, 123, 150, 163, 167-8, 177, 227, 306, 311, 334, 408.
—— 'Alí b. 'Abdalláh al-Gurgání, 49, 150, 169-70, 206, 234, 339.
—— al-Gurgání. *See* Abu 'l-Qásim 'Alí b. 'Abdalláh al-Gurgání.
—— al-Ḥakím, 338.
—— Ibráhím b. Muḥammad b. Maḥmúd al-Naṣrábádí, 150, 159-60, 162.
—— Junayd, 5, 23, 27, 39, 57, 74, 103, 106, 110, 115, 118, 123, 124, 128-30, 131, 132, 134, 135, 137, 138, 143, 144, 145, 147, 148, 149, 150, 151, 154, 156, 157, 166, 182, 185-9, 194, 200, 206, 208, 216, 225, 228, 249, 250, 251, 260,

N.

O.

P.

Q.

II.

Subjects, Oriental Words, and Technical Terms.

Arabic and Persian words are printed in italics. In their arrangement no account is taken of the definite article *al.*

A.

'abá, 48, 52, 133.
abad, 386.
Abdál, 214.
Abrár, 214.
Actions, the Divine, 14.
adab, *ádáb*, 334, 341.
ádáb-i ẓáhir, 292.
'adam, 28, 168, 253, 373.
ádamiyyat, 246, 254.
'adl, 387.
áfát, 281.
aghyár, 31.
aḥdáth, 416.
ahl-i dargáh, 169.
—— *ḥaqá'iq*, 225.
—— *ḥaqíqat*, 25.
—— *ḥaqq*, 62, 402.
—— *ḥashw*, 316, 416.
—— *himmat*, 167.
—— *'ibárat*, 59.
ahl al-'ilm, 253.
ahl-i ma'ní, 403.
—— *maqámát*, 61.
—— *minan*, 265.
—— *mu'ámalat*, 225.
—— *rusúm*, 172.
—— *wafá*, 265.
aḥrár, 43.
aḥwál, 33, 110, 157, 177. See *ḥál* and States of Mystics.
á'ib, 391.
'ajz, 276.
akhláq, 42.
Akhyár, 214.
'alá'iq, 165, 384.
'álam, 385, 386.
álat-i mawsúm, 199.
'álim, 382, 383.
'álim-i rabbání, 151.
Alms, 314–17.
amír, 388.
amn, 216.
anfás, 164.
angalyún, 407.
Angels, 239–41, 302, 303, 351.
Annihilation, 20, 23, 25, 28, 36, 37, 40, 48, 58–60, 95, 170, 171, 205, 241–6. See *faná*.
'aql, 309.
'araḍ, 261, 264, 386.
arbáb-i aḥwál, 302.
—— *ḥál*, 32.
—— *laṭá'if*, 353.
—— *ma'ání*, 38, 59.
'árif, 79, 100, 265, 267, 382–3, 414.
'arsh, 33.
Ascension of Báyazíd, 238.
—— of Muḥammad, 186, 215, 240, 259, 262, 277, 283, 302, 330, 331, 336, 368.
—— of Prophets and Saints, 238.
Asceticism, 17, 37, 86. *See* Mortification and *zuhd*.
Asking, rules in, 357–60.
asrár, 255.
Association. *See* Companionship.
—— with the wicked, 86.

N.

T.

U.

III.

Books.

A.

B.

G.

K.

L.

M.

N.

R.

T.

CORRECTIONS AND ADDITIONS.

Page 2, penult. *For* (p. 3) *read* (p. 1).

p. 3, line 14 and l. 30. *For* (p. 3) *read* (p. 1).

p. 4, l. 18. *For* (p. 3) *read* (p. 1).

p. 4; l. 26. *For* just as the veil destroys revelation (*mukáshafat*) *read* just as veiling destroys the unveiled object (*mukáshaf*).

p. 6, l. 4 and l. 16. *For* (p. 3) *read* (p. 1).

p. 51, l. 6. *For* Parg *read* Burk *or* Purg, and correct the note accordingly. See Guy Le Strange, *The Lands of the Eastern Caliphate*, p. 292.

p. 54, l. 28. *For* the infectious cankers of the age *read* the cankers which infect age after age.

p. 85, l. 19. For (*sáḥib al-qulúb*) read (*ṣáḥi 'l-qulúb*). *Ṣáḥí*, "sober," is the antithesis of *maghlúb*, "enraptured."

p. 127, l. 17. *For* AL-INṬÁKÍ *read* AL-ANṬÁKÍ.

p. 130, l. 27. Although some writers give "Abu 'l-Ḥasan" as the *kunya* of Núrí, the balance of authority is in favour of "Abu 'l-Ḥusayn".

p. 131, n. 2. *Add*, See Goldziher in *ZDMG.*, 61, 75 ff., and a passage in Yáqút's *Irshád al-Aríb*, ed. by Margoliouth, vol. iii, pt. i, 153, 3 ff.; cited by Goldziher in *JRAS.* for 1910, p. 888.

p. 140, l. 19. *For* ABÚ MUḤAMMAD 'ABDALLÁH *read* ABÚ 'ABDALLÁH.

p. 155, l. 26. *Omit* B. *before* DULAF.

p. 169, l. 1. *Omit* B. *before* 'ALÍ.

p. 173, l. 11. *For* Pádsháh-i *read* Pádisháh-i.

p. 182, l. 26. *Sháhmurghí* is probably a mistake for *siyáh murghí*, "a blackbird." Cf. my edition of the *Tadhkirat al-Awliyá*, ii, 259, 23.

p. 257, l. 1. For *t'aṭíl* read *ta'ṭíl*.

p. 323, l. 10. *For* Miṣṣíṣí *read* Maṣṣíṣí.

ADDITIONAL CORRECTIONS AND NOTES.

Preface, p. x. On the date of Hujwírí's death, see Massignon, *Passio* ch. 15, p. 44.*

Preface, p. xi, l. 18. After Lahore add, "where he is known by the name of Dátá Ganj-bakhsh".

Preface, p. xiii, l. 2. "Annihilation" is not a good rendering of the term *faná*, "passing away," which (as used by Hujwírí) implies transformation rather than extinction.

Preface, p xv. 3 fr. foot. Schukovski's edition was published at Leningrad in 1926.

p. 2, penult. *For* (p. 3) *read* (p. 1), and so on p. 3, l. 14 and l. 4. fr. foot; p. 4, l. 18; and p. 6, l. 4 and l. 16.

p. 25, last l. Schukovski reads: *al-faqir lá yastaghni 'anhu*, which is explained by Hujwírí: " The faqir is he who is never rich " (*Kashf*, 29, penult.).

p. 42, 9 foll. " Morals " (*akhláq*) i.e. innate moral and spiritual dispositions with which God has endowed the elect.

p. 62, l. 3. Sufis call themselves *ahl-i-Haqq*, " the followers of the Real," i.e. " the people of God," as well as *ahl-i-Haqiqat*, the followers of Reality ".

p. 63, l. 9 fr. foot. " Under My cloak " (*tahta qabá'i*). None of Schukovski's MSS. (*Kashf*, 70, 14) gives the variant reading *tahta qibábi*, " under My tents ".

p. 118, 6 fr. foot. *Kashf*, 148, 2, reads *fasala* has separated (himself from God) " instead of *dalla* " has gone astray." The former reading makes a better antithesis to *wasaltu*.

p. 150, note 1. Cf. Massignon, *Esquisse d'une bibliographie Qarmate* in the Browne Presentation Volume, p. 331.

p. 153, l. 9. *Al-alsinat mustantiqát*, etc., i.e. " our tongues serve to articulate and (gradually) perish in the process of articulation." For the mystical sense of this saying, which is entirely misunderstood by Hujwírí, see Massignon, *Passion*, 921 *seq.*

p. 159, l. 8 fr. foot. *Bashariyyat*, the carnal nature of man.

p. 163, l. 9. Al-Khurqání. The correct form of the *nisba* seems to be Kharaqání. So Sam 'ání and Yáqút.

p. 163, l. 14. *For* Mu'addib *read* Mu'addab.

p. 172, l. 10. *For* al-Misbáh *read* al-Sabbáh.

p. 172, l. 13. Some MSS. have: " and I have read some works by him."

p. 178, l. 21. *For* from the Giver to the gift *read* from the gift to the Giver.

p. 178, l. 23. *For* from the gift to the Giver *read* from the Giver to the gift.

p. 206, l. 6. *For* 'Ulyán *read* 'Ulayyán.

p. 214. l. 10 fr. foot. According to Qushayrí, Abú Bakr b. Fúrak held that the saint does *not* know himself to be a saint.

p. 216. l. 11 fr. foot. " The son of his time," *i.e.* conscious of nothing but the spiritual state by which he is dominated at the moment, " the eternal Now."

p. 218, l. 10 fr. foot. " Both parties," i.e. scholastic theologians (*mutakallimún*) and jurists (*fuqahá*).

p. 219, l. 4. *For* they do not admit *read* they admit. Cf. Qushayrí (Cairo A. H. 1318) 187, 12 foll. " Abú Isháq Isfará'iní used to say " The saints have miracles, such as the answering of (their) prayers, but not miracles of the evidentiary kind which belong to the prophets (exclusively)."

p. 232, note 1, l. 3. *For* George *read* Gregory.

p. 238, l. 13 fr. foot. *For* Purification *read* Transcendence.

p. 248, l. 14. *For* formal authority *read* subjection to forms.

p. 250, l. 3 foll. These lines are not verse, but rhymed prose (*saj'*).

p. 260, note 2. According to Massignon, *Passion*, ch. 15, p. 44,* the person referred to is Abu 'l-Fadl Muhammad b. Táhir al-Maqdisí (Brockelmann, I. 335).

ADDITIONAL CORRECTIONS AND NOTES.—*continued.*

p. 262, l. 8 fr. foot. *Chashm-i-dil* is the *oculus cordis* of medieval Christian mysticism.

p. 276, l. 12. " Because inability ('ajz) is search." The meaning seems to be that real search for God involves inability to seek Him, i.e. complete self-abandonment.

p. 283, l. 7 and l. 10. *For* atom *read* ant.

p. 286, l. 15 (and p. 307, l. 23). *For* sects *read* schools. Presumably the Ahl-i hadíth and the Ahl-i ra'y are meant.

p. 300, penult. See Qur'án, xxxiii, 72.

p. 301, l. 11. " Salutation," i.e. the blessing (salám) which concludes the ritual prayer.

p. 311, l. 18 foll. See Massignon, *Passion*, 327. The Persian text (*Kashf*, 402, 9 seq.) runs as follows: *muhibb-rá án pasandah báshad ki hasti-yi ú az ráh-i dústí pák gardad ú waláyat-i nafs andar wajd-i vay bursad.* All Schukovski's MSS. read *hasti-yi ú*, not *himmat-i ú*, and the former reading, which I have translated, is unquestionably right. The verb *bursídan*, " to come to an end," " to be annihilated," occurs several times in the *Kashf* and also in the *Tadhkiratu 'l-Awliyá*.

p. 325. l. 4. " The novice, etc." In *Qút al-qulúb* (Cairo, A.H. 1310) I, 95, 21 what is here prescribed for the *muríd* is said to be characteristic of the saints: *wa-min sifati 'l-Abdál an yakúna akluhum fáqatan wa-nawmuhum ghalabatan wa-kalámuhum darúratan*.

p. 326, l. 4 fr. foot. *For* purification *read* transcendence.

p. 349, l. 5 fr. foot. For *al-zillat* read *al-zallat*.

p. 404, last line. *For* entirely *read* on even terms (i.e., with neither loss nor gain). See *Luma'*, 272, 11 and Glossary under *ra'san bi-ra'sin*.

p. 408, l. 4 fr. foot. *Read* Ibn al-Fuwatí and cf. *Luma'*, 286, 1 foll.

p. 412, l. 1. *For* 'Azrá'íl *read* 'Azázíl.

p. 419, note 1. Schukovski reads (*Kashf*, 545, 12) *ú mar ú-rá bad-án niyyat-i ú bi-sanjad*, " and (he should) judge him by his intention," but this does not agree with the words which follow. I think we must read *bi-nasanjad* and translate : " he should not weigh his (the auditor's) intention i.e., ponder whether it is good or bad, for such behaviour brings no luck to the person who subjects him (the auditor) to a test of that kind."

ADDITIONAL CO[illegible]

[illegible] with the [illegible]

[illegible]

[illegible] These [illegible]

[illegible]

[illegible] the [illegible]

[illegible]

[illegible] and [illegible]

[illegible] and the [illegible]

[illegible] should [illegible] the [illegible]

[illegible] the [illegible]